Nonlinear System Modelling and Control

Nonlinear System Modelling and Control

Guest Editor

Chathura Wanigasekara

MDPI

Basel • Beijing • Wuhan • Barcelona • Belgrade • Novi Sad • Cluj • Manchester

Guest Editor
Chathura Wanigasekara
Institute of Maritime Technologies
and Propulsion Systems
German Aerospace Center (DLR)
Geesthacht
Germany

Editorial Office
MDPI AG
Grosspeteranlage 5
4052 Basel, Switzerland

This is a reprint of the Special Issue, published open access by the journal *Computation* (ISSN 2079-3197), freely accessible at: https://www.mdpi.com/journal/computation/special_issues/898LB30YPN.

For citation purposes, cite each article independently as indicated on the article page online and as indicated below:

Lastname, A.A.; Lastname, B.B. Article Title. *Journal Name* **Year**, *Volume Number*, Page Range.

ISBN 978-3-7258-7951-9 (Hbk)
ISBN 978-3-7258-7952-6 (PDF)
https://doi.org/10.3390/books978-3-7258-7952-6

Contents

About the Editor

Chathura Wanigasekara

Chathura Wanigasekara received a B.Sc. degree in electrical and electronic engineering from the University of Peradeniya, Sri Lanka, in 2013, and the M.E. degree in electrical and electronic engineering and the Ph.D. degree in control engineering from the University of Auckland, New Zealand, in 2016 and 2020, respectively. From 2020 to 2022, he was a Postdoctoral Researcher with the Centre for Industrial Mathematics, University of Bremen, Germany. Since 2022, he has been working for the German Aerospace Centre, previously at the Institute for the Protection of Maritime Infrastructures, Bremerhaven, Germany and now at the Institute of Maritime Technologies and Propulsion Systems, Geesthacht, Germany. He also has been serving as a Lecturer at the University of Bremen since 2023. His current research interests include nonlinear system identification and control, machine learning, and networked control systems. He is the author and coauthor of more than 70 scientific publications in various reputed journals and conferences. He was a recipient of the Fowlds Memorial Prize for the most distinguished student in M.E. studies, in 2016, and has been a Senior member of IEEE since 2023.

computation

MDPI

Editorial

Nonlinear System Modelling and Control: Trends, Challenges, and Future Perspectives

Chathura Wanigasekara

Institute of Maritime Technologies and Propulsion Systems, German Aerospace Centre (DLR), 21502 Geesthacht, Germany; chathura.wanigasekara@dlr.de

1. Introduction

Nonlinear systems engineering has undergone a profound transformation with the rapid development of computational tools and advanced analytical methods. In the past, engineers often relied on simplified linear approximations or hand-derived models, but modern computational techniques have become indispensable for modelling, analysing, and controlling complex nonlinear dynamics [1,2]. As digital computation matured, nonlinear system theory evolved from a mathematically challenging niche to a central pillar of modern engineering practice. Numerical solvers, symbolic tools, and high-performance computing environments have enabled rigorous treatment of behaviours such as multistability, bifurcations, saturation effects, time delays, and hybrid dynamics—phenomena that linear models cannot adequately capture [3]. This shift has transformed how researchers design controllers, predict system responses, and ensure stability in increasingly complex applications ranging from robotics and energy systems to transportation and cyber–physical infrastructures [4,5]. By integrating dynamical systems theory, numerical optimisation, and computational algorithms, nonlinear modelling and control have matured into a powerful framework capable of addressing challenges that were previously intractable using classical methods.

Equally transformative has been the rise of optimisation-driven control design within the field of nonlinear systems [6]. Modern optimisation algorithms allow engineers to compute control laws that explicitly account for constraints, uncertainties, and nonlinearities. While early applications focused on optimal feedback laws for low-dimensional systems, the field truly accelerated with the development of nonlinear model predictive control (NMPC), an approach that repeatedly solves finite-horizon optimisation problems in real time. NMPC has enabled high-performance tracking, safety enforcement, and constraint handling across a wide variety of systems, from chemical processes and autonomous vehicles to large-scale energy networks [7]. Foundational contributions in optimal and predictive control provided systematic ways to handle multivariable nonlinear systems, while advances in numerical methods and convexification techniques have made online optimisation far more tractable [8,9]. Over the past two decades, numerous studies have demonstrated the practical viability of NMPC and related optimisation-based methods, showing their effectiveness in applications with complex dynamics, strong coupling, and nonlinearity [10]. Whether implemented through gradient-based solvers, sequential quadratic programming, or learning-enhanced optimisation, these methods have reshaped modern control design and continue to inspire new research at the intersection of computation, control, and decision-making.

In parallel, performance-driven and safety-critical control paradigms have emerged as modern cornerstones of nonlinear systems engineering, particularly in robotics [11],

 https://doi.org/10.3390/computation14020044

autonomous systems [12], and energy management. These approaches rely on iterative computational frameworks that enforce stability and safety margins under uncertain or extreme operating conditions. They frequently incorporate nonlinear simulations, Lyapunov analysis, and probabilistic verification, all of which have become feasible only through advances in computational power and numerical algorithms. Sophisticated nonlinear models now capture complex physical interactions, actuator limits, and hybrid transitions with unprecedented fidelity. From multi-rotor drones and ground robots to flexible energy assets and distributed microgrids, computationally empowered nonlinear modelling and control have enabled reliable operation in domains where analytical solutions remain out of reach [13].

In recent years, the rapid rise of machine learning (ML) and artificial intelligence has further expanded the toolkit available to the field of nonlinear systems [14,15]. Data-driven modelling approaches such as neural networks, Koopman-based lifted models, Gaussian processes, and hybrid physics-informed learning can now approximate complex nonlinear behaviors that are difficult to capture analytically [16]. ML techniques have gained traction in tasks such as state estimation, fault diagnosis, adaptive control, and real-time prediction [17]. Unlike classical first-principles modelling, ML models can learn high-dimensional relationships directly from data, making them effective surrogates for computationally expensive simulation routines [18]. Researchers have used ML to accelerate NMPC computations, compensate for unmodelled disturbances, estimate unknown system parameters, or support digital twins operating in real time [19]. ML-enhanced models and control schemes are especially useful for handling sensor noise, unstructured environments, and time-varying nonlinearities [20]. While challenges remain regarding stability guarantees, interpretability, and robustness, the integration of AI into nonlinear system modelling and control is rapidly advancing and reshaping many engineering workflows.

Control-oriented monitoring and diagnosis frameworks also represent one of the most active research fronts. Modern systems increasingly rely on advanced observer designs, fault detection algorithms, and health-aware control to ensure safe and reliable operation [21]. With the integration of ML and high-frequency sensor data, these frameworks can detect anomalies, identify changes in system dynamics, and support predictive maintenance strategies [22]. Such advancements are essential for autonomous vehicles, industrial automation, smart grids, and other cyber–physical systems where real-time decision-making is critical [23]. Their inclusion in this Special Issue reflects the field's growing emphasis on bridging online monitoring, computational modelling, and nonlinear control synthesis.

Another important frontier in nonlinear systems engineering lies in the advancement of stochastic modelling and robust analysis techniques. Real-world systems are inherently affected by uncertainties in parameters, disturbances, and environmental conditions, making uncertainty quantification and robust control essential components of modern design workflows [24]. Approaches such as stochastic stability analysis, probabilistic reachability, and robust MPC provide rigorous ways to account for variability while ensuring performance and safety under realistic operating conditions [25,26]. In parallel, high-precision numerical methods and advanced solvers have improved the accuracy and efficiency of classical nonlinear analysis techniques, enabling the treatment of multi-scale dynamics, time delays, and hybrid switching behaviours with greater fidelity [27,28]. Together, these developments underscore the growing importance of computational innovation in advancing nonlinear system modelling and control.

Motivated by these advancements, this Special Issue, "Nonlinear System Modelling and Control", was conceived to showcase recent developments and emerging applications at the forefront of the field. The call for papers invited contributions across a broad

 https://doi.org/10.3390/computation14020044

spectrum of topics, including nonlinear modelling frameworks, advanced control strategies, distributed and networked control, observer and estimation methods, learning-based approaches, and applications in robotics, energy systems, electric drives, autonomous systems, and other complex engineering domains. Nine peer-reviewed papers that highlight important research trends are included in this Special Issue. These contributions address a wide range of topics, including advanced nonlinear modelling and estimation techniques, robust and adaptive controllers for uncertain systems, optimisation-based and data-driven methods for real-time control, and application-oriented studies that demonstrate the practical value of nonlinear system theory in modern engineering. In the following sections, we summarise each contribution to this Special Issue, situating its significance within the broader evolution of nonlinear system modelling and control.

2. Overview of the Special Issue

This Special Issue brings together nine diverse and insightful contributions that reflect the growing depth and breadth of research in nonlinear system modelling and control.

Contribution 1 ([29]). *A Finite-Time Extended State Observer with Prediction Error Compensation for PMSM Control.*

This paper proposes a finite-time extended state observer (FTESO) integrated with model predictive control (MPC) for high-performance control of permanent magnet synchronous motors (PMSMs). A disturbance-aware predictive model is constructed by incorporating lumped disturbances into the PMSM current equations, addressing load fluctuations and parameter uncertainties. The FTESO, designed with nonlinear gains and Lyapunov stability, ensures rapid disturbance estimation and is embedded into a feedforward-compensated MPC with a composite cost function considering current error and voltage increment. Simulations show that under sudden load disturbances, FTESO-MPC achieves faster recovery and a smaller steady-state error than LESO-MPC; when inductance triples, FTESO-MPC maintains smooth convergence, whereas LESO-MPC exhibits oscillations with d-axis current peaks near 200 A. Under resistance or flux variations, FTESO-MPC sustains stable regulation with less ripple, confirming its superior tracking accuracy and robustness compared to LESO-MPC.

Contribution 2 ([30]). *An Energy Saving MTPA-Based Model Predictive Control Strategy for PMSM in Electric Vehicles Under Variable Load Conditions.*

To promote energy efficiency and support sustainable electric transportation, this study addresses the challenge of real-time and energy-optimal control of permanent magnet synchronous motors (PMSMs) in electric vehicles operating under variable load conditions, proposing a novel Laguerre-based model predictive control (MPC) strategy integrated with maximum torque per ampere (MTPA) operation. Traditional MPC methods often suffer from limited prediction horizons and high computational burden when handling strong coupling and time-varying loads, compromising real-time performance. To overcome these limitations, a Laguerre function approximation is employed to model the dynamic evolution of control increments using a set of orthogonal basis functions, effectively reducing the control dimensionality while accelerating convergence. Furthermore, to enhance energy efficiency, the MTPA strategy is embedded by reformulating the current allocation process using d- and q-axis current variables and deriving equivalent reference currents to simplify the optimisation structure. A cost function is designed to simultaneously ensure current accuracy and achieve maximum torque per unit current. The simulation results under typical electric vehicle conditions demonstrate that the proposed Laguerre-MTPA MPC con-

 https://doi.org/10.3390/computation14020044

troller significantly improves steady-state performance, reduces energy consumption, and ensures faster response to load disturbances compared to traditional MTPA-based control schemes. This work provides a practical and scalable control framework for energy-saving applications in sustainable electric transportation systems.

Contribution 3 ([31]). *Advanced Deep Learning Framework for Predicting the Remaining Useful Life of Nissan Leaf Generation 01 Lithium-Ion Battery Modules.*

Accurate estimation of the remaining useful life (RUL) of lithium-ion batteries (LIBs) is essential for ensuring safety and enabling effective battery health management systems. To address this challenge, data-driven solutions leveraging advanced machine learning and deep learning techniques have been developed. This study introduces a novel framework, Deep Neural Networks with Memory Features (DNNwMF), for predicting the RUL of LIBs. The integration of memory features significantly enhances the model's accuracy, and an autoencoder is incorporated to optimize the feature representation. The focus of this work is on feature engineering and uncovering hidden patterns in the data. The proposed model was trained and tested using lithium-ion battery cycle life datasets from NASA's Prognostic Centre of Excellence and CALCE Lab. The optimized framework achieved an impressive RMSE of 6.61%, and with suitable modifications, the DNN model demonstrated a prediction accuracy of 92.11% for test data, which was used to estimate the RUL of Nissan Leaf Gen 01 battery modules.

Contribution 4 ([32]). *Subsequential Continuity in Neutrosophic Metric Space with Applications.*

This paper introduces two concepts, subcompatibility and subsequential continuity, which are, respectively, weaker than the existing concepts of occasionally weak compatibility and reciprocal continuity. These concepts are studied within the framework of neutrosophic metric spaces. Using these ideas, a common fixed point theorem is developed for a system involving four maps. Furthermore, the results are applied to solve the Volterra integral equation, demonstrating the practical use of these findings in neutrosophic metric spaces. These results provide foundational tools that can inform modelling, estimation, and stability analysis in practical nonlinear control applications.

Contribution 5 ([33]). *FPGA Implementation of Synergetic Controller-Based MPPT Algorithm for a Standalone PV System.*

Photovoltaic (PV) energy is gaining traction due to its direct conversion of sunlight to electricity without harming the environment. It is simple to install, adaptable in size, and has low operational costs. The power output of PV modules varies with solar radiation and cell temperature. To optimize system efficiency, it is crucial to track the PV array's maximum power point. This paper presents a novel fixed-point FPGA design of a nonlinear maximum power point tracking (MPPT) controller based on synergetic control theory for autonomous standalone photovoltaic systems. The proposed solution addresses the chattering issue associated with the sliding mode controller by introducing a new strategy that generates a continuous control law rather than a switching term. Because it requires a lower sample rate when switching to the invariant manifold, its controlled switching frequency makes it better suited for digital applications. The suggested algorithm is first emulated to evaluate its performance, robustness, and efficacy under a standard benchmarked MPPT efficiency calculation regime. FPGA has been used for its capability to handle high-speed control tasks more efficiently than traditional micro-controller-based systems. The high-speed response is critical for applications where rapid adaptation to changing conditions,

https://doi.org/10.3390/computation14020044

such as fluctuating solar irradiance and temperature levels, is necessary. To validate the effectiveness of the implemented synergetic controller, the system responses under variant meteorological conditions have been analysed. The results reveal that the synergetic control algorithm provides smooth and precise MPPT.

Contribution 6 ([34]). *Model Predictive Control of Spatially Distributed Systems with Spatio-Temporal Logic Specifications.*

In this paper, for spatially distributed systems, we propose a new method of model predictive control with spatio-temporal logic specifications. We formulate the finite-time control problem with specifications described by SSTLf (signal spatio-temporal logic over finite traces) formulas. In the problem formulation, the feasibility is guaranteed by representing control specifications as a penalty in the cost function. Time-varying weights in the cost function are introduced to satisfy control specifications. The finite-time control problem can be written as a mixed integer programming (MIP) problem. According to the policy of model predictive control (MPC), the control input can be generated by solving the finite-time control problem at each discrete time. The effectiveness of the proposed method is presented through a numerical example.

Contribution 7 ([35]). *The Effect of Proportional, Proportional-Integral, and Proportional-Integral-Derivative Controllers on Improving the Performance of Torsional Vibrations on a Dynamical System.*

The primary goal of this research is to lessen the high vibration that the model causes by using an appropriate vibration control. Thus, we begin by implementing various controller types to investigate their impact on the system's reaction and evaluate each control's outcomes. The controller types are presented as proportional (P), proportional–integral (PI), and proportional–integral–derivative (PID) controllers. PID control was employed to regulate the torsional vibration behaviour on a dynamical system. The PID controller aims to increase system stability after seeing the impact of P and PI control. This kind of control ensures that there are no unstable components in the system. By using the multiple-time-scale perturbation (MTSP) technique, a first-order approximate solution has been obtained. Using the frequency response function approach, the stability and steady-state response of the system under the primary resonance condition, representing the worst-case resonance, are addressed. The nonlinear dynamical system's chaotic response and the numerical solution for various parameter values are also addressed. MATLAB programs are utilized to attain simulation outcomes.

Contribution 8 ([36]). *Assessment of computational tools for analysing the observability and accessibility of nonlinear models.*

Accessibility and observability are two properties of dynamic models that provide insights into the structural relationships between their input, output, and state variables. They are closely related to controllability and structural local identifiability, respectively. Observability and identifiability determine, respectively, the possibility of inferring the unmeasured state variables and parameters of a model from output measurements; accessibility and controllability describe the possibility of driving its state by changing its input. Analysing these structural properties in nonlinear models of ordinary differential equations can be challenging, particularly when dealing with large systems. Two main approaches are currently used for their study: one based on differential geometry, which uses symbolic computation, and another one based on sensitivity calculations, which use

 https://doi.org/10.3390/computation14020044

numerical integration. These approaches are implemented in two MATLAB software tools: the differential geometry approach in STRIKE-GOLDD, and the sensitivity-based method in StrucID. These toolboxes differ significantly in their features and capabilities. Until now, their performance had not been thoroughly compared. This paper present a comprehensive comparative study of these two approaches, elucidating their differences in applicability, computational efficiency, and robustness compared to computational issues. Our core finding is that StrucID has a substantially lower computational cost than STRIKE-GOLDD; however, it may occasionally yield inconsistent results due to numerical issues.

Contribution 9 ([37]). *Approximate Analytical Solutions of Nonlinear Jerk Equations Using the Parameter Expansion Method.*

The parameter expansion method (PEM) is employed to study nonlinear Jerk equations, which are often difficult to solve because of their strong nonlinearity. This method provides higher accuracy and broader applicability, enabling analytical insights and closed form approximations. This study explores the use of Prof. J. H. He's PEM to derive approximate analytical solutions of the nonlinear third-order Jerk equation, a model commonly encountered in the analysis of complex dynamical systems across physics and engineering. Owing to the strong nonlinearity inherent in Jerk-type equations, exact solutions are often unattainable. The PEM provides a simple, effective framework by expanding the solution with respect to an embedding parameter, allowing accurate approximations without the need of small parameters or linearisation. The method's reliability and precision are validated through comparisons with numerical simulations, demonstrating its practicality and robustness for tackling nonlinear problems. It is found that the parameter expansion method yields highly accurate approximate solutions for the nonlinear third-order Jerk equation, closely matching numerical simulations and outperforming several alternative analytical techniques in terms of simplicity and effectiveness. The approximate solutions derived using this method offer insights that can help control practitioners, simplify nonlinear models, and support robust controller or observer design.

3. Emerging Themes in Nonlinear System Modelling and Control

Although the contributions in this Special Issue span a wide range of systems, methodologies, and application domains, several unifying themes emerge across them. Taken together, the papers reveal how modern nonlinear modelling and control increasingly integrate data-driven methods, advanced observers, predictive and optimisation-based frameworks, and rigorous analytical tools to address uncertainty, complexity, and real-time constraints. The following subsections synthesise these cross-cutting ideas highlighting common modelling philosophies, control strategies, and application trends that collectively characterise current developments in nonlinear system research. Note that the themes discussed in the following sections reflect the contributions of this Special Issue and are not meant to represent a comprehensive survey of all modelling and control approaches for nonlinear systems. Some trade-offs are evident across the contributions. Controllers that achieve high performance or fast disturbance rejection often require more computation, while methods designed for real-time implementation may simplify models and reduce predictive accuracy. Data-driven approaches offer adaptability but must balance robustness and interpretability. Highlighting these trade-offs helps readers understand the practical strengths and limitations of the presented works.

Across these contributions, clear trade-offs emerge. For example, methods that achieve high control performance or rapid disturbance rejection often require higher computational effort or more complex observers, while approaches that emphasise real-time implementability sometimes sacrifice modelling fidelity or predictive accuracy. Similarly,

 https://doi.org/10.3390/computation14020044

data-driven models and learning-enhanced controllers offer flexibility and adaptability but must balance interpretability, robustness, and stability guarantees. Highlighting these complementary strengths and limitations helps contextualise the contributions and provides readers with a practical understanding of the design decisions inherent in modern nonlinear system modelling and control.

3.1. Modelling Approaches

A variety of modelling paradigms are represented in this Special Issue, reflecting the diversity of nonlinear systems seen in modern engineering and applied science. Several contributions advance data-driven and hybrid modelling, where computational and learning-based tools supplement classical physics-based models. For example, the deep neural network with memory features for lithium-ion battery prognosis demonstrates how latent representations and feature-enhanced learning can uncover degradation patterns not easily captured by first-principles models. Similarly, the fractional fixed-point and neutrosophic-metric-space formulation for solving Volterra equations highlights the emergence of hybrid mathematical frameworks that blend nonlinear analysis with uncertainty-aware modelling.

Reduced-order and structure-aware models appear prominently as well. Works focusing on structural observability and identifiability provide computational tools to assess whether complex nonlinear models can support reliable state and parameter estimation. Such studies are essential for large-scale systems where full-order modelling becomes intractable. Likewise, the parameter expansion method applied to nonlinear Jerk equations shows how analytical approximations can derive tractable surrogate models that retain essential nonlinear behaviour.

Across several papers, explicit treatment of uncertainties, disturbances, and parameter variations is a central theme. The finite-time extended state observer for PMSMs models lumped disturbances directly, enabling robust current prediction despite load changes and parameter drift. In energy systems, irradiance variability is captured through nonlinear MPPT models designed for digital hardware, emphasising the need for models that reflect fast-changing environmental conditions.

These modelling approaches align strongly with the computational focus of the journal: they rely on numerical optimisation, nonlinear solvers, embedded digital implementation, or simulation-driven evaluation. Collectively, the modelling contributions in the Special Issue illustrate the growing trend of integrating advanced numerical methods, machine learning, and rigorous nonlinear analysis to produce models that are accurate, uncertainty-aware, and suitable for real-time control.

3.2. Control Strategies

The contributions to this Special Issue illustrate several complementary nonlinear control strategies, each designed to address robustness, performance, and implementability in different application domains. Many papers focus on robust and adaptive control, tackling challenges such as parameter drift, disturbances, and strong nonlinear coupling. The finite-time ESO–MPC controller for PMSMs, for instance, uses a nonlinear disturbance observer to compensate for sudden load changes, achieving fast recovery and improved steady-state accuracy. Likewise, the Laguerre-based MPC method reduces the computational burden of long-horizon optimisation, enabling energy-efficient control in electric vehicle drives.

Nonlinear model predictive control (MPC) appears prominently in both methodological and application-driven settings. Beyond electric drive systems, one contribution formulates an MPC framework grounded in spatio-temporal logic specifications, demonstrating how logical constraints can be embedded into mixed-integer predictive optimisation for distributed spatial processes.

 https://doi.org/10.3390/computation14020044

Other papers highlight continuous nonlinear control laws such as synergetic control for photovoltaic MPPT and PID-based vibration suppression. The synergetic MPPT controller offers a smooth alternative to classic sliding-mode methods, reducing chattering while preserving robustness under irradiance fluctuations. The PID vibration control study emphasises the importance of classical nonlinear control analysis resonance response, stability boundaries, and chaotic behaviour analysis within high-speed mechanical systems.

Several contributions push the boundary in terms of linking nonlinear control with computation, such as FPGA-based implementations, optimisation-enhanced observers, or hybrid control frameworks for epidemiological systems. Across the papers, the trade-offs between performance, robustness, computational complexity, and real-time feasibility remain central. Collectively, these works demonstrate that modern nonlinear control is increasingly characterised by a careful synthesis of rigorous analysis, algorithmic innovation, and hardware-aware design.

3.3. *Applications and Case Studies*

Beyond methodological advances, the Special Issue highlights the broad reach of nonlinear modelling and control across several impactful application domains. Power and energy systems feature prominently, with contributions on photovoltaic MPPT under variable irradiance, nonlinear control of PMSM electric drives, and lithium-ion battery health prognostics. These systems are inherently nonlinear due to electromagnetic coupling, temperature effects, and complex electrochemical dynamics. The presented control strategies ranging from predictive control to synergetic and observer-based schemes demonstrate how nonlinear methods can enable higher energy efficiency, reliability, and real-time adaptability.

Transportation and electrified mobility applications appear through advanced control of PMSMs in electric vehicles and investigations relevant to maritime and autonomous systems via battery prognostics and digital twin-inspired modelling frameworks. These contributions underscore the importance of nonlinear control in ensuring safe, efficient, and disturbance-resilient operation in dynamic environments.

This Special Issue also includes application studies in mechanical systems, where PID-based vibration control is validated through analysis of resonance, stability, and chaotic behaviour. Across the applications, validation ranges from detailed numerical experiments to FPGA-based hardware tests and real-world datasets. Collectively, these case studies highlight the significance and applicability of nonlinear modelling and control in addressing real-world challenges related to safety, sustainability, and resilience.

4. Bridging Theory, Computation, and Real-World Deployment

The contributions in this Special Issue collectively underline the increasingly critical link between theoretical nonlinear systems research, computational tools, and practical deployment in real-world systems. Across many papers, the role of advanced numerical methods and optimisation frameworks is explicit. Model predictive control relies on efficient solvers, mixed-integer programming, and reduced-order parametrisations such as Laguerre functions to satisfy real-time requirements. Nonlinear observers, such as finite-time ESOs, also depend on careful numerical tuning and stability analysis to perform reliably under rapidly varying conditions.

The synergy between high-fidelity models and real-time feasibility is a recurring theme. Battery RUL estimation and MPPT control demonstrate how learning-enhanced or synergetic models can produce accurate predictions while remaining computationally tractable for deployment on embedded platforms. FPGA-based implementation of nonlinear controllers further highlights the importance of hardware-aware design, where sampling rates, fixed-point arithmetic, and power constraints shape the controller architecture.

 https://doi.org/10.3390/computation14020044

Several contributions align with the broader vision of digital twin systems, where accurate modelling, estimation, and prediction enable online monitoring and decision support. Although digital twins are not explicitly developed in the papers, many contributions such as battery ageing models, observer-based PMSM estimation, and spatio-temporal logic MPC provide the foundational elements necessary for building real-time intelligent system representations.

Time delays, communication constraints, and robustness are addressed in MPC, observer design, and parameter identification studies. These factors are essential for cyber–physical systems such as electric transportation, renewable energy assets, and distributed sensing networks. This Special Issue reinforces that nonlinear modelling and control sit at the core of efficient, safe, and sustainable operation. As systems become more electrified and interconnected, the need for robust nonlinear models, real-time observers, and predictive controllers will continue to grow. The contributions in this issue illustrate the increasing integration of theory, computation, and practical implementation, moving the field closer to dependable and intelligent real-world nonlinear control systems.

5. Open Challenges and Future Directions

While the papers in this Special Issue make significant advances, several open problems remain at the frontier of nonlinear system modelling and control. Scalability remains a central challenge, particularly for large-scale nonlinear systems such as multi-energy networks, autonomous-vehicle fleets, or epidemiological systems with spatial heterogeneity. Methods such as spatio-temporal logic MPC and structural identifiability analysis offer promising directions, but further progress is needed to extend nonlinear control to systems with high dimensionality and interconnection complexity.

Building on these challenges, several near-term research priorities emerge in the field of nonlinear systems. These include improving scalability and computational efficiency for high-dimensional and interconnected systems; integrating robust and learning-enabled control while ensuring stability, interpretability, and safety; and developing hardware-aware real-time implementations for embedded platforms or FPGAs. Establishing standardised benchmarking protocols and openly available datasets such as battery cycle-life datasets for predictive control or PV system datasets for MPPT evaluation can further accelerate progress and enable systematic comparison of new methods.

Robustness under uncertainty continues to be an important concern. The papers in this issue highlight the impact of parameter variability, disturbances, and environmental fluctuations. The finite-time observer and synergetic MPPT controller address these aspects, but a more unified framework that integrates robust optimisation, adaptive estimation, and stochastic modelling remains an open direction. The integration of learning-enabled control presents opportunities and risks. Battery RUL estimation demonstrates the power of deep learning for complex nonlinear systems, but ensuring stability, safety, and interpretability in learning-based controllers remains a challenge. Safe reinforcement learning, certifiable neural-network approximations, and verifiable learning architectures represent promising research avenues. Hybrid and cyber–physical systems pose ongoing challenges due to switching dynamics, mode-dependent behaviours, and digital/physical interaction layers. Applications such as vibration control and epidemiological modelling show the importance of addressing nonlinear dynamics under changing conditions. Future work must consider cyber-security, resilience to sensor and communication attacks, and fault-tolerant nonlinear control. Achieving real-time computation for advanced nonlinear control laws is another critical area. MPC with spatio-temporal logic, high-order observers, and nonlinear optimisation must meet tight computational budgets on embedded or resource-constrained hardware. Research in algorithmic acceleration, reduced-order models, surrogate solvers,

https://doi.org/10.3390/computation14020044

and hardware-aware control code generation will remain crucial. Finally, the field lacks standardised benchmarks and openly available datasets for the systematic evaluation of competing nonlinear modelling and control methods. While existing battery and power electronics datasets provide useful starting points, the development of broader, community-accepted benchmarks would significantly enhance comparability and accelerate progress. From a societal perspective, nonlinear modelling and control will play a key role in addressing sustainability, energy transition, and resilient infrastructure. Electrified transportation, renewable generation, and smart autonomous systems all rely on accurate nonlinear models and robust controllers. The contributions in this Special Issue point toward these broader impacts and motivate continued innovation in the years to come.

6. Concluding Remarks

This Special Issue on "Nonlinear System Modelling and Control" presented nine contributions advancing the theory, computation, and applications of nonlinear systems, spanning topics such as advanced observers, model predictive and vibration control, MPPT design, identifiability analysis, learning-based battery prognosis, and analytical methods for nonlinear differential equations. Common themes include the integration of physics-based and data-driven modelling, control strategies balancing robustness and computational feasibility, and applications across energy systems, electrified transport, and mechanical systems, while also highlighting ongoing challenges in scalability, real-time implementation, uncertainty management, and the reliable deployment of learning-enabled controllers.

We thank the authors, reviewers, and editorial team for their support and hope this collection stimulates continued research and collaboration in the field of nonlinear systems.

Funding: This editorial received no external funding.

Acknowledgments: The author thanks all contributors to the Special Issue "Nonlinear System Modelling and Control", as well as the reviewers and the editorial staff of *Computation* for their efforts.

Conflicts of Interest: The author declares no conflicts of interest.

References

1. De Persis, C.; Tesi, P. Learning controllers for nonlinear systems from data. *Annu. Rev. Control* **2023**, *56*, 100915. [CrossRef]
2. Wanigasekara, C.; Zhang, L.; Swain, A.; Nguang, S.K. Delta-Modulator-Based Quantised State Feedback Controller for T–S Fuzzy Networked Systems. *Int. J. Fuzzy Syst.* **2021**, *23*, 642–656. [CrossRef]
3. Schweidtmann, A.M.; Zhang, D.; von Stosch, M. A review and perspective on hybrid modeling methodologies. *Digit. Chem. Eng.* **2024**, *10*, 100136. [CrossRef]
4. Gamage, D.; Zhang, X.; Ukil, A.; Wanigasekara, C.; Swain, A. Distributed Co-ordinated Consensus Control for Multi-Energy Storage of DC Microgrid. In *2021 IEEE Power & Energy Society General Meeting (PESGM)*; IEEE: New York, NY, USA, 2021; pp. 1–5.
5. Gowrienanthan, B.; Kiruthihan, N.; Rathnayake, K.D.I.S.; Kiruthikan, S.; Logeeshan, V.; Kumarawadu, S.; Wanigasekara, C. Deep Learning Based Non-Intrusive Load Monitoring for a Three-Phase System. *IEEE Access* **2023**, *11*, 49337–49349. [CrossRef]
6. Zhang, X.; Liniger, A.; Borrelli, F. Optimization-Based Collision Avoidance. *IEEE Trans. Control Syst. Technol.* **2021**, *29*, 972–983. [CrossRef]
7. Meng, C.; Li, H. Learning-Based Nonlinear MPC with Integrated Moving Horizon Estimation of Quadrotors. *IEEE Trans. Ind. Electron.* **2025**, *72*, 9560–9568. [CrossRef]
8. Malikopoulos, A.A. A Multiobjective Optimization Framework for Online Stochastic Optimal Control in Hybrid Electric Vehicles. *IEEE Trans. Control Syst. Technol.* **2016**, *24*, 440–450. [CrossRef]
9. Chen, Y.; Braun, D.J. Hardware-in-the-Loop Iterative Optimal Feedback Control Without Model-Based Future Prediction. *IEEE Trans. Robot.* **2019**, *35*, 1419–1434. [CrossRef]
10. Wang, T.; Gao, H.; Qiu, J. A Combined Adaptive Neural Network and Nonlinear Model Predictive Control for Multirate Networked Industrial Process Control. *IEEE Trans. Neural Netw. Learn. Syst.* **2016**, *27*, 416–425. [CrossRef]

 https://doi.org/10.3390/computation14020044

11. Milutinović, D.; Lima, P. Modeling and Optimal Centralized Control of a Large-Size Robotic Population. *IEEE Trans. Robot.* **2006**, *22*, 1280–1285. [CrossRef]
12. Zong, Y.; Chen, L.; Canyelles-Pericas, P.; Lu, N.; Jiang, B. Resilient Time Synchronisation for Aerial Swarms by Distributed Graph Neural Networks. *IEEE Trans. Netw. Sci. Eng.* **2026**, *13*, 179–193. [CrossRef]
13. Panjavarnam, K.; Ismail, Z.H.; Tang, C.H.H.; Sekiguchi, K.; Casas, G.G. Model Predictive Control for Autonomous UAV Landings: A Comprehensive Review of Strategies, Applications and Challenges. *J. Eng.* **2025**, *2025*, e70085. [CrossRef]
14. Oromiehie, E.; Prusty, B.G.; Rajan, G.; Wanigasekara, C.; Swain, A. Machine learning based process monitoring and characterisation of automated composites. In Proceedings of the SAMPE, Seattle, WA, USA, 22–25 May 2017; pp. 1–6.
15. Jayasinghe, J.A.R.R.; Malindi, J.H.E.; Rajapaksha, R.M.A.M.; Logeeshan, V.; Wanigasekara, C. Classification and Localization of Faults in AC Microgrids Through Discrete Wavelet Transform and Artificial Neural Networks. *IEEE Open Access J. Power Energy* **2024**, *11*, 303–313. [CrossRef]
16. Boscaino, V.; Vitale, G.; Rizzo, R. Review and Outlook on Power Converters Exploiting Artificial Neural Networks: Recent Advances and Perspectives. *IEEE Access* **2025**, *13*, 200069–200097. [CrossRef]
17. Vidal, C.; Malysz, P.; Kollmeyer, P.; Emadi, A. Machine Learning Applied to Electrified Vehicle Battery State of Charge and State of Health Estimation: State-of-the-Art. *IEEE Access* **2020**, *8*, 52796–52814. [CrossRef]
18. Zhang, L.; Li, K.; Du, D.; Guo, Y.; Fei, M.; Yang, Z. A Sparse Learning Machine for Real-Time SOC Estimation of Li-ion Batteries. *IEEE Access* **2020**, *8*, 156165–156176. [CrossRef]
19. Wang, S.; Dragicevic, T.; Gontijo, G.F.; Chaudhary, S.K.; Teodorescu, R. Machine Learning Emulation of Model Predictive Control for Modular Multilevel Converters. *IEEE Trans. Ind. Electron.* **2021**, *68*, 11628–11634. [CrossRef]
20. Zhao, H.; Diaz, J.C.G.; Hoyos, S. Multi-Channel Nonlinearity Mitigation Using Machine Learning Algorithms. *IEEE Trans. Mob. Comput.* **2024**, *23*, 2535–2550. [CrossRef]
21. Bani-Ahmed, A.; Rashidi, M.; Nasiri, A.; Hosseini, H. Reliability Analysis of a Decentralized Microgrid Control Architecture. *IEEE Trans. Smart Grid* **2019**, *10*, 3910–3918. [CrossRef]
22. Anand, H.; Sammuli, B.S.; Olofsson, K.E.J.; Humphreys, D.A. Real-Time Magnetic Sensor Anomaly Detection Using Autoencoder Neural Networks on the DIII-D Tokamak. *IEEE Trans. Plasma Sci.* **2022**, *50*, 4126–4130. [CrossRef]
23. Nassif, A.B.; Talib, M.A.; Nasir, Q.; Dakalbab, F.M. Machine Learning for Anomaly Detection: A Systematic Review. *IEEE Access* **2021**, *9*, 78658–78700. [CrossRef]
24. Wang, D.; He, H.; Liu, D. Adaptive Critic Nonlinear Robust Control: A Survey. *IEEE Trans. Cybern.* **2017**, *47*, 3429–3451. [CrossRef] [PubMed]
25. Babayomi, O.; Madonski, R.; Zhang, Z.; Rodriguez, J.; Davidson, I.; Kim, D.S. Robust Model Predictive Control of Converter-Based Microgrids. *IEEE Trans. Power Electron.* **2025**, *40*, 17124–17146. [CrossRef]
26. Ghosh, A.; Cortes-Aguirre, C.; Chen, Y.A.; Khurram, A.; Kleissl, J. Adaptive Relaxation-Based Nonconservative Chance Constrained Stochastic MPC. *IEEE Trans. Control Syst. Technol.* **2025**, *33*, 1543–1559. [CrossRef]
27. Pang, N.; Wang, X.; Wang, Z. Event-Triggered Adaptive Control of Nonlinear Systems with Dynamic Uncertainties: The Switching Threshold Case. *IEEE Trans. Circuits Syst. II Express Briefs* **2022**, *69*, 3540–3544. [CrossRef]
28. Zhang, Y.; Niu, H.; Tao, J.; Li, X. Novel Data and Neural Network-Based Nonlinear Adaptive Switching Control Method. *IEEE Trans. Neural Netw. Learn. Syst.* **2022**, *33*, 789–797. [CrossRef]
29. Gao, L.; Zhang, G.; Lv, X.; Wang, Y.; Shi, Z. A Finite-Time Extended State Observer with Prediction Error Compensation for PMSM Control. *Computation* **2025**, *13*, 247. [CrossRef]
30. Gao, L.; Lv, X.; Ma, K.; Shi, Z. An Energy Saving MTPA-Based Model Predictive Control Strategy for PMSM in Electric Vehicles Under Variable Load Conditions. *Computation* **2025**, *13*, 231. [CrossRef]
31. Wickramaarachchi, S.M.; Suraweera, S.A.D.; Akalanka, D.M.P.; Logeeshan, V.; Wanigasekara, C. Advanced Deep Learning Framework for Predicting the Remaining Useful Life of Nissan Leaf Generation 01 Lithium-Ion Battery Modules. *Computation* **2025**, *13*, 147. [CrossRef]
32. Gupta, V.; Garg, N.; Shukla, R. Subsequential Continuity in Neutrosophic Metric Space with Applications. *Computation* **2025**, *13*, 87. [CrossRef]
33. Al-Hussein, A.B.A.; Tahir, F.R.; Pham, V.T. FPGA Implementation of Synergetic Controller-Based MPPT Algorithm for a Standalone PV System. *Computation* **2025**, *13*, 64. [CrossRef]
34. Komizu, I.; Kobayashi, K.; Yamashita, Y. Model Predictive Control of Spatially Distributed Systems with Spatio-Temporal Logic Specifications. *Computation* **2024**, *12*, 196. [CrossRef]
35. Alluhydan, K.; EL-Sayed, A.T.; El-Bahrawy, F.T. The Effect of Proportional, Proportional-Integral, and Proportional-Integral-Derivative Controllers on Improving the Performance of Torsional Vibrations on a Dynamical System. *Computation* **2024**, *12*, 157. [CrossRef]

 https://doi.org/10.3390/computation14020044

36. Shams Falavarjani, M.; González Vázquez, A.; Villaverde, A.F. Assessment of Computational Tools for Analysing the Observability and Accessibility of Nonlinear Models. *Computation* **2025**, *13*, 281. [CrossRef]
37. Ismail, G.M.; Moatimid, G.M.; Kontomaris, S.V. Approximate Analytical Solutions of Nonlinear Jerk Equations Using the Parameter Expansion Method. *Computation* **2026**, *14*, 17. [CrossRef]

https://doi.org/10.3390/computation14020044

computation

MDPI

Article

Approximate Analytical Solutions of Nonlinear Jerk Equations Using the Parameter Expansion Method

Gamal M. Ismail [1,*], Galal M. Moatimid [2] and Stylianos V. Kontomaris [3,*]

[1] Department of Mathematics, Faculty of Science, Islamic University of Madinah, Madinah 42351, Saudi Arabia
[2] Department of Mathematics, Faculty of Education, Ain Shams University, Roxy, Cairo 11566, Egypt; gal_moa@edu.asu.edu.eg
[3] School of Sciences, European University Cyprus, Nicosia 2404, Cyprus
* Correspondence: gamalm2010@yahoo.com (G.M.I.); s.kontomaris@research.euc.ac.cy (S.V.K.)

Abstract

The Parameter Expansion Method (PEM) is employed to study nonlinear Jerk equations, which are often difficult to solve because of their strong nonlinearity. This method provides higher accuracy and broader applicability, enabling analytical insights and closed-form approximations. This study explores the use of Prof. He's PEM to derive approximate analytical solutions of the nonlinear third-order Jerk equation, this model is commonly encountered in the analysis of complex dynamical systems across physics and engineering. Owing to the strong nonlinearity inherent in Jerk equations, exact solutions are often unattainable. The PEM provides a simple, effective framework by expanding the solution with respect to an embedding parameter, allowing accurate approximations without the need of small parameters or linearization. The method's reliability and precision are validated through comparisons with numerical simulations, demonstrating its practicality and robustness in tackling nonlinear problems. The results indicate that PEM provides highly accurate approximations of nonlinear Jerk equation, showcasing greater simplicity and efficiency relative to other analytical methods, along with excellent concordance with numerical simulations. Additionally, the nonlinear Jerk equation demonstrates exact approximate solutions via PEM, closely mirroring numerical results and surpassing several contemporary analytical techniques in efficiency and usability. Furthermore, the study indicates that PEM is a straightforward and effective approach in solving nonlinear Jerk equation. It generates accurate estimates that nearly align with numerical simulations and surpass numerous other analytical methods.

Keywords: Jerk equation; analytical and numerical solutions; conservative oscillators; cantilever beam

1. Introduction

Nonlinear third-order differential equations play a significant role in modeling a wide range of physical and engineering systems, particularly those involving higher-order dynamics such as Jerk (a third-order derivative of displacement), which is essential in characterizing smooth transitions in acceleration. There are several key applications of nonlinear Jerk equations across various fields, such as robotics, motion control, vehicle dynamics, biomechanics, structural engineering, plasma physics, nonlinear circuits, dynamical systems, MEMS/NEMS devices, and seismology [1–3]. Due to their inherent nonlinearity and higher order, exact analytical solutions of such equations are often difficult or impossible to achieve. Traditional techniques such as perturbation methods have been widely applied to solve weakly nonlinear differential equations [4]. However, their effectiveness diminishes when dealing with strongly nonlinear problems. This has motivated the development of alternative analytical and semi-analytical approaches capable of handling stronger nonlinearities without requiring small parameters. Among these, He's PEM has emerged as a simple yet powerful analytical tool [5,6]. The PEM constructs approximate solutions by expanding the response in terms of an artificial parameter, enabling effective handling of nonlinearities with minimal computational effort.

Analytical solutions of nonlinear Jerk equations are infrequently obtainable due to the strong nonlinearity inherent in their structure. Consequently, researchers have developed various analytical and semi-analytical methods to approximate periodic solutions and analyze system dynamics [7–10]. More specifically, Wang et al. [11] applied He's PEM to obtain analytical solutions of nonlinear Jerk equations. Hu [12] applied the Lindstedt–Poincaré perturbation method to a class of nonlinear Jerk equations, deriving approximate frequency–amplitude relations of systems with cubic nonlinearity. Similarly, Ma et al. [13] employed He's Homotopy perturbation method (HPM) to obtain analytical approximations of Jerk oscillators, accomplishing results that agreed well with numerical simulations. In an effort to enhance flexibility and accuracy, Marinca et al. [14] introduced the optimal auxiliary functions method to tackle nonlinear Jerk systems, effectively reducing residual errors through optimally selected auxiliary terms. Hu et al. [15] proposed a modified Mickens iteration procedure to handle nonlinear Jerk equations, which demonstrated rapid convergence and accurate estimation of periodic solutions, even of strongly nonlinear cases. Ramos [16] applied the Lindstedt–Poincaré method to analyze Jerk equations. While Leung and Guo [17] applied the residue harmonic balance approach. Ismail and Abu-Zinadah [18] extend the global error minimization method to obtain analytic approximations of nonlinear Jerk equations. El-Dib [19,20] used the non-perturbative approach and Galerkin's method, respectively, to solve the nonlinear Jerk oscillator.

More recently, Ismail and Yamani [21] presented a hybrid approach based on the Modified Iteration Method and He's PEM, offering an efficient framework for solving complex Jerk equations without resorting to linearization or small parameter assumptions. Nonlinear Jerk equations, when examined through PEM, possess significant experimental and practical applications in science and engineering. In mechanical systems, Jerk equations are essential in creating smoother motion profiles in robotics, computer numerical control (CNC) machining, and transportation systems, as abrupt changes in acceleration can lead to wear, vibration, or discomfort. Nonlinear Jerk models in electrical engineering characterize specific chaotic oscillators and nonlinear circuits, facilitating the advancement of secure communication systems and signal processing devices. In biomechanics, Jerk is significant in modeling human or animal movement, contributing to ergonomic design, prosthetics, and sports performance analysis. The PEM improves these applications by delivering precise analytical approximations that can be empirically tested, diminishing dependence on solely numerical simulations and facilitating real-time implementation in control systems. In experimental contexts, PEM-based models facilitate parameter optimization, forecast system behavior under diverse conditions, and enhance designs for stability and performance, serving as a potent instrument in connecting theoretical nonlinear dynamics with practical breakthroughs.

The present study aims to explore the application of PEM to a class of nonlinear third-order differential equations, often referred to as Jerk equations. The focus is on deriving accurate approximate solutions and comparing them with the known results to demonstrate the method's efficiency, reliability, and simplicity. The findings contribute to the growing

 https://doi.org/10.3390/computation14010017

body of literature on analytical methods of nonlinear systems, offering a valuable tool for researchers who working with higher-order nonlinear differential equations.

Jerk equations feature complex displacement–velocity–acceleration coupling and high-order nonlinearities that complicate their analysis. This study is very significant to demonstrate the systematic application of PEM to derive highly accurate analytical approximations of strongly nonlinear Jerk equations. The PEM solutions not only match numerical simulations with remarkable precision, but also successfully capture elusive phenomena like amplitude-dependent frequency shifts and higher-harmonic content features that often missed by traditional perturbation methods. These findings establish PEM as an efficient and reliable analytical tool in exploring Jerk equations in various engineering and physical contexts.

To crystallize the presentation of the paper, its remainder is organized as follows: Section 2 is devoted to introducing the implementation of PEM. This section involves two special cases. The results and discussion are presented in Section 3. Lastly, the conclusions are presented in Section 4.

2. Implementation of PEM

The general third-order nonlinear Jerk equation, according to Gottlieb [22], can be described as

$$\dddot{x} + \alpha\dot{x} + \beta\dot{x}^3 + \gamma x^2\dot{x} - \delta x\dot{x}\ddot{x} + \mu\dot{x}\ddot{x}^2 = 0, \tag{1}$$

with the initial conditions of

$$x(0) = 0,\ \dot{x}(0) = A,\ \ddot{x}(0) = 0. \tag{2}$$

Equation (1) is highly versatile. It applies to mechanical vibrations, nonlinear circuits, chaos theory, control and robotics, human motion, biomechanics, and aerospace systems.

According to PEM [23,24], the solution is expanded in a series of artificial parameters, p, in the following form:

$$x = x_0 + px_1 + p^2x_2 + \cdots, \tag{3}$$

in which the parameter $\alpha, \beta, \gamma, \delta$, and μ can be expanded as x in Equation (3):

$$\alpha = \omega^2 + p\omega_1 + p^2\omega_2 + \cdots, \tag{4}$$

$$\beta = pa_1 + p^2a_2 + \cdots, \tag{5}$$

$$\gamma = pb_1 + p^2b_2 + \cdots, \tag{6}$$

$$\delta = pc_1 + p^2c_2 + \cdots, \tag{7}$$

$$\mu = pd_1 + p^2d_2 + \cdots. \tag{8}$$

Substituting Equations (3)–(8) into Equation (1) and equating the terms of the identical powers of p, we have

$$\dddot{x}_0 + \omega^2\dot{x}_0 = 0, \tag{9}$$

$$\dddot{x}_1 + \omega^2\dot{x}_1 + b_1\dot{x}_0x_0^2 + \omega_1\dot{x}_0 + a_1\dot{x}_0^3 - c_1x_0\dot{x}_0\ddot{x}_0 + d_1\dot{x}_0\ddot{x}_0^2 = 0, \tag{10}$$

 https://doi.org/10.3390/computation14010017

$$\dddot{x}_2 + \omega^2\dot{x}_2 + b_1 2x_0x_1\dot{x}_0 + b_2x_0^2\dot{x}_0 + \omega_2\dot{x}_0 + a_2\dot{x}_0^3 + b_1x_0^2\dot{x}_1 + \omega_1\dot{x}_1 + 3a_1\dot{x}_0^2\dot{x}_1 - c_1x_1\dot{x}_0\ddot{x}_0 - c_2x_0\dot{x}_0\ddot{x}_0$$
$$-c_1x_0\dot{x}_0\ddot{x}_0 + d_2\dot{x}_0\ddot{x}_0^2 + d_1\dot{x}_1\ddot{x}_0^2 - c_1x_0\dot{x}_0\ddot{x}_1 + 2d_2\dot{x}_0\ddot{x}_0\ddot{x}_1 = 0. \quad (11)$$

The solution of Equation (9), in light of the initial conditions, is given as

$$x_0 = \frac{A}{\omega}\sin(\omega t). \quad (12)$$

Substituting Equation (12) into Equation (10), then solving the results after eliminating the secular terms, we obtain the following:

$$x_1 = A^3\left(\frac{a_1}{96\omega^3} - \frac{b_1}{96\omega^5} + \frac{c_1}{96\omega^3} - \frac{d_1}{96\omega}\right)\sin(3\omega t), \quad (13)$$

$$\omega_1 = -\frac{A^2(3\omega^2a_1 + b_1 - \omega^2c_1 + \omega^4d_1)}{4\omega^2}. \quad (14)$$

Similar to the previous step, we can obtain x_2 and ω_2 in the same manner:

$$x_2 = \left(\frac{A^5a_1^2}{512\omega^5} + \frac{A^3a_2}{96\omega^3} - \frac{A^5a_1b_1}{768\omega^7} - \frac{A^5b_1^2}{1536\omega^9} - \frac{A^3b_2}{96\omega^5} + \frac{A^5a_1c_1}{384\omega^5} + \frac{A^5c_1^2}{1536\omega^5} - \frac{A^3c_2}{96\omega^3} - \frac{A^5a_1d_1}{768\omega^3} - \frac{A^5b_1d_1}{768\omega^5} - \frac{A^5d_1^2}{1536\omega} - \frac{A^3d_2}{96\omega} + \right.$$
$$\left.\frac{A^3a_1\omega_1}{768\omega^5} - \frac{A^3b_1\omega_1}{768\omega^7} + \frac{A^3c_1\omega_1}{768\omega^5} - \frac{A^3d_1\omega_1}{768\omega^3}\right)\mathrm{Sin}(3\omega t) + \left(\frac{A^5a_1^2}{5120\omega^5} - \frac{7A^5a_1b_1}{23{,}040\omega^7} + \frac{A^5b_1^2}{9216\omega^9} - \frac{A^5a_1c_1}{11{,}520\omega^5} + \frac{A^5b_1c_1}{5760\omega^7} - \frac{13A^5c_1^2}{46{,}080\omega^5} - \right.$$
$$\left.\frac{A^5a_1d_1}{1536\omega^3} + \frac{13A^5b_1d_1}{23{,}040\omega^5} - \frac{A^5c_1d_1}{5760\omega^3} + \frac{7A^5d_1^2}{15{,}360\omega}\right)\sin(5\omega t). \quad (15)$$

$$\omega_2 = \frac{1}{384\omega^6}A^2(-9A^2\omega^4a_1^2 - 288\omega^6a_2 + 10A^2\omega^2a_1b_1 - A^2b_1^2 - 96\omega^4b_2 - 16A^2\omega^4a_1c_1 + 8A^2\omega^2b_1c_1$$
$$-7A^2\omega^4c_1^2 - 96\omega^6c_2 - 6A^2\omega^6a_1d_1 + 14A^2\omega^4b_1d_1 - 8A^2\omega^6c_1d_1 + 15A^2\omega^8d_1^2 - 96\omega^8d_2). \quad (16)$$

The higher-order approximate solutions to Equation (1) for $x(t)$ and ω can be established in a similar manner.

Now, we shall study some different relevant cases considering main Equation (1).

2.1. Special Case 1: Jerk Equation Based on Displacement–Velocity–Acceleration Interaction

Putting $\beta = \gamma = \mu = 0$, and $\alpha = \delta = 1$, in Equation (1), we obtain the Jerk function involving displacement–velocity–acceleration product and velocity term in the following form [22]:

$$\dddot{x} + \dot{x} - x\dot{x}\ddot{x} = 0,\ x(0) = 0,\ \dot{x}(0) = A,\ \ddot{x}(0) = 0. \quad (17)$$

Equation (17) describes a system where a competition between linear velocity effects and a nonlinear product of displacement, velocity, and acceleration governs the rate of change in acceleration (Jerk). This makes it a model for nonlinear oscillators with strong displacement–velocity–acceleration coupling, relevant in mechanical vibrations, nonlinear circuits, and complex dynamical systems.

Inserting Equations (3), (4) and (7) into Equation (17), a new trial function is proposed for the first-order approximation as

$$\dddot{x}_0 + \omega^2\dot{x}_0 = 0, \quad (18)$$

$$\dddot{x}_1 + \omega^2\dot{x}_1 + \omega_1\dot{x}_0 - c_1x_0\dot{x}_0\ddot{x}_0 = 0, \quad (19)$$

$$\dddot{x}_2 + \omega^2\dot{x}_2 + \omega_2\dot{x}_0 + \omega_1\dot{x}_1 - c_1x_1\dot{x}_0\ddot{x}_0 - c_2x_0\dot{x}_0\ddot{x}_0 - c_1x_0\dot{x}_1\ddot{x}_1 - c_1x_0\dot{x}_0\ddot{x}_1 = 0. \quad (20)$$

https://doi.org/10.3390/computation14010017

A new trial function is proposed for the first-order approximation, Equation (18), as

$$x_0(t) = \frac{A}{\omega}\sin\omega t. \tag{21}$$

Substituting Equation (21) into Equation (19), we can write

$$\dddot{x}_1 + \omega^2\dot{x}_1 + \frac{1}{4}(A^3c_1 + 4A\omega_1)\cos(\omega t) - \frac{1}{4}A^3c_1\cos(3\omega t) = 0. \tag{22}$$

Solving the above results after eliminating the secular term, and choosing $c_1 = 0$ and $c_2 = 0$, we obtain

$$x_1(t) = -\frac{A^3}{96\omega^3}\sin(3\omega t),\ \omega_1 = -\frac{1}{4}A^2, \tag{23}$$

$$x_2(t) = -\frac{A^5}{3072\omega^5}\sin(3\omega t) + \frac{13A^5}{46,080\omega^5}\sin(5\omega t),\ \omega_2 = \frac{7A^4}{384\omega^2}. \tag{24}$$

Applying the same procedure, we can find x_3, x_4, ... and so on.

Now using Equations (21), (23) and (24), we obtain the third-order solution for $x(t)$, as follows

$$x(t) = \frac{A}{\omega}\sin(\omega t) - \left(\frac{A^3}{96\omega^3} + \frac{A^5}{3072\omega^5}\right)\sin(3\omega t) + \frac{13A^5}{46,080\omega^5}\sin(5\omega t), \tag{25}$$

$$\omega = \frac{1}{4}\sqrt{8 + 2A^2 + \sqrt{64 + 32A^2 - \frac{2A^4}{3}}}. \tag{26}$$

Equations (25) and (26) represent the effects of strong nonlinearity: amplitude-dependent frequency and wave forming across higher harmonics, both of which are a direct result of the three-way feedback between x, $\dot{x}$, and $\ddot{x}$ that controls the Jerk equation. These features characterize nonlinear oscillators in mechanical systems, circuits, and elsewhere, and determine their response under different excitation amplitudes.

2.2. Special Case 2: Jerk Function, Involving the Product of Velocity and the Square of Acceleration, Along with a Term Proportional to Velocity

Putting $\beta = \gamma = \delta = 0$, and $\alpha = \mu = 1$, in Equation (1), then we obtain the Jerk function involving velocity times acceleration squared, and velocity in the following form [22]:

$$\dddot{x} + \dot{x} + \dot{x}\ddot{x}^2 = 0,\ x(0) = 0,\ \dot{x}(0) = A,\ \ddot{x}(0) = 0. \tag{27}$$

Equation (27) describes a system where Jerk is governed by a balance between a linear velocity effect and a nonlinear velocity–acceleration interaction. The nonlinear term makes the system highly sensitive to bursts of acceleration: the faster and more forcefully the system accelerates, the stronger feedback on Jerk. This means that the system behaves like a dynamical amplifier of rapid motion, showing strong nonlinear resistance or amplification depending on the motion's phase and intensity.

Following the same procedure as the previous case, after performing many calculations, we can finally obtain the general solution up to third order in the following form:

$$x(t) = \frac{A}{\omega}\sin(\omega t) - (\frac{A^3}{96\omega} + \frac{A^5}{3072\omega})\sin(3\omega t) + (\frac{7A^5}{15,360\omega})\sin(5\omega t), \tag{28}$$

$$\omega = \frac{64}{\sqrt{4096 - 1024A^2 + 160A^4 - 13A^6}}. \tag{29}$$

https://doi.org/10.3390/computation14010017

To assess the accuracy of the solutions obtained in cases 1 and 2, we compared the approximate analytical results derived using PEM with numerical solutions obtained via the fourth-order Runge–Kutta method. Figures 1 and 2 illustrate these comparisons, corresponding to the present solutions (25) and (28), respectively.

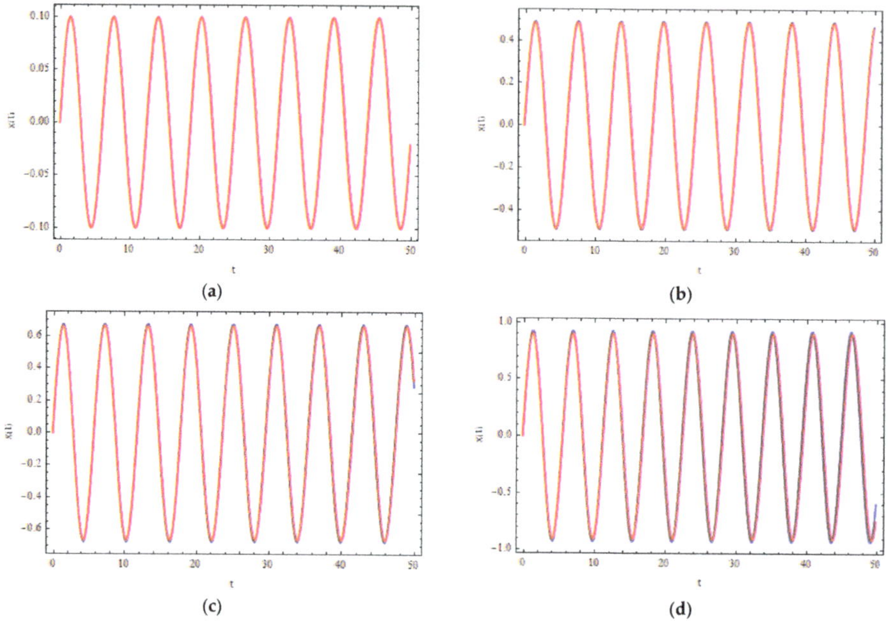

Figure 1. Shows comparison between analytical solution (red line) and numerical solution (blue line) for Equation (25). (**a**) $A = 0.1$; (**b**) $A = 0.5$; (**c**) $A = 0.7$; (**d**) $A = 1$.

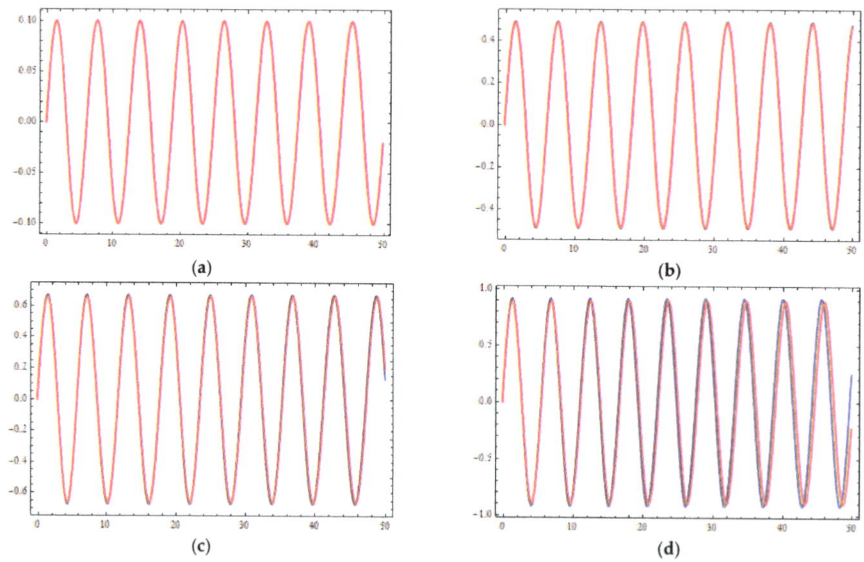

Figure 2. Displays a comparison between analytical solution (red line) and numerical solution (blue line) for Equation (28). (**a**) $A = 0.1$; (**b**) $A = 0.5$; (**c**) $A = 0.7$; (**d**) $A = 1$.

https://doi.org/10.3390/computation14010017

3. Results and Discussion

The PEM was effectively applied to the nonlinear third-order Jerk equation, yielding accurate and consistent approximate analytical solutions. Two specific cases are explored: one involving displacement–velocity–acceleration interactions and another involving velocity coupled with acceleration-squared terms. The third-order approximations demonstrated strong agreement with numerical results obtained via the Runge–kutta method, as shown in Figures 1 and 2, particularly for low to moderate oscillation amplitudes. Frequency–amplitude response curves indicated significant nonlinearity-induced shifts, showing both hardening and softening behavior depending on the nature of the Jerk function. The analytical expressions also successfully captured higher-order harmonic contributions—such as third and fifth harmonics—especially at larger amplitudes.

These findings highlight PEM's effectiveness as a semi-analytical approach in solving the nonlinear Jerk-type. Unlike traditional perturbation methods, PEM does not depend on small parameters or linearization assumptions, making it well-suited for systems with strong nonlinearities. The method accurately models amplitude-dependent frequency behavior and provides deeper insights into the dynamics of nonlinear Jerk equations. The inclusion of higher-order harmonics reflects the impact of nonlinearity on waveform shape and energy distribution. Furthermore, PEM delivers closed-form solutions that support further theoretical investigations and sensitivity analyses. Overall, PEM proves to be a robust and flexible method in analyzing nonlinear oscillatory systems in areas such as applied mechanics, vibration analysis, and control engineering.

In contrast to perturbation methods that require small parameters or linearization, PEM directly incorporates nonlinear coupling terms, allowing it to capture amplitude-dependent frequency shifts and higher-harmonic contributions, while maintaining excellent agreement with numerical simulations. Figures 1 and 2, therefore, serve not only as visual comparisons but also as demonstrations of PEM's effectiveness, providing a compact analytical framework that accurately tracks nonlinear distortions in both frequency and waveform—an advantage over traditional perturbation approaches.

Figure 1: Shows comparison between the analytical solutions obtained using PEM (red line) and the numerical solution (blue line) for Equation (25). The numerical solution is generated using the classical fourth-order Runge–Kutta method to ensure stability and accuracy. The PEM solution closely follows the numerical response, reproducing the fundamental oscillation as well as nonlinear effects such as amplitude-dependent frequency shifts and higher-harmonic components.

Figure 2: Displays comparison between the analytical solutions obtained using PEM (red line) and the numerical solution (blue line) for Equation (28). The numerical solution is obtained using the fourth-order Runge–Kutta method under identical initial conditions and time-stepping parameters. The strong agreement highlights PEM's ability to reproduce nonlinear distortions, including hardening/softening frequency shifts and waveform modifications arising from third- and fifth-order harmonics.

Taken together, Figures 1 and 2 demonstrate PEM's strength in handling strongly nonlinear Jerk equations. The method successfully models nonlinear frequency shifts—showing hardening or softening depending on the governing Jerk function—and naturally captures the emergence of higher harmonics that reshape the waveform at larger amplitudes. These features, often inaccessible to conventional perturbation methods, are clearly resolved within the PEM framework. The near-complete overlap with numerical simulations further confirms its robustness as a semi-analytical approach, making PEM a reliable tool in investigating nonlinear oscillators in applied mechanics and engineering contexts.

In addition, Tables 1 and 2 provide quantitative evidence by comparing the third approximate period T_3 obtained from the PEM with the exact values and other analytical

 https://doi.org/10.3390/computation14010017

methods. The deviations are remarkably small, for example, at amplitude 0.1, the PEM period is 6.275347 compared with the exact 6.275346837, an error of less than 10^{-6} Even at larger amplitudes, discrepancies remain minimal. Together with Figures 1 and 2, these results provide both numerical and graphical validation of PEM's accuracy and convergence, reinforcing the claim that PEM is a simple yet highly effective tool in capturing nonlinear frequency shifts and higher-harmonic behavior.

Table 1. Displays a comparison between the exact and approximate values of the period for Equation (17).

A	T_e	Current T_3	RHBM [17]	HPM [13]	LPM [16]	HBM [22]	PEM [11]
0.1	6.275347	6.275350 (4.78×10^{-5})	6.275346837 (2.59×10^{-6})	6.27534684 (2.55×10^{-6})	6.275348 (1.59×10^{-5})	6.275346 (1.59×10^{-5})	6.275326 (3.35×10^{-4})
0.2	6.252016	6.2520924 (0.001222)	6.25201599 (1.59×10^{-7})	6.25201599 (2.59×10^{-7})	6.252028 (1.92×10^{-4})	6.252003 (2.08×10^{-4})	6.251690 (0.00521)
0.5	6.096061	6.09866 (0.042634)	6.09606050 (8.20×10^{-6})	6.09605904 (3.12×10^{-5})	6.096491 (0.00706)	6.095585 (0.00781)	6.083668 (0.20329)
1	5.626007	5.653322 (0.485513)	5.62599289 (2.51×10^{-4})	5.62579479 (0.00377)	5.630343 (0.07707)	5.619852 (0.10940)	5.441398 (3.28135)

Table 2. Shows a comparison between the exact and approximate values of the period for Equation (27).

A	T_e	Current T_3	RHBM [17]	HPM [13]	LPM [16]	HBM [22]
0.1	6.2753338	6.275338 0	6.2753338 0	6.27533378 0	6.275329 (7.61×10^{-5})	6.2753264 (1.18×10^{-4})
0.2	6.251809	6.251887 (0.001247)	6.25180911 (1.76×10^{-6})	6.25182078 (1.88×10^{-4})	6.251740 (0.00110)	6.251690 (0.00190)
0.5	6.088449	6.0914236 (0.048856)	6.08848374 (5.71×10^{-4})	6.08815979 (0.00475)	6.085649 (0.04599)	6.083668 (0.07853)
1	5.527200	5.570066 (0.775546)	5.52994105 (0.04959)	5.50818960 (0.343943)	5.477174 (0.90509)	5.441398 (1.55236)
1.5	4.690247	4.863291 (3.689443)	4.72603111 (0.76295)	4.44735707 (5.17847)	4.412733 (5.91683)	4.155936 (11.39196)

To validate the accuracy, we calculated the percentage error (%) according to its definition:

$$\text{Error} = \left| \frac{T_{\text{exact}} - T_{\text{App}}}{T_{\text{exact}}} \right| \times 100\%, \tag{30}$$

where various approximate periods obtained by T_{App} and T_{exact} represent the corresponding exact period of the oscillator.

Finally, while earlier studies, such as Ismail and Yamani [21], employed hybrid schemes that combine PEM with Modified Iteration Methods to enhance convergence, the present work deliberately applies PEM in its pure form. This choice emphasizes PEM's intrinsic ability to capture amplitude-dependent frequency shifts, higher-harmonic distortions, and nonlinear waveform modifications without auxiliary corrections. The results confirm that PEM alone provides a concise yet robust analytical framework, delivering accuracy comparable to more complex hybrid approaches while retaining greater simplicity and transparency. This highlights the dual contribution of the paper: establishing PEM as both a practical analytical tool for nonlinear Jerk equations and a benchmark framework against which hybrid or modified methods can be evaluated.

https://doi.org/10.3390/computation14010017

To assess the accuracy of the analytical approximations for the nonlinear Jerk Equations (17) and (27) against the corresponding reference solutions in Equations (25) and (28), three quantitative error indicators were utilized: the Root Mean Square Error (RMSE), the Relative RMSE, and the Maximum Absolute Error (Max Abs Error). The equations were first solved numerically using a high-order Runge–Kutta integration scheme to obtain the reference solution $x_{num}(t)$, while the analytical approximation $x_{approx}(t)$ was evaluated at the same discrete time points t_i. The RMSE, which quantifies the average deviation magnitude between the two solutions, was calculated as follows:

$$\text{RMSE} = \sqrt{\frac{1}{N} + \sum_{i=1}^{N} \left[x_{num}(t_i) - x_{approx}(t_i)\right]^2}, \tag{31}$$

where N represents the total number of sampled points. To obtain a dimensionless and scale-independent indicator, the RMSE was normalized by the root-mean-square amplitude of the numerical solution, resulting in the Relative RMSE, which is defined as

$$\text{Relative RMSE} = \frac{\text{RMSE}}{N\sqrt{\frac{1}{N} + \sum_{i=1}^{N} \left[x_{num}(t_i) - x_{approx}(t_i)\right]^2}}. \tag{32}$$

Furthermore, the Maximum Absolute Error was determined as

$$\text{Max Abs Error} = max\left|x_{num}(t_i) - x_{approx}(t_i)\right|, \tag{33}$$

to capture the largest pointwise deviation between the two solutions within the considered time interval. Collectively, these three metrics provide a comprehensive evaluation of both the overall and peak discrepancies, where lower values indicate stronger agreement and higher accuracy of the analytical approximation in reproducing the true system dynamics, as shown in Tables 3 and 4.

Table 3. Computes RMSE, Relative RMSE, and Maximum Absolute Error for Equation (17).

A	**RMSE**	**Relative RMSE**	**Max Abs Error**
0.1	0.0000220515	0.000311564	0.0000313245
0.5	0.0050616	0.0146871	0.0110108
1	0.0997455	0.1527548	0.2300944
1.5	0.4753127	0.5284609	1.0796243
2	1.1507117	1.0622366	2.5387488

Table 4. Computes RMSE, Relative RMSE, and Maximum Absolute Error for Equation (25).

A	**RMSE**	**Relative RMSE**	**Max Abs Error**
0.1	0.0000221	0.000312677	0.0000315208
0.5	0.0065785	0.0190583	0.0148713
1	0.178973	0.279584	0.4200002
1.5	0.98505	1.15267	2.15964
2	1.42245	1.48123	2.80166

To quantify the largest pointwise deviation between the two solutions over the considered time interval. Together, these three metrics offer a comprehensive assessment of both the overall and peak discrepancies, where smaller values signify closer agreement and higher accuracy of the analytical approximation in capturing the true system dynamics, as presented in Tables 3 and 4.

https://doi.org/10.3390/computation14010017

Tables 3 and 4 present a quantitative assessment of the PEM accuracy through the RMSE, Relative RMSE, and Maximum Absolute Error for the two nonlinear Jerk equations. The outcomes demonstrate that PEM maintains excellent consistency with the numerical (Runge–Kutta) results, particularly for small and moderate amplitudes where the errors remain below 10^{-3}. As anticipated, the discrepancies increase with amplitude due to the intensification of nonlinear effects at larger oscillation levels. A comparative analysis reveals that the second case (Table 4) exhibits slightly higher errors than the first, suggesting that the velocity–acceleration-squared coupling produces stronger nonlinearity than the displacement–velocity–acceleration interaction. In general, the low RMSE and Maximum Absolute Error values confirm the robustness and convergence of PEM, while the gradual error increase at high amplitudes indicates that higher-order extensions or hybrid formulations—such as combining PEM with the Modified Iteration Method—could further enhance accuracy.

4. Conclusions

This paper introduced a straightforward and effective analytical technique, parameter expansion, to estimate the frequencies and periodic solutions of highly nonlinear oscillators described by a third-order nonlinear differential equation. The method's key benefit lies in its simplicity, and the results it produced closely match numerical solutions, regardless of whether the oscillations have small or large amplitudes. In conclusion, this study successfully employed PEM to analyze complex dynamics of slender cantilever beams with flexible roots and intermediate lumped masses, systems governed by a highly nonlinear differential equation. The PEM provides a straightforward and accurate approximate analytical solution, demonstrating superior performance compared to other approximation techniques, particularly in physically realistic scenarios. By directly yielding analytical solutions while bypassing complex computations, PEM offers a quicker and more efficient approach in understanding and predicting the behavior of these challenging nonlinear oscillators, making it a valuable tool for engineering applications.

As a future study, coupled Jerk systems can be studied in multi-body mechanical constructions, interconnected electrical circuits, synchronized robotic arms, and physiological systems such as coupled neuromuscular reflexes. These systems frequently display complex behavior, including chaos, synchronization, bifurcations, and wave propagation, which are challenging to analyze using conventional linearization or perturbation techniques. PEM offers a systematic method for obtaining precise approximate solutions without limiting the research to minor parameters, facilitating a more profound understanding of stability, resonance, and control attributes. Utilizing PEM in coupled Jerk equations enables researchers to more accurately forecast system behavior across diverse conditions, optimize design parameters, and improve performance in both experimental and industrial contexts, thereby connecting theoretical nonlinear dynamics with practical engineering applications.

Author Contributions: Conceptualization, G.M.I.; methodology, G.M.I. and G.M.M.; software, G.M.I. and G.M.M.; validation, G.M.I., G.M.M. and S.V.K.; investigation, G.M.I., G.M.M. and S.V.K.; resources, G.M.I. and G.M.M.; writing—original draft preparation, G.M.I.; writing—review and editing, G.M.I., G.M.M. and S.V.K. All authors have read and agreed to the published version of the manuscript.

Funding: This research received no external funding.

Data Availability Statement: The original contributions presented in this study are included in the article. Further inquiries can be directed to the corresponding authors.

https://doi.org/10.3390/computation14010017

Acknowledgments: The researchers wish to extend their sincere gratitude to the Deanship of Scientific Research at the Islamic University of Madinah for the support provided to the Post-Publishing Program.

Conflicts of Interest: The authors declare no conflicts of interest.

References

1. Sommer Iii, H.J. Kinematic jerk and jounce for multibody dynamics with joint constraints. *Mech. Mach. Theory* **2024**, *196*, 105613. [CrossRef]
2. Nayfeh, A.H.; Mook, D.T. *Nonlinear Oscillations*; Wiley-Interscience: New York, NY, USA, 1979.
3. Holm, D.D.; Schmah, T.; Stoica, C. *Geometric Mechanics and Symmetry*; Oxford University Press: Oxford, UK, 2009.
4. Mickens, R.E. *Truly Nonlinear Oscillations*; World Scientific: Singapore, 2006.
5. He, J.H. Homotopy perturbation technique. *Comput. Math. Appl.* **2006**, *37*, 257–262. [CrossRef]
6. He, J.H. Some asymptotic methods for strongly nonlinear equations. *Int. J. Mod. Phys. B* **2006**, *20*, 1141–1199. [CrossRef]
7. Cveticanin, L. Exact Solutions for Strong Nonlinear Oscillators with Linear Damping. *Mathematics* **2025**, *13*, 1662. [CrossRef]
8. Farea, N.M.; Ismail, G.M. Analytical solution for strongly nonlinear vibration of a stringer shell. *J. Low Freq. Noise Vib. Act. Control* **2025**, *44*, 81–87. [CrossRef]
9. Mohammadian, M.; Ismail, G.M. Improved harmonic balance method for analyzing asymmetric restoring force functions in nonlinear vibration of mechanical systems. *Phys. Scr.* **2024**, *99*, 075280. [CrossRef]
10. Big-Alabo, A. Frequency response of a mass grounded by linear and nonlinear springs in series: An exact analysis. *J. Low Freq. Noise Vib. Act. Control* **2023**, *43*, 813–830. [CrossRef]
11. Wang, Y.X.; Ren, Z.F.; Mo, L.F. Application of He's parameter-expansion method to Jerk equation. *J. Phys. Conf. Series* **2008**, *96*, 012215. [CrossRef]
12. Hu, H. Perturbation method for periodic solutions of nonlinear jerk equations. *Phys. Lett. A* **2008**, *372*, 4205–4209. [CrossRef]
13. Ma, X.Y.; Wei, L.P.; Guo, Z.J. He's homotopy perturbation method to periodic solutions of nonlinear Jerk equations. *J. Sound Vib.* **2008**, *314*, 217–227. [CrossRef]
14. Marinca, V.; Herisanu, N.; Marinca, B. *Optimal Auxiliary Functions Method for Nonlinear Dynamical Systems*; Springer: Cham, Switzerland, 2021.
15. Hu, H.; Zheng, M.Y.; Guo, Y.J. Iteration calculations of periodic solutions to nonlinear jerk equations. *Acta Mech.* **2010**, *209*, 269–274. [CrossRef]
16. Ramos, J.I. Approximate methods based on order reduction for the periodic solutions of nonlinear third-order ordinary differential equations. *Appl. Math. Comput.* **2010**, *215*, 4304–4319. [CrossRef]
17. Leung, A.Y.T.; Guo, Z.J. Residue harmonic balance approach to limit cycles of nonlinear Jerk equations. *Int. J. Non-Linear Mech.* **2011**, *46*, 898–906. [CrossRef]
18. Ismail, G.M.; Abu-Zinadah, H. Analytic approximations to nonlinear third-order Jerk equations via modified global error minimization method. *J. King Saud Univ. Sci.* **2021**, *33*, 101219. [CrossRef]
19. El-Dib, Y.O. The simplest approach to solving the cubic nonlinear Jerk oscillator with the non-perturbative method. *Math. Meth. Appl. Sci.* **2022**, *45*, 5165–5183. [CrossRef]
20. El-Dib, Y.O.; Elgazery, N.S.; Alyousef, H.A. Galerkin's method to solve a fractional time-delayed Jerk oscillator. *Arch. Appl. Mech.* **2023**, *93*, 3597–3607. [CrossRef]
21. Ismail, G.M.; Yamani, M.I. A novel analytical approximate solution for strongly nonlinear third-order Jerk equations using a modified iteration method. *Eur. J. Pure Appl. Math.* **2024**, *17*, 3622–3641. [CrossRef]
22. Gottlieb, H.P.W. Harmonic balance approach to periodic solution of nonlinear Jerk equation. *J. Sound Vib.* **2004**, *271*, 671–683. [CrossRef]
23. He, J.H. An elementary introduction to recently developed asymptotic methods and nanomechanics in textile engineering. *Int. J. Mod. Phys. B* **2008**, *22*, 3487–3578. [CrossRef]
24. He, J.H. Bookkeeping parameter in perturbation methods. *Int. J. Nonlinear Sci. Numer. Simul.* **2001**, *2*, 257–264. [CrossRef]

 https://doi.org/10.3390/computation14010017

computation

MDPI

Article

Assessment of Computational Tools for Analysing the Observability and Accessibility of Nonlinear Models

Mahmoud Shams Falavarjani [1], Adriana González Vázquez [1] and Alejandro F. Villaverde [1,2,*]

[1] Universidade de Vigo, Department of Systems Engineering and Control, 36310 Vigo, Galicia, Spain; mahmoud.shamsfalavarjani@uvigo.gal (M.S.F.); adriana.gonzalez@uvigo.gal (A.G.V.)
[2] CITMAga, Galician Centre for Mathematical Research and Technology, 15782 Santiago de Compostela, Galicia, Spain
* Correspondence: afvillaverde@uvigo.gal

Abstract

Accessibility and observability are two properties of dynamic models that provide insights into the structural relationships between their input, output, and state variables. They are closely related to controllability and structural local identifiability, respectively. Observability and identifiability determine, respectively, the possibility of inferring the unmeasured state variables and parameters of a model from output measurements; accessibility and controllability describe the possibility of driving its state by changing its input. Analysing these structural properties in nonlinear models of ordinary differential equations can be challenging, particularly when dealing with large systems. Two main approaches are currently used for their study: one based on differential geometry, which uses symbolic computation, and another one based on sensitivity calculations that uses numerical integration. These approaches are implemented in two MATLAB (R2024b) software tools: the differential geometry approach in STRIKE-GOLDD, and the sensitivity-based method in StrucID. These toolboxes differ significantly in their features and capabilities. Until now, their performance had not been thoroughly compared. In this paper we present a comprehensive comparative study of them, elucidating their differences in applicability, computational efficiency, and robustness against computational issues. Our core finding is that StrucID has a substantially lower computational cost than STRIKE-GOLDD; however, it may occasionally yield inconsistent results due to numerical issues.

Keywords: control theory; nonlinear systems; dynamic modelling; observability; identifiability; controllability; accessibility; computational methods; software

1. Introduction

Structural local identifiability and observability are theoretical properties that characterize the ability to infer, respectively, the parameters and the states of a dynamic model from knowledge of its inputs and outputs [1–3]. Structural identifiability is a necessary but not sufficient condition for model calibration, i.e., for parameter estimation [4]. Similarly, observability is a prerequisite for designing state observers and, consequently, for real-time monitoring of the model's internal states. In the linear case, observability is analysed by computing the rank of the observability matrix, which can be readily obtained through matrix multiplications [5]. In nonlinear systems, observability depends on the operating point and can also be assessed via the rank of an observability matrix [6]. However, the computation of nonlinear observability in this way becomes more involved, as it requires

Lie derivatives [7]. Observability and structural identifiability are closely related concepts; in fact, by treating model parameters as constant state variables, the identifiability problem can be reformulated as an observability problem [8]. As a result, both properties can be analysed jointly; we will refer to Structural Identifiability and Observability with the acronym SIO. Note that in this work we consider these properties from a structural viewpoint, which is sometimes also referred to as "a priori". Their practical counterparts can be approached using methods for practical identifiability analysis [9,10] and uncertainty quantification [11,12].

Historically, the main challenges in analysing SIO have been the limited applicability of some methods for specific models and problem conditions, and the computational burden associated with large-scale models. However, over the past decade, several methods for performing structural identifiability analysis along with publicly available implementations have been developed [13]. Due to these recent advances, it has been argued that the analysis of SIO no longer represents an obstacle in the development of useful mathematical models [10]. The availability of fast and reliable methods for detecting structurally unidentifiable parameters enables researchers to perform this analysis repeatedly throughout the model development process and across various programming environments. One approach, previously mentioned, relies on constructing an observability and identifiability matrix and computing its rank. This test, known as the Observability Rank Condition (ORC), draws on concepts from differential geometry, namely Lie derivatives, and it is implemented in the MATLAB toolbox STRIKE-GOLDD [14,15]. While the ORC is theoretically powerful, its computational cost can be high, especially for complex models with a large number of unknowns (parameters and states) relative to the number of outputs. As an alternative, numerical approaches have been proposed, such as the one presented in [16], which is based on computing the sensitivity matrix and applying singular value decomposition (SVD). A MATLAB implementation is available as the StrucID toolbox [17].

Controllability, like observability, is a property that depends on a model's structure [7,18–20]. Broadly speaking, it describes the possibility of driving a system from an initial state to a final state within a specified period of time. A related property, local accessibility, refers to the possibility of driving a system from an initial state to a full-dimensional target set, i.e., it means that the system can be steered from an initial state to any point in its neighbourhood [21]. For linear models at equilibrium points, controllability and accessibility coincide, and they can be determined by checking whether the controllability matrix has full rank, which implies that the reachable set at time T has a non-empty interior. In contrast, for nonlinear models, these concepts may differ. In particular, nonlinear controllability at non-equilibrium points is associated with a property sometimes called strong accessibility, which means that the accessible set has a non-empty interior exactly at time T. Accessibility has also been referred to in the literature as local weak controllability [7] or simply accessibility.

The analysis of Nonlinear Accessibility and Controllability (NAC) resembles that of structural identifiability and observability (SIO) in that it can also be performed with methods based on differential geometry or sensitivities [22,23]. Except for the simplest cases, such analyses typically involve complex computations and require algorithmic implementations of the associated tests. The differential geometric approach to NAC analysis involves the computation of Lie brackets, instead of the Lie derivatives used for SIO analysis. A number of conditions can be used to analyse NAC (see [15,24]); like the ORC test for SIO analyses, they are also implemented in the aforementioned STRIKE-GOLDD toolbox. Thus, this software tool provides a comprehensive differential geometry approach to SIO and NAC analysis. Likewise, the StrucID toolbox was initially designed for SIO analysis and later extended to NAC [25], thus providing a unified implementation for performing sensitivity-based analyses of SIO and NAC. It should be noted that, although many specialised software tools exist for testing SIO [13], there are comparatively fewer tools for analysing NAC. This gap may be one of the reasons why the controllability of nonlinear models remains underexplored in domains such as biological modelling, biomedicine, or bioprocesses [26].

Until now, the trade-off between computational accuracy and efficiency in these tools has not yet been evaluated in sufficient detail. Some partial results have been published: for example, Wang and Qi [27] presented a method based on automatic differentiation and compared its performance on two models with STRIKE-GOLDD and StrucID; however, they did not share a software implementation, nor did they disclose key details of the comparisons. Rey Barreiro and Villaverde [13] conducted an extensive comparison of SIO analysis tools but limited to symbolic computation methods, and therefore not considering StrucID. Heinrich and colleagues [28] reviewed recent advances in identifiability analysis and compared a number of tools, including StrucID and STRIKE-GOLDD, but focusing only on their computational speed. Moreover, we have also performed preliminary comparisons of these two tools, as well as of the empirical Gramian framework [29], although we only examined their performance for SIO analysis [30].

To fill this gap, our aim in this paper is to compare the performance of the two main tools that are currently available for the analysis of structural local identifiability, observability, accessibility and controllability of nonlinear models: STRIKE-GOLDD and StrucID. We consider models described by ordinary differential equations (ODEs), and examine three criteria: the applicability of the methods, the reliability of their results, and the computational time taken by the calculations. The remainder of this paper is organised as follows: First, in Section 2, we introduce the modelling framework and the methods. Then, in Section 3 we present the results of the evaluations and discuss them. Lastly, we provide our conclusions in Section 4.

2. Materials and Methods

2.1. Modelling Framework

We study dynamic models described by systems of ordinary differential equations (ODEs) of the general form

$$\mathcal{M}: \begin{cases} \dot{x}(t) = f(x(t), u(t), \theta), \\ y(t) = h(x(t), \theta). \end{cases} \tag{1}$$

where f and h are analytic functions. Here, $\theta \in \mathbb{R}^p$ denotes the parameter vector, $u(t) \in \mathbb{R}^r$ represents the input vector, $x(t) \in \mathbb{R}^n$ the state vector, and $y(t) \in \mathbb{R}^m$ the output vector. In this paper, we may sometimes omit the dependence on time to simplify the notation, i.e., we write $\dot{x} = f(x, u, \theta)$ and $y = h(x, \theta)$, for example.

Very often, models are affine in the inputs, i.e., their dynamics can be expressed in the following form:

$$\dot{x} = f(x, \theta) + \sum_{i=1}^{r} u_i g_i(x, \theta), \tag{2}$$

where u_i are the control inputs and, as before, f and g_i are analytic vector fields. This type of model can adequately describe many systems and processes, including biological ones [31,32]. Many theoretical conditions about accessibility and controllability obtained with differential geometric approaches—including those reviewed in Section 2.4.2—are not applicable to models of the general nonlinear form (1), and instead require that the model under study is affine in the inputs.

2.2. Concepts

2.2.1. Structural Identifiability and Observability (SIO)

A parameter $\theta_i \in \theta$ is *structurally locally identifiable* [33,34] if, for almost every $\theta^* \in \mathbb{R}^q$ (except for a set of measure zero), there exists a neighbourhood $\mathcal{N}(\theta^*)$ such that for all $\hat{\theta} \in \mathcal{N}(\theta^*)$,

$$y(t,\theta^*) = y(t,\hat{\theta}) \Longleftrightarrow \theta_i^* = \hat{\theta}_i, \tag{3}$$

If this condition does not hold in any neighbourhood of θ^*, then θ_i is *structurally unidentifiable*. In this work, we will use the word "identifiability" to refer specifically to structural local identifiability.

Similarly, a state variable $x_i(\tau)$ is said to be *observable* if it can be locally determined from the output $y(t)$ and the input $u(t)$ over a finite interval $t_0 \leq \tau \leq t \leq t_f$ ($x_i(\tau)$ is the ith state variable evaluated at time τ, and $\theta_i \in \theta$ denotes the ith model parameter. The symbols t_0 and t_f correspond to the initial and final times of the observation interval) as discussed in [3]. The observability of a state variable is equivalent to the identifiability of its initial condition, if the latter is treated as a parameter. (Note that observability is also a structural and local property, in the same way as the version of identifiability that we study here.) A model as a whole is said to be identifiable (respectively, observable) if all its parameters (respectively, state variables) satisfy the corresponding property. Otherwise, it is called unidentifiable (respectively, unobservable) [10]. We use the acronym SIO to refer to structural local identifiability and observability.

2.2.2. Nonlinear Accessibility and Controllability (NAC)

A system has the *accessibility* property (i.e., it is called *accessible*) if it can be steered from an initial state x_0 to a full-dimensional final set $x(t_f) = x_f$, using appropriate control inputs $u(t)$ [35]. A system is said to be *locally controllable* if it can be steered from an initial state x_0 to any neighbouring point and back. The definition of controllability entails that the initial state lies within the accessible neighbourhood [24]. Thus, accessibility is a less demanding property than controllability, which is why it is sometimes referred to as weak local controllability [7]. Therefore, while every controllable system is necessarily accessible, the reverse is not always true [24]. We will use the acronym NAC to refer to nonlinear accessibility and controllability.

2.3. StrucID

StrucID is a MATLAB toolbox for which the source code, as well as a compiled version that enables its use without a MATLAB installation, is available on Github (https://github.com/jdstigter/StrucID, accessed on 1 November 2025). It is also integrated in the D2D-framework (https://github.com/Data2Dynamics/d2d, accessed on 1 November 2025). StrucID is designed for the structural analysis of nonlinear dynamic models. It evaluates structural identifiability, observability, and accessibility (for which it uses the equivalent term "reachability"). It can test for the identifiability of unknown initial conditions (i.e., observability), while known initial conditions can also be provided in the input file and are used to inform the numeric integration. The input to a StrucID analysis is provided in a single .txt file [17,36]. Figure 1 shows the interface of this software.

The tests provided by StrucID are based on sensitivity calculations. Sensitivities have the advantageous property of being governed by linear dynamics, even when the system itself is nonlinear. By integrating these linear dynamics over a short time interval and sampling the resulting trajectories, a sensitivity matrix can be formed. If this matrix satisfies a specific rank condition, the local structural property of the system under investigation is confirmed. Moreover, performing a singular value decomposition (SVD) on the sensitivity matrix not only determines its rank but also pinpoints the exact system components responsible for any failure to satisfy the local structural property.

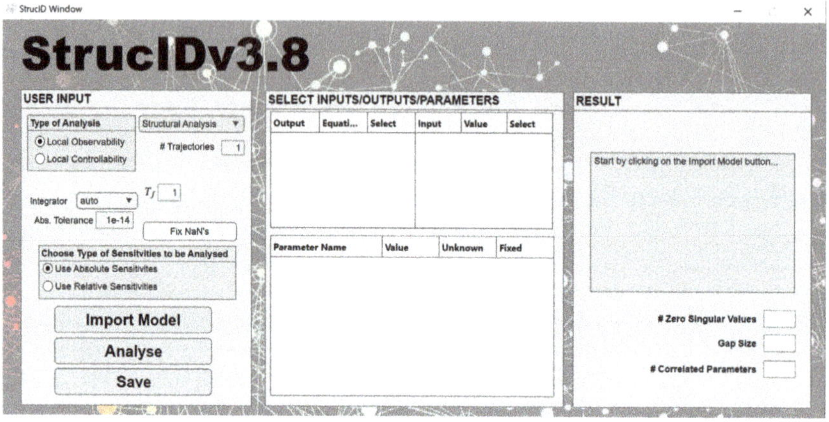

Figure 1. Screenshot of the StrucID software interface.

2.3.1. SIO Analysis with StrucID

The parametric state and output sensitivity matrix functions, denoted by $\frac{\partial x}{\partial \theta}(t)$ and $\frac{\partial y}{\partial \theta}(t)$, respectively, play a central role. For convenience of notation, these matrix functions are represented as $x_\theta(t)$ and $y_\theta(t)$, having dimensions $n \times p$ and $m \times p$, respectively. At any given time t, $x_\theta(t)$ and $y_\theta(t)$ quantify the sensitivity of the state vector $x(t)$ and the output vector $y(t)$ with respect to the parameter vector θ. By differentiating Equation (1) with respect to the parameter vector θ, and by interchanging differentiation with respect to the independent parameters, it can be shown that the dynamics of these sensitivity matrices are governed by the following relations:

$$\frac{dx_\theta}{dt} = \frac{\partial f}{\partial x} x_\theta + \frac{\partial f}{\partial \theta}, \tag{4}$$

$$y_\theta = \frac{\partial h}{\partial x} x_\theta + \frac{\partial h}{\partial \theta}. \tag{5}$$

Simultaneous integration of the differential Equations (1) and (4), starting from initial conditions $x(t_0)$, yields the trajectories $x(t)$ and $x_\theta(t)$. Substituting these into Equation (5) provides the corresponding output sensitivity matrix $y_\theta(t)$. A necessary and sufficient condition for unique parameter determination from the measured output $y(t)$ of the system (Equation (1)), under a given set of initial conditions, is that $y_\theta(t)$ possesses the full column rank, i.e., p linearly independent columns. This rank condition can be verified by evaluating $y_\theta(t)$ at discrete time instants $t_0 < t_1 < \cdots < t_N$, forming the *parametric output sensitivity matrix*:

$$Y_\theta = \begin{bmatrix} y_\theta(t_0) \\ y_\theta(t_1) \\ \vdots \\ y_\theta(t_N) \end{bmatrix} \in \mathbb{R}^{(N+1)m \times p}. \tag{6}$$

The rank condition, referred to as the *Sensitivity Equation Rank Condition* (SERC), is

$$\text{rank}(Y_\theta) = p.$$

StrucID evaluates the SERC by performing a singular value decomposition (SVD) of the sensitivity matrix Y_θ. If this matrix is rank deficient, its SVD will yield one or more zero singular values. Each zero singular value corresponds to a singular vector obtained from the decomposition, and the nonzero elements of this vector identify the parameters that are mutually correlated and therefore cannot be uniquely estimated.

By interpreting the initial state $x(t_0)$ as a set of parameters, the local observability of the state can be analysed as the local structural identifiability of the initial condition $x(t_0)$ from the system output $y(t)$ for $t \geq t_0$. Thus, the state vector $x(t_0)$ plays the same role as the parameter vector θ in Equations (1)–(8). Since in Equations (7) and (8) the functions f and h do not explicitly depend on x_0, these equations simplify to

$$\frac{dx_{x_0}}{dt} = \frac{\partial f}{\partial x} x_{x_0}, \tag{7}$$

$$y_{x_0} = \frac{\partial h}{\partial x} x_{x_0}, \tag{8}$$

where $x_{x_0}(t)$ and $y_{x_0}(t)$ denote the parametric sensitivity matrix functions of $x(t)$ and $y(t)$ with respect to the initial state x_0. The simultaneous integration of the differential Equations (1) and (7), subject to the initial condition and

$$x_{x_0}(t_0) = I_n, \tag{9}$$

yields the trajectories $x(t)$ and $x_{x_0}(t)$. In Equation (9), I_n represents the $n \times n$ identity matrix, corresponding to the sensitivity of $x(t_0) = x_0$ with respect to itself. Substituting $x(t)$ and $x_{x_0}(t)$ into Equation (8) yields $y(t)$ and $y_{x_0}(t)$. The sensitivity matrix function $y_{x_0}(t)$ having n linearly independent columns is a necessary and sufficient condition to uniquely determine x_0 from the system output $y(t)$, given a choice of the initial conditions. Analogously to Equation (6), to verify this rank condition, the sensitivity matrix function $y_{x_0}(t)$ is evaluated at discrete time instants $t_0 < t_1 < \cdots < t_N$ to form the concatenated sensitivity matrix:

$$Y_{x_0} = \begin{bmatrix} y_{x_0}(t_0) \\ y_{x_0}(t_1) \\ \vdots \\ y_{x_0}(t_N) \end{bmatrix} \in \mathbb{R}^{(N+1)m \times n}. \tag{10}$$

Thus, the Sensitivity Equation Rank Condition (SERC) for local observability is

$$\text{rank}(Y_{x_0}) = n.$$

The SERC is necessary and sufficient. If Y_{x_0} does not have full rank n, the nonzero components of the singular vectors associated with zero singular values indicate state variables that are mutually correlated and therefore cannot be uniquely identified.

2.3.2. NAC Analysis with StrucID

By considering sensitivities, an important equivalence was established between the observability of the initial state x_0 from those trajectories and the observability of the linear dynamics along trajectories. This dual relationship extends naturally to controllability, showing that accessibility of a nonlinear system can likewise be analysed through the controllability of the linearised dynamics along trajectories. The duality between observability and controllability is established by linearising the nonlinear system around a trajectory [37], giving the perturbation dynamics

$$\delta \dot{x} = \frac{\partial f}{\partial x}\delta x + \frac{\partial f}{\partial u}\delta u. \tag{11}$$

By applying the substitutions

$$t \to t_N - t, \quad y \to u, \quad Y \to U, \quad x(t_0) = x_0 \to x(t_N) = x_N, \quad \frac{\partial f}{\partial x} \to \left(\frac{\partial f}{\partial x}\right)^T, \quad \frac{\partial h}{\partial x} \to \left(\frac{\partial f}{\partial u}\right)^T,$$

the dual system is obtained as

$$\frac{dx_{xN}}{dt} = \left(\frac{\partial f}{\partial x}\right)^T x_{xN}, \tag{12}$$

$$u_{xN} = \left(\frac{\partial f}{\partial u}\right)^T x_{xN}, \tag{13}$$

$$x_{xN}(t_N) = I_n. \tag{14}$$

The resulting sensitivity matrix,

$$U_{xN} = \begin{bmatrix} u_{xN}(t_N) \\ u_{xN}(t_{N-1}) \\ \vdots \\ u_{xN}(t_0) \end{bmatrix} \in \mathbb{R}^{(N+1)r \times n}, \tag{15}$$

serves as the dual counterpart of the output sensitivity matrix Y_{x0} introduced for observability analysis [25]. Its structure captures how infinitesimal variations in the input sequence affect the final state x_N, thus providing a basis for evaluating the local controllability and strong accessibility of the nonlinear system. For both local structural identifiability and local observability, the singular value decomposition (SVD) of the sensitivity matrix Y_{x_0} plays a central role in the analysis. Analogously, for the assessment of local strong accessibility, an SVD of the sensitivity matrix U_{x_N} serves this same fundamental purpose. The SVD of this matrix can be expressed as

$$U_{x_N} = \sum_{i=1}^{n} u_i r_i v_i^T, \qquad U_{x_N} \in \mathbb{R}^{(N+1)r \times n}, \; u_i \in \mathbb{R}^{(N+1)r}, \; r_i \in \mathbb{R}, \; v_i \in \mathbb{R}^n. \tag{16}$$

This decomposition represents U_{x_N} as a sum of equally sized matrices $u_i v_i^T$, each weighted by its corresponding singular value $r_i \geq 0$. If one or more of the singular values r_i are (numerically) zero, the matrix U_{x_N} becomes rank deficient. The column vectors v_i associated with zero singular values form a basis for the null space of U_{x_N}. These vectors define directions in the state space along which the terminal state x_N cannot be locally controlled.

2.4. STRIKE-GOLDD

STRIKE-GOLDD is a MATLAB toolbox originally developed for analysing structural identifiability and observability. Since version 4.1.0 [?], it can also analyse accessibility and controllability, thanks to the functions in the module NLControllability. It can be downloaded from GitHub at https://github.com/afvillaverde/strike-goldd, (accessed on 1 November 2025). Figure 2 illustrates the main interfaces of this software.The analysis of SIO with STRIKE-GOLDD can be performed with three algorithms—FISPO [39], ORC-DF [40], and ProbObsTest [15]—of which we use FISPO and ProbObsTest in this study. For analysing NAC, up to four algorithms are available [15]: LC, ARC, LARC, and GSC. Of these, the latter two are used in this study. These methods are described in the remainder of this section.

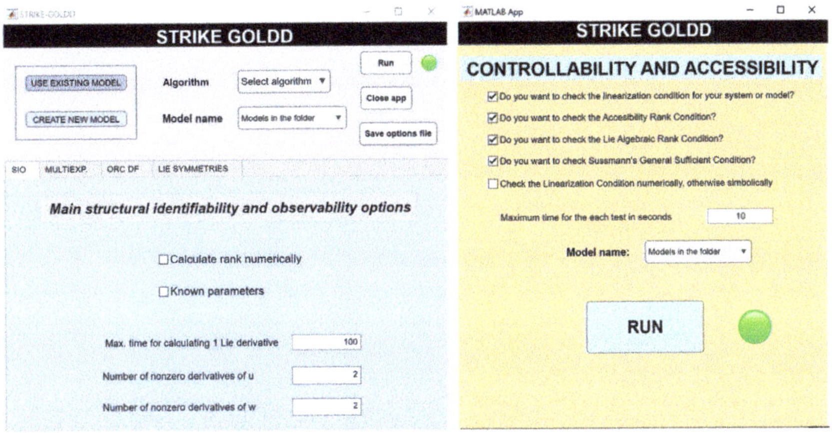

(a) Structural Identifiability and Observability **(b) Controllability and Accessibility**

Figure 2. Screenshots of the STRIKE-GOLDD software interface displaying: (**a**) options for structural identifiability and observability analysis, and (**b**) options for controllability and accessibility analysis.

2.4.1. SIO Analysis in STRIKE-GOLDD

FISPO

The FISPO algorithm is an advanced implementation of the ORC test mentioned in the Introduction, which can be applied to rational and non-rational models. The ORC, which was introduced in [7], provides the theoretical differential geometric basis for determining observability as well as—by considering the parameters as state variables—structural local identifiability. The FISPO algorithm is an extended computational implementation of the ORC. One key feature is its iterative nature, i.e., only a minimum number of Lie derivatives is calculated initially, with higher-order derivatives being computed only if necessary [14]. Another important extension of FISPO with respect to the original ORC is that it can take into account the effect of time-varying inputs explicitly [41], as well as analysing models with unknown inputs [39].

To analyse SIO, the parameters θ_i are considered constant state variables, thus extending the state vector as $\tilde{x} = \tilde{x}(x,\theta)$. The algorithm builds the observability -identifiability matrix:

$$\mathcal{OI}(x) = \begin{pmatrix} \frac{\partial h(\tilde{x})}{\partial \tilde{x}} \\ \frac{\partial (L_f h(\tilde{x}))}{\partial \tilde{x}} \\ \frac{\partial (L_f^2 h(\tilde{x}))}{\partial \tilde{x}} \\ \vdots \\ \frac{\partial (L_f^{n+q-1} h(\tilde{x}))}{\partial \tilde{x}} \end{pmatrix}. \quad (17)$$

which is obtained from Lie derivatives that, in their general form, can be calculated as

$$L_f h(\tilde{x}) = \frac{\partial h(\tilde{x})}{\partial \tilde{x}} f(\tilde{x}, u) \quad (18)$$

$$L_f^i h(\tilde{x}) = \frac{\partial (L_f^{i-1} h(\tilde{x}))}{\partial \tilde{x}} f(\tilde{x}, u) + \sum_{j=0}^{i-2} \frac{\partial (L_f^{i-1} h(\tilde{x}))}{\partial u^{(j)}} u^{(j+1)}, \quad i > 1. \quad (19)$$

The $\mathcal{OI}$ matrix must have full rank, i.e., equal to $n+q$, for the system to be fully identifiable and observable. If rank < $n+q$, the identifiability/observability of each variable is determined by removing each column and re-calculating the rank. If this operation decreases the rank, the variable associated to the column is identifiable/observable; otherwise, it is not [39].

The calculation of Lie derivatives is performed symbolically, and its computational cost increases steeply with i. One alternative to alleviate this computational complexity is the ProbObsTest algorithm.

ProbObsTest

This algorithm speeds up the ORC test by avoiding the symbolic calculations of Lie derivatives. It is based on the algorithm proposed by Sedoglavic [42] and, like it, is applicable to rational models. Unlike classical methods based on algebraic symbolic theory, which typically have exponential time complexity, this algorithm uses semi-numerical methods and performs the analysis in polynomial time. Sedoglavic's variational system is used to avoid symbolic computations, and symbolic variables are replaced with random numerical values [15]. The output derivatives $Y^{(j)}$ are generated up to a certain order ν, using derivatives with respect to the vector field F. The partial derivatives of the outputs with respect to the state variables and parameters form a Jacobian matrix:

$$J = \frac{\partial(Y^{(j)}),\ 0 \le j \le \nu}{\partial(X,\Theta)}$$

Power series of the output are obtained, and the Jacobian is computed numerically. As in FISPO, variables and parameters that reduce the rank are considered unobservable. The algorithm uses modular arithmetic, and its probability of success can be made arbitrarily large by tuning a precision parameter.

2.4.2. NAC Analysis with STRIKE-GOLDD

STRIKE-GOLDD provides four algorithms for testing NAC conditions: LC, ARC, LARC, and GSC. In this study, we focus exclusively on the LARC and GSC algorithms, which test, respectively, for accessibility and controllability. The other two, LC and ARC, can be useful in specific case studies but are not essential and thus not considered here for simplicity. We describe the LARC and GSC algorithms below.

Lie Algebra Rank Condition (LARC)

The LARC test computes a control distribution Δ_c recursively, starting with $\Delta_0 = \text{span}(\mathcal{F})$, where $\mathcal{F} = \{f, g_1, \ldots, g_m\}$, and updating it at subsequent steps as $\Delta_{i+1} = \text{span}(\Delta_i \cup \{[v,h] \mid v \in \mathcal{F},\ h \in \Delta_i\})$. After each step, it checks whether the distribution is invariant with respect to the set $\mathcal{F}$, i.e., if for every $h \in \Delta_i$ and $v \in \mathcal{F}$, the Lie bracket $[v,h] \in \Delta_i$. If this condition is satisfied, the algorithm stops, and Δ_i is the final control distribution, Δ_c. Then, the system is accessible at x_0 if and only if, at the end of the process, $\Delta_c(x_0)$ has full rank (i.e., $\dim(\Delta_c(x_0)) = n$).

The LARC test can be computationally intensive due to the exponential growth in the number of Lie brackets and the need to check the non-invariance condition at every step. The LARC implementation in STRIKE-GOLDD includes modifications to alleviate its computational complexity [15].

General Sufficient Condition (GSC)

Sussmann's GSC [43] assigns to each Lie bracket generated from the set $F = \{f, g_1, \ldots, g_m\}$ a type in the form of a numerical vector $(k, \ell_1, \ldots, \ell_m)$, where k denotes the number of occurrences of the vector f, and ℓ_i denotes the number of occurrences of g_i. Brackets in which f appears an odd number of times and each g_i appears an even number of times are called "bad" brackets. If the system is at equilibrium at the point x_0 (i.e., $f(x_0) = 0$) and the LARC condition holds, then the system is STLC if each bad bracket can be expressed as a smooth linear combination of brackets of the lower type. This lower type is defined in weighted terms, $\theta k_j + \ell_{j1} + \cdots + \ell_{jm} < \theta k + \ell_1 + \cdots + \ell_m$, where $\theta \in [0, 1]$ is an arbitrary weight (typically chosen close to zero to minimize the weight of f).

In STRIKE-GOLDD, the GSC is verified through a sequence of steps. First, the control distribution is generated by applying the LARC algorithm. Next, "bad" Lie brackets are detected. Lastly, it is verified whether each bad bracket can be expressed as a linear combination of brackets of the lower type; this is checked using algebraic operations in vector spaces such as computing the null space.

2.5. Case Studies

In this study, we analysed the SIO and NAC of a set of 32 nonlinear models that cover a wide range of processes, including gene regulatory networks, enzymatic reactions, signalling pathways, metabolic systems, and synthetic biology circuits. The name of each model, a brief description, and the corresponding references are summarised in Table 1. More detailed information can be found in the original references listed in the table. We analysed the SIO of all of these models (for one of them, the "Bioprocess", we analysed several versions with different number of experiments, thus increasing the number of cases to 35). However, we did not analyse the NAC of all models because some of them do not have control inputs.

Table 1. Summary of the 32 biological models analysed in this study. The table includes each model's short name, its description, and the original reference.

Model	Description	Ref.
1_A_integral	Linear circuit with integral feedback	[44]
1B_Prob_integral	Linear circuit with proportional-integral feedback	[44]
1C_nonlinear	Nonlinear circuit model of hormonal reactions	[44]
2DOF	A mechanical system with two independent motions	[40]
Arabidopsis	Circadian rhythm in the plant *Arabidopsis thaliana*	[45]
Bolie	Glucose-insulin regulatory system in humans	[46]
C2M	Compartmental model with two compartments	[41]
Fujita	Epidermal Growth Factor-dependent Protein Kinase B signalling pathway	[47]
HIV_known input	HIV infection dynamics	[4]
Bioprocess	Biochemical reactions	[48]
TS_Known input	Genetic toggle switch	[49]
1D_BIG	Glucose-insulin regulation via β-cell and insulin	[44]
NFKB (Merkt)	NF-κB (Nuclear Factor kappa B) signalling pathway	[50]
PC (hSRPsIPr)	A phage cocktail, describing bacteriophage-bacteria interactions and the host immune response	[?]
Raia_jakstat	JAK/STAT signalling pathway in lymphoma cells	[51]
MAPK	Mitogen Activated Protein Kinase signalling pathway	[52]

Table 1. *Cont.*

Model	Description	Ref.
BioSD_I	Two-species synthetic biology circuit for signal differentiation	[53]
BioSD_II	Three-species synthetic biology circuit for signal differentiation	[53]
BioSD_III	Three-species synthetic biology circuit for signal differentiation with positive and negative feedback	[53]
BioSD_II_MM_simple	Three-species synthetic biology circuit for signal differentiation with simple kinetics	[53]
BioSD_II_MM_complex	Three-species synthetic biology circuit for signal differentiation with complex kinetics	[53]
Dichotomous_Feedback_BettaRR	Synthetic biology circuit implementing dichotomous feedback—RR molecules (Response Regulator)	[54]
Dichotomous_Feedback_BettaSR	Synthetic biology circuit implementing dichotomous feedback—SR molecules (Sequestering Regulator)	[54]
Dichotomous_Feedback_kap	Synthetic biology circuit with input signal *kap*	[54]
Dichotomous_Feedback_I_BettaRR	Synthetic biology circuit with dichotomous feedback, input I, and RR molecules	[54]
Dichotomous_Feedback_I_BettaSR	Synthetic biology circuit with dichotomous feedback, input I, and SR molecules	[54]
Dichotomous_Feedback_I	Synthetic biology circuit with dichotomous feedback, with input signal I	[54]
Kelly_1	Synthetic biology circuit implementing negative feedback via sRNA-tuned autorepression	[55]
Kelly_1_gr	Synthetic biology circuit with generalised regulatory dynamics	[55]
Kelly_2	Synthetic biology circuit implementing negative feedback via closed-loop sRNA regulation	[55]
Kelly_2_gxgr	Synthetic biology circuit with generalised regulatory dynamics	[55]
CSTR_observer	Continuous Stirred Tank Reactor with High Gain Observer	[56]

3. Results

In this study, to provide a clear and comprehensive understanding of the investigation, when discussing the results of both families of analyses, SIO and NAC, we focused on three key aspects:

(i) Applicability: we assessed whether each model could be fully analysed by both tools, and identified which algorithms were capable of performing the analyses.

(ii) Reliability of the results: we compared the results obtained from the two software tools, to detect differences in their outputs, and investigated the potential reasons behind such discrepancies.

(iii) Computational efficiency: we measured the time required to complete the analyses.

The results of the analyses are presented and discussed below.

3.1. Observability and Identifiability Analyses

We first analysed the SIO of all the models with StrucID and STRIKE-GOLDD (in the latter case with the ProbObsTest and FISPO algorithms).

3.1.1. Applicability

According to the applicability of the methods, the models can be classified into four categories.

First category: models that can be successfully analysed by all three algorithms. Of the 35 models considered, 14 fell into this category.

Second category: models that can be analysed by StrucID and ProbObsTest but not by FISPO due to their computational cost. Of the 35 models considered, 13 fell into this category. The main reason behind the failure of FISPO in these cases is the high dimensionality of the models, characterised by a large number of state variables, parameters, and equations.

Third category: models that can be analysed by StrucID and the FISPO algorithm but not by ProbObsTest due to the models being non-rational. Of the 35 models considered, 2 fell into this category.

Fourth category: models that can only be analysed using StrucID. Of the 35 models considered, 6 fell into this category. Similar to the second category, the excessive computational load is the primary factor preventing the algorithms in STRIKE-GOLDD from completing the analysis.

3.1.2. Reliability

Table 2 summarizes the results of the SIO analyses. For 11 models, we obtained different results with StrucID and STRIKE-GOLDD. Specifically, STRIKE-GOLDD classified certain parameters as identifiable, while StrucID reported them as non-identifiable. This pattern was consistent across the eleven models. To address these discrepancies, we used a third tool, the SIAN algorithm, implemented in Julia [57]. The corresponding results are presented in Table 3, which shows that the results obtained with SIAN are in full agreement with those obtained with the FISPO and ProbObsTest algorithms within the STRIKE-GOLDD toolbox (1 of the 11 models could not be analysed using SIAN).

These findings hint at the existence of numerical issues in StrucID. One explanation is that the sensitivity calculations performed by the methods in this toolbox rely on numerical integrations, without mechanisms to control the propagation of numerical errors due to double precision operations. Furthermore, the rank of the resulting observability matrix is determined by calculating its singular values numerically, which leads to a well-known issue: this procedure cannot result in singular values that are exactly equal to zero; instead, the singular values will always be positive, and it is necessary to choose a threshold to decide which of them correspond to the zeros of a symbolic algorithm. A recent discussion of this issue can be found, for example, in [58].

Table 2. Results of the SIO analyses using the FISPO and Prob_Obs_Test algorithms from the STRIKE-GOLDD and the StrucID toolboxes. The table classifies model parameters and state variables into four categories: Identifiable, Non-identifiable (Non-Id), Observable (Obs), and Non-observable (Non-Obs).

Models	FISPO (STRIKE-GOLDD)				Prob_Obs_Test (STRIKE-GOLDD)				StrucID			
	Identifiable	Non-Id	Obs	Non-Obs	Identifiable	Non-Id	Obs	Non-Obs	Identifiable	Non-Id	Obs	Non-Obs
1_A_integral	All		All		All		All		All		All	
1B_Prob_integral	All		All		All		All		All		All	
2DOF	All		All		All		All		All		All	
C2M	All		All		All		All		x4	x3, x5, x6	x1	x2
Fujita	All		All		All		All		R_2_k2, R_3_k1, R_4_k1, R_5_k2, R_6_k1, R_7_k1, R_8_k1	SF_p, SF_pAkt, SF_pS6,EGFR_turnover, R_1_k1, R_1_k2, R_2_k1, R_5_k1, R_9_k1		pS6, EGFR, pEGFR, pEGFR_Akt, Akt, pAkt, S6, pAkt_S6, EGF_EGFR
MAPK	All		All		not rational				All		All	
HIV	All		All		All		All		All		All	
PC	All		All		All		All		All		All	
1C-nonlinear		p1, p2	x1	x2, x3		p1, p2	x1	x2, x3		p1, p2	x1	x2, x3
Bolie	Vp, p1, p3	p2, p4	q1	q2	p1, p3, Vp	p2, p4	q1	q2		p1, p2, p3, p4, Vp		q1, q2
Raia-jakstat	t1, t10, t12, t13, t14, t16, t18, t19, t2, t20, t3, t4, t5, t6, t7, t8, t9	t11, t15, t17, t21, t22	x1, x11, x2, x3, x4, x5, x6, x8	x10	t1, t2, t3, t4, t5, t6, t7, t8, t9, t10, t12, t13, t14, t16, t18, t19, t20	t11, t15, t17, t21, t22	x1, x2, x3, x4, x5, x6, x8, x11, x13	x10	t1, t2, t3, t4, t5, t6, t7, t8, t9, t10, t12, t13, t14, t16, t18, t19, t20	t11, t15, t17, t21, t22, x10	x1, x2, x3, x4, x5, x6, x8, x11, x13	x10
BioSD-I	p1, p2	p3, p4, p5, p6	x1	x2	p1, p2	p3, p4, p5, p6	x1	x2		p1, p2, p3, p4, p5, p6		x2
BioSD-II	p1, p2, p4	p3, p5, p6, p7	x1	x2, x3	p1, p2, p4	p3, p5, p6, p7	x1	x2, x3	p4	p1, p2, p3, p5, p6, p7	x1	x2, x3
BioSD-III	p1, p2	p3, p4, p5, p6, p7	x1	x2, x3	p1, p2	p3, p4, p5, p6, p7	x1	x2, x3		p1, p2, p3, p4, p5, p6, p7		x2, x3
TS-Known input	All		All		not rational				k01, k1, ntetr, k02, k2, nlaci	tatc, natc, tiptg, niptg	x1, x2	
1D-BIG	p3, p4, p5	p1, p2	x1	x2, x3	p3, p4, p5	p1, p2	x1	x2, x3	p3, p4, p5	p1, p2	x1	x2, x3
NFKB					t1, t2, c3a, c4a, c5, k1, k3, kprod, kdeg, i1, e2a, i1a, a1, a2, a3, c1a, c2a, c5a, c6a, c1, c2, c3, kv, e1a	k2, c4, c1c, c2c, c3c	x1, x3, x4, x5, x6, x10, x11, x13, x14	x8, x15	t1, t2, c3a, c4a, c5, k1, k3, kprod, kdeg, i1, e2a, i1a, a1, a2, a3, c1a, c2a, c5a, c6a, c1, c2, c3, kv, e1a	k2, c4, c1c, c2c, c3c	x1, x3, x4, x5, x6, x10, x11, x13, x14	x8, x15

Table 2. *Cont.*

Models	FISPO (STRIKE-GOLDD)				Prob_Obs_Test (STRIKE-GOLDD)				StrucID			
	Identifiable	**Non-Id**	**Obs**	**Non-Obs**	**Identifiable**	**Non-Id**	**Obs**	**Non-Obs**	**Identifiable**	**Non-Id**	**Obs**	**Non-Obs**
BioSD-II-MM-simple					p1, p2, p4, p6	p3, p5, p7, p8	x1	x2, x3	p4, p6	p1, p2, p3, p5, p7, p8	x1	x2, x3
BioSD-II-MM-complex					p1, p2, p4, p5, p7	p3, p6, p8, p9	x1	x2, x3	p4, p5, p7	p1, p2, p3, p6, p8, p9	x1	x2, x3
Dichotomous-F-BettaRR					All		All		All		All	
Dichotomous-F-BettaSR					All		All		All		All	
Dichotomous-F-kap					All		All		All		All	
Dichotomous-F-I					All		All		p1, p2, p3, p4, p5, p6, p7, p8, p9	p10, p11	All	
Kelly-1					All		All		p1, p5, p6, p7, p10, p13, p14	p2, p3, p4, p8, p9, p11, p12	t,s	c, T
CSTR-observer					All		All		All		All	
Dichotomous-F-I-BettaRR					p1, p2, p4, p5, p7, p8, p9	p3, p10, p11	All		p1, p2, p4, p5, p7, p8, p9	p3, p10, p11	All	
Dichotomous-F-I-BettaSR					p1, p2, p4, p5, p6, p7, p9	p3, p10, p11	All		p1, p2, p4, p5, p6, p7, p9	p3, p10, p11	All	
Kelly-2					p2, p3, p4, p8, p10, p11	p1, p5, p6, p7, p9		r,s,c	p4, p8, p11	p1, p2, p3, p5, p6, p7, p9, p10	R	r, s, c
Kelly-2-gxgr					p4, p5, p7, p8, p11	p6	r, s	c	p4, p5, p7, p8, p11	p6	r,s,R	c
Arabidopsis					not rational				a, n1, r3, k1, k4, m1, m4, n2, q2, r1, r2, r4	g1, g2, k2, k3, k5, k6, k7, m2, m3, m5, m6, m7, p1, p2, p3, q1	x1, x4	x2, x3, x5, x6, x7
Bioprocess					not rational				p1, p2, p3, p4, p5, p6, p7, p8		x1, x2, x3, x4, x5	
Bioprocess2xp					not rational					p1, p2, p3, p4, p5, p6, p7, p8	x1E1, x2E1, x3E1, x4E1, x5E1, x1E2, x2E2, x3E2, x4E2, x5E2	

Table 2. *Cont.*

Models	FISPO (STRIKE-GOLDD)				Prob_Obs_Test (STRIKE-GOLDD)				StrucID			
	Identifiable	Non-Id	Obs	Non-Obs	Identifiable	Non-Id	Obs	Non-Obs	Identifiable	Non-Id	Obs	Non-Obs
Bioprocess3xp					not rational				p1, p2, p3	p4, p5, p6, p7	x1E1, x2E1, x3E1, x4E1, x5E1, x1E2, x2E2, x3E2, x4E2, x5E2, x1E3, x2E3, x3E3, x4E3, x5E3	
Bioprocess4xp					not rational				All		All	
Kelly-1-gr					not rational				p1, p5, p6, p7, p10, p13, p14	p2, p3, p4, p11, p12	t,s	c, T

Table 3. Comparison of structural identifiability and observability results for models with discrepancies between STRIKE-GOLDD and StrucID analyses, including the results obtained using the Julia-based SIAN algorithm as a third reference. For the Kelly_1 model, SIAN cannot analyse it and returns an error because it contains non-rational functions, specifically exponential or power terms with parameters in the exponents.

Models	STRIKE_GOLDD				StrucID	SIAN	
	FISPO		Prob_Obs_Test		Non-Id.	Id.	Non-Id.
	Id.	Non-Id.	Id.	Non-Id.			
C2M	All		All		x3, x5, x6, x2	All	
Fujita	All		All		scaleFactor_p, EGFR, scaleFactor_p, Akt, scaleFactor_pS6, EGFR_turnover, R_1_k1, R_1_k2, R_2_k1, R_5_k1, R_9_k1, EGFR, pEGFR, pEGFR_Akt, Akt, pAkt, S6, pAkt_S6, pS6, EGF_EGFR	All	
Bolie	Vp, p1, p3, q1	p2, p4, q2	Vp, p1, p3, q1	p2, p4, q2	p1, p2, p3, p4, Vp, q1, q2	p1, p3, Vp, q1	q2, p4, p2
BioSD_I	p2, p1, x1	p4, p3, p6, p5, x2	p2, p1, x1	p4, p3, p6, p5, x2	p1, p2, p3, p4, p5, p6, x2	p2, p1, x1	p4, p3, p6, p5, x2
BioSD_II	p2, p1, p4, x1	p3, p6, p7, p5, x3, x2	p2, p1, p4, x1	p3, p6, p7, p5, x3, x2	p1, p2, p3, p5, p6, p7, x2, x3	p2, p1, p4, x1	p3, p6, p7, p5, x3, x2

Table 3. *Cont.*

Models	STRIKE_GOLDD				StrucID	SIAN	
	FISPO		Prob_Obs_Test		Non-Id.	Id.	Non-Id.
	Id.	Non-Id.	Id.	Non-Id.			
BioSD_III	p2, p1, x1	p4, p3, p6, p7, p5, x3, x2	p2, p1, x1	p4, p3, p6, p7, p5, x3, x2	p1, p2, p3, p4, p5, p6, p7, x2, x3	p2, p1, x1	p4, p3, p6, p7, p5, x3, x2
BioSD_II_MM_simple			p2, p1, p4, p6, x1	p3, p5, p7, p8, x3, x2	p1, p2, p3, p6, p8, p9, x2, x3	p2, p1, p4, p6, x1	p3, p5, p7, p8, x3, x2
BioSD_II_MM_complex			p2, p4, p5, p1, p7, x1	p3, p6, p8, p9, x3, x2	p1, p2, p3, p6, p8, p9, x2, x3	p2, p4, p5, p1, p7, x1	p3, p6, p8, p9, x3, x2
Dichotomous_Feedback_I			All		p10, p11	All	-
Kelly_1			All		p2, p3, p4, p8, p9, p11, p12, c, T	error	
Kelly_2			p2, p3, p4, p8, p10, p11	p9, p5, p1, p6, p7, s, c, r	p1, p2, p3, p5, p6, p7, p9, p10, r, s, c	p10, p4, p2, p3, p11, p8	p9, p5, p1, p6, p7, s, c, r

3.1.3. Computational Efficiency

Figure 3 plots the CPU time required to analyse each model with the three SIO methods considered. A clear conclusion can be extracted: StrucID is consistently faster than both of the STRIKE-GOLDD methods, FISPO and ProbObsTest. While the difference can be small in absolute terms for small models, for larger models it becomes substantial. Furthermore, some models could only be analysed with StrucID.

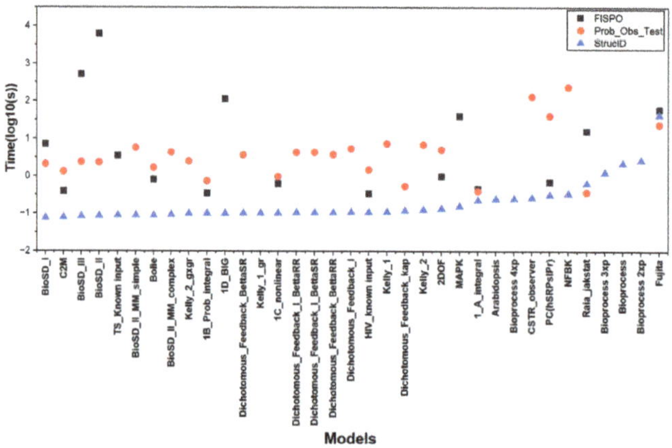

Figure 3. Comparative chart of the computational time required to analyse different models using the FISPO and ProbObsTest algorithms from the STRIKE-GOLDD toolbox and the methods available in the StrucID toolbox. As shown, the analysis time varies depending on the model complexity and the algorithm applied.

3.2. *Accessibility and Controllability Analyses*

We analysed the NAC of the models with control inputs using the LARC and GSC algorithms from STRIKE-GOLDD, along with the sensitivity-based algorithm in StrucID. Table 4 summarizes the results.

Table 4. Comparison of the results of different Controllability and local Accessibility analysis methods for the case studies. The columns show the case name, Lie algebraic rank condition (LARC), generalised Sussmann condition (GSC), and the outcome of the StrucID tool. "not Affine in 'U"' refers to models not affine in the input, which makes them impossible to analyse with the algorithms included in STRIKE-GOLDD.

Case Study	LARC	GSC	StrucID
1_A_integral	Accessible	STLC	Accessible
1B_Prob_integral	Accessible	STLC	Accessible
1C_nonlinear	Accessible	STLC	Accessible
2DOF	Accessible	STLC	Accessible
Arabidopsis	Accessible	—	Accessible
Boile	Accessible	—	Accessible
C2M	Accessible	STLC	Accessible
CSTR_observer	Accessible	STLC	Accessible
BioSD_I	Accessible	STLC	Accessible
BioSD_II	Accessible	STLC	Accessible

Table 4. *Cont.*

Case Study	LARC	GSC	StrucID
BioSD_II_MM_simple	Accessible	STLC	Accessible
Kelly_1_gr	Accessible	STLC	inAccessible
Kelly_2_gxgr	Accessible	STLC	inAccessible
BioSD_III	Accessible	STLC	inAccessible
Dichotomous_Feedback_BettaRR	Accessible	STLC	Accessible
Dichotomous_Feedback_BettaSR	Accessible	STLC	Accessible
Dichotomous_Feedback_kap	Accessible	STLC	Accessible
Dichotomous_Feedback_I_BettaRR	Accessible	STLC	Accessible
Dichotomous_Feedback_I_BettaSR	Accessible	STLC	Accessible
Raia_jakstat	Accessible	—	inAccessible
Fujita	inAccessible	—	inAccessible
HIV	—	—	Accessible
Dichotomous_Feedback_I	not Affine in "U"		Accessible
BioSD_II_MM_complex	not Affine in "U"		Accessible
Kelly_1	not Affine in "U"		inAccessible
Kelly_2	not Affine in "U"		inAccessible
Bioprocess	not Affine in "U"		inAccessible
Bioprocess 2xp	not Affine in "U"		Accessible
Bioprocess 3xp	not Affine in "U"		inAccessible
Bioprocess 4xp	not Affine in "U"		Accessible
TS	not Affine in "U"		inAccessible
1D_BIG	computation limit		inAccessible
Bachman jackstat	computation limit		inAccessible
NFKB (Merkt)	computation limit		Accessible
PC	computation limit		Accessible

3.2.1. Applicability

A fundamental difference between the capabilities of the StrucID and STRIKE-GOLDD toolboxes in analysing NAC stems from the fact that STRIKE-GOLDD cannot analyse models that are not affine with respect to the inputs. In STRIKE-GOLDD, models are first checked for this characteristic; if a model is not affine, the toolbox automatically attempts to convert it into an affine form using an internal algorithm in order to proceed with the analysis. If this conversion fails, STRIKE-GOLDD reports that it is unable to analyse the controllability and accessibility of the model. In contrast, StrucID is capable of analysing all models regardless of their structure.

Additionally, some affine models could not be analysed with STRIKE-GOLDD due to their excessive complexity, given by a high number of state variables or the complexity of their equations. This limitation depends on the available computing resources; we set a predefined time limit of 3600 s, beyond which we reported that a method has reached its computation limit.

3.2.2. Reliability

Among the models that were successfully analysed by both toolboxes, similarities and differences were observed in the results. STRIKE-GOLDD and StrucID agreed on the results of 17 models, most of which (all but one, the 'Fujita' model) were classified as accessible. For other models, however, discrepancies arose. The biosd_III, Kelly_1_gr, Kelly_2_gxgr and Raia_JAKSTAT models were classified as accessible by the LARC algorithm and as inaccessible by StrucID. However, in all cases in which a model was classified as accessible by StrucID, it was also accessible according to LARC.

Unlike in the SIO case, we could not find a third tool on which to rely to verify the results of the two approaches. However, since in each tool the SIO and NAC analyses share the same methodological foundations, we hypothesize that the discrepancies between both tools regarding NAC can be explained in the same way as those regarding SIO—that is, they might be caused by numerical issues affecting the algorithms in StrucID.

3.2.3. Computational Efficiency

The time required for the NAC analyses of the models included in this study is shown in Figure 4. As for SIO, the results indicate that StrucID performs the analysis in a shorter time. An important remark is that, within the STRIKE-GOLDD framework, there exists some dependency between the NAC algorithms, and several computational steps are shared among them: specifically, the LARC test is a prerequisite for checking the GSC.

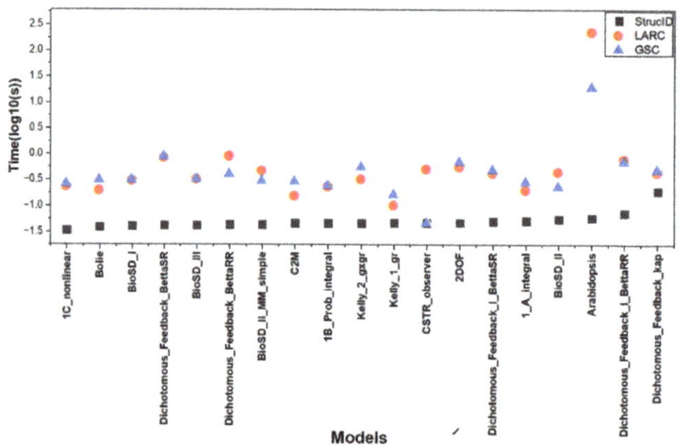

Figure 4. Comparison of the computational time required for analysing different models using three algorithms: LARC and GSC (both included in STRIKE-GOLDD), and StrucID. The x-axis lists the analysed models, and the y-axis shows the computation time in seconds, in logarithmic scale.

3.3. Discussion

In our analyses, we focused on three key aspects: applicability, reliability, and computational efficiency. Our results allow us to derive clear takeaways about them.

In regard to the first aspect, StrucID is the most widely applicable tool since it can handle nonlinear ODE models of a very general type. In contrast, STRIKE-GOLDD does provide one algorithm with the same applicability for SIO analyses (FISPO), but all of their algorithms for NAC analysis are limited to systems that are affine in the inputs. Furthermore, its other SIO algorithm, ProbObsTest, which is much faster than FISPO, requires models to be rational.

In regard to the second aspect, reliability, we found some interesting results. For SIO analysis, StrucID and STRIKE-GOLDD usually produced consistent results, but we found some cases in which they differ. All parameters classified as identifiable by StrucID were also classified as identifiable by STRIKE-GOLDD. However, some parameters classified as identifiable by STRIKE-GOLDD were classified as unidentifiable by StrucID. Given the different methodological foundations of their algorithms, it would seem reasonable to assume that STRIKE-GOLDD yields more accurate results than StrucID since it is based on symbolic computations instead of numerical ones. We confirmed this intuition by using a third tool, SIAN, which follows a different approach (differential algebra) than the other toolboxes examined here. The results obtained with SIAN coincided with those yielded by STRIKE-GOLDD, thus reinforcing the conclusion that it is more reliable than StrucID. For NAC analyses, we do not have an alternative verification tool, unlike for SIO. However, it should be noted that for each toolbox the foundations of the NAC and SIO analyses are the same: STRIKE-GOLDD relies on symbolic calculations of Lie derivatives (for SIO) and Lie brackets (for NAC), which are obtained in a similar way. Likewise, StrucID decides SIO and NAC based on the same type of sensitivity-based numerical calculations. Hence, it is reasonable to assume that the discrepancies in the NAC results produced by both approaches have the same causes as the discrepancies in the SIO results, i.e., they can be attributed to numerical issues that affect the reliability of the sensitivity-based calculations.

In regard to the third aspect, computational efficiency, StrucID is the clear winner. Its numerical approach yields extremely fast calculations, and for most models the computation time is at least an order of magnitude lower than the STRIKE-GOLDD algorithms. For this latter toolbox, there is a clear difference between the two SIO algorithms: ProbObsTest is more efficient, with computation times that are sometimes comparable to StrucID, while FISPO is slower and more demanding in terms of computational resources. However, this superior efficiency of ProbObsTest with respect to FISPO comes at the expense of inferior applicability since it cannot handle rational models. As for the NAC tests, again we conclude that the StrucID sensitivity-based approach is faster than the geometric control conditions that can be checked by STRIKE-GOLDD.

4. Conclusions

In this article, we report the results of a systematic analysis of the performance of two computational tools for analysing control-theoretic properties of nonlinear models, StrucID and STRIKE-GOLDD. While a few studies have already been published in this regard [27,28,30], our motivation for the work presented in this paper was to extend them in a number of ways, namely by applying the tools to a much larger set of models, discussing their applicability in detail, comparing their computational efficiency both for identifiability/observability and accessibility/controllability, assessing the correctness of their results, and providing practical guidance for tool selection in complex nonlinear models.

Some remarks are in order regarding the set of case studies selected for this assessment. Obviously, the choice of models to be analysed can and will affect the results. However, we note that the aim of this study was to obtain clear guidance in the form of qualitative conclusions, as opposed to quantitative measures, about the performance of the two tools being examined. That is, we did not intend to quantify exactly how much faster a tool is when compared to another, nor did we attempt to calculate the percentage of models for which their results disagree. Instead, our aim was to establish if a given tool is clearly faster than the other (as we indeed found to be the case, often by several orders of magnitude); or, regarding reliability, to find cases in which a tool gives wrong results and to explain their cause (as we have done here). Thus, the set of models that we used should not be considered a representative selection of those found in the literature—they just need to be realistic and sufficiently diverse to account for the different situations that can arise.

In short, our results show the existence of a trade-off: STRIKE-GOLDD is more reliable than StrucID, but StrucID is more generally applicable and computationally more efficient than STRIKE-GOLDD. Model users should choose between these tools accordingly when working on a particular application.

It should be noted that the two tools evaluated here are implemented in MATLAB. To the best of our knowledge, there are no other open research tools capable of performing these analyses in other programming languages. Their development would be a valuable addition to the set of resources available to the user.

Author Contributions: Conceptualisation, A.F.V.; software, M.S.F.; formal analysis, M.S.F., A.G.V., A.F.V.; investigation, M.S.F.; validation, A.G.V.; writing—original draft preparation, M.S.F., A.G.V., A.F.V.; supervision, A.F.V.; funding acquisition, A.F.V. All authors have read and agreed to the published version of the manuscript.

Funding: This work has received funding from grant PID2023-146275NB-C21 funded by MICIU/AEI/10.13039/501100011033 and ERDF/EU.

Data Availability Statement: All the files required to reproduce the analyses can be found in GitHub at https://github.com/MahmoudSh9/Models-data.git, accessed on 1 November 2025. They consist of the input files for the StrucID and STRIKE-GOLDD toolboxes that implement the models considered as case studies in this paper.

Conflicts of Interest: The authors declare no conflicts of interest. The funders had no role in the design of the study; in the collection, analyses, or interpretation of data; in the writing of the manuscript; or in the decision to publish the results.

References

1. Bellman, R.; Åström, K.J. On structural identifiability. *Math. Biosci.* **1970**, 7, 329–339. [CrossRef]
2. Anstett-Collin, F.; Denis-Vidal, L.; Millérioux, G. A priori identifiability: An overview on definitions and approaches. *Annu. Rev. Control* **2020**, 50, 139–149. [CrossRef]
3. Chatzis, M.; Chatzi, E.; Smyth, A. On the observability and identifiability of nonlinear structural and mechanical systems. *Struct. Control Health Monit.* **2014**, 22, 574–593. [CrossRef]
4. Miao, H.; Xia, X.; Perelson, A.S.; Wu, H. On identifiability of nonlinear ODE models and applications in viral dynamics. *SIAM Rev.* **2011**, 53, 3–39. [CrossRef] [PubMed]
5. Kalman, R. Contribution to the Theory of Optimal Control. *Bol. Soc. Mat. Mex.* **2001**, 5, 102–119 .
6. Martinelli, A. *Observability: A New Theory Based on the Group of Invariance*; SIAM: Philadelphia, PA, USA, 2020.
7. Hermann, R.; Krener, A. Nonlinear controllability and observability. *IEEE Trans. Autom. Control* **1977**, 22, 728–740. [CrossRef]
8. Tunali, E.; Tarn, T.J. New Results for Identifiability of Nonlinear Systems. *Autom. Control. IEEE Trans.* **1987**, 32, 146–154. [CrossRef]
9. Lam, N.N.; Docherty, P.D.; Murray, R. Practical identifiability of parametrised models: A review of benefits and limitations of various approaches. *Math. Comput. Simul.* **2022**, 199, 202–216. [CrossRef]
10. Wieland, F.G.; Hauber, A.L.; Rosenblatt, M.; Tönsing, C.; Timmer, J. On structural and practical identifiability. *Curr. Opin. Syst. Biol.* **2021**, 25, 60–69. [CrossRef]
11. Mitra, E.D.; Hlavacek, W.S. Parameter estimation and uncertainty quantification for systems biology models. *Curr. Opin. Syst. Biol.* **2019**, 18, 9–18. [CrossRef]
12. Plank, M.J.; Simpson, M.J. Structured methods for parameter inference and uncertainty quantification for mechanistic models in the life sciences. *R. Soc. Open Sci.* **2024**, 11, 240733. [CrossRef] [PubMed]
13. Rey Barreiro, X.; Villaverde, A.F. Benchmarking tools for a priori identifiability analysis. *Bioinformatics* **2023**, 39, btad065. [CrossRef]
14. Villaverde, A.; Barreiro, A.; Papachristodoulou, A. Structural Identifiability of Dynamic Systems Biology Models. *PLoS Comput. Biol.* **2016**, 12, e1005153. [CrossRef]
15. Díaz-Seoane, S.; Rey Barreiro, X.; Villaverde, A.F. STRIKE-GOLDD 4.0: User-friendly, efficient analysis of structural identifiability and observability. *Bioinformatics* **2023**, 39, btac748. [CrossRef]
16. Stigter, H.; Molenaar, J. A Fast Algorithm to Assess Local Structural Identifiability. *Automatica* **2015**, 58, 118–124. [CrossRef]

17. Stigter, H.; Joubert, D. Computing Measures of Identifiability, Observability, and Controllability for a Dynamic System Model with the StrucID App. *IFAC-PapersOnLine* **2021**, *54*, 138–143. [CrossRef]
18. Isidori, A. *Nonlinear Control Systems*; Communications and Control Engineering; Springer: London, UK, 2013.
19. Nijmeijer, H.; van der Schaft, A. *Nonlinear Dynamical Control Systems*; Springer: New York, NY, USA, 2013.
20. Sontag, E.D. *Mathematical Control Theory: Deterministic Finite Dimensional Systems*; Springer Science & Business Media: Berlin/Heidelberg, Germany, 2013; Volume 6.
21. Sontag, E.D. Controllability is Harder to Decide than Accessibility. *SIAM J. Control Optim.* **1988**, *26*, 1106–1118. [CrossRef]
22. Haynes, G.; Hermes, H. Nonlinear controllability via Lie theory. *SIAM J. Control* **1970**, *8*, 450–460. [CrossRef]
23. Sussmann, H.J. *Nonlinear Controllability and Optimal Control*; Routledge: London, UK, 2017.
24. Díaz-Seoane, S.; Barreiro Blas, A.; Villaverde, A.F. Controllability and accessibility analysis of nonlinear biosystems. *Comput. Methods Programs Biomed.* **2023**, *242*, 107837. [CrossRef]
25. van Willigenburg, G.; Stigter, H.; Molenaar, J. Establishing local strong accessibility of large-scale nonlinear systems by replacing the Lie algebraic rank condition. In Proceedings of the 2021 European Control Conference (ECC), Virtual, 29 June–2 July 2021; pp. 2645–2650. [CrossRef]
26. Szederkényi, G.; Kovács, M.; Hangos, K. Reachability of nonlinear fed-batch fermentation processes. *Int. J. Robust Nonlinear Control* **2002**, *12*, 1109–1124. [CrossRef]
27. Wang, L.; Qi, J. Efficient Structural Parameter Identifiability Analysis for Generator Dynamic Models. In Proceedings of the IEEE 2024 56th North American Power Symposium (NAPS), El Paso, TX, USA, 13–15 October 2024; pp. 1–6.
28. Heinrich, M.; Rosenblatt, M.; Wieland, F.G.; Stigter, H.; Timmer, J. On structural and practical identifiability: Current status and update of results. *Curr. Opin. Syst. Biol.* **2025**, *41*, 100546. [CrossRef]
29. Himpe, C. emgr—The Empirical Gramian Framework. *Algorithms* **2018**, *11*, 91. [CrossRef]
30. Leoca, D.A.I.; Falavarjani, M.S.; Villaverde, A.F. Comparativa de metodologías de análisis de identificabilidad estructural y observabilidad para modelos no lineales. *Jornadas De Automática* **2025**, *46*, 72.
31. DiStefano, J., III. *Dynamic Systems Biology Modeling and Simulation*; Academic Press: Cambridge, MA, USA, 2015.
32. Iglesias, P.A.; Ingalls, B.P. *Control Theory and Systems Biology*; MIT Press: Cambridge, MA, USA, 2010.
33. Walter, E.; Pronzato, L. *Identification of Parametric Models: From Experimental Data*; Springer: Berlin/Heidelberg, Germany, 1997.
34. Oana, C.; Banga, J.; Balsa-Canto, E. Structural Identifiability of Systems Biology Models: A Critical Comparison of Methods. *PLoS ONE* **2011**, *6*, e27755. [CrossRef]
35. Sarafrazi, M.A.; Kotta, Ü.; Bartosiewicz, Z. Finite determination of accessibility and singular points of nonlinear systems: An algebraic approach. *Syst. Control Lett.* **2020**, *136*, 104600. [CrossRef]
36. Stigter, J.H.; van Willigenburg, L.G. Model Reduction of Complex Dynamical Systems: A Sensitivity Based Approach. *IFAC-PapersOnLine* **2025**, *59*, 457–462. [CrossRef]
37. Stigter, J.; van Willigenburg, L.; Molenaar, J. An Efficient Method to Assess Local Controllability and Observability for Non-Linear Systems. *IFAC-PapersOnLine* **2018**, *51*, 535–540. [CrossRef]
38. Díaz-Seoane, S.; Sellán, E.; Villaverde, A.F. Structural Identifiability and Observability of Microbial Community Models. *Bioengineering* **2023**, *10*, 483. [CrossRef] [PubMed]
39. Villaverde, A.F.; Tsiantis, N.; Banga, J.R. Full observability and estimation of unknown inputs, states and parameters of nonlinear biological models. *J. R. Soc. Interface* **2019**, *16*, 20190043. [CrossRef]
40. Maes, K.; Chatzis, M.; Lombaert, G. Observability of nonlinear systems with unmeasured inputs. *Mech. Syst. Signal Process.* **2019**, *130*, 378–394. [CrossRef]
41. Villaverde, A.F.; Evans, N.D.; Chappell, M.J.; Banga, J.R. Input-Dependent Structural Identifiability of Nonlinear Systems. *IEEE Control Syst. Lett.* **2019**, *3*, 272–277. [CrossRef]
42. Sedoglavic, A. A Probabilistic Algorithm to Test Local Algebraic Observability in Polynomial Time. *J. Symb. Comput.* **2002**, *33*, 735–755. [CrossRef]
43. Sussmann, H.J. A general theorem on local controllability. *SIAM J. Control Optim.* **1987**, *25*, 158–194. [CrossRef]
44. Villaverde, A.; Banga, J. Dynamical compensation and structural identifiability of biological models: Analysis, implications, and reconciliation. *PLoS Comput. Biol.* **2017**, *13*, e1005878. [CrossRef]
45. Locke, J.; Millar, A.; Turner, M. Modelling genetic networks with noisy and varied experimental data: The circadian clock in Arabidopsis thaliana. *J. Theor. Biol.* **2005**, *234*, 383–393. [CrossRef]
46. Bolie, V.W. Coefficients of normal blood glucose regulation. *J. Appl. Physiol.* **1961**, *16*, 783–788. [CrossRef] [PubMed]
47. Fujita, K.A.; Toyoshima, Y.; Uda, S.; Ozaki, Y.; Kubota, H.; Kuroda, S. Decoupling of Receptor and Downstream Signals in the Akt Pathway by Its Low-Pass Filter Characteristics. *Sci. Signal.* **2010**, *3*, ra56. [CrossRef]
48. Neddermeyer, F.; Marhold, V.; Menzel, C.; Krämer, D.; King, R. Modelling the production of soluble hydrogenase in Ralstonia eutropha by on-line optimal experimental design. *IFAC-PapersOnLine* **2016**, *49*, 627–632. [CrossRef]

49. Lugagne, J.B.; Sosa Carrillo, S.; Kirch, M.; Köhler, A.; Batt, G.; Hersen, P. Balancing a genetic toggle switch by real-time feedback control and periodic forcing. *Nat. Commun.* **2017**, *8*, 1671. [CrossRef]
50. Merkt, B.; Timmer, J.; Kaschek, D. Higher-order Lie symmetries in identifiability and predictability analysis of dynamic models. *Phys. Rev. E Stat. Nonlinear Soft Matter Phys.* **2015**, *92*, 012920. [CrossRef]
51. Raia, V.; Schilling, M.; Böhm, M.; Hahn, B.; Roller, A.; Raue, A.; Sticht, C.; Bohl, S.; Saile, M.; Möller, P.; et al. Dynamic Mathematical Modeling of IL13-Induced Signaling in Hodgkin and Primary Mediastinal B-Cell Lymphoma Allows Prediction of Therapeutic Targets. *Cancer Res.* **2011**, *71*, 693–704. [CrossRef] [PubMed]
52. Nguyen, L.; Degasperi, A.; Cotter, P.; Kholodenko, B. DYVIPAC: An integrated analysis and visualisation framework to probe multi-dimensional biological networks. *Sci. Rep.* **2015**, *5*, 12569. [CrossRef] [PubMed]
53. Alexis, E.; Schulte, C.C.; Cardelli, L.; Papachristodoulou, A. Biomolecular mechanisms for signal differentiation. *iScience* **2021**, *24*, 103462. [CrossRef] [PubMed]
54. Sootla, A.; Delalez, N.; Alexis, E.; Norman, A.; Steel, H.; Wadhams, G.; Papachristodoulou, A. Dichotomous feedback: A signal sequestration-based feedback mechanism for biocontroller design. *J. R. Soc. Interface* **2022**, *19*, 20210737. [CrossRef]
55. Kelly, C.; Harris, A.; Steel, H.; Hancock, E.; Heap, J.; Papachristodoulou, A. Synthetic negative feedback circuits using engineered small RNAs. *Nucleic Acids Res.* **2018**, *46*, 9875–9889. [CrossRef]
56. Mursyitah, D.; Faizal, A.; Aini, Z. Performance of High-Gain Observer (HGO) For Level Estimation in Continuous Stirred Tank Reactor (CSTR). *J. Ecotipe (Electron. Control. Telecommun. Inf. Power Eng.)* **2024**, *11*, 117–124. [CrossRef]
57. Hong, H.; Ovchinnikov, A.; Pogudin, G.; Yap, C. SIAN: Software for structural identifiability analysis of ODE models. *Bioinformatics* **2019**, *35*, 2873–2874. [CrossRef]
58. Chatzis, M.; Maes, K.; Lombaert, G. Observability of nonlinear discrete-time systems with unmeasured inputs. *Mech. Syst. Signal Process.* **2025**, *238*, 113142. [CrossRef]

computation

MDPI

Article

A Finite-Time Extended State Observer with Prediction Error Compensation for PMSM Control

Lihua Gao [1,2], Guangming Zhang [2,*], Xiaodong Lv [2], Yan Wang [1] and Zhihan Shi [2]

[1] College of Electrical Engineering and Control Science, Nanjing Polytechnic Institute, Nanjing 210048, China; gaolihua@njpi.edu.cn (L.G.); wyan@njpi.edu.cn (Y.W.)
[2] College of Electrical Engineering and Control Science, Nanjing Tech University, Nanjing 211816, China; lxd@njtech.edu.cn (X.L.); szh@njtech.edu.cn (Z.S.)
* Correspondence: zgm@njtech.edu.cn

Abstract

This paper proposes a finite-time extended state observer (FTESO) integrated with model predictive control (MPC) for high-performance control of permanent magnet synchronous motors (PMSMs). A disturbance-aware predictive model is constructed by incorporating lumped disturbances into the PMSM current equations, addressing load fluctuations and parameter uncertainties. The FTESO, designed with nonlinear gains and Lyapunov stability, ensures rapid disturbance estimation and is embedded into a feedforward-compensated MPC with a composite cost function considering current error and voltage increment. Simulations show that under sudden load disturbances, FTESO-MPC achieves faster recovery and a smaller steady-state error than LESO-MPC; when inductance triples, FTESO-MPC maintains smooth convergence, whereas LESO-MPC exhibits oscillations with d-axis current peaks near 200 A. Under resistance or flux variations, FTESO-MPC sustains stable regulation with less ripple, confirming its superior tracking accuracy and robustness compared with LESO-MPC.

Keywords: finite-time extended state observer; model predictive control; permanent magnet synchronous motor; disturbance rejection

1. Introduction

In recent years, the rapid growth of global transportation demand has significantly increased the deployment of electric drive systems. Among various applications, electric vehicles (EVs), electric buses, and urban rail transit are typical examples. In these systems, electric drives play a crucial role in ensuring reliable and efficient operation [1,2]. At the heart of these applications lies the electric drive system, which directly determines the dynamic performance and operational reliability of the equipment. Particularly, permanent magnet synchronous motors (PMSMs) have gained widespread application due to their high power density, excellent responsiveness, and suitability for advanced control. However, in real-world operating conditions, PMSM-driven systems are frequently subjected to load disturbances, parameter uncertainties, and unmodeled dynamics [3]. These challenges necessitate the development of advanced control strategies that can achieve strong disturbance rejection and maintain stable speed performance under practical operating conditions.

Traditional speed control strategies, such as proportional–integral (PI) control and feedforward decoupling methods [4–8], have demonstrated satisfactory performance in

https://doi.org/10.3390/computation13100247

light-load or steady-state conditions. However, these methods typically assume that external disturbances and model uncertainties are negligible, which becomes invalid under dynamic operating conditions. In scenarios with significant parameter variations or abrupt load changes, such controllers often fail to adjust the control law in a timely manner, resulting in increased output deviations and degraded regulation performance. To address this issue, control strategies with built-in disturbance estimation and compensation mechanisms have attracted increasing research attention. The Extended State Observer (ESO) [9–13] has emerged as a widely used technique in nonlinear control systems, owing to its ability to dynamically estimate generalized disturbances—including external perturbations, modeling errors, and unmodeled dynamics—by augmenting the system state. By incorporating these estimated disturbances into the control loop, ESO-based methods can effectively mitigate the impact of uncertainties, allowing the controller to operate as if under ideal model conditions. This significantly enhances the robustness and adaptability of the control system under complex and uncertain environments.

Despite the theoretical clarity and implementation simplicity of conventional ESO structures, which are mostly based on linear state-space models and finite-difference estimations, their performance deteriorates in the presence of high-speed disturbances or rapid state transitions. In applications such as coal unloading crawlers, where load impacts are abrupt and disturbances occur frequently, the inherent estimation delay of linear ESOs often becomes a limiting factor [14–16]. To address this limitation, recent studies have introduced various structural improvements, among which the Finite-Time Convergent Extended State Observer (FTESO) [17–22] has gained significant attention. FTESO incorporates nonlinear feedback gains and sliding-mode terms into the observer design, enabling the estimated disturbance to converge to its true value within a finite time. This structure offers substantial improvements in estimation speed and tracking accuracy compared to conventional ESOs, especially in scenarios with rapidly changing system states or high-frequency disturbances. As demonstrated in [22], FTESO-based control systems exhibit significantly reduced current and speed recovery times, lower overshoot, and minimized steady-state errors under dynamic disturbance conditions. These advantages make FTESO particularly suitable for enhancing the robustness and dynamic performance of electric drive systems.

Although Model Predictive Control (MPC) has demonstrated excellent capabilities in dynamic optimization and multi-objective control, its performance remains highly dependent on the accuracy of the internal model. Under non-ideal modeling conditions, such as parameter uncertainties or external disturbances, MPC may generate prediction deviations that lead to suboptimal control actions. To address this limitation, an effective solution is to incorporate disturbance estimates provided by an ESO into the MPC framework, forming a disturbance-observation–based predictive compensation structure [23–25]. This integrated ESO-MPC architecture enhances the model adaptation capability of MPC by dynamically correcting prediction errors induced by unmodeled dynamics. In practical applications, such a scheme improves the controller's ability to respond rapidly to and recover stably from sudden load disturbances. Recent studies have explored several variants of this approach, including ESO-MPC, Finite-Time ESO-MPC (FTESO-MPC), and disturbance-compensated rolling optimization schemes, with promising results in motor drives, power converters, and other dynamic systems [26–28]. In these frameworks, the ESO is typically used to estimate current disturbances, voltage shifts, or internal state fluctuations, and feed these estimates into the MPC optimization process. This enables the cost function to be adaptively corrected in real time, thereby improving decision-making accuracy. Moreover, due to the real-time estimation capability of the ESO, its outputs can be directly utilized as feedback to update the internal prediction model, enhancing the robustness and adaptability of the control system under complex operating conditions.

While the integration of FTESO and MPC successfully combines the multi-variable optimization capability of predictive control with the disturbance estimation and adaptation strengths of finite-time observers, its effectiveness still relies on certain assumptions regarding model accuracy and parameter availability. In practice, the design, tuning, and real-time implementation of the observer–controller structure can introduce additional complexity and computational burden, which may limit its applicability in highly dynamic and resource-constrained systems [29–31]. This challenge becomes more pronounced in scenarios such as coal unloading equipment, where strong nonlinearities, multiple concurrent disturbances, and significant system uncertainties are present. Under such conditions, the system model may deviate considerably from reality, and the behavior of external disturbances may be difficult to model explicitly. Consequently, FTESO-MPC–based control strategies may exhibit limited robustness and adaptability, especially when faced with rapidly changing or unknown operating conditions. Motivated by these limitations, further enhancement of disturbance-resilient control design is required to ensure reliable operation in complex industrial systems.

In this context, the proposed control strategy can be interpreted as an integrated-architecture (IA)-based control scheme, in which the finite-time extended state observer (FTESO) and the model predictive controller (MPC) are designed within a unified framework rather than as separated modules. This integrated architecture allows the observer and controller to interact in real time: the FTESO rapidly estimates lumped disturbances and feeds them directly into the MPC optimization process, while the MPC updates its cost function and prediction model based on these estimations. Such mutual coupling forms a closed-loop coordination between disturbance observation and predictive compensation, significantly improving dynamic adaptability and robustness. By combining the fast finite-time convergence of the observer with the optimal decision-making of predictive control, the IA-based FTESO–MPC scheme achieves superior disturbance rejection, faster transient response, and smoother control action compared with conventional cascaded approaches. This integration highlights the key innovation of the present work and provides a more systematic foundation for robust and adaptive PMSM control.

To address the challenges of strong external disturbances and parameter uncertainties commonly encountered in electric drive systems, this paper develops a disturbance-aware current prediction model for PMSMs, which incorporates a lumped disturbance term to represent unmodeled dynamics and external perturbations. An FTESO is designed based on nonlinear feedback gain, enabling rapid and accurate estimation of current disturbances within a finite convergence time. The estimated disturbance is then embedded into the MPC framework, forming a disturbance-compensated composite controller. A multi-objective cost function is constructed, which simultaneously considers current tracking error and voltage increment regulation, thereby enabling real-time feedforward compensation of system disturbances and smooth voltage response adjustment. The proposed IA-based FTESO–MPC scheme significantly improves robustness and dynamic performance under complex conditions, providing an effective solution for robust and stable PMSM operation.

The main contributions of this study can be summarized as follows:

(1) A finite-time extended state observer (FTESO) is developed to achieve rapid and accurate estimation of lumped disturbances in PMSM drives, ensuring convergence within a finite time under strong nonlinear and time-varying conditions.

(2) A novel affine-interval-based nonlinear gain function is introduced into the observer design, which guarantees global smoothness and eliminates the chattering phenomenon commonly observed in conventional sliding-mode ESOs.

(3) A disturbance-aware current prediction model is constructed, incorporating parameter perturbations and unmodeled dynamics as lumped disturbances to enhance model fidelity under practical uncertainties.
(4) A multi-objective cost function is formulated to simultaneously minimize current tracking error and voltage increment, improving both dynamic response and energy efficiency.
(5) An integrated-architecture (IA)-based FTESO–MPC control framework is established, allowing real-time interaction between disturbance estimation and predictive optimization, thereby improving robustness, convergence speed, and steady-state accuracy compared with conventional ESO–MPC or deadbeat control approaches.

2. Disturbance-Aware Modeling of PMSM for Control Design

Accurately modeling the behavior of PMSMs under complex and dynamic load conditions is crucial for developing advanced control strategies that ensure robust performance and effective disturbance rejection. Conventional PMSM current models are often based on idealized assumptions and fail to capture parameter variations, mechanical disturbances, and environmental influences—factors that significantly affect control accuracy in practical applications. In real-world industrial and transportation scenarios, PMSMs frequently operate under harsh and variable conditions. Motor parameters such as inductance and resistance may change due to temperature fluctuations, magnetic saturation, and manufacturing deviations. At the same time, load disturbances can be introduced by uneven mass distribution, mechanical shocks, friction changes, or transmission backlash. These effects lead to strong nonlinearities and uncertainties in the system, greatly increasing control complexity and posing challenges for achieving stable and reliable motor operation. To better capture these real-world uncertainties and to provide a reliable foundation for sustainable and disturbance-resilient control design, this study incorporates aggregated disturbance terms f_d and f_q into the standard PMSM current model [32]:

$$\begin{aligned} L_d \frac{di_d}{dt} &= -Ri_d + PL_q\omega_m i_q + u_d + f_d \\ L_q \frac{di_q}{dt} &= -Ri_q - PL_d\omega_m i_d - P\omega_m\phi_f + u_q + f_q \end{aligned} \tag{1}$$

where these terms represent the unmodeled dynamics and disturbance effects along the d-axis and q-axis, respectively. The modified model offers a more realistic and energy-aware representation of PMSM dynamics, enabling the design of predictive controllers tailored to the demands of efficient electric drive systems in modern transportation applications.

Assuming further that the incremental variations of the stator resistance, d-axis inductance, q-axis inductance, and permanent magnet flux linkage are denoted by ΔR_s, ΔL_d, ΔL_q, and $\Delta\phi_f$, respectively, the current model in Equation (1) can be reformulated to incorporate parameter perturbations as follows:

$$\begin{aligned} (L_d + \Delta L_d)\frac{di_d}{dt} &= -(R + \Delta R)i_d + P(L_q + \Delta L_q)\omega_m i_q + u_d \\ (L_q + \Delta L_q)\frac{di_q}{dt} &= -(R + \Delta R)i_q - P(L_d + \Delta L_d)\omega_m i_d - P\omega_m\left(\phi_f + \Delta\phi_f\right) + u_q \end{aligned} \tag{2}$$

Building upon Equation (2), the model can be further reformulated to explicitly incorporate both motor parameter variations and external disturbance effects, yielding the following extended representation:

$$\begin{aligned} \frac{di_d}{dt} &= -\frac{R}{L_d}i_d + F_d + \frac{u_d}{L_d} \\ \frac{di_q}{dt} &= -\frac{R}{L_q}i_q + F_q + \frac{u_q}{L_q} \end{aligned} \tag{3}$$

where F_d and F_q represent the lumped disturbances that result from the combined effects of motor parameter variations and external perturbations. It should be noted that in practical PMSM drive systems, inverter nonlinearities such as dead-time, switching delay, and voltage saturation inevitably introduce additional voltage distortion. These effects can be equivalently regarded as lumped disturbances acting on the stator voltage model. Therefore, their influence is implicitly included in the total disturbance term of the system dynamics.

$$\begin{array}{l} F_d = -\frac{\Delta L_d}{L_d}\frac{di_d}{dt} - \frac{\Delta R}{L_d}i_d + \frac{P(L_q+\Delta L_q)}{L_d}\omega_m i_q + \frac{f_d}{L_d} \\ F_q = -\frac{\Delta L_q}{L_q}\frac{di_q}{dt} - \frac{\Delta R}{L_q}i_q - \frac{P(L_d+\Delta L_d)}{L_q}\omega_m i_d - \frac{P\omega_m(\phi_f+\Delta\phi_f)}{L_q} + \frac{f_q}{L_q} \end{array} \tag{4}$$

By setting the sampling period as T_s, Equation (4) can be discretized as follows:

$$\begin{array}{l} i_d(k+1) = -\frac{T_s R}{L_d}i_d(k) + T_s F_d(k) + \frac{T_s}{L_d}u_d(k) \\ i_q(k+1) = -\frac{T_s R}{L_q}i_q(k) + T_s F_q(k) + \frac{T_s}{L_q}u_q(k) \end{array} \tag{5}$$

Based on Equation (5), a disturbance prediction model for the PMSM is constructed by treating the d-axis current i_d, q-axis current i_q, and the lumped disturbances F_d and F_q as system state variables. It is assumed that the disturbance terms F_d and F_q remain constant over the prediction horizon N_p. Accordingly, an extended state-space model is formulated to capture both system dynamics and disturbance evolution:

$$\begin{array}{l} x(k+1) = Ax(k) + Bu(k) \\ y(k) = Cx(k) \end{array} \tag{6}$$

where

$$x(k) = \begin{bmatrix} i_d(k) \\ i_q(k) \\ F_d(k) \\ F_q(k) \end{bmatrix}, y(k) = \begin{bmatrix} i_d(k) \\ i_q(k) \end{bmatrix}, u(k) = \begin{bmatrix} u_d(k) \\ u_q(k) \end{bmatrix} \tag{7}$$

$$A = \begin{bmatrix} -\frac{T_s R}{L_d} & 0 & 0 & 0 \\ 0 & -\frac{T_s R}{L_q} & 0 & 0 \\ 0 & 0 & T_s & 0 \\ 0 & 0 & 0 & T_s \end{bmatrix}, B = \begin{bmatrix} \frac{T_s}{L_d} \\ \frac{T_s}{L_q} \end{bmatrix}, C = \begin{bmatrix} 1 & 0 & 0 & 0 \\ 0 & 1 & 0 & 0 \end{bmatrix} \tag{8}$$

Let $\Delta i_d(k)$ and $\Delta i_q(k)$ denote the incremental errors of the d-axis and q-axis currents, and $\Delta F_d(k)$ and $\Delta F_q(k)$ represent the incremental disturbance estimation errors. Based on Equation (6), the incremental prediction model of the stator currents can be derived as follows:

$$\begin{array}{l} x_e(k+1) = A_e x_e(k) + B_e \Delta u(k) \\ y(k) = C_e x_e(k) \end{array} \tag{9}$$

where

$$\begin{array}{l} x_e(k) = \begin{bmatrix} \Delta i_d(k) \\ \Delta i_q(k) \\ \Delta F_d(k) \\ \Delta F_q(k) \\ i_d(k) \\ i_q(k) \end{bmatrix}, y(k) = \begin{bmatrix} i_d(k) \\ i_q(k) \end{bmatrix}, \Delta u(k) = \begin{bmatrix} \Delta u_d(k) \\ \Delta u_q(k) \end{bmatrix} \\ A_e = \begin{bmatrix} -\frac{T_s R}{L_d} & 0 & 0 & 0 & 0 & 0 \\ 0 & -\frac{T_s R}{L_q} & 0 & 0 & 0 & 0 \\ 0 & 0 & T_s & 0 & 0 & 0 \\ 0 & 0 & 0 & T_s & 0 & 0 \\ -\frac{T_s R}{L_d} & 0 & 0 & 0 & 0 & 0 \\ 0 & -\frac{T_s R}{L_q} & 0 & 0 & 0 & 0 \end{bmatrix}, B_e = \begin{bmatrix} \frac{T_s}{L_d} & 0 \\ 0 & \frac{T_s}{L_q} \\ 0 & 0 \\ 0 & 0 \\ \frac{T_s}{L_d} & 0 \\ 0 & \frac{T_s}{L_q} \end{bmatrix}, \\ C_e = \begin{bmatrix} 0 & 0 & 0 & 0 & 1 & 0 \\ 0 & 0 & 0 & 0 & 0 & 1 \end{bmatrix} \end{array} \tag{10}$$

3. Feedforward-Based Compound Control Design

3.1. Finite-Time Convergent Extended State Observer

To enhance the disturbance rejection capability of the PMSM control system under complex and time-varying conditions, and to improve the accuracy of model predictive control, this study develops an FTESO. The observer is designed to estimate, in real time, the d-axis and q-axis currents of the PMSM along with the corresponding lumped disturbances. These estimated disturbances are incorporated as extended state variables into the predictive control framework, enabling proactive and efficient compensation. By enhancing disturbance suppression and dynamic adaptability, the proposed method contributes to more robust and stable motor drive performance under complex operating conditions.

Design of an FTESO for d-axis current:

$$\begin{cases} e_{1d} = \hat{i}_d - i_d, e_{2d} = \phi_{1d} - F_{0d} \\ \dot{\hat{i}}_d = F_{0d} - \frac{R}{L_d} i_d + \frac{1}{L_d} u_d \\ F_{0d} = \phi_{1d} - k_{1d}\left(\theta e_{1d}^{\frac{\beta}{2}} + (b-\theta) e_{1d}^{1-\frac{\beta}{2}}\right)^2 sign(e_{1d}) \\ \dot{\phi}_{1d} = -k_{2d}\left(\theta e_{2d}^{\frac{\beta}{2}} + (b-\theta) e_{2d}^{1-\frac{\beta}{2}}\right)^2 sign(e_{2d}) \end{cases} \tag{11}$$

Design of an FTESO for q-axis current:

$$\begin{cases} e_{1q} = \hat{i}_q - i_q, e_{2q} = \phi_{1q} - F_{0q} \\ \dot{\hat{i}}_q = F_{0q} - \frac{R}{L_q} i_q + \frac{1}{L_q} u_q \\ F_{0q} = \phi_{1q} - k_{1q}\left(\theta e_{1q}^{\frac{\beta}{2}} + (b-\theta) e_{1q}^{1-\frac{\beta}{2}}\right)^2 sign(e_{1q}) \\ \dot{\phi}_{1q} = -k_{2q}\left(\theta e_{2q}^{\frac{\beta}{2}} + (b-\theta) e_{2q}^{1-\frac{\beta}{2}}\right)^2 sign(e_{2q}) \end{cases} \tag{12}$$

where $\hat{i}_d$ and $\hat{i}_q$ represent the estimated values of the d-axis and q-axis currents, respectively, while F_{od} and F_{0q} denote the estimated disturbance components along the d-axis and q-axis. The parameters k_{1d}, k_{2d}, k_{1q} and k_{2q} are adjustable gains within the FTESO design. Regardless of the initial magnitude of current or disturbance estimation errors, the observer ensures that all deviations converge to their reference values or predefined bounds within a finite time. These bounds can be arbitrarily small, demonstrating the high precision and fast convergence characteristics of the proposed finite-time extended observer. Some details are in Figure 1.

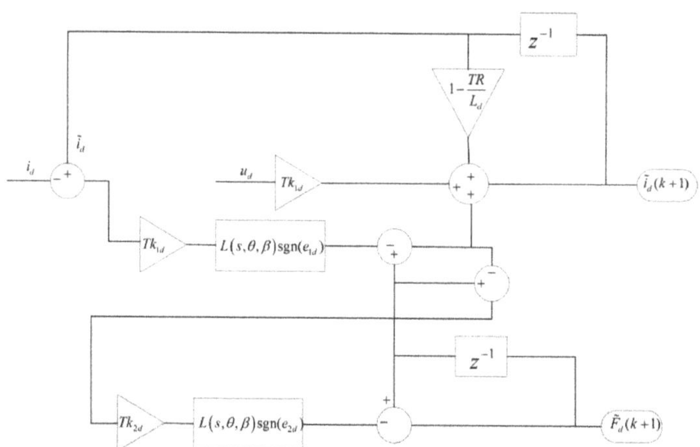

Figure 1. Block Diagram of FTESO.

3.2. Stability Analysis

Theorem 1. *The nonlinear dynamics can be expressed as:*

$$\dot{s}(t) = -L(s,\theta,\beta) = -\left(\theta s(t)^{\frac{\beta}{2}} + (b-\theta)s(t)^{1-\frac{\beta}{2}}\right)^2, s(0) = s_0 \tag{13}$$

where, given that $\theta > 0$, $b - \theta > 0$, and $0 < \beta < 1$, the nonlinear function exhibits finite-time convergence. For any initial value s_0, the time required for the function to converge to the origin and to ρ can be respectively expressed as:

$$\begin{aligned} t_0 &= \tfrac{1}{1-\beta}\left(\tfrac{1}{\theta(b-\theta)} - \tfrac{1}{\theta^2 s_0^{1-\beta} + \theta(b-\theta)}\right) \\ t_\rho &= \tfrac{1}{1-\beta}\left(\tfrac{1}{\theta\rho^{1-\beta} + (b-\theta)} - \tfrac{1}{\theta^2 s_0^{1-\beta} + \theta(b-\theta)}\right) \end{aligned} \tag{14}$$

The upper bound of the convergence time is given by:

$$T_{\max} = \frac{1}{\theta(b-\theta)(1-\beta)} \tag{15}$$

In contrast to the conventional finite-time extended state observers that employ the discontinuous fal(·) function [9], the proposed FTESO introduces a redesigned nonlinear gain term inspired by the definition of affine intervals in convex affine subspace theory. This nonlinear mapping ensures global differentiability, thereby eliminating the non-smooth transition near the origin that commonly causes chattering and numerical instability in traditional designs. By reformulating the nonlinear feedback law into an affine-type continuous structure, the observer achieves smooth finite-time convergence [33–35] and enhanced robustness against system uncertainties and external disturbances. Moreover, the continuous nature of the affine-interval-based function improves the numerical stability of the discrete-time implementation, reducing sensitivity to sampling noise and quantization errors. The redesigned nonlinearity preserves the fast finite-time convergence characteristics while ensuring global smoothness, which facilitates both digital realization and theoretical analysis. As a result, the proposed FTESO provides a balanced structure that combines the advantages of finite-time convergence, robustness, and computational smoothness, making it more suitable for high-performance PMSM drive control.

Proof of Theorem 1. Let the Lyapunov candidate function be defined as $V(s) = \frac{s^2}{2} \geq 0$. Taking the time derivative of V, we obtain:

$$\begin{aligned} \dot{V} &= s\dot{s} \\ &= -s\left(\theta s^{\frac{\beta}{2}} + (b-\theta)s^{1-\frac{\beta}{2}}\right)^2 \\ &= -V^{\frac{1+\beta}{2}}\left(\theta + (b-\theta)V^{\frac{1-\beta}{2}}\right)^2 \end{aligned} \tag{16}$$

Since $\theta > 0, b - \theta > 0$, it follows that $(b-\theta)V^{\frac{1-\beta}{2}} > 0$. Therefore, the time derivative of the Lyapunov function satisfies $\dot{V} \leq -\theta^2 V^{\frac{1+\beta}{2}}$. Given that $0 < \beta < 1$, we have $1 < 1 + \beta < 2$, which implies $0 < \frac{1+\beta}{2} < 1$. This confirms that the nonlinear function converges to the equilibrium point in finite time.

When $V \neq 0$, then:

$$\frac{1}{V^{\frac{1+\beta}{2}}}\frac{dV}{dt} = \left(\theta + (b-\theta)V^{\frac{1-\beta}{2}}\right)^2 \tag{17}$$

Let $m = V^{\frac{1-\beta}{2}}$, then:

$$\begin{aligned} &\int_{m(0)}^{m(t)} \frac{dm}{(\theta + (b-\theta)m)^2} = \int_0^t (\beta - 1)dt \\ &s^{1-\beta}(t) = m(t) = \frac{1}{\theta^2(\beta-1)t + \dfrac{\theta^2}{\theta(b-\theta)+\theta^2 m(0)}} - \frac{\theta(b-\theta)}{\theta^2} \end{aligned} \tag{18}$$

Case 1:

For any initial condition s_0, the settling time of s to reach the origin can be derived from Equation (18) as follows:

$$t = \frac{1}{1-\beta}\left(\frac{1}{\theta(b-\theta)} - \frac{1}{\theta^2 s_0^{1-\beta} + \theta(b-\theta)}\right) \tag{19}$$

Case 2:

For any initial state s_0, the convergence time of s to a predefined threshold ρ can be determined based on Equation (18) as follows:

$$t_\rho = \frac{1}{\theta(1-\beta)}\left(\frac{1}{\theta\rho^{1-\beta} + (b-\theta)} - \frac{1}{\theta^2 s_0^{1-\beta} + (b-\theta)}\right) \tag{20}$$

where the convergence rate increases as the value of β decreases.

Case 3:

Based on the above two scenarios, the convergence time is a strictly increasing function of the initial value s_0. Therefore, the convergence time $T_{\max}$ is bounded:

$$T_{\max} = \frac{1}{\theta(b-\theta)(1-\beta)} \tag{21}$$

From Equations (3) and (11), the following expression can be derived:

$$\begin{aligned} \dot{e}_{1d} &= \dot{\hat{i}}_d - \dot{i}_d \\ &= F_{0d} - F_d \\ &= \phi_{1d} - F_d - k_{1d}\left(\theta e_{2d}^{\frac{\beta}{2}} + (b-\theta)e_{2d}^{1-\frac{\beta}{2}}\right)^2 sign(e_{2d}) \end{aligned} \tag{22}$$

$$\begin{aligned} e_{2d} &= \phi_{1d} - F_{0d} \\ &= \phi_{1d} - \left(\dot{\hat{i}}_d - \tfrac{R}{L_d} i_d + \tfrac{1}{L_d} u_d\right) \\ &= \phi_{1d} - (\dot{e}_{1d} + F_d) \end{aligned} \tag{23}$$

Let $e_{3d} = \phi_{1d} - F_d$, then:

$$\begin{aligned} \dot{e}_{3d} &= \dot{\phi}_{1d} - \dot{F}_d \\ &= -k_{2d}\left(\theta(e_{3d} - \dot{e}_{1d})^{\frac{\beta}{2}} + (b-\theta)(e_{3d} - \dot{e}_{1d})^{1-\frac{\beta}{2}}\right)^2 sign(e_{3d} - \dot{e}_{1d}) - \dot{F}_d \end{aligned} \tag{24}$$

It follows from the preceding analysis that both e_{1d} and e_{3d} achieve finite-time convergence. Upon system stabilization, the condition $\dot{e}_{1d} = 0$ is satisfied, and Equation (24) is thereby evaluated as:

$$\begin{aligned} \dot{e}_{3d} &= \dot{\phi}_{1d} - \dot{F}_d \\ &= -k_{2d}\left(\theta(e_{3d})^{\frac{\beta}{2}} + (b-\theta)(e_{3d})^{1-\frac{\beta}{2}}\right)^2 sign(e_{3d}) - \dot{F}_d \end{aligned} \tag{25}$$

It can thus be concluded that:

$$\left(\theta(e_{3d})^{\frac{\beta}{2}} + (b-\theta)(e_{3d})^{1-\frac{\beta}{2}}\right)^2 \leq \xi \tag{26}$$

For $\theta(e_{3d})^{\frac{\beta}{2}} > (b-\theta)(e_{3d})^{1-\frac{\beta}{2}}$, then:

$$\left(2(b-\theta)(e_{3d})^{1-\frac{\beta}{2}}\right)^2 \leq \xi, |e_{3d}| \leq \left(\frac{\xi}{4(b-\theta)^2}\right)^{\frac{1}{2-\beta}} \tag{27}$$

For $\theta(e_{3d})^{\frac{\beta}{2}} < (b-\theta)(e_{3d})^{1-\frac{\beta}{2}}$, then:

$$\left(2\theta(e_{3d})^{\frac{\beta}{2}}\right)^2 \leq \xi, |e_{3d}| \leq \left(\frac{\xi}{4\theta^2}\right)^{\frac{1}{\beta}} \tag{28}$$

According to Equations (27) and (28), by appropriately tuning the parameters θ and b, the estimated values produced by the observer can accurately approximate the true system states, with the estimation error reduced to an arbitrarily small level. This capability enables precise state feedback, supporting disturbance suppression and dynamic adaptability of PMSMs under dynamic operating conditions. □

3.3. Composite Controller Design

Assuming a sampling period of T_s, the extended state observer models defined in Equations (11) and (12) are discretized using the zero-order hold method.

A discrete-time finite-time convergent extended state observer is developed for the d-axis current channel:

$$\begin{cases} e_{1d}(k) = \hat{i}_d(k) - i_d(k), e_{2d}(k) = \phi_{1d}(k) - F_{0d}(k) \\ \hat{i}_d(k+1) = \hat{i}_d(k) + TF_{0d}(k) - \frac{TR}{L_d} i_d(k) + \frac{T}{L_d} u_d(k) \\ F_{0d}(k) = \phi_{1d}(k) - Tk_{1d}\left(\theta e_{1d}^{\frac{\beta}{2}}(k) + (b-\theta)e_{1d}^{1-\frac{\beta}{2}}(k)\right)^2 sign(e_{1d}(k)) \\ \phi_{1d}(k+1) = \phi_{1d}(k) - Tk_{2d}\left(\theta e_{2d}^{\frac{\beta}{2}}(k) + (b-\theta)e_{2d}^{1-\frac{\beta}{2}}(k)\right)^2 sign(e_{2d}(k)) \end{cases} \tag{29}$$

A discrete-time finite-time convergent extended state observer is developed for the q-axis current channel:

$$\begin{cases} e_{1q}(k) = \hat{i}_q(k) - i_q(k), e_{2q}(k) = \phi_{1q}(k) - F_{0q}(k) \\ \hat{i}_q(k+1) = \hat{i}_q(k) + TF_{0q}(k) - \frac{TR}{L_q} i_q(k) + \frac{T}{L_q} u_q(k) \\ F_{0q}(k) = \phi_{1q}(k) - Tk_{1q}\left(\theta e_{1q}^{\frac{\beta}{2}}(k) + (b-\theta)e_{1q}^{1-\frac{\beta}{2}}(k)\right)^2 sign(e_{1q}(k)) \\ \phi_{1q}(k+1) = \phi_{1q}(k) - Tk_{2q}\left(\theta e_{2q}^{\frac{\beta}{2}}(k) + (b-\theta)e_{2q}^{1-\frac{\beta}{2}}(k)\right)^2 sign(e_{2q}(k)) \end{cases} \tag{30}$$

To ensure precise tracking of the reference current trajectory while mitigating voltage oscillations caused by power device switching, a multi-objective cost function is constructed based on current tracking error and voltage increment minimization. This formulation not only enhances dynamic current response and reduces transient overshoot, but also minimizes copper losses and thermal stress, thereby improving the overall disturbance suppression and dynamic adaptability of the PMSM drive system in electric drive system applications.

$$
\begin{aligned}
J(i,\Delta u) &= \sum_{j=1}^{Np}\left(\hat{i}(k+j)-i_{ref}(k+j)\right)^T Q\left(\hat{i}(k+j)-i_{ref}(k+j)\right) \\
&+\sum_{j=1}^{Nc}\Delta u(k+j)^T R\Delta u(k+j)
\end{aligned}
\tag{31}
$$

At the current sampling instant k, the prediction horizon is defined as N_p, and the control horizon as N_c. The time index $k+j$ denotes the j-th prediction step starting from moment k. The predicted current vector at $k+j$ is given by $\hat{i}(k+j) = \begin{bmatrix}\hat{i}_d(k+j)\\ \hat{i}_q(k+j)\end{bmatrix}$ representing the estimated d-axis and q-axis currents of the PMSMs. The reference current vector is denoted as $i_{ref}(k+j) = \begin{bmatrix} i_{dref}(k+j)\\ i_{qref}(k+j)\end{bmatrix}$, which corresponds to the desired d-axis and q-axis currents at time $k+j$. The control increment of voltage input is defined as $\Delta u(k+j) = \begin{bmatrix}\Delta u_d(k+j)\\ \Delta u_q(k+j)\end{bmatrix}$, where Δu_d and Δu_q represent the incremental voltage inputs for the d- and q-axes, respectively. To balance current tracking precision and input effort, Q is introduced as the weighting matrix for current tracking errors, and R is the weighting matrix for voltage increments. This formulation lays the foundation for optimizing the control input in a predictive framework that improves dynamic response and ensures stable current regulation—critical for reliable high-performance electric drive systems.

According to the predictive control strategy adopted in the relevant literature [36], the incremental control inputs for the d-axis and q-axis voltages are parameterized using Laguerre functions:

$$
\begin{aligned}
\Delta u(k+j) &= \begin{bmatrix}\Delta u_d(k+j)\\ \Delta u_q(k+j)\end{bmatrix} \\
&= \begin{bmatrix} l_1^d(k) & \dots & l_N^d(k) & 0 & \dots & 0 \\ 0 & \dots & 0 & l_1^q(k) & \dots & l_N^q(k)\end{bmatrix} \\
&* \begin{bmatrix} c_1^d(k) & \dots & c_N^d(k) & c_1^q(k) & \dots & c_N^q(k)\end{bmatrix}
\end{aligned}
\tag{32}
$$

where this approach expresses the control input sequence as a weighted combination of orthonormal Laguerre basis functions, enabling a compact representation with significantly fewer decision variables. Specifically, the voltage increments $\Delta u_d(k+j)$ and $\Delta u_q(k+j)$ over the prediction horizon are mapped to a set of Laguerre coefficients, which serve as the new optimization variables. By leveraging the orthogonality and recursive structure of Laguerre functions, the method achieves a notable reduction in computational complexity, thereby enhancing the real-time applicability of the predictive controller. Furthermore, this coefficient-based formulation enables smoother control transitions and more stable voltage regulation, which helps maintain consistent system performance and prolong component lifespan.

The composite control law based on the finite-time convergent observer and disturbance compensation can be derived by substituting Equations (1), (11), (12), and (32) into Equation (31).

$$
\begin{aligned}
u(k+1) &= u(k)+\Delta u(k+1) \\
&= u(k) - L^T\Omega^{-1}\psi(x_e(k)-\hat{x}_e(k))
\end{aligned}
\tag{33}
$$

Let $\Delta u(k+1) = \begin{bmatrix}\Delta u_d(k+j)\\ \Delta u_q(k+j)\end{bmatrix}$ represent the incremental voltages along the d-axis and q-axis at prediction step $k+j$. The matrix Ω denotes the weight assigned to the current tracking error, while R represents the weight assigned to the control voltage increment.

Therefore, the structure of the predictive control scheme incorporating the designed FTESO is illustrated in Figure 2.

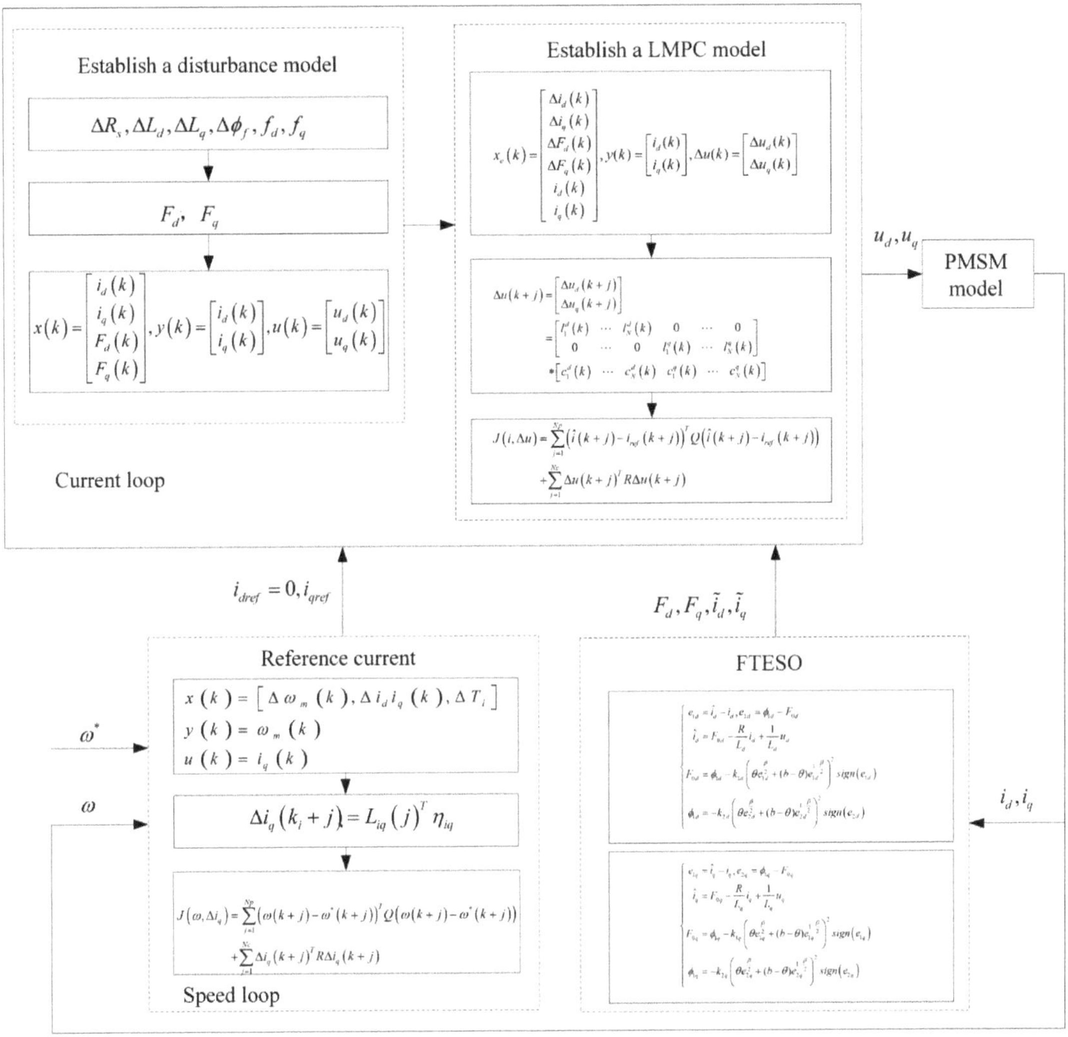

Figure 2. Flowchart of FTESO-MPC Controller.

4. Result Analysis

To validate the disturbance rejection capability of the proposed FTESO-based predictive controller, this section presents both simulation and experimental evaluations. A comparative analysis is conducted against the LESO-based predictive controller reported in the literature. Emphasis is placed on assessing not only the tracking accuracy and dynamic performance but also the control system's contribution to enhanced disturbance suppression and dynamic adaptability under complex load conditions, which aligns with the overarching goal of advancing robust control strategies for high-performance electric drive systems.

To assess the dynamic response characteristics of the control system under realistic operating conditions, simulation experiments were conducted considering both time-varying load disturbances and parametric uncertainties in the PMSM. Two control strategies—FTESO-based predictive control and conventional LESO-based predictive control—were evaluated and compared. The simulation settings, including motor parameters, observer configurations, and disturbance profiles, are detailed in Tables 1–3. These scenarios are designed to reflect typical working conditions in electric vehicle applications, where external load variation and parameter drift pose challenges to stable and reliable motor operation. By observing current regulation, control smoothness, and torque response under these variations, the effectiveness of the proposed controller in enhancing robustness and maintaining high-performance operation is quantitatively analyzed.

Table 1. Speed Loop LMPC Controller Parameters.

Parameter	Description	Value
N_p	Prediction horizon	1
a	Laguerre factor	0.5
N	Number of Laguerre terms	4
q_ω	Speed error weighting factor	1,000,000
r	Control input increment weighting factor	0.1

Table 2. Current Loop LMPC Controller Parameters.

Parameter	Description	Value
N_p	Prediction horizon	1
N_c	Control horizon	1
a_1	Laguerre factor for d-axis current	0.5
a_2	Laguerre factor for q-axis current	0.5
N_1	Number of Laguerre terms for d-axis current	4
N_2	Number of Laguerre terms for q-axis current	4
q_{i_d}	Weighting factor for d-axis current tracking error	100,000
q_{i_q}	Weighting factor for q-axis current tracking error	100,000
r	Weighting factor for input increment	0.01

Table 3. FTESO-MPC and LESO-MPC Parameters.

FTESO	k_{1d} 5000	k_{2d} 0.01	k_{1q} 0.01	k_{2q} 0.01	θ 0.1	β 0.9	b 1
Linear ESO	k_{1d} 5000	k_{2d} 0.01	k_{1q} 0.01	k_{2q} 0.01			

Under the condition of load increase, the dynamic response curves of different control strategies are illustrated in Figure 3. This figure presents the simulated speed response of the proposed FTESO-MPC and the benchmark LESO-MPC controllers when the PMSM is subjected to a sudden external load disturbance. Specifically, Figure 3b depicts the load profile: the PMSM is initially set to track a reference speed of 100 rad/s and starts from no-load conditions. At a specific time instant, an external torque load of 5 N·m is suddenly applied. As shown in Figure 3a, both FTESO-MPC and LESO-MPC demonstrate satisfactory speed tracking performance during the no-load start-up and acceleration phase. However, the FTESO-MPC exhibits superior dynamic performance. In the initial acceleration phase (0~0.1 s), FTESO-MPC responds significantly faster than LESO-MPC, quickly converging to the reference speed with a smaller steady-state error. This indicates that FTESO-MPC possesses enhanced dynamic response characteristics and regulation precision. When the external load is abruptly increased, the LESO-MPC controller shows a larger speed dip and a longer recovery time. In contrast, the FTESO-MPC maintains better disturbance rejection, with less speed fluctuation and faster recovery to steady-state. These results verify that FTESO-MPC achieves more effective compensation against load perturbations, offering improved robustness and faster transient recovery. Such advantages are particularly beneficial for electric drive systems, where precise and rapid adaptation to variable load conditions contributes directly to improved stability and enhanced control reliability.

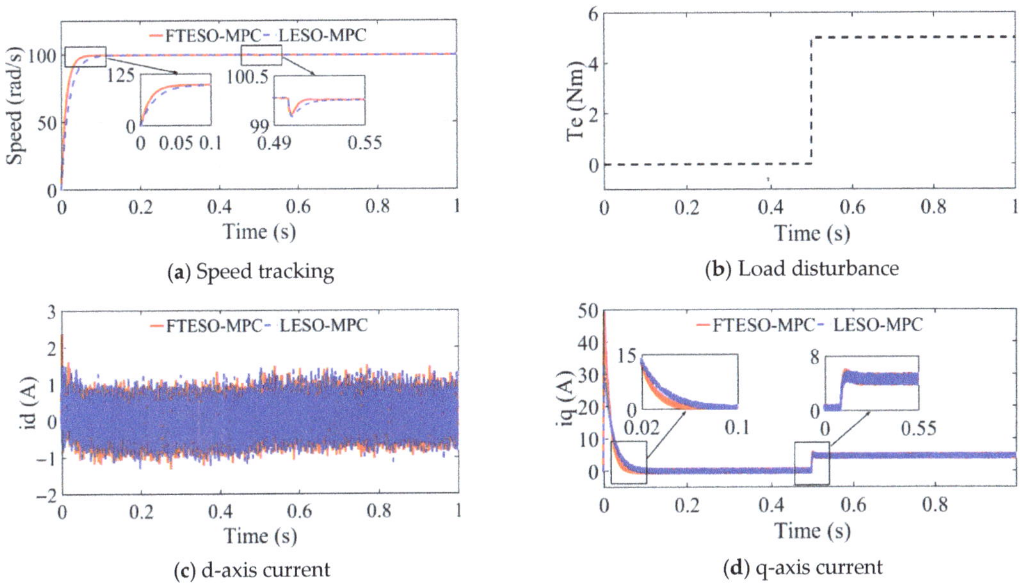

Figure 3. Dynamic Response Simulation Curves of Different Control Strategies under Load Increase Condition.

Corresponding to this is the analysis shown in Figure 3d. During the motor start-up phase, the d-axis current experiences an initial surge followed by a rapid decrease toward its steady-state value. The FTESO-MPC controller exhibits a faster current decay rate and reaches the steady state within a shorter time frame compared to the LESO-MPC, which takes noticeably longer to stabilize. When the external load suddenly increases to 5 N·m, a sharp transient occurs in the d-axis current. FTESO-MPC promptly adjusts the current to a new steady-state value, while LESO-MPC responds with slower current convergence and more pronounced oscillations. This demonstrates the superior transient performance of FTESO-MPC in quickly compensating for current disturbances, ensuring system stability, and minimizing overshoot. In particular, FTESO-MPC leads to smaller current deviation and reduced settling time, whereas LESO-MPC shows larger current fluctuations and a slower recovery. These observations further confirm that FTESO-MPC provides faster dynamic adaptation to abrupt load changes, maintaining system stability and reducing the risk of excessive current stress, which is critical for ensuring system reliability and energy efficiency. Figure 4 presents the dynamic response of both controllers under a load-decreasing scenario. The trends remain consistent with those in Figure 3, further validating the disturbance rejection capability of FTESO-MPC across various operating conditions. This robustness under load transients is essential for electric drive systems, where high-frequency load variations frequently occur under real-world operating conditions.

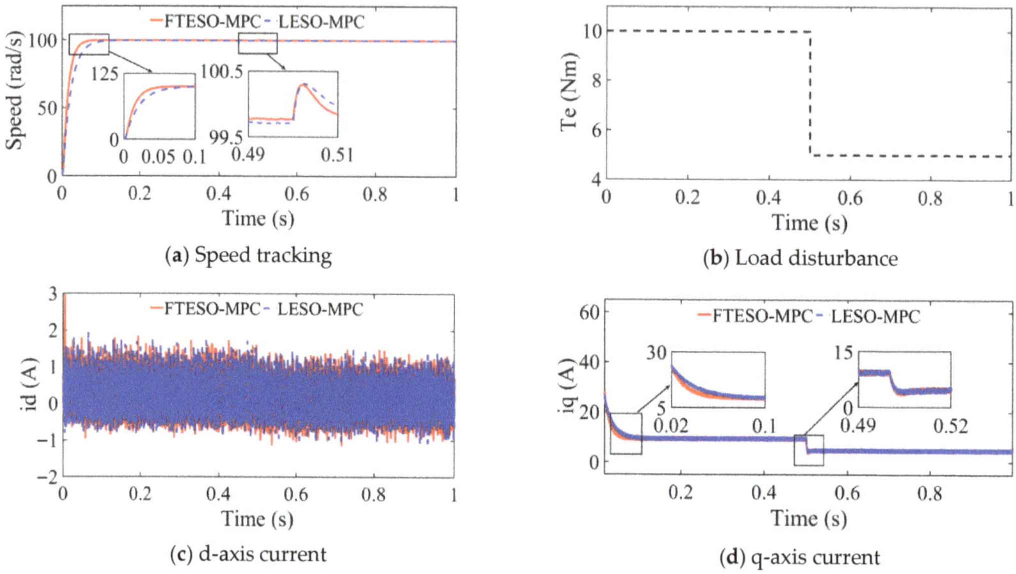

Figure 4. Dynamic Response Simulation Curves of Different Control Strategies under Load Decrease Condition.

Figure 5 illustrates the dynamic response curves of different control strategies under varying inductance conditions. Specifically, the figure compares the performance of FTESO-MPC and LESO-MPC when system inductance is subject to step changes, with all other load conditions consistent with those in Figure 3b. The purpose of this simulation is to evaluate how well each controller adapts to inductance variations, which are common in practical electric drive systems due to temperature fluctuations, magnetic saturation, or structural uncertainties. As observed in Figure 5a, the FTESO-MPC maintains robust dynamic performance across all inductance scenarios. When the inductance is reduced to 0.5 times its nominal value, the system exhibits fast rise time and minimal overshoot, indicating strong regulation capabilities. With a doubled inductance (2×), the system still achieves smooth convergence toward the target speed without noticeable overshoot, demonstrating good control stability. Even under a more challenging condition of triple inductance (3×), the FTESO-MPC maintains a stable response, with only a moderate increase in settling time and no observable oscillation. These results underscore the controller's robustness and adaptability to parameter uncertainties, which are crucial in energy-efficient electric drive systems operating under dynamic environments. In contrast, Figure 5b shows that while LESO-MPC performs adequately under small inductance variations (0.5× and 2×), its control performance degrades significantly when inductance increases to 3×. The system exhibits pronounced oscillations during the initial phase and takes considerably longer to stabilize, reflecting poor disturbance rejection and limited adaptability to parameter shifts. This sensitivity to inductance variation highlights the limitations of LESO-MPC in handling system uncertainty, which may compromise both stability and energy efficiency in practical applications. Overall, the comparison confirms that FTESO-MPC offers superior robustness and dynamic adaptability, making it a more suitable solution for high-performance electric drive systems, where varying electrical parameters and external disturbances are prevalent.

This observation is further supported by the current response curves in Figure 5e,f, which reveal significant differences between FTESO-MPC and LESO-MPC under varying inductance conditions, particularly in terms of the d-axis current behavior. The two control strategies exhibit noticeably different response characteristics as the inductance multiplier changes. In the initial transient phase of the d-axis current response, FTESO-MPC demonstrates superior dynamic performance by more effectively suppressing abrupt current surges and enabling faster convergence to the steady-state value. In contrast, LESO-MPC shows a considerable current overshoot under the 3× inductance condition, with peak current values approaching 200 A—significantly higher than in other scenarios. This excessive overshoot indicates that LESO-MPC struggles to mitigate current shocks when faced with drastic inductance variations, leading to pronounced current fluctuations that compromise system stability. During the steady-state phase, FTESO-MPC maintains relatively stable d-axis current levels across all inductance cases, with minimal ripple, highlighting its robust disturbance rejection capability. On the other hand, LESO-MPC continues to exhibit substantial current oscillations under the 3× inductance condition. The steady-state error under such a condition is also noticeably larger for LESO-MPC, reflecting its limited adaptability to substantial parameter uncertainties. Overall, these results further validate the effectiveness of FTESO-MPC in ensuring reliable current regulation under changing inductance environments. Such robustness is particularly crucial in electric drive systems, where maintaining stable current control not only ensures operational safety and efficiency but also prevents excessive current fluctuations that can compromise reliability.

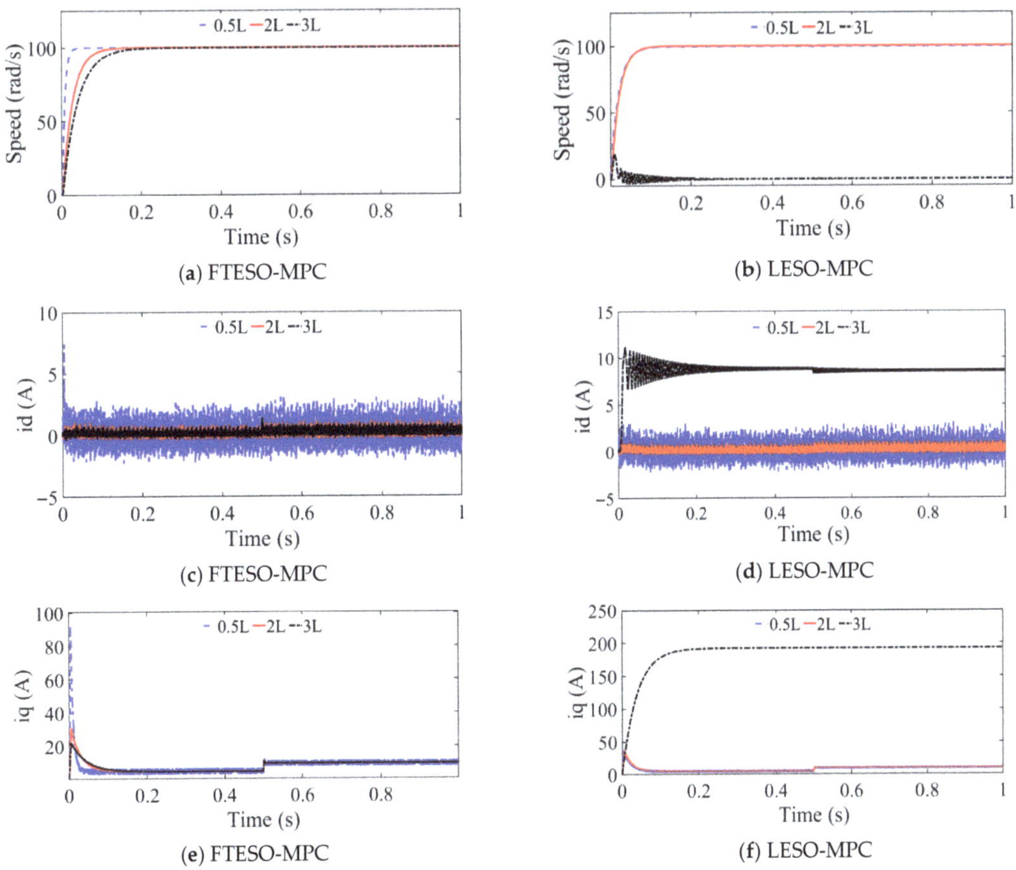

Figure 5. Dynamic Response Simulation Curves of Different Control Strategies under Inductance Variation Condition.

Figure 6 illustrates the simulation results comparing the dynamic responses of FTESO-MPC and LESO-MPC controllers under varying stator resistance conditions. The purpose of this comparison is to assess each controller's ability to maintain stable system performance in the presence of parameter uncertainty, a critical concern for energy-efficient electric drive systems operating in sustainable transportation environments. The external load conditions are consistent with those specified in Figure 3b. As shown in Figure 6a, during the startup phase (0~0.2 s), both FTESO-MPC and LESO-MPC controllers successfully accelerate the motor from standstill to the reference speed of 100 rad/s. Under nominal resistance, the two controllers exhibit similar transient performance. However, as the resistance increases to 2× and 3× the nominal value, noticeable differences emerge. The FTESO-MPC maintains smooth and responsive tracking behavior with minimal overshoot or oscillation. In contrast, the LESO-MPC shows a slower dynamic adjustment, especially under 3× resistance, indicating reduced adaptability. The superior robustness of FTESO-MPC stems from its use of a finite-time convergent observer, which enables rapid and accurate disturbance estimation. This enhances the control system's resilience under varying resistive conditions, a feature especially valuable for electric vehicles where operating conditions and thermal environments frequently change. Further validation is presented in Figure 6e,f, which show the corresponding d-axis current responses. The FTESO-MPC demonstrates superior dynamic current regulation, quickly adapting to resistance changes with smaller transient deviations and faster convergence to steady-state values. Conversely, the LESO-MPC exhibits greater current ripple and significant overshoot, particularly under 0.5× and 3× resistance conditions. These findings confirm that FTESO-MPC not only enhances transient current control but also ensures greater system reliability and thermal stability, aligning with the broader goal of improving robust performance in electric drive systems.

Figure 7 illustrates the dynamic response curves of FTESO-MPC and LESO-MPC under varying flux linkage conditions. This set of simulations aims to evaluate the adaptability of both control strategies to flux linkage deviations, which are common in real-world electric vehicle operations due to temperature effects, magnetic saturation, or aging of motor materials. The load conditions used in this analysis follow the settings depicted in Figure 3b. As shown in Figure 7a, when the flux linkage decreases to 0.5 times its nominal value, both controllers exhibit fast transient response with minimal overshoot. However, under increased flux linkage conditions (2× and 3×), differences between the two controllers become more evident. While both controllers ensure system convergence to the target speed, LESO-MPC shows slower dynamic response. In contrast, FTESO-MPC demonstrates shorter rise times and a more efficient convergence process, indicating superior responsiveness and enhanced adaptability to system variations. Corresponding observations from Figure 7e,f reveal significant distinctions in q-axis current behavior. FTESO-MPC maintains smoother current responses across all flux linkage variations, even under extreme deviations. On the other hand, LESO-MPC suffers from larger current fluctuations, particularly at the onset of flux disturbances. When flux linkage is reduced (0.5×), LESO-MPC exhibits considerable q-axis current overshoot, reflecting its limited capability to cope with rapid magnetic weakening. Conversely, FTESO-MPC quickly stabilizes the current and achieves better damping, contributing to reduced energy losses and improved thermal reliability. Moreover, in high-flux scenarios (2× and 3×), FTESO-MPC continues to deliver consistent and stable q-axis current control, minimizing ripple and ensuring optimal current utilization. LESO-MPC, however, shows persistent instability in current regulation, which can negatively impact overall system reliability. These results confirm that FTESO-MPC not only enhances disturbance rejection but also supports the development of resilient PMSM drive systems—critical for ensuring stable and robust operation in practical applications.

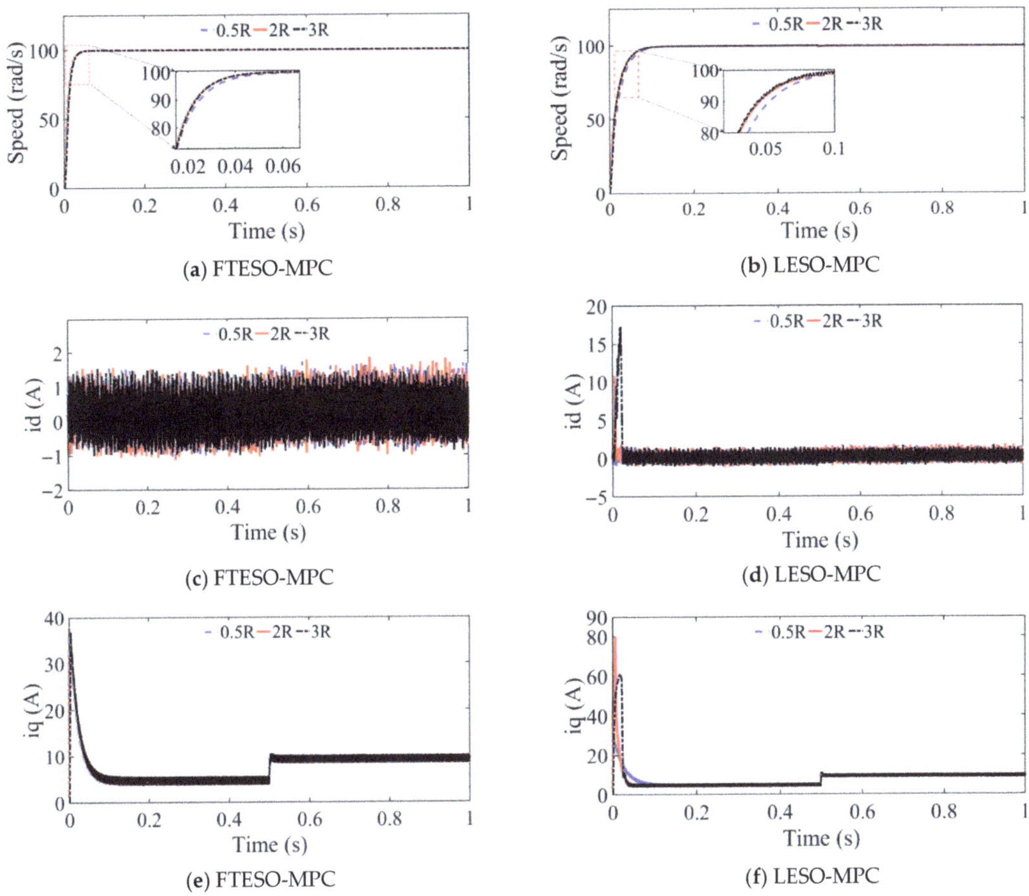

Figure 6. Dynamic Response Simulation Curves of Different Control Strategies under Resistance Variation Condition.

Table 4 summarizes the comparative performance of the proposed FTESO-MPC and the conventional LESO-MPC under representative disturbance scenarios. As can be seen, FTESO-MPC achieves faster recovery and smaller steady-state error under sudden load disturbances, maintains smooth current convergence without oscillation when the inductance increases threefold, and exhibits stable regulation with reduced ripple under resistance and flux linkage variations. In contrast, LESO-MPC suffers from slower recovery, larger current peaks, and instability in these cases. This table highlights the overall advantages of FTESO-MPC in terms of disturbance rejection, transient stability, and robustness under parameter uncertainties.

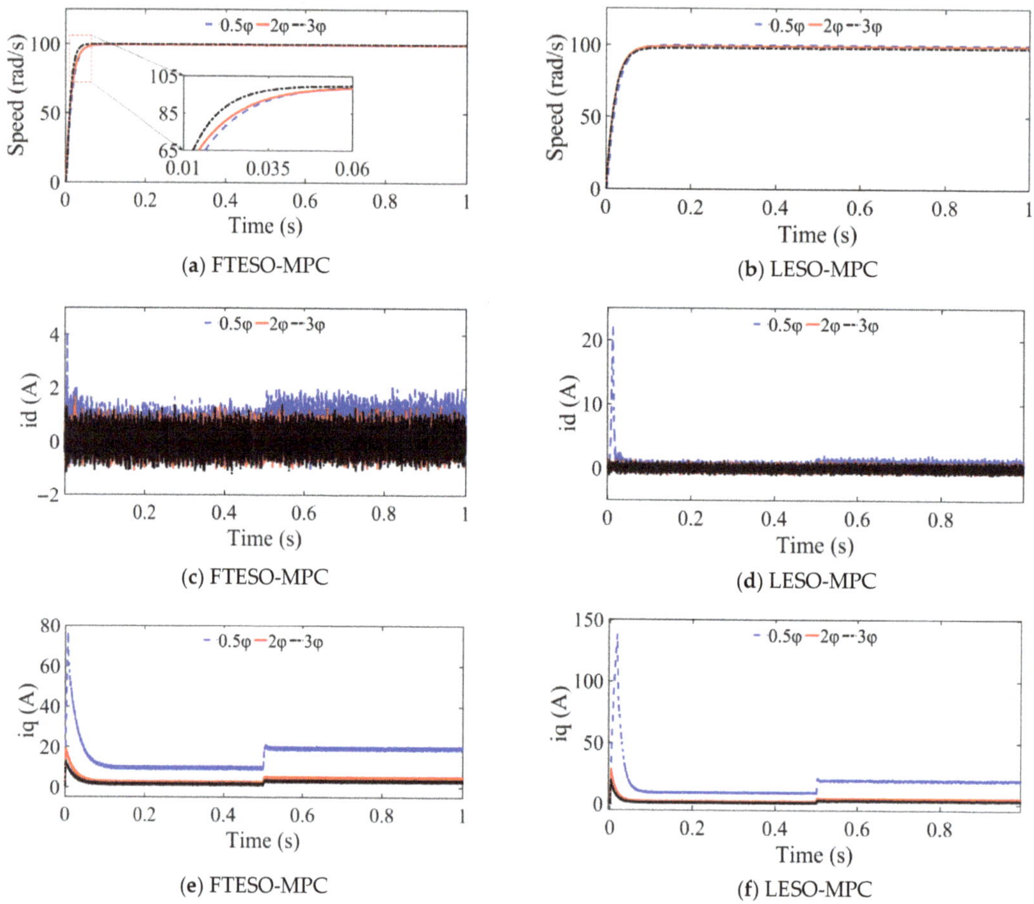

Figure 7. Dynamic Response Simulation Curves of Different Control Strategies under Flux Linkage Variation Condition.

Table 4. Performance comparison between FTESO-MPC and LESO-MPC under representative scenarios.

Scenario	Metric/Observation	LESO-MPC	FTESO-MPC
Sudden load disturbance	Recovery time	Longer, larger speed drop	Faster recovery, smaller speed drop
	Steady-state error	Noticeable residual error	Very small, almost eliminated
Inductance ↑ 3×	Current response	Pronounced oscillations; d-axis peak ≈ 200 A	Smooth convergence; no oscillation
Resistance ↑ 3×	Current regulation	Slower response, large ripple	Stable response, reduced ripple
Flux linkage variations (0.5×–3×)	Transient stability	Overshoot and instability	Smooth convergence, stable tracking
Overall robustness	Under parameter uncertainties & disturbances	Limited robustness	Strong robustness and adaptability

↑ indicates an increase in the parameter.

5. Conclusions

This paper addresses the robust control of PMSMs in nonlinear disturbance environments, focusing on a composite control strategy that integrates disturbance observation and predictive compensation. To cope with typical challenges—such as sudden load fluctuations, parameter variations, and external disturbances—a current prediction model incorporating lumped disturbance terms was established based on the conventional PMSM framework. This model captures the coupled influence of electromagnetic perturbations, parameter uncertainties, and flux linkage variations, thereby providing a more realistic representation of motor dynamics under practical operating conditions.

To overcome the estimation delays and slow convergence typically observed in conventional LESOs, an FTESO with a nonlinear gain structure was proposed. By employing exponential-type feedback and Lyapunov-based stability design, the observer guarantees global finite-time convergence, enabling rapid and accurate estimation of current disturbances. These estimations are then directly integrated into the MPC for real-time compensation and control input updates, significantly enhancing the system's disturbance rejection capability and control precision. Furthermore, a composite cost function was designed by incorporating both current tracking error and voltage increment, enabling dynamic optimization of the control input based on the disturbance observations. To meet the requirements for real-time digital controller implementation, the FTESO was discretized and embedded into a fully integrated feedforward-compensated FTESO-MPC control framework suitable for engineering applications.

Finally, the effectiveness of the proposed strategy was validated through comprehensive simulation studies under a range of representative disturbance scenarios, including abrupt load changes and severe variations in resistance, inductance, and flux linkage. Comparative results with the LESO-MPC approach demonstrate that the FTESO-MPC controller consistently achieves superior speed tracking accuracy, faster disturbance convergence, and improved transient performance. Notably, under significant parameter uncertainties, the controller is able to promptly estimate and compensate for disturbances, thereby ensuring robust and adaptive control of PMSMs—laying a solid foundation for practical engineering applications. Despite these contributions, this study still has some limitations. First, the proposed FTESO-MPC framework has only been validated through simulations, and experimental verification on real hardware platforms (e.g., DSPs or FPGAs) remains to be carried out. Second, the design and tuning of observer gains and cost-function weights involve empirical choices, which may limit generalization across different PMSM drive systems. Third, the additional computational cost introduced by the integrated FTESO-MPC structure may pose challenges for implementation in real-time embedded environments. Future work will address these limitations by developing systematic co-tuning approaches, performing hardware-in-the-loop tests, and extending the method to sensorless and multi-motor applications.

Author Contributions: Conceptualization, L.G.; methodology, Z.S.; software, X.L.; validation, Y.W. and X.L.; formal analysis, Y.W.; investigation, G.Z. and X.L.; resources, Y.W. and X.L.; data curation, L.G.; writing—original draft preparation, L.G.; writing—review and editing, Z.S. and G.Z.; visualization, X.L.; supervision, Z.S.; project administration, Y.W.; funding acquisition, L.G. and G.Z. All authors have read and agreed to the published version of the manuscript.

Funding: This research was funded by the Research Development Project of Nanjing Polytechnic Institute under Grant NJPI-YB-2025-06.

Data Availability Statement: The original contributions presented in this study are included in the article. Further inquiries can be directed to the corresponding author.

Acknowledgments: The authors would like to express their gratitude to all those who helped them during the writing of this paper.

Conflicts of Interest: The authors declare no conflicts of interest.

References

1. Wei, F.; Walls, W.D.; Zheng, X.; Li, G. Evaluating Environmental Benefits from Driving Electric Vehicles: The Case of Shanghai, China. *Transp. Res. Part D-Transp. Environ.* **2023**, *119*, 103749. [CrossRef]
2. Cavus, M.; Allahham, A. Spatio-Temporal Attention-Based Deep Learning for Smart Grid Demand Prediction. *Electronics* **2025**, *14*, 2514. [CrossRef]
3. Saleh, S.A. Development and Performance Testing of a V/F Control for Permanent Magnet Synchronous Motor Drives with Wavelet Modulated Power Electronic Converters. *IEEE Trans. Ind. Appl.* **2024**, *60*, 5025–5037. [CrossRef]
4. Ganapathee, M.; Alavandar, S.; Kasinathan, P.; Sowmmiya, U.; Ramachandaramurthy, V.K.; Pachaivannan, N. Evaluation of Hybrid Controllers for Space Vector Modulation-Inverter Driven Permanent Magnet Synchronous Motor-Pump Assembly. *ISA Trans.* **2022**, *128*, 635–649. [CrossRef] [PubMed]
5. Liu, Z.; Mao, K.; Lei, X.; Zheng, S.; Zhang, H. Loss Minimization Control Based on Bivariate Extreme Value Theory for Pmsms. *IEEE Trans. Power Electron.* **2024**, *39*, 2004–2012. [CrossRef]
6. Depeng, Z.; Ren, Y.; Gao, P.; Guo, K.; Wang, Z. Harmonic Suppression Strategy for Dual Three-Phase Permanent Magnet Synchronous Machines Based on a Multi-Input Multi-Output Controller. *IEEE Trans. Appl. Supercond.* **2024**, *34*, 5209305.
7. Hong, Y.; Yang, R.; Hu, W.; Huang, Z. Fpga-Based Sensorless Speed Control of Pmsm Using Enhanced Performance Controller Based on the Reduced-Order Ekf. *IEEE J. Emerg. Sel. Top. Power Electron.* **2021**, *9*, 289–301.
8. Shijiao, W.; Jiang, C.; Tu, Q.; Shu, H.; Zhu, C. Particle Swarm Optimization of Fuzzy Pi Control for Pmsms. *J. Power Electron.* **2023**, *23*, 1585–1593. [CrossRef]
9. Han, J. From Pid to Active Disturbance Rejection Control. *IEEE Trans. Ind. Electron.* **2009**, *56*, 900–906. [CrossRef]
10. Ling, Z.; Liu, X.; Zhang, J.; Wang, T. Angle Tracking Control for Double-Joint Dexterous Hand Systems Based on a Piecewise Extended State Observer. *Control Eng. Pract.* **2021**, *110*, 104754.
11. Chang, J.-L. Applying Sliding Mode Technique to Design Extended State Observer for Nonlinear Systems. *Asian J. Control* **2022**, *24*, 2127–2139. [CrossRef]
12. Yu, R.; He, P.; Li, H.; Cao, J.; Deng, F. Consensus of Multiagent Systems with Intermittent Communication Via Extended State Observer. *IEEE Trans. Circuits Syst. II-Express Briefs* **2023**, *70*, 231–235. [CrossRef]
13. Li, L.; Hu, Y.; Liu, X. Smooth and Fast Speed Control of Dual Three-Phase Pmsm Drives Using Integrated Extended State Observer. *IEEE Trans. Transp. Electrif.* **2024**, *10*, 9996–10005. [CrossRef]
14. Shuo, C.; Ding, W.; Hu, R.; Wu, X.; Shi, S. Sensorless Control of Pmsm Drives Using Reduced Order Quasi Resonant-Based Eso and Newton-Raphson Method-Based Pll. *IEEE Trans. Power Electron.* **2023**, *38*, 229–244.
15. Xie, F.; Ni, S.; Wang, H. Speed Fluctuation Suppression of Permanent Magnet Synchronous Motor Based on Double Extended State Observer. *J. Electr. Eng. Technol.* **2024**, *19*, 3079–3088. [CrossRef]
16. Wei, W.; Zhang, Z.; Zuo, M. Phase Leading Active Disturbance Rejection Control for a Nanopositioning Stage. *ISA Trans.* **2021**, *116*, 218–231. [CrossRef]
17. Hamid, R.; Shafiei, M.H.; Abdi, E. A Novel Continuous Finite-Time Extended State Observer Design for a Class of Uncertain Nonlinear Systems. *IEEE Access* **2020**, *8*, 228289–228302. [CrossRef]
18. Ling, Z.; Zheng, C.; Wang, Y.; Liu, B. A Finite-Time Control for a Pneumatic Cylinder Servo System Based on a Super-Twisting Extended State Observer. *IEEE Trans. Syst. Man Cybern.-Syst.* **2021**, *51*, 1164–1173.
19. Ling, Z.; Liu, L.; Li, X.; Cao, X. High-Precision Finite-Time Positioning Control for an Inertial Reference Unit with Asymmetric Loads and Mover Sideslip. *IEEE Trans. Ind. Electron.* **2023**, *70*, 2971–2981.
20. Liu, C.; Luo, G.; Chen, Z.; Tu, W. Finite-Time Convergent Multiple Disturbance Rejection Control for Electromechanical Actuators. *IEEE Trans. Power Electron.* **2021**, *36*, 6863–6878. [CrossRef]
21. Shao, X.; Yue, X.; Li, J. Event-Triggered Robust Control for Quadrotors with Preassigned Time Performance Constraints. *Appl. Math. Comput.* **2021**, *392*, 125667. [CrossRef]
22. Lei, C.; Zhou, Q.; Jin, N. Fixed-Time Backstepping Distributed Cooperative Control for Multiple Unmanned Aerial Vehicles. *Asian J. Control* **2023**, *25*, 1981–1990.
23. Hao, C.; Lv, C. Incorporating Eso into Deep Koopman Operator Modeling for Control of Autonomous Vehicles. *IEEE Trans. Control Syst. Technol.* **2024**, *32*, 1854–1864.
24. Gu, W.; Yao, J.; Yao, Z.; Zheng, J. Output Feedback Model Predictive Control of Hydraulic Systems with Disturbances Compensation. *ISA Trans.* **2019**, *88*, 216–224. [CrossRef]

25. Zhang, Z.; Ran, M.; Dong, C. Safe Mpc-Based Disturbance Rejection Control for Uncertain Nonlinear Systems with State Constraints. *ISA Trans.* **2024**, *153*, 233–242. [CrossRef]
26. Hou, X.; Yue, M.; Zhao, J.; Zhang, X. An Eso-Based Integrated Trajectory Tracking Control for Tractor-Trailer Vehicles with Various Constraints and Physical Limitations. *Int. J. Syst. Sci.* **2018**, *49*, 3202–3215. [CrossRef]
27. Liu, X.; Qiu, L.; Wu, W.; Ma, J.; Wang, D.; Peng, Z.; Fang, Y. Finite-Time Eso-Based Cascade-Free Fcs-Mpc for Nnpc Converter. *Int. J. Electr. Power Energy Syst.* **2023**, *148*, 108939. [CrossRef]
28. Zhang, L.; Liu, R.; Shi, M.; Wang, J.; Zhang, C. Finite-Time Eso-Based Two-Stage Robust Model-Free Predictive Control for Flexible Interconnecting Device. *Electr. Eng.* **2025**, *107*, 6099–6106. [CrossRef]
29. Mousavi, M.S.; Davari, S.A.; Nekoukar, V.; Garcia, C.; Rodriguez, J. A Robust Torque and Flux Prediction Model by a Modified Disturbance Rejection Method for Finite-Set Model-Predictive Control of Induction Motor. *IEEE Trans. Power Electron.* **2021**, *36*, 9322–9333. [CrossRef]
30. Benjamin, D.; Hosseini, A.; Rossa, C. Model Predictive Control of an Active Ankle-Foot Orthosis with Non-Linear Actuation Constraints. *Control Eng. Pract.* **2023**, *136*, 105538.
31. Oluleke, B.; Zhang, Z.; Li, Z. Model-Free Predictive Control of Dcdc Boost Converters: Sensor Noise Suppression with Hybrid Extended State Observers. *IEEE Trans. Power Electron.* **2024**, *39*, 245–259.
32. Guo, T.; Sun, Z.; Wang, X.; Li, S.; Zhang, K. A Simple Current-Constrained Controller for Permanent-Magnet Synchronous Motor. *IEEE Trans. Ind. Inform.* **2019**, *15*, 1486–1495. [CrossRef]
33. Luo, S.X.; Deng, F.Q.; Yu, X.H. Unified Stability Analysis for Ito Stochastic Systems: From Almost Surely Asymptotic to Finite-Time Convergence. *IEEE Trans. Autom. Control* **2022**, *67*, 406–412. [CrossRef]
34. Wen, H.S.; He, X.; Huang, T.W.; Yu, J.Z. Neurodynamic Algorithms with Finite/Fixed-Time Convergence for Sparse Optimization Via L1 Regularization. *IEEE Trans. Syst. Man Cybern.-Syst.* **2024**, *54*, 131–142. [CrossRef]
35. Weng, Y.P.; Tian, M.; Wang, N. Finite-Time Model-Free Adaptive Control for Mimo Nonlinear Systems with Adjustable Fast Convergence Domain: Theory and Experiment. *IEEE Trans. Ind. Electron.* **2025**, *72*, 10542–10552. [CrossRef]
36. Gao, L.; Zhang, G.; Yang, H.; Mei, L. A Novel Method of Model Predictive Control on Permanent Magnet Synchronous Machine with Laguerre Functions. *Alex. Eng. J.* **2021**, *60*, 5485–5494. [CrossRef]

computation

MDPI

Article

An Energy Saving MTPA-Based Model Predictive Control Strategy for PMSM in Electric Vehicles Under Variable Load Conditions

Lihua Gao [1,2], Xiaodong Lv [2,*], Kai Ma [1] and Zhihan Shi [2]

[1] College of Electrical Engineering and Control Science, Nanjing Polytechnic Institute, Nanjing 210048, China; gaolihua@njpi.edu.cn (L.G.); mak@njpi.edu.cn (K.M.)

[2] College of Electrical Engineering and Control Science, Nanjing Tech University, Nanjing 211816, China; szh@njtech.edu.cn

* Correspondence: lxd@njtech.edu.cn

Abstract

To promote energy efficiency and support sustainable electric transportation, this study addresses the challenge of real-time and energy-optimal control of permanent magnet synchronous motors (PMSMs) in electric vehicles operating under variable load conditions, proposing a novel Laguerre-based model predictive control (MPC) strategy integrated with maximum torque per ampere (MTPA) operation. Traditional MPC methods often suffer from limited prediction horizons and high computational burden when handling strong coupling and time-varying loads, compromising real-time performance. To overcome these limitations, a Laguerre function approximation is employed to model the dynamic evolution of control increments using a set of orthogonal basis functions, effectively reducing the control dimensionality while accelerating convergence. Furthermore, to enhance energy efficiency, the MTPA strategy is embedded by reformulating the current allocation process using d- and q-axis current variables and deriving equivalent reference currents to simplify the optimization structure. A cost function is designed to simultaneously ensure current accuracy and achieve maximum torque per unit current. Simulation results under typical electric vehicle conditions demonstrate that the proposed Laguerre-MTPA MPC controller significantly improves steady-state performance, reduces energy consumption, and ensures faster response to load disturbances compared to traditional MTPA-based control schemes. This work provides a practical and scalable control framework for energy-saving applications in sustainable electric transportation systems.

Keywords: energy efficiency; electric vehicles; model predictive control; maximum torque per ampere

1. Introduction

In electric vehicle applications, which are increasingly regarded as a cornerstone of energy-saving and sustainable transportation, the energy efficiency and thermal reliability of permanent magnet synchronous motors (PMSMs) largely depend on the proper coordination of d-axis and q-axis stator currents. When the current distribution deviates from the optimal condition, such as when the d-axis and q-axis components are not effectively coordinated, the motor must increase the total current amplitude to sustain the required torque output [1–3]. This non-optimal operation results in higher copper losses, increased energy consumption, and accelerated temperature rise, thereby imposing greater thermal stress on the system. Over time, such conditions can significantly compromise the long-term reliability and operational lifespan of PMSMs. As electric vehicles continue to evolve toward greener and more efficient mobility solutions, optimizing current allocation has become a critical aspect in the development of energy-efficient control strategies for sustainable electric transportation systems.

Achieving efficient current allocation under dynamic load conditions is a key challenge for improving the overall energy efficiency and operational stability of PMSM drive systems. This issue becomes particularly critical in electric vehicle scenarios, where the motor is frequently subjected to high-load, nonlinear disturbances and rapidly shifting operating points. In such environments, it is essential for the motor to maintain the required torque output while minimizing current consumption to prevent unnecessary energy losses and thermal runaway. As a result, energy-optimized control strategies that aim to minimize current amplitude without compromising torque performance have emerged as a vital direction in the evolution of advanced motor control technologies [4,5].

The Maximum Torque Per Ampere (MTPA) [6–8] control strategy has been widely adopted as a classical and effective method for the energy-efficient control of PMSMs under steady-state or quasi-steady-state conditions. Its core principle lies in precisely adjusting the ratio between the d-axis and q-axis currents to achieve the maximum electromagnetic torque output per unit of stator current, thereby minimizing copper losses and improving system efficiency. This strategy is particularly effective for PMSMs with saliency, where magnetic flux linkage coupling exists between the axes. Studies [9] have shown that compared to traditional vector control methods based solely on q-axis orientation, MTPA control can significantly reduce current consumption, suppress thermal buildup, and improve operational stability, especially in applications characterized by stringent current constraints or prolonged high-load conditions.

In practical engineering applications, the most commonly implemented MTPA method is based on a dual closed-loop PI vector control structure, which includes an outer speed loop and an inner current loop. The speed controller first generates a desired torque command, and then, using the MTPA characteristic curve, the optimal reference values of d-axis and q-axis currents are computed. These reference currents are regulated via PI controllers to generate the appropriate control voltages for the inverter. Owing to its clear structure and well-established implementation, this approach has been widely applied in industrial servos, CNC machine tools, and electric vehicle drives [10–13]. However, the PI-based implementation suffers from critical limitations under varying operating conditions, primarily due to its high sensitivity to motor parameter variations. As the motor parameters shift with temperature, load, or prolonged operation, the fixed gain settings of the PI controller may become suboptimal, leading to degraded dynamic performance. Furthermore, the accuracy of MTPA reference current calculation heavily depends on motor parameters such as flux linkage and inductance. Modeling inaccuracies and parameter drifts can cause deviations from the optimal current trajectory, resulting in torque fluctuations and reduced energy efficiency [14–16].

To further enhance dynamic response and control robustness, model predictive control (MPC) has been increasingly integrated into MTPA strategies in recent years as a promising alternative to traditional PI-based control structures [17–21]. MPC operates by predicting the system's future behavior over a finite time horizon based on current state measurements and solving an optimization problem at each control interval. This rolling optimization explicitly accounts for system constraints and multiple performance objectives, enabling more accurate and adaptive control. Depending on whether the switching states of the inverter are explicitly considered, MPC methods are generally categorized into finite control set MPC (FCS-MPC) [22–24] and continuous control set MPC (CCS-MPC) [25]. FCS-MPC is widely used in motor control applications due to its simplicity and high computational efficiency. It directly searches for the optimal switching state within a finite set, eliminating the need for modulation. However, the discrete nature of the control input leads to coarse control granularity, which may result in steady-state errors and limited robustness to parameter variations. In contrast, CCS-MPC computes a continuous-valued control voltage that must be applied through a modulation scheme, offering smoother control signals and superior robustness to system uncertainties. Nevertheless, CCS-MPC typically incurs a significantly higher computational burden, posing challenges for real-time implementation in high-frequency motor drive systems.

In existing studies [26], MTPA reference current trajectories are typically derived through analytical expressions or numerical approximation methods and incorporated into the MPC cost function as part of the control optimization objective. One representative FCS-MPC approach introduces the MTPA current error into a single-objective cost function, selecting control inputs that guide the current trajectory as close as possible to the optimal MTPA path [27]. To improve control accuracy and system consistency, subsequent research has formulated multi-objective cost functions that combine torque error, MTPA tracking error, and current constraint penalties [28]. However, due to the inherent nonlinearity of MTPA characteristics, the resulting cost functions often involve high-order terms, leading to increased computational complexity and posing challenges for real-time optimization. Alternative approaches have attempted to incorporate absolute or squared trajectory deviation terms into the cost function, sometimes combined with dynamic weighting mechanisms to enhance control smoothness. Yet, these formulations often suffer from structural inconsistency and convergence instability, which limit the practical deployment of MTPA–MPC strategies in industrial motor drives [29]. Furthermore, while FCS-MPC generally lacks the adaptive capability to cope with motor parameter variations, resulting in steady-state errors, CCS-MPC offers better robustness due to its embedded integral action. Nevertheless, CCS-MPC remains constrained in real-world applications by its high computational load and strong dependence on hardware performance. As such, recent research efforts are increasingly focused on developing MTPA–MPC schemes that are lightweight in structure, analytically tractable in cost function formulation, and capable of dynamically adjusting current trajectories. The ultimate goal is to achieve accurate MTPA current tracking and optimal control performance while maintaining low computational overhead suitable for real-time electric drive applications.

In this study, a low-dimensional, high-response Laguerre-based model predictive control algorithm is developed within the MPC framework to address the computational challenges of real-time motor control. By parameterizing the control input sequence using Laguerre functions, the proposed method significantly reduces the number of optimization variables, thereby lowering the computational burden and improving the online solving efficiency of the controller. This dimensionality reduction enables the practical implementation of continuous control set MPC in high-frequency applications such as electric vehicle drives. Building upon this foundation, the proposed strategy further integrates the MTPA control principle to enhance current utilization and torque density. Specifically, the d-axis and q-axis currents are selected as the primary predictive state variables, and an equivalent current construction method is introduced to simplify the generation of MTPA reference currents. A current allocation cost function is designed to balance tracking accuracy and energy efficiency, enabling the motor to produce maximum torque per unit current. As a result, the proposed Laguerre-MTPA MPC approach achieves energy-efficient, high-performance torque control under dynamic load conditions, offering a promising solution for sustainable and real-time electric transportation systems.

2. The PMSM Model and MTPA-Based Model Predictive Control

2.1. PMSM Model

The continuous-time electrical dynamics equations and mechanical equation of a PMSM in the dq0 rotating reference frame can be described by [30]:

$$\begin{aligned} \frac{di_d}{dt} &= -\frac{R_s}{L_d} i_d + \frac{L_q}{L_d} P\omega_m i_q + \frac{u_d}{L_d} \\ \frac{di_q}{dt} &= -\frac{R_s}{L_q} i_q + \frac{L_d}{L_q} P\omega_m i_d - \frac{\phi_f}{L_q} P\omega_m + \frac{u_q}{L_q} \end{aligned} \tag{1}$$

$$T_e = \frac{3}{2} P[\phi_f i_q + (L_d - L_q) i_d i_q] \tag{2}$$

where i_d is the stator current of the d-axis; i_q is the stator current of the q-axis; ω_m is the mechanical angular speed of the rotor; ϕ_f is the base electromotive force constant; R_s is the stator winding resistance; L_d is the stator inductance of the d-axis; L_q is the stator inductance component of the q-axis; P is the number of pole pairs; u_d is the stator voltage of the d-axis; u_q is the stator voltage of the q-axis; and T_e is the electromagnetic torque.

Assuming the sampling interval is T_s, the items $\omega_m i_q(k)$ and $\omega_m i_d(k)$ are considered as constant variables in a sampling interval; then, (1) can be discretized as:

$$\begin{aligned} i_d(k+1) &= \frac{L_d - T_s R_s}{L_d} i_d(k) + \frac{L_q}{L_d} T_s P\omega_m i_q(k) + \frac{T_s}{L_d} u_d(k) \\ i_q(k+1) &= \frac{L_q - T_s R_s}{L_q} i_q(k) - \frac{L_d}{L_q} T_s P\omega_m i_d(k) - T_s P \frac{\phi_f}{L_q} \omega_m(k) + \frac{T_s}{L_q} u_q(k) \end{aligned} \tag{3}$$

Assume the d-axis current i_d, q-axis current i_q, mechanical angular speed ω_m, the product of i_d and ω_m, and the product of i_q and ω_m are the state variables. Assuming the d-axis voltage u_d and q-axis voltage u_q are the input variables and d-axis current i_d and q-axis current i_q are the output variables, then (3) can be described in the state space model:

$$\begin{aligned} x(k+1) &= Ax(k) + Bu(k) \\ y(k) &= Cx(k) \end{aligned} \tag{4}$$

$$\begin{gathered} x(k) = \begin{bmatrix} i_d(k) \\ i_q(k) \\ \omega_m(k) \\ \omega_m i_d(k) \\ \omega_m i_q(k) \end{bmatrix}, y(k) = \begin{bmatrix} i_d(k) \\ i_q(k) \end{bmatrix}, u(k) = \begin{bmatrix} u_d(k) \\ u_q(k) \end{bmatrix}, \\ B = \begin{bmatrix} \frac{T_s}{L_d} & 0 & 0 & 0 & 0 \\ 0 & \frac{T_s}{L_q} & 0 & 0 & 0 \end{bmatrix}^T, C = \begin{bmatrix} 1 & 0 & 0 & 0 & 0 \\ 0 & 1 & 0 & 0 & 0 \end{bmatrix}^2 \end{gathered} \tag{5}$$

$$A = \begin{bmatrix} \frac{L_d - T_s R_s}{L_d} & 0 & 0 & 0 & \frac{T_s P L_q}{L_d} \\ 0 & \frac{L_q - T_s R_s}{L_q} & -\frac{T_s P L_d}{L_q} & 0 & -\frac{T_s P \phi_f}{L_q} \\ 0 & 0 & 1 & 0 & 0 \\ 0 & 0 & 0 & 1 & 0 \\ 0 & 0 & 0 & 0 & 1 \end{bmatrix} \tag{6}$$

2.2. MTPA Strategy

From (2), it can be seen that the torque of a PMSM consists of two parts: the first part is the electromagnetic torque, and the second part is the reluctance torque. When using the $i_d = 0$ control strategy, only electromagnetic torque takes effect, and the torque is determined by the q-axis current. However, this control strategy will reduce the motor operating efficiency and the torque performance. In order to better utilize reluctance torque, the control strategy of MTPA can be adopted to control the motor.

The MTPA control method refers to the minimum stator current of the motor under the same electromagnetic torque, which means (2) is subject to [31]:

$$i_s = \min\sqrt{i_d^2 + i_q^2} \tag{7}$$

In order to obtain the d-axis and q-axis currents of the PMSM under the MTPA control method, the following Lagrange function is usually constructed:

$$F = \sqrt{i_d^2 + i_q^2} + \lambda\left(T_e - \frac{3}{2}P\left(\phi_f i_q + (L_d - L_q)i_d i_q\right)\right) \tag{8}$$

Considering $i_d \leq 0$, $i_q \geq 0$, note that the constraints $i_d \leq 0$ and $i_q \geq 0$ are introduced only for the forward-driving operation of the traction system. A negative i_d is a common requirement in MTPA control of IPMSMs to utilize the reluctance torque, and it does not lead to demagnetization as long as the current remains within the safe operating range defined by the machine design. The constraint $i_q \geq 0$ corresponds to forward torque generation. If motor reversal is required, the condition can be relaxed to $i_q < 0$, which produces negative torque. In this paper, only the forward-driving case is considered for clarity.

λ is the Lagrange factor.

Then, take the partial derivative of function F with respect to the variables i_d, i_q, and λ.

$$\begin{cases} \frac{\partial F}{\partial i_d} = \frac{i_d}{\sqrt{i_d^2+i_q^2}} - \frac{3}{2}\lambda P(L_d - L_q)i_q = 0 \\ \frac{\partial F}{\partial i_q} = \frac{i_q}{\sqrt{i_d^2+i_q^2}} - \frac{3}{2}\lambda P\phi_f - \frac{3}{2}\lambda P(L_d - L_q)i_d = 0 \\ \frac{\partial F}{\partial \lambda} = T_e - \frac{3}{2}P[\phi_f i_q + (L_d - L_q)i_q i_q] = 0 \end{cases} \tag{9}$$

By solving the equations, the relationship between the d-axis and q-axis currents under the MTPA control method can be described as [32]:

$$\left(i_d - \frac{\phi_f}{2(L_q - L_d)}\right)^2 = \left(\frac{\phi_f}{2(L_q - L_d)}\right)^2 + i_q^2 \tag{10}$$

considering that $i_d \leq 0$, $i_q \geq 0$.

From (7) and (10), it can be seen that the relationship between d-axis and q-axis currents is not linear and is difficult to solve. Therefore, a simpler method for solving d-axis and q-axis currents is needed under the MTPA control method.

2.3. Traditional MTPA Model Predictive Control

Based on the mathematical model of PMSM described in (4), the MPC of PMSM usually calculates the system behavior under different control sequences within a finite predictive period. A preset cost function is used to obtain the optimal control sequence; then, the first control variable in the optimal control sequence is applied on the PMSM control to achieve rolling optimization.

The traditional MTPA-based MPC algorithm first calculates the MTPA reference currents through (7) and (10) and then obtains the optimal voltage by solving the cost function. The cost function usually includes current errors, or MTPA curve errors, or a combination of both described in (10) [33,34].

$$J = \sum_{m=1}^{N_P} \left(\begin{bmatrix} i_d(k+m) \\ i_q(k+m) \end{bmatrix} - \begin{bmatrix} i_d^* \\ i_q^* \end{bmatrix} \right)^T q_i \left(\begin{bmatrix} i_d(k+m) \\ i_q(k+m) \end{bmatrix} - \begin{bmatrix} i_d^* \\ i_q^* \end{bmatrix} \right) + q_{mtpa} \sum_{m=1}^{N_P} \left| i_d^2(k+m) + \frac{\varphi_f}{(L_d - L_q)} i_d(k+m) - i_q^2(k+m) \right| \tag{11}$$

where i_d^* and i_q^* are the references of the d-axis current and q-axis current, respectively; m is the future m-th predictive period starting from k; n is the future n-th control period starting from k; q_i is the weight of current errors; and q_{mpta} is the weight of MTPA curve errors.

From (11), it can be seen that the second item is an absolute expression, which needs to be segmented according to the situation when solving the optimal control variable. Moreover, it differs from the standard quadratic programming cost function and cannot be directly solved using the quadratic programming solutions, which increase the difficulty of the solution. Therefore, a more convenient cost function is needed for MTPA-based MPC control for PMSM.

3. The Proposed MTPA-Based MPC Method

3.1. The Proposed MTPA Method

At every sampling period k, the d-axis and q-axis currents of PMSM can be represented by a unique variable i_N:

$$i_N(k) = i_q(k) - i_d(k) \tag{12}$$

Considering that $i_N(k) = \begin{cases} (i_q(k) - i_d(k)) > 0 & i_q(k) > 0 \\ 0 & i_q(k) = 0 \end{cases}$.

First, (10) can be transformed into:

$$\left(i_d(k) - \Lambda + i_q(k)\right)\left(i_d(k) - \Lambda - i_q(k)\right) = \Lambda^2 \tag{13}$$

where $\Lambda = \frac{\phi_f}{2(L_q - L_d)}$.

Then, substituting (12) into (10), we obtain:

$$-(i_d(k) - \Lambda + i_q(k))(i_N(k) + \Lambda) = \Lambda^2 \tag{14}$$

Next, combining (12) and (14), an equation system is constructed as follow:

$$\begin{cases} i_d(k) + i_q(k) = \Lambda - \frac{\Lambda^2}{i_N(k)+\Lambda} \\ i_q(k) - i_d(k) = i_N(k) \end{cases} \tag{15}$$

By solving (15), we can obtain:

$$\begin{cases} i_q^*(k) = \frac{i_N^2(k)+2\Lambda i_N(k)}{2(i_N(k)+\Lambda)} \\ i_d^*(k) = -\frac{i_N^2(k)}{2(i_N(k)+\Lambda)} \end{cases} \tag{16}$$

The $i_d^*(k)$ and $i_q^*(k)$ in (16) is the reference current under the MTPA control method. Compared with (7) and (10), (16) is used to calculate the current of the d-axis and q-axis, which reduces the load of calculation. Figure 1 shows the schematic diagram of the proposed MTPA algorithm.

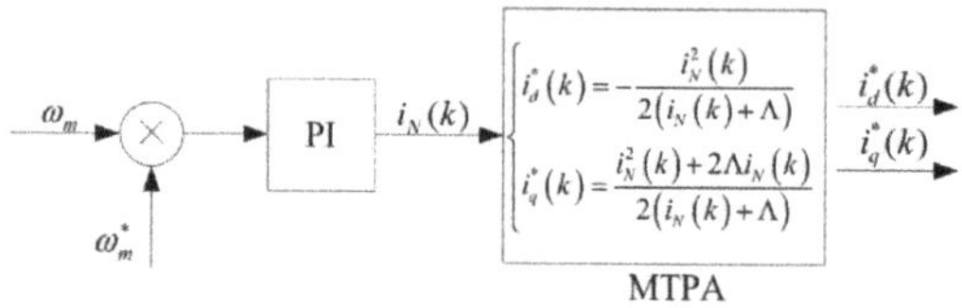

Figure 1. The proposed MTPA schematic diagram.

3.2. The Proposed Cost Function

There is a segmented function in (11), which is complex to calculate. Then, a new cost function is designed according to the MTPA characteristics as follows:

$$\begin{aligned} J = &\sum_{m=1}^{N_p}\left(\begin{bmatrix} i_d(k+m) \\ i_q(k+m) \end{bmatrix} - \begin{bmatrix} i_d^*(k+m) \\ i_q^*(k+m) \end{bmatrix}\right)^T q_i \left(\begin{bmatrix} i_d(k+m) \\ i_q(k+m) \end{bmatrix} - \begin{bmatrix} i_d^*(k+m) \\ i_q^*(k+m) \end{bmatrix}\right) \\ &+q_{mtpa}\sum_{m=1}^{N_p}\left(i_d(k+m)-\Lambda)^2-\Lambda^2-i_q^2(k+m)\right)^2 \\ &+\sum_{n=1}^{N_c}\Delta u^T(k+n-1)r\Delta u(k+n-1) \end{aligned} \tag{17}$$

The cost function in (17) consists of three parts: total current errors within N_p predictive periods, MTPA curve errors within N_p predictive periods, and voltage increment errors within Nc control periods. The total current errors refers to the errors between the operating current of the PMSM and the reference currents of the PMSM under MTPA control. The purpose of this item is to make the currents of the PMSM follow the reference currents as much as possible, that is, the reference currents of the PMSM under MTPA control. The second MTPA curve errors is to ensure that the d-axis and q-axis current trajectories of the PMSM are as close as possible to the MTPA curve during operation, further ensuring that the PMSM operates in MTPA mode. When the PMSM becomes stable, the voltage increments should approach zero as soon as possible to ensure the steady-state performance and dynamic response of the PMSM.

In the second item of (17), the power of expression J is 4. To simplify calculations, the power of the cost function must be reduced.

First, the second item in (17) can be reconstructed:

$$\begin{aligned} &(i_d(k+m)-\Lambda)^2-\Lambda^2-i_q^2(k+m) \\ &=(i_d(k+m)-\Lambda-i_q(k+m))(i_d(k+m)-\Lambda+i_q(k+m))-\Lambda^2 \end{aligned} \tag{18}$$

Substitute (12) into (17), then:

$$\begin{aligned} &(i_d(k+m)-\Lambda)^2-\Lambda^2-i_q^2(k+m) \\ &=-(i_N(k+m)+\Lambda)(i_d(k+m)+i_q(k+m)-\Lambda)-\Lambda^2 \end{aligned} \tag{19}$$

When a PMSM is running, the current should be kept as close to the MTPA curve as possible. Therefore, the following equation is true:

$$\begin{aligned} -(i_N(k+m)+\Lambda)(i_d(k+m)+i_q(k+m)-\Lambda)-\Lambda^2=0 \\ i_d(k+m)+i_q(k+m)=\tfrac{\Lambda i_N(k+m)}{\Lambda+i_N(k+m)} \end{aligned} \tag{20}$$

According to the analysis above, the cost function (16) is equal to:

$$
\begin{aligned}
J = & \sum_{m=1}^{N_p} \left(\begin{bmatrix} i_d(k+m) \\ i_q(k+m) \end{bmatrix} - \begin{bmatrix} i_d^* \\ i_q^* \end{bmatrix} \right)^T q_i \left(\begin{bmatrix} i_d(k+m) \\ i_q(k+m) \end{bmatrix} - \begin{bmatrix} i_d^* \\ i_q^* \end{bmatrix} \right) \\
& + q_{mtpa} \sum_{m=1}^{N_p} \left(i_d(k+m) + i_q(k+m) - \frac{\Lambda i_N(k+m)}{\Lambda + i_N(k+m)} \right)^2 \\
& + \sum_{n=1}^{N_c} \Delta u^T(k+n-1) r \Delta u(k+n-1)
\end{aligned} \tag{21}
$$

Furthermore, the cost function (21) can be changed to:

$$
\begin{aligned}
J = & \sum_{m=1}^{Np} \left(\begin{bmatrix} i_d(k+m) \\ i_q(k+m) \\ i_d(k+m) + i_q(k+m) \end{bmatrix} - \begin{bmatrix} i_d^* \\ i_q^* \\ i_{mtpa}^* \end{bmatrix} \right)^T q \left(\begin{bmatrix} i_d(k+m) \\ i_q(k+m) \\ i_d(k+m) + i_q(k+m) \end{bmatrix} - \begin{bmatrix} i_d^* \\ i_q^* \\ i_{mtpa}^* \end{bmatrix} \right) \\
& + \sum_{n=1}^{Nc} \Delta u^T(k+n-1) r \Delta u(k+n-1)
\end{aligned} \tag{22}
$$

where $q = \begin{bmatrix} q_{id} & 0 & 0 \\ 0 & q_{iq} & 0 \\ 0 & 0 & q_{mtpa} \end{bmatrix}$, $i_{mtpa}^* = \frac{\Lambda i_N(k+m)}{\Lambda + i_N(k+m)}$.

Assume the following:

$$
\begin{aligned}
y_m(k+m) &= \begin{bmatrix} i_d(k+m) \\ i_q(k+m) \\ i_d(k+m) + i_q(k+m) \end{bmatrix} = \begin{bmatrix} i_d(k+m) \\ i_q(k+m) \\ i_{mtpa}(k+m) \end{bmatrix} \\
y_m^*(k+m) &= \begin{bmatrix} i_d^*(k+m) \\ i_q^*(k+m) \\ i_{mtpa}^*(k+m) \end{bmatrix} = \begin{bmatrix} i_N^2(k+m) + 2\Lambda i_N(k+m) \\ 2(i_N(k+m) + \Lambda) \\ -\frac{i_N^2(k+m)}{2(i_N(k+m)+\Lambda)} \\ \frac{\Lambda i_N(k+m)}{\Lambda + i_N(k+m)} \end{bmatrix}
\end{aligned} \tag{23}
$$

Then, substituting (23) into (22), we can obtain:

$$
\begin{aligned}
J = & \sum_{m=1}^{N_p} (y_m(k+m) - y_m^*(k+m))^T q (y_m(k+m) - y_m^*(k+m)) \\
& + \sum_{n=1}^{N_c} \Delta u^T(k+n-1) r \Delta u(k+n-1)
\end{aligned} \tag{24}
$$

Equation (24) is the proposed cost function for solving the optimal control variables.

3.3. The Proposed PMSM Model

From (22) and (23), it can be seen that the sum of the d-axis current and q-axis current has been added to the output variables and cost function. In order to find the solution of the optimal variables, it is necessary to modify the state space model of PMSM described in (4).

First, modify the state space model of PMSM described in (4) to the 1st state space model, namely the incremental model.

$$
\begin{aligned}
\Delta x(k+1) &= A_1 \Delta x(k) + B_1 \Delta u(k) \\
y(k) &= C_1 \Delta x(k)
\end{aligned} \tag{25}
$$

where $\Delta x(k) = \begin{bmatrix} \Delta i_d(k) \\ \Delta i_q(k) \\ \Delta \omega_m(k) \\ \Delta \omega_m i_d(k) \\ \Delta \omega_m i_q(k) \\ i_d(k) \\ i_q(k) \end{bmatrix}$, $y(k) = \begin{bmatrix} i_d(k) \\ i_q(k) \end{bmatrix}$, $\Delta u(k) = \begin{bmatrix} \Delta u_d(k) \\ \Delta u_q(k) \end{bmatrix}$,

$B_1 = \begin{bmatrix} \frac{T_s}{L_d} & 0 & 0 & 0 & 0 & \frac{T_s}{L_d} & 0 \\ 0 & \frac{T_s}{L_q} & 0 & 0 & 0 & 0 & \frac{T_s}{L_q} \end{bmatrix}^T$, $C_1 = \begin{bmatrix} 0 & 0 & 0 & 0 & 0 & 1 & 0 \\ 0 & 0 & 0 & 0 & 0 & 0 & 1 \end{bmatrix}$,

$$A_1 = \begin{bmatrix} \frac{L_d - T_s R_s}{L_d} & 0 & 0 & 0 & \frac{T_s P L_q}{L_d} & 0 & 0 \\ 0 & \frac{L_q - T_s R_s}{L_q} & -\frac{T_s P L_d}{L_q} & 0 & -\frac{T_s P \phi_f}{L_q} & 0 & 0 \\ 0 & 0 & 1 & 0 & 0 & 0 & 0 \\ 0 & 0 & 0 & 1 & 0 & 0 & 0 \\ 0 & 0 & 0 & 0 & 1 & 0 & 0 \\ \frac{L_d - T_s R_s}{L_d} & 0 & 0 & 0 & 0 & 1 & 0 \\ 0 & \frac{L_q - T_s R_s}{L_q} & 0 & 0 & 0 & 0 & 1 \end{bmatrix}.$$

Next, add the sum of the d-axis current and q-axis current to the 1st state space model (25), and the 2nd state space model is formed in (25).

$$\begin{aligned} x_m(k+1) &= A_m x_m(k) + B_m \Delta u(k) \\ y_m(k) &= C_m x_m(k) \end{aligned} \tag{26}$$

where $x_m(k) = \begin{bmatrix} \Delta i_d(k) \\ \Delta i_q(k) \\ \Delta \omega(k) \\ \Delta i_d \omega(k) \\ \Delta i_q \omega(k) \\ i_d(k) \\ i_q(k) \\ i_d(k) + i_q(k) \end{bmatrix}$, $y_m(k) = \begin{bmatrix} i_d(k) \\ i_q(k) \\ i_d(k) + i_q(k) \end{bmatrix}$, $\Delta u(k) = \begin{bmatrix} \Delta u_d(k) \\ \Delta u_q(k) \end{bmatrix}$,

$A_m = \begin{bmatrix} A_1 & 0 & 0 \\ C_1 A_1 & 1 & 0 \\ C_z C_1 A_1 & 0 & 1 \end{bmatrix}$, $B_m = \begin{bmatrix} B_1 \\ C_1 B_1 \\ C_z C_1 B_1 \end{bmatrix}$, $C_m = [0_{3\times5} \; I_{3\times3}]$, $C_z = [1 \; 1]$.

3.4. The Improved PMSM Model Using the LAGUERRE Function

A stable linear system can be represented by a series of Laguerre functions. The differences of voltage $\Delta u(k)$ described in (26) will be zero when the PMSM becomes steady; in order to accelerate the rate of voltage increment decay to zero, a Laguerre function is introduced to represent the voltage increment. By adjusting the parameters of the Laguerre function, we can reduce the number of predictive periods and speed up the system response.

$$\Delta u(k) = \begin{bmatrix} \Delta u_d(k) \\ \Delta u_d(k) \end{bmatrix} = \begin{bmatrix} L_d(0)\eta_d \\ L_q(0)\eta_q \end{bmatrix} = L_u(0)^T \eta_I \tag{27}$$

where $\eta_I = \begin{bmatrix} \eta_d \\ \eta_q \end{bmatrix} = \begin{bmatrix} c_1^d & \cdots & c_{Nd}^d & c_1^q & \cdots & c_{Nq}^q \end{bmatrix}^T$,

$L_u(0) = \begin{bmatrix} L_d(0) \\ L_q(0) \end{bmatrix} = \begin{bmatrix} l_1^d(0) & \cdots & l_N^d(0) & 0 & 0 & 0 \\ 0 & 0 & 0 & l_1^q(0) & \cdots & l_N^q(0) \end{bmatrix}$.

η_I is the Laguerre coefficients matrix. $c_1^d, c_2^d \ldots c_{N_d}^d$ are the Laguerre coefficients of the d-axis voltage; $c_1^q, c_2^q \ldots c_{N_q}^q$ are the Laguerre coefficients of the q-axis. N_d is the number of items of the d-axis voltage Laguerre functions. N_q is the number of items of the q-axis voltage Laguerre functions. $L_u(0)$ is the Laguerre vector of the d-axis voltage and q-axis voltage.

To ensure analytical clarity, the assumptions used in transforming the cost function are as follows: (i) the MTPA deviation term is replaced by a quadratic surrogate to guarantee differentiability and compatibility with quadratic programming; (ii) the sum of i_d and i_q is introduced into the outputs so that the MTPA manifold can be softly enforced within the cost; and (iii) an incremental model with Laguerre parameterization is employed to represent input increments, which preserves convexity while reducing dimensionality. Under these assumptions, the final cost function can be written as a quadratic form in the optimization vector, with a positive semidefinite Hessian. When the increment weight $r_u > 0$ and the Laguerre embedding has full column rank, the Hessian is strictly positive definite, ensuring convexity and uniqueness of the solution. For closed-loop stability, the incremental MPC framework yields an ISS-type Lyapunov decrease condition, since the smoothing term $\sum r_u \parallel \Delta u \parallel^2$ guarantees the boundedness of increments and the Laguerre factor $a \in (0,1)$ ensures exponential decay. Finally, the tuning criteria of the weights are summarized as follows: q_d, q_q balance d- and q-axis current tracking; r_{mtpa} determines the adherence to the analytical MTPA curve; and r_u provides smoothness and stability margin. A sensitivity test shows that varying each weight by one order of magnitude changes current RMS, overshoot, and settling time in a predictable monotonic fashion, which confirms robustness of the proposed settings without additional graphical evidence.

The cost function weights have distinct physical roles: q_d and q_q penalize tracking errors of the d- and q-axis currents, q_{mtpa} enforces proximity to the analytical MTPA trajectory, and r penalizes voltage increments to smooth the control action and improve closed-loop stability. In practice, the weights are tuned empirically: larger q_d and q_q accelerate current tracking at the expense of overshoot, larger q_{mtpa} enhance efficiency but slow down the transient, and larger r reduce torque/current ripple but lead to slower dynamic response. In the following simulation parameter settings, the nominal values are used ($q_d = q_q = q_{\text{MTPA}} = 10^4, r = 0.1$), which were found to balance accuracy, efficiency, and robustness. Sensitivity analysis shows that varying each weight by one order of magnitude results in monotonic and predictable changes in RMS current, overshoot, and settling time, confirming the robustness of the tuning strategy.

3.5. The Constrains of Currents

It is well known that the currents of PMSM must satisfy

$$i_d^2 + i_q^2 \leq I_{max}^2 \tag{28}$$

where i_d, i_q are the d-/q-axis stator currents obtained from the Clarke–Park transformation, and $I_{\max}$ is the maximum admissible current amplitude. Since (28) is nonlinear, it must be linearized before embedding into the quadratic programming framework.

Combining (10), (13), and (28), we obtain:

$$\left(i_d - \frac{\Lambda}{2}\right)^2 \leq \frac{I_{max}^2}{2} + \frac{a^2}{4} \tag{29}$$

where $a = \Lambda$, and Λ is in (13). In addition, a common approach is to apply the $\updownarrow_1$-norm inner approximation, $|i_d| + |i_q| \leq I_{\max}$, which guarantees that if it holds, then (28) also holds. Expanding the absolute values gives four linear inequalities:

$i_d + i_q \leq I_{\max}, i_d - i_q \leq I_{\max}, -i_d + i_q \leq I_{\max}, -i_d - i_q \leq I_{\max}$, or in compact form, $S_4\mathbf{i} \leq I_{\max}\mathbf{1}_4$, where $\mathbf{I}_{\text{stack}} = \left[\mathbf{i}(k+1)^\top, \ldots, \mathbf{i}(k+N_p)^\top\right]^\top$. This procedure results in a conservative inner approximation; the feasible set changes from a circular disk of radius $I_{\max}$ (nonlinear) to an inscribed diamond (linear). Although this reduces the feasible region slightly, it ensures that the true current limit is never violated.

By solving (29), we can obtain:

$$\begin{cases} i_d \leq \frac{\Lambda}{2} + \sqrt{\frac{I_{max}^2}{2} + \frac{a^2}{4}} \\ -i_d \leq \sqrt{\frac{I_{max}^2}{2} + \frac{a^2}{4}} - \frac{\Lambda}{2} \end{cases} \tag{30}$$

According to (12), we can obtain:

$$\begin{cases} i_q \leq \frac{\Lambda}{2} + \sqrt{\frac{I_{max}^2}{2} + \frac{a^2}{4}} + i_N \\ -i_q \leq \sqrt{\frac{I_{max}^2}{2} + \frac{a^2}{4}} - \frac{\Lambda}{2} - i_N \end{cases} \tag{31}$$

Then, combining (10), (30), and (31), the constraints of the d-axis and q-axis current can be described as follows:

$$\begin{cases} i_d \leq 0 \\ -i_d \leq \sqrt{\frac{I_{max}^2}{2} + \frac{a^2}{4}} - \frac{\Lambda}{2} \\ i_q \leq \frac{\Lambda}{2} + \sqrt{\frac{I_{max}^2}{2} + \frac{a^2}{4}} + i_N \\ -i_q \leq \sqrt{\frac{I_{max}^2}{2} + \frac{a^2}{4}} - \frac{\Lambda}{2} - i_N \end{cases} \quad \text{subject to: } \sqrt{\frac{I_{max}^2}{2} + \frac{a^2}{4}} - \frac{\Lambda}{2} - i_N \leq 0 \tag{32}$$

or

$$\begin{cases} i_d \leq 0 \\ -i_d \leq \sqrt{\frac{I_{max}^2}{2} + \frac{a^2}{4}} - \frac{\Lambda}{2} \\ i_q \leq \frac{\Lambda}{2} + \sqrt{\frac{I_{max}^2}{2} + \frac{a^2}{4}} + i_N \\ -i_q \leq 0 \end{cases} \quad \text{subject to: } \sqrt{\frac{I_{max}^2}{2} + \frac{a^2}{4}} - \frac{\Lambda}{2} - i_N > 0 \tag{33}$$

Based on the 2nd space state model (26), cost function (24) and (27), constraints (32) and (33), the incremental optimal control variable Δu can be obtained. The proposed MTPA-based MPC method is presented in Figure 2.

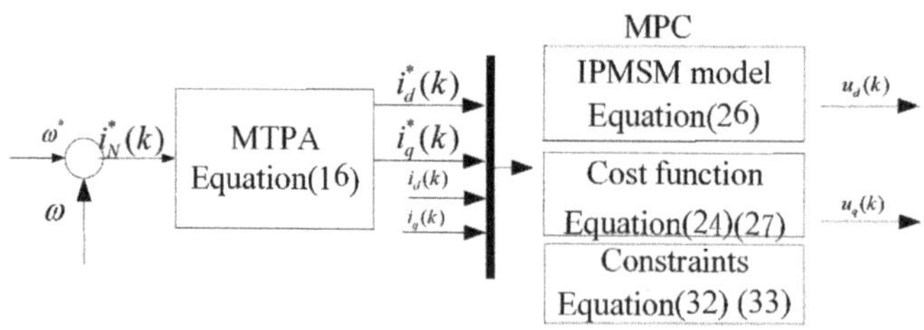

Figure 2. The proposed MTPA-based MPC schematic diagram.

4. Results

To validate the effectiveness of the proposed Laguerre-MTPA MPC, extensive simulation experiments were conducted using MATLAB/Simulink R2017a. Two types of PMSMs were selected to evaluate the performance of the proposed method under different saliency conditions. The motor parameters were designed according to Tables 1–3. Motor 1 exhibits a large difference between the d-axis and q-axis inductances, representing a high-saliency machine, while Motor 2 features a relatively small inductance difference, representing a low-saliency configuration. This setup allows for a comprehensive assessment of Laguerre-MTPA MPC adaptability and performance across various motor types. The listed weights were chosen to balance tracking accuracy, efficiency, and smoothness, as discussed in Section 3.4.

Table 1. Motor 1 parameters.

Parameter	Description	Value
P_n	Pole pair number	4
R_s	Stator winding resistance	0.958 Ω
L_d	Inductance along d-axis	0.00525 mH
L_q	Inductance along q-axis	0.012 mH
ψ_f	Permanent magnet flux linkage	0.1827 Wb
J	Moment of inertia	$0.003\ \mathrm{kg} \cdot \mathrm{m}^2$
B	Viscous friction coefficient	$0.0038\ \mathrm{N} \cdot \mathrm{m} \cdot \mathrm{s}$

Table 2. Motor 2 parameters.

Parameter	Description	Value
P_n	Pole pair number	6
R_s	Stator winding resistance	0.00423 Ω
L_d	Inductance along d-axis	0.171 mH
L_q	Inductance along q-axis	0.391 mH
ψ_f	Permanent magnet flux linkage	0.1039 Wb

Table 3. Laguerre-MTPA MPC controller parameters.

Parameter	Description	Value
k_{p_ω}	Speed proportional gain	5
k_{i_ω}	Speed integral gain	1000
N_p	Prediction horizon	4
N_c	Control interval	1
a_1	Laguerre factor for d-axis voltage	0.9
a_2	Laguerre factor for q-axis voltage	0.9
N_1	Number of Laguerre terms for d-axis voltage	4
N_2	Number of Laguerre terms for q-axis voltage	4
q_{i_d}	Weight of d-axis current error	10,000
q_{i_q}	Weight of q-axis current error	10,000
q_{mtpa}	Weight of MTPA trajectory error	10,000
r	Weight of voltage increment error	0.1

The MTPA tracking performance of Motor 2 under load variation is illustrated in Figure 3, which presents the dynamic current response trajectories of three control strategies: the proposed Laguerre-MTPA MPC, the traditional MTPA method, and standard MPC without MTPA integration. In this simulation, the reference speed of Motor 2 is set to 100 rad/s with an initial external load torque of $10\ \mathrm{N} \cdot \mathrm{m}$. At $t = 0.3$ s, the load increases to $20\ \mathrm{N} \cdot \mathrm{m}$, and at $t = 0.6$ s, it decreases back to $10\ \mathrm{N} \cdot \mathrm{m}$. Figure 3 shows the current trajectories in the d-q plane, which are used to evaluate the tracking capability of each control method with respect to the theoretical MTPA trajectory calculated from Equation (9). It is observed that the traditional MTPA method exhibits noticeable current fluctuations and significant deviation from the optimal trajectory. In contrast, the standard MPC without MTPA exhibits a wide and scattered current distribution, lacking consistency and alignment with the desired torque-per-ampere path. The proposed Laguerre-MTPA MPC strategy, however, demonstrates a highly concentrated current trajectory that closely follows the theoretical MTPA curve, indicating superior tracking accuracy and improved control consistency under dynamic loading conditions.

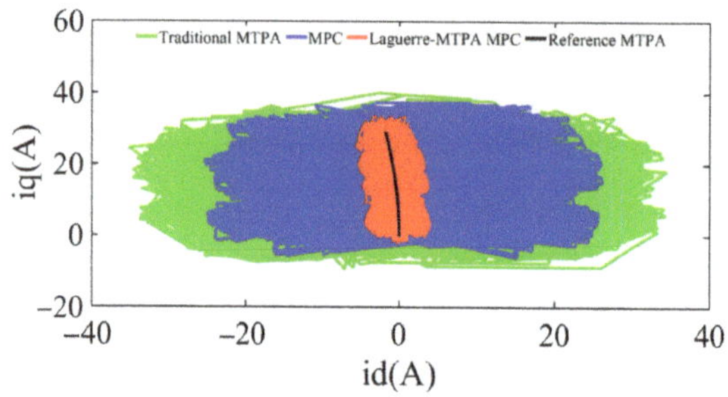

Figure 3. MTPA response of Motor 2 under varying load conditions.

In contrast to Figure 3, the MTPA tracking performance of Motor 1 under load variation is shown in Figure 4. To further verify the generality and robustness of the proposed Laguerre-MTPA MPC strategy across different types of PMSMs, Motor 1 is selected for comparative simulation. The load variation scenario is kept identical to that in Figures 3–5 for consistency. Unlike Motor 1, which features similar d-axis and q-axis inductances and thus a minimal contribution from reluctance torque, Motor 2 exhibits a significant difference between the two inductances (i.e., $L_d \neq L_q$), resulting in a pronounced magnetic saliency and a noticeably nonlinear MTPA trajectory. As shown in the d-q current distribution plot in Figure 4, the intrinsic motor characteristics clearly influence the performance of each control strategy. For Motor 2, although both the traditional MTPA control and the standard MPC show deviations from the ideal MTPA path, the overall current distribution remains relatively compact. However, for Motor 1 with its stronger reluctance torque characteristics, the traditional MTPA control results in greater deviations from the theoretical trajectory, while the current point cloud under standard MPC becomes highly scattered and unstable, severely compromising current utilization and torque output precision. In contrast, the proposed Laguerre-MTPA MPC algorithm demonstrates consistent tracking performance across both motor types. Even in the presence of dominant reluctance torque effects in Motor 1, the current trajectory remains closely aligned with the theoretical MTPA path. No significant current deviation or instability is observed, highlighting the superior adaptability and robustness of the proposed method under varying magnetic saliency conditions.

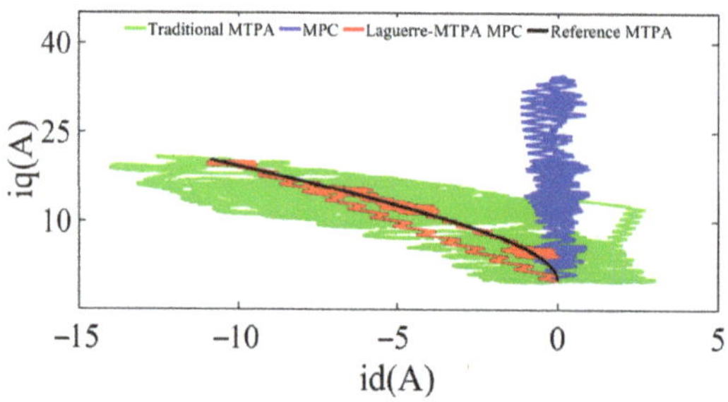

Figure 4. MTPA response of Motor 1 under varying load conditions.

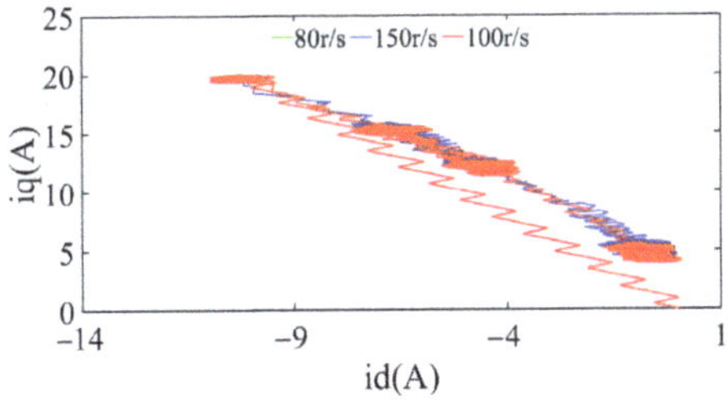

Figure 5. MTPA response of Motor 1 under varying speed conditions.

The MTPA tracking performance of Motor 1 under varying speeds is illustrated in Figure 5. This figure presents the current distribution trajectories of the proposed Laguerre-MTPA MPC strategy under different speed conditions, while keeping the load variation scenario identical to that described in Figure 3. Three representative operating points, 80 rad/s, 100 rad/s, and 150 rad/s, are selected for comparative simulation, and the corresponding current paths are plotted in the d-q plane. As shown in Figure 5, the current trajectories at all three speeds are well aligned with the theoretical MTPA curve and exhibit high compactness and consistency, indicating strong speed adaptability of the proposed controller. Specifically, as the speed increases, the spread of the current along the d-axis becomes slightly wider due to the increased torque demand and system dynamics. Nevertheless, the Laguerre-MTPA MPC controller consistently maintains accurate tracking of the MTPA trajectory without exhibiting notable deviation or oscillatory behavior. Notably, under the high-speed condition of 150 rad/s, where system dynamics are more pronounced, the controller still generates prompt and stable current commands that closely follow the optimal torque-per-ampere path. This reflects the effectiveness of Laguerre function-based parametrization in maintaining optimization stability even at elevated speeds. These results confirm that the proposed Laguerre-MTPA MPC strategy is not only effective under steady-state or low-speed conditions but also exhibits excellent trajectory tracking accuracy and robustness at high speeds, making it well-suited for wide-speed-range electric drive applications.

The electromagnetic torque performance under load variation is compared in Figure 6, which illustrates the response of three control strategies: the proposed Laguerre-MTPA MPC, the traditional MTPA-MPC, and the standard Laguerre-based MPC (LMPC). The test scenario mirrors the one used in previous sections; Motor 1 operates at a reference speed of 100 rad/s with an initial external load torque of 10 N·m. At $t = 0.3$ s, the load increases to 20 N·m, and at $t = 0.6$ s, it decreases back to 10 N·m. As observed in Figure 6, although all three control strategies are capable of responding to load variations, their performance differs significantly. The standard LMPC (without MTPA integration) exhibits a slower response speed, noticeable overshoot, and persistent steady-state oscillations. The traditional MTPA–MPC improves the response speed but shows slight oscillations at moments of abrupt load change. In contrast, the proposed Laguerre-MTPA MPC achieves superior dynamic performance with faster response, reduced overshoot, and smoother torque convergence during both disturbance events. For instance, in the load step-up scenario at $t = 0.3$ s, the Laguerre-MTPA MPC stabilizes the electromagnetic torque near the new setpoint within approximately 10 ms, about 30% faster than the traditional MTPA–MPC method. Similarly, during the load drop at $t = 0.6$ s, the proposed controller demonstrates lower response delay and quicker recovery to steady state, further confirming its effectiveness in handling abrupt load disturbances with high precision and robustness.

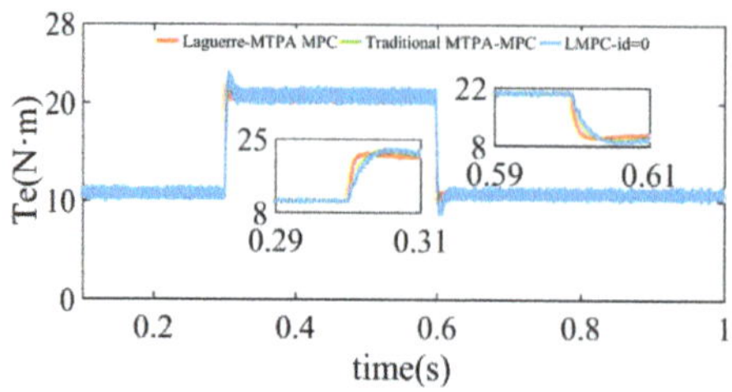

Figure 6. Electromagnetic torque response comparison under load changes.

Figure 7 presents the current magnitude response curves under load disturbance for different control strategies, aiming to evaluate their impact on current utilization efficiency. The load variation scenario is identical to that described in Figure 6. As shown in the figure, all three control methods exhibit significant changes in current magnitude during load transients, but their dynamic behaviors differ markedly. The standard LMPC maintains relatively high current magnitudes throughout the entire process, with sharp fluctuations during load transitions, indicating poor current utilization and lower efficiency. The traditional MTPA-MPC strategy shows improved performance in steady-state phases, demonstrating some degree of current optimization. However, it still suffers from abrupt current spikes and minor oscillations during load disturbances. In contrast, the proposed Laguerre-MTPA MPC consistently achieves lower current magnitude responses, with faster convergence and smaller fluctuations during transient periods. Notably, during the load increase phase at $t = 0.3$ s, the current under Laguerre-MTPA MPC rapidly rises to the new steady-state level and stabilizes quickly, demonstrating excellent dynamic current control capability. Moreover, in steady-state operation, the proposed method reduces the average current magnitude by approximately 12–18% compared to the other methods, shortens the transient settling time by around 25%, and exhibits smoother amplitude transitions. Figure 7 shows that the proposed Laguerre–MTPA MPC achieves a reduction of approximately 12–18% in the average current magnitude compared with the baselines. Since copper loss is given by $P_{Cu} = 3I^2R_s$ (with R_s listed in Table 2), this directly corresponds to a 12–18% reduction in copper loss and, thus, in winding thermal stress. The smoother current trajectories also imply fewer transient spikes, contributing to lower cumulative energy consumption over drive cycles. These improvements directly contribute to lower copper losses, higher system energy efficiency, and reduced thermal stress.

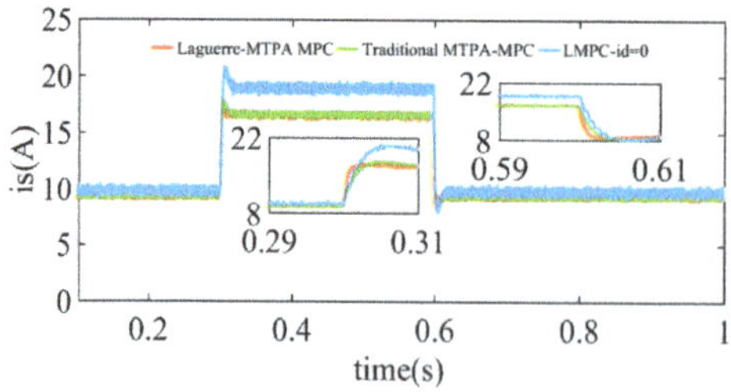

Figure 7. Current magnitude response comparison under load changes.

Figure 8 illustrates the speed response of the motor under the same load disturbance conditions, comparing the ability of each control strategy to reject disturbances and maintain speed stability. Although all controllers maintain generally stable speed outputs, varying degrees of speed fluctuations occur during sudden load changes. The standard LMPC strategy shows the largest deviations, with significant speed dips and overshoots at both disturbance moments, along with the longest recovery time. The traditional MTPA-MPC demonstrates improved disturbance rejection but still exhibits notable speed deviations when subjected to abrupt load changes. In comparison, the proposed Laguerre-MTPA MPC controller achieves the smallest speed fluctuations and the fastest dynamic recovery during both disturbance events. As shown in the detailed insets, during the sudden load increase at $t = 0.3$ s, the proposed controller results in the smallest speed drop and restores the steady-state value within approximately 10 ms. Similarly, during the load decrease at $t = 0.6$ s, it produces the smallest overshoot and exhibits a smooth convergence trend, outperforming both benchmark methods. These results indicate that the proposed Laguerre–MTPA MPC not only improves electromagnetic torque control precision but also significantly enhances the system's disturbance rejection capability under variable operating conditions.

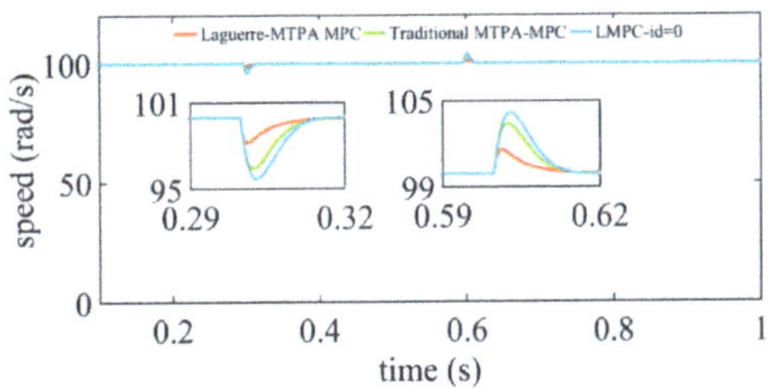

Figure 8. Speed tracking response comparison under load changes.

Figures 9 and 10 illustrate the responses of the d-axis and q-axis currents, respectively, under the load variation scenario described in Figure 6. These current trajectories are used to assess the ability of different control strategies to adapt to changing torque demands, particularly reflected in the behavior of the q-axis current, which is directly related to electromagnetic torque generation. As shown in Figure 10, the standard LMPC (configured with baseline parameters) exhibits the largest q-axis current fluctuations at both disturbance moments, accompanied by pronounced oscillations during the transient phases and poor overall stability. The traditional MTPA-MPC strategy offers some improvement in suppressing fluctuations but still shows brief overshoots during load transitions. In contrast, the proposed Laguerre-MTPA MPC demonstrates the most stable q-axis current response under both disturbance events. The current transitions are smooth, with minimal fluctuations, and the steady-state values accurately align with the torque levels corresponding to the external load changes. A closer examination of the detailed insets reveals that during the load increase at $t = 0.3$ s, the q-axis current under the proposed controller rises rapidly and settles smoothly, whereas the other strategies exhibit either delay or oscillatory behavior. Similarly, during the load decrease at $t = 0.6$ s, the Laguerre-MTPA MPC shows a faster downward response with the smallest overshoot.

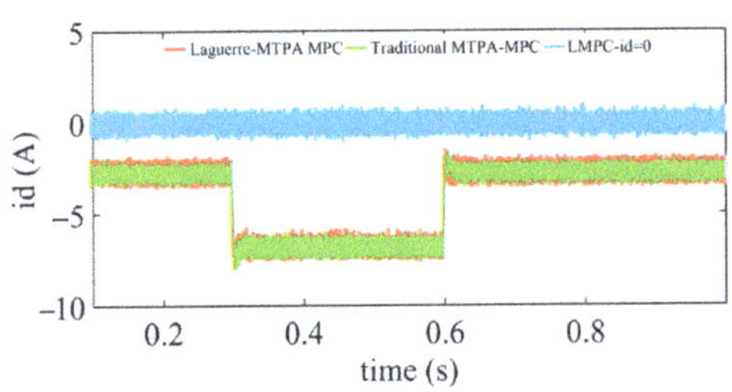

Figure 9. d-axis current response under load changes.

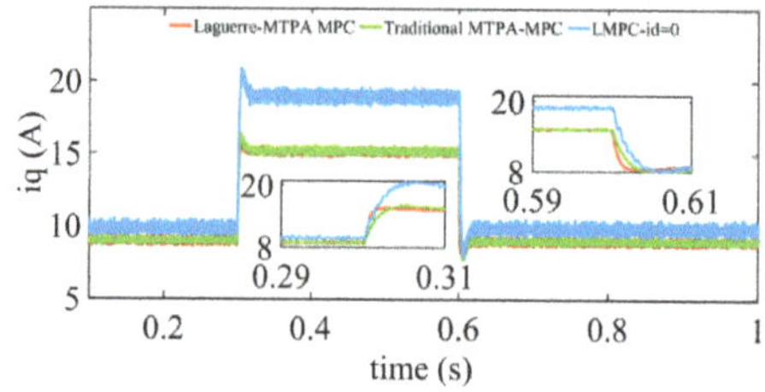

Figure 10. q-axis current response under load changes.

Overall, these results confirm that the proposed controller not only refines the current trajectory for torque generation but also significantly improves the system's dynamic responsiveness and steady-state precision under load disturbances. This highlights the superior electromagnetic control capability and dynamic consistency of the Laguerre–MTPA MPC strategy.

5. Conclusions

This paper presents a novel energy-efficient control strategy that integrates Laguerre function-based modeling with MTPA optimization to enhance the performance of PMSM drive systems in electric vehicles. By compressing the control input sequence using Laguerre orthogonal functions, the proposed method significantly reduces the dimensionality of the optimization problem, thereby improving the real-time computational efficiency and enabling practical online deployment of the MPC controller. In addition, an equivalent MTPA current trajectory is dynamically constructed to generate optimal current references that maximize torque output per unit current. This integration not only enhances the responsiveness of the controller but also improves the current utilization efficiency and aligns with energy-saving objectives. In this work, the proposed Laguerre–MTPA MPC framework has been shown to reduce the current magnitude, improve dynamic performance, and enhance robustness under parameter variations and load disturbances. These improvements translate directly into copper loss reduction and energy savings. In future work, we plan to extend the evaluation to full drive-cycle energy accounting (e.g., WLTP-like torque–speed profiles), including cumulative kWh calculation, inverter switching losses, and iron/core loss estimation. Such studies will further confirm the practical energy-saving potential of the proposed controller in realistic automotive applications.

Author Contributions: Conceptualization, L.G.; methodology, X.L.; software, Z.S.; validation, K.M.; formal analysis, K.M.; investigation, Z.S.; resources, K.M.; data curation, L.G.; writing—original draft preparation, L.G.; writing—review and editing, X.L.; visualization, Z.S.; supervision, X.L.; project administration, K.M.; funding acquisition, L.G. All authors have read and agreed to the published version of the manuscript.

Funding: This research was funded by the Research Development Project of Nanjing Polytechnic Institute under Grant NJPI-YB-2025-06.

Data Availability Statement: The original contributions presented in this study are included in the article. Further inquiries can be directed to the corresponding author.

Acknowledgments: The authors would like to express their gratitude to all those who helped them during the writing of this paper.

Conflicts of Interest: The authors declare no conflicts of interest.

References

1. Wang, Y.; Wang, C.; Xue, H. A Novel Capacity Configuration Method of Flywheel Energy Storage System in Electric Vehicles Fast Charging Station. *Electr. Power Syst. Res.* **2021**, *195*, 107185. [CrossRef]
2. Wang, K.; Wu, Z. Simplified Current Control Strategy for Permanent-Magnet Synchronous Motors with Rotor Flux Distortion. *IEEE Trans. Ind. Electron.* **2022**, *69*, 3407–3417. [CrossRef]
3. Lai, C.; Feng, G.; Tjong, J.; Kar, N.C. Direct Calculation of Maximum-Torque-Per-Ampere Angle for Interior Pmsm Control Using Measured Speed Harmonic. *IEEE Trans. Power Electron.* **2018**, *33*, 9744–9752. [CrossRef]
4. Chen, B.; Shen, A.; Luo, X.; Dou, Z.; Luo, P. Novel Mtpa Control Strategy for Ipmsm Based on Multiple Virtual Signals Injection. *IET Electr. Power Appl.* **2020**, *14*, 457–463. [CrossRef]
5. Feng, G.; Lu, Y.; Lai, C.; Ding, B.; Kar, N.C. Fault Tolerant Maximum Torque Per Ampere (Ft-Mtpa) Control for Dual Three-Phase Interior Pmsms under Open-Phase Fault. *IEEE Trans. Ind. Electron.* **2022**, *69*, 12030–12041. [CrossRef]
6. Choi, S.; Lee, W.; Kang, A.; Baek, S.; Lee, J.S. Accuracy Improvement of Maximum Torque Per Ampere Control for Interior Permanent Magnet Synchronous Motor Drives Reflecting Pm Flux Linkage Variations. *J. Power Electron.* **2023**, *23*, 1678–1687. [CrossRef]
7. Huang, K.; Peng, W.; Lai, C.; Feng, G. Efficient Maximum Torque Per Ampere (Mtpa) Control of Interior Pmsm Using Sparse Bayesian Based Offline Data-Driven Model with Online Magnet Temperature Compensation. *IEEE Trans. Power Electron.* **2023**, *38*, 5192–5203. [CrossRef]
8. Zuo, K.; Wang, F.; Li, Z.; Ke, D.; Kennel, R.; Heldwein, M.L. A Robust Unified Strategy for Maximum Torque Per Ampere and Field Weakening in Permanent Magnet Synchronous Motor. *IEEE Trans. Power Electron.* **2024**, *39*, 5286–5297. [CrossRef]
9. Liu, J.; Gong, C.; Han, Z.; Yu, H. Ipmsm Model Predictive Control in Flux-Weakening Operation Using an Improved Algorithm. *IEEE Trans. Ind. Electron.* **2018**, *65*, 9378–9387. [CrossRef]
10. Liao, G.; Zhang, W.; Cai, C. Research on a Pmsm Control Strategy for Electric Vehicles. *Adv. Mech. Eng.* **2021**, *13*, 16878140211051462. [CrossRef]
11. Alzayed, M.; Chaoui, H. Efficient Simplified Current Sensorless Dynamic Direct Voltage Mtpa of Interior Pmsm for Electric Vehicles Operation. *IEEE Trans. Veh. Technol.* **2022**, *71*, 12701–12710. [CrossRef]
12. Xu, W.; Cao, C.; Zhang, Y.; Huang, S.; Gao, J. Improved Flux-Weakening Method with Excitation Current Distribution for Hybridly Excited Asymmetric Stator Pole Doubly Salient Machine Based on Electrical Vehicle. *IEEE J. Emerg. Sel. Top. Power Electron.* **2023**, *11*, 1385–1396. [CrossRef]
13. Elhaj, A.; Alzayed, M.; Chaoui, H. Direct Voltage Mtpa Control of Interior Permanent Magnet Synchronous Motor Driven Electric Vehicles. *Control Eng. Pract.* **2025**, *156*, 106197. [CrossRef]
14. Li, K.; Wang, Y. Maximum Torque Per Ampere (Mtpa) Control for Ipmsm Drives Using Signal Injection and an Mtpa Control Law. *IEEE Trans. Ind. Inform.* **2019**, *15*, 5588–5598. [CrossRef]
15. Li, K.; Wang, Y. Maximum Torque Per Ampere (Mtpa) Control for Ipmsm Drives Based on a Variable-Equivalent-Parameter Mtpa Control Law. *IEEE Trans. Power Electron.* **2019**, *34*, 7092–7102. [CrossRef]
16. Kim, H.-S.; Yoo, J.; Sul, S.-K. Online Mtpa Operation of Ipmsm Based on Dual-Loop Control in Polar Coordinates. *IEEE Trans. Power Electron.* **2022**, *37*, 4431–4441. [CrossRef]
17. Xu, W.; Elmorshedy, M.F.; Liu, Y.; Rodriguez, J.; Garcia, C. Maximum Thrust Per Ampere of Linear Induction Machine Based on Finite-Set Model Predictive Direct Thrust Control. *IEEE Trans. Power Electron.* **2020**, *35*, 7366–7378. [CrossRef]
18. Elmorshedy, M.F.; Xu, W.; Allam, S.M.; Rodriguez, J.; Garcia, C. Mtpa-Based Finite-Set Model Predictive Control without Weighting Factors for Linear Induction Machine. *IEEE Trans. Ind. Electron.* **2021**, *68*, 2034–2047. [CrossRef]
19. An, X.; Liu, G.; Chen, Q.; Zhao, W.; Song, X. Adjustable Model Predictive Control for Ipmsm Drives Based on Online Stator Inductance Identification. *IEEE Trans. Ind. Electron.* **2022**, *69*, 3368–3381. [CrossRef]
20. Xu, W.; Tang, Y.; Dong, D.; Xiao, X.; Rashad, E.E.M.; Junejo, A.K. Optimal Reference Primary Flux Based Model Predictive Control of Linear Induction Machine with Mtpa and Field-Weakening Operations for Urban Transit. *IEEE Trans. Ind. Appl.* **2022**, *58*, 4708–4721. [CrossRef]
21. Gao, J.; Gui, W.; Yang, C.; Peng, T.; Yang, Y.; Luo, J.; Yang, C. Modeling, Analysis, and Suppression of Demagnetization for Mtpa-Driven Permanent Magnet Motors with Distributed Windings. *IEEE Trans. Power Electron.* **2024**, *39*, 9430–9445. [CrossRef]
22. Shen, W.; Shao, L.; Liu, D.; Wang, J.; Ge, C. Event-Triggered Fcs-Mpc with Sliding Mode Observer for Permanent Magnet Synchronous Motor Servo Motion Systems. *IEEE Trans. Autom. Sci. Eng.* **2025**, *22*, 2257–2268. [CrossRef]
23. Ma, C.; Yao, X.; Li, H.; De Belie, F. Setting up Reference Variants to Comply with Current Boundary Settings in Finite Set Model Predictive Pmsm Control. *IEEE J. Emerg. Sel. Top. Power Electron.* **2021**, *9*, 5377–5389. [CrossRef]
24. Chen, Z.; Qiu, J. Adjacent-Vector-Based Model Predictive Control for Permanent Magnet Synchronous Motors with Full Model Estimation. *IEEE J. Emerg. Sel. Top. Power Electron.* **2023**, *11*, 1317–1331. [CrossRef]

25. Yang, Y.; Xiao, Y.; Fan, M.; Wang, K.; Zhang, X.; Hu, J.; Fang, G.; Zeng, W.; Vazquez, S.; Rodriguez, J. A Novel Continuous Control Set Model Predictive Control for Lc-Filtered Three-Phase Four-Wire Three-Level Voltage-Source Inverter. *IEEE Trans. Power Electron.* **2023**, *38*, 4572–4584. [CrossRef]
26. Malekpour, M.; Azizipanah-Abarghooee, R.; Terzija, V. Maximum Torque Per Ampere Control with Direct Voltage Control for Ipmsm Drive Systems. *Int. J. Electr. Power Energy Syst.* **2019**, *116*, 105509. [CrossRef]
27. Gade, C.R.; Sultana, R.W. Control of Permanent Magnet Synchronous Motor Using Mpc-Mtpa Control for Deployment in Electric Tractor. *Sustainability* **2022**, *14*, 12428. [CrossRef]
28. Liu, G.; Song, C.; Chen, Q. Fcs-Mpc-Based Fault-Tolerant Control of Five-Phase Ipmsm for Mtpa Operation. *IEEE Trans. Power Electron.* **2020**, *35*, 2882–2894. [CrossRef]
29. Zhong, B.; Su, J.; Yang, G.; Sun, G.; Tan, K. Unified Optimal Control Method for Synrm in Full-Speed Region Considering Magnetic Saturation. *IEEE J. Emerg. Sel. Top. Power Electron.* **2025**, *13*, 675–689. [CrossRef]
30. Zhang, X.; Li, H.; Shao, M. Fixed-Time-Convergent Sliding Mode Control with Sliding Mode Observer for Pmsm Speed Regulation. *Sensors* **2024**, *24*, 1561. [CrossRef]
31. Mohamed, E.E.M.; Saeed, M.S.R. T-Type Multilevel Inverter-Fed Interior Pm Machine Drives Based on the Voltage Regulation Feedback and the Model Predictive Control. *Electr. Eng.* **2024**, *106*, 2749–2763. [CrossRef]
32. Kumar, K.B.; Kumar, K.V.P. An Enhanced Predictive Current Control Technique for Interior Permanent Magnet Synchronous Motor Drives with Extended Voltage Space Vectors for Electric Vehicles. *Int. J. Circuit Theory Appl.* **2024**, *52*, 4234–4253. [CrossRef]
33. Agoro, S.; Husain, I. Robust Deadbeat Finite-Set Predictive Current Control with Torque Oscillation and Noise Reduction for Pmsm Drives. *IEEE Trans. Ind. Appl.* **2022**, *58*, 365–374. [CrossRef]
34. Feng, G.; Lai, C.; Han, Y.; Kar, N.C. Fast Maximum Torque Per Ampere (Mtpa) Angle Detection for Interior Pmsms Using Online Polynomial Curve Fitting. *IEEE Trans. Power Electron.* **2022**, *37*, 2045–2056. [CrossRef]

computation

Article

Advanced Deep Learning Framework for Predicting the Remaining Useful Life of Nissan Leaf Generation 01 Lithium-Ion Battery Modules

Shamaltha M. Wickramaarachchi [1], S. A. Dewmini Suraweera [1], D. M. Pasindu Akalanka [1], V. Logeeshan [1] and Chathura Wanigasekara [2,*]

1 Department of Electrical Engineering, University of Moratuwa, Moratuwa 10400, Sri Lanka; shamalthamangala@gmail.com (S.M.W.); dewminisuraweeras@gmail.com (S.A.D.S.); dm.pasindu.akalanka@gmail.com (D.M.P.A.); logeeshanv@uom.lk (V.L.)
2 Institute of Maritime Energy Systems, German Aerospace Centre (DLR), 21502 Geesthacht, Germany
* Correspondence: chathura.wanigasekara@dlr.de

Abstract: The accurate estimation of the remaining useful life (RUL) of lithium-ion batteries (LIBs) is essential for ensuring safety and enabling effective battery health management systems. To address this challenge, data-driven solutions leveraging advanced machine learning and deep learning techniques have been developed. This study introduces a novel framework, Deep Neural Networks with Memory Features (DNNwMF), for predicting the RUL of LIBs. The integration of memory features significantly enhances the model's accuracy, and an autoencoder is incorporated to optimize the feature representation. The focus of this work is on feature engineering and uncovering hidden patterns in the data. The proposed model was trained and tested using lithium-ion battery cycle life datasets from NASA's Prognostic Centre of Excellence and CALCE Lab. The optimized framework achieved an impressive RMSE of 6.61%, and with suitable modifications, the DNN model demonstrated a prediction accuracy of 92.11% for test data, which was used to estimate the RUL of Nissan Leaf Gen 01 battery modules.

Keywords: autoencoder; deep learning; lithium-ion battery; memory features; Nissan Leaf battery; PCA; remaining useful life

1. Introduction

This an extended version of the "Accurate Prediction of Remaining Useful Life for Lithium-ion Battery Cells Using Deep Neural Networks" conference paper published by *IEEE* [1]. The commercialization of lithium-ion battery technology by Sony in 1991 was a significant milestone given the increasing demand for sophisticated energy storage systems that primarily depend on technology, mobility, and energy efficiency [2]. Due to their comparatively high energy and power density, remarkable efficiency, low self-discharge rate, and extended lifespan [3,4] compared to other batteries, LIBs have since found extensive applications in a variety of industries, including electric vehicles, household appliances, communication applications, aerospace, cell phones, and other fields [5]. The main energy source for the most recent iterations of the Tesla, Chevrolet Volt, Nissan Leaf, and BYD E6 is lithium-ion batteries.

As lithium-ion batteries continually experience cycles of charge and discharge, their overall capacity gradually reduces—a process known as "health degradation". This aging process is influenced by various aspects. As the lithium ions migrate between the anode and cathode and induce capacity fading, a solid layer known as the Electrolyte Interface (SEI) layer repeatedly forms on the electrode's surface. Another factor is lithium plating, which occurs when a battery is overcharged in cold conditions, turning lithium ions into lithium metal. Additionally, capacity degradation is brought on by an increase in internal impedance [3,4,6].

Because LIBs deteriorate, safety and dependability have become increasingly important; battery failures can harm an entire system and potentially result in serious injuries and considerable financial losses. An explosion or fire may result from a lithium-ion battery malfunction in electric vehicles [7]. The RUL is a crucial indicator that supports safety concerns and is used to assess the dependability of electronic systems and optimize LIB performance [3]. Complex degradation mechanisms, noisy operation settings, and capacity regeneration noise pose challenges to RUL prediction [8].

A lithium-ion battery's remaining usable life (RUL) is expressed as the number of cycles left before the capacity decreases to less than 70% of its initial capacity [9].

In recent years, significant advancements have been made in the field of RUL prediction, particularly through the application of deep learning (DL) techniques. Models such as Convolutional Neural Networks (CNNs), Recurrent Neural Networks (RNNs), Long Short-Term Memory (LSTM), Gated Recurrent Units (GRUs), and Transformer architectures have been widely adopted to capture complex degradation patterns and temporal dependencies in lithium-ion batteries [10–12]. Attention mechanisms and hybrid models combining physics-based and data-driven approaches have also emerged to enhance prediction robustness and accuracy. In parallel, research on battery safety has focused on identifying failure modes such as thermal runaway, overcharging, and internal short circuits, and integrating early warning systems into battery management systems (BMSs). DL-based anomaly detection and safety-aware RUL prediction models are being explored to address these concerns. Despite these advancements, challenges remain in practical implementation, including model interpretability, generalization across different battery chemistries and usage patterns, data scarcity for extreme conditions, and computational constraints for real-time deployment. Addressing these issues is critical for the development of reliable and safe DL-based RUL prediction systems suitable for real-world applications [13].

Because of this, estimating RUL is still crucial, and there is currently no totally accurate way to anticipate RUL. The goal of this study is to combine an autoencoder with Deep Neural Networks (DNNs) that use memory features in order to create an accurate prediction model that addresses these problems. Using previous data on battery health, operating conditions, and degradation patterns—which offer practical insights for optimizing battery usage and maintenance strategies—the model will learn to estimate the RUL effectively. The project advances the creation of sophisticated battery management systems that facilitate more effective use and increase the longevity of lithium-ion batteries across a range of applications.

Model-based and data-driven methods are the two categories into which the approaches to RUL prediction can be divided [10]. Model-based methods rely on comparable circuit models, dynamic models, and electrochemical concepts. Despite the great accuracy of model-based strategies, data-driven approaches have garnered significant attention [10] because of their limited applications and complexity [3]. Nevertheless, the accuracy of these machine learning models is rather moderate [3].

(A) Related work

(1) Model-Based Approach

The models are computationally sophisticated and follow a stringent structure tailored to a particular framework. Xu and Chen estimated the RUL of LIBs by developing a state–space model, also referred to as a dynamic model [14]. The model parameters and states are refined through the integration of expectation maximization (EM) and the Extended Kalman Filter algorithm. Heng et al. propose an enhanced approach for forecasting the remaining useful life of LIBs by leveraging an improved unscented particle filter (UPF) algorithm combined with linear-optimizing combination resampling [11].

(2) Data-Driven Approach

The data-driven method, in comparison to the model-based approach, is faster, less complex, and more convenient. Zhang et al. introduced a technique for estimating the remaining useful life (RUL) based on the Box–Cox transformation (BCT), a statistical method typically applied in Linear Regression and Time Series Analysis to stabilize variance and normalize the data distribution [15]. They leveraged this technique in predicting the RUL of lithium-ion batteries (LIBs). Similarly, Nuhic et al. employed Support Vector Machines (SVMs) to diagnose and predict system health, particularly focusing on estimating the state of health and RUL of LIBs [16]. However, due to the inherent limitations of SVM models, such as the requirement for the Kernel Function to satisfy Mercer Conditions, calculating the loss function can be challenging.

Currently, researchers are exploring Neural Network (NN)-based models, including Deep Neural Networks (DNNs) and Recurrent Neural Networks (RNNs) with Long Short-Term Memory (LSTM) [10,12]. Zhang et al. utilized LSTM to predict the RUL of LIBs [11]. Although RNN and LSTM models demonstrate superior accuracy compared to other machine learning models, they present certain challenges, including high computational requirements, significant memory consumption, and extended training times [17]. Additionally, implementing dropouts in LSTM models is complex.

To mitigate these challenges, we introduced a deep learning approach that integrates memory-based features, which have been rarely explored in the literature. Given the degradation patterns observed in LIBs, these patterns can be harnessed for Time Series Analysis, allowing memory-based features to be incorporated into the model. In this study, we prioritized feature engineering and proposed an optimized model architecture to enhance accuracy. The proposed method was benchmarked against SVM and Linear Regression models.

The novelty of this paper lies in utilizing auto-encoded memory features integrated with a Deep Neural Network (DNN) for the accurate prediction of remaining useful life (RUL). This approach is applied to real-world field data collected from Nissan Leaf batteries, demonstrating the model's practical effectiveness. Additionally, the novelty of this project lies in its ability to predict the RUL of a Nissan Leaf Gen 1 battery module, which shares similar charge–discharge characteristic graphs with the model's trained dataset. This is achieved by performing the charge–discharge process while maintaining key factors consistent with the training dataset. Furthermore, we introduce a novel data normalization method, enabling comparisons to be made between lithium-ion batteries with different capacities. Notably, this method has been applied to real-world data, showcasing its utility in practical applications, such as predicting the RUL of Nissan Leaf car batteries, even in the absence of structured or consistent charge patterns.

2. Materials and Methods

2.1. Proposed RUL Prediction Approach

The suggested model framework for predicting the RUL is shown in Figure 1. Initially, the original data's insightful properties were retrieved, exposing important trends and patterns that might be used to predict the batteries' RUL.

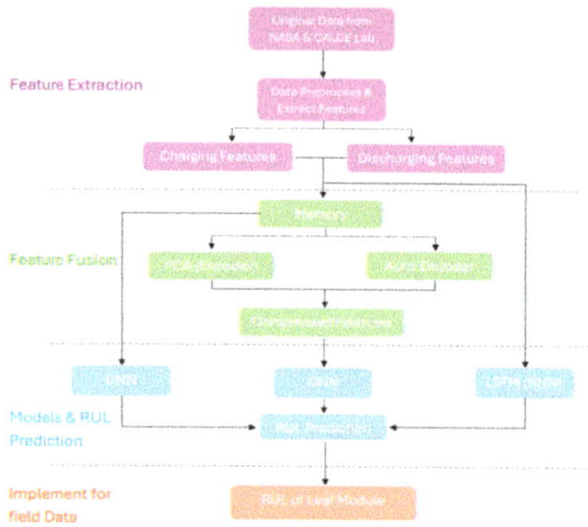

Figure 1. Proposed Methodology.

After that, a PCA with memory feature integration was used to complete feature fusion. In order to forecast the RUL as the output, the encoded features were finally given into the DNN model.

A. Dataset (Original Signal)

A set of four lithium-ion batteries (B0005, B0006, B0007, and B0018) from the NASA dataset were subjected to three distinct operational profiles: charge, discharge, and impedance, all conducted at room temperature. These batteries were selected for predicting the remaining useful life (RUL). The NASA dataset provides time series data for each charge and discharge cycle, including measurements of voltage, current, temperature, and impedance. Each cycle follows the widely adopted constant current–constant voltage (CC-CV) pattern for both charging and discharging.

The testing process was repeated until the battery capacity degraded to 70% of its initial value. A complete cycle comprises both a charge and a discharge sequence. Figure 2 illustrates a typical charge–discharge cycle of a lithium-ion battery. All charge–discharge cycles were compared against this reference pattern and those that deviated significantly were excluded from the dataset, as such anomalies could negatively impact the performance of the neural network.

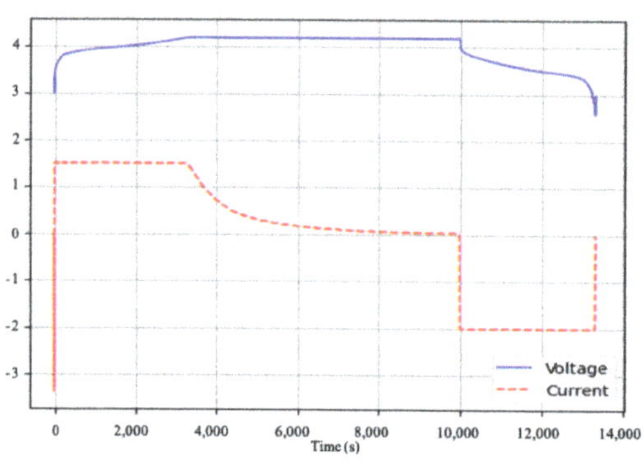

Figure 2. Typical complete cycle of a lithium-ion battery.

- Charging process: Initially, the battery is charged with a constant current (CC) until the voltage is raised to a maximum upper limit. Then, the voltage is kept constant (CV) while the current drops to a certain lower limit.

- Discharging process: The entire discharge process is at a constant current (CC) of a specific value until the voltage drops to a certain lower limit.

B. Feature Extraction

In Deep Neural Networks, feature engineering plays a pivotal role in the success of prediction models, especially in complex scenarios like battery life prediction. The dataset gathered from charging and discharging cycles of batteries presents a significant challenge: the number of data points varies across cycles, with some having as few as 800 data points and others as many as 5000. This disparity makes it impractical to directly feed raw data into the neural network, necessitating data preprocessing and feature extraction to ensure consistent and meaningful input.

Feature extraction is crucial because, in theory, incorporating a broader set of features enhances the model's accuracy. A well-structured representation of the data is essential for identifying trends and key features that contribute to better predictions.

As batteries undergo repeated charge and discharge cycles, they degrade due to several mechanisms, including the loss of active lithium ions, lithium plating, electrode degradation, metal dissolution, and an increase in internal impedance [18]. These factors lead to a reduction in the battery's capacity over time. Consequently, time series data of current, voltage, and temperature during charging and discharging cycles reveal distinct patterns when analyzed against the cycle count.

For instance, the figures for a B0005 battery, depicted in Figure 3, illustrate the variation in voltage, current, and temperature of the battery cell B0005 over time during the charging and discharging processes across multiple cycles. Figure 3a–c corresponds to the discharge cycles while Figure 3d–f corresponds to the charge cycles. By analyzing these curves, it is evident that certain parameters of lithium-ion batteries are highly sensitive to the cycle count and exhibit clear trends. For instance, Figure 3a highlights whether all discharging cycles follow a typical pattern, as shown in Figure 2, and highlights how the time taken to reach the minimum terminal voltage decreases as the cycle count increases. Similarly, Figure 3e highlights how the constant current (CC) charging time shortens with each successive cycle.

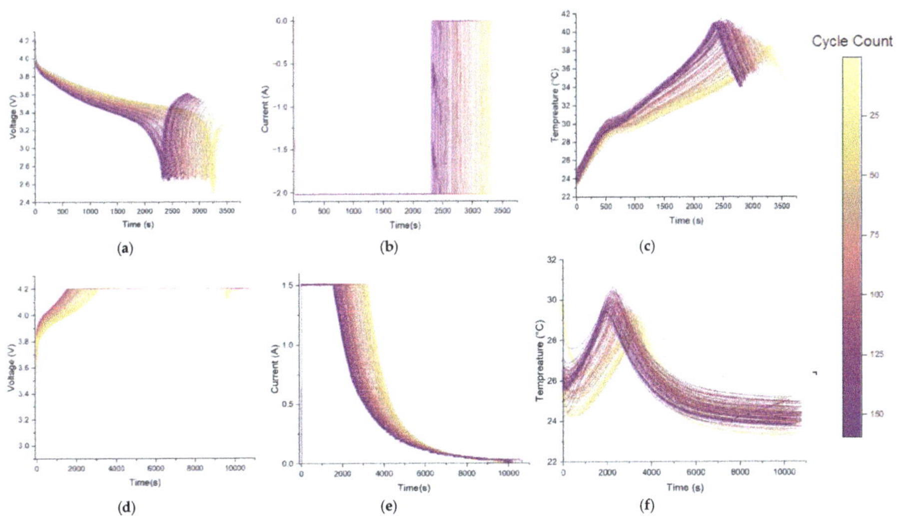

Figure 3. B0005. (**a**) Discharging voltage vs. time; (**b**) discharging current vs. time; (**c**) discharging temperature vs. time; (**d**) charging voltage vs. time; (**e**) charging current vs. time; (**f**) charging temperature vs. time.

These characteristic features, extracted from the original data for each cycle, serve as critical inputs for predicting the battery's remaining useful life (RUL). Identifying and leveraging these features enables the neural network to make more accurate and reliable predictions.

These distinguishing characteristics were taken from the original data for every battery cycle in order to forecast the RUL. While plotting each cycle for each battery, we observed errors in some battery cycles, such as missing data points and graphs showing abnormalities compared to others. These cycles were skipped during model training to prevent potential errors in the model. However, some of these cycles were retained to evaluate the model's accuracy. The following features are extracted from the charging and discharging operation.

Charging Features:

Upper Cut-off Voltage Time

$(t_{min(i)}, V_i)$, $V_i \geq$ Upper Cut off Voltage, i = 1, 2, 3, ... where $t_{min(i)}$ represents the time when the battery terminal voltage reaches the maximum value first and V_i represents the value of output voltage in the ith cycle.

Constant Current Charging Time (CCCT)

$(t_{min(i)}, A_i)$, $A_i \leq$ Constant Current Value, i = 1, 2, 3, ... A_i represents the value of the current value in the ith cycle.

Constant Voltage Charging Time (CVCT)

$(t_{min(i)}, V_i)$, V_i £ Constant Voltage Value, i = 1, 2, 3, ... where V_i represents the value of the output voltage in the ith cycle.

Maximum Charging Voltage Time

The time required to reach the maximum battery-measured voltage. $(t_{max}, V_{max}) = \{(t_i, V_i \mid max(V_i))\}$, i = 1, 2, 3, ..., m, where t_{max} is the time stamp for which the maximum voltage Vmax is measured in the ith cycle.

Maximum Temperature Time

Time when the battery reaches its maximum temperature. $(t_{max}, T_{max}) = \{(t_i, T_i \mid max(T_i))\}$, i = 1, 2, 3, ..., m, where t_{max} is the time stamp for which the maximum temperature T_{max} is measured at the ith cycle

Area Under Voltage Curve

Area covered by the voltage vs. time curve.

Area Under Current Curve

Area covered by the current curve vs. time.

Maximum Power Time

$(t_{max}, (V^*I)_{max}) = \{(t_i, V^*I \mid max(V^*I))\}$, i = 1, 2,..., m, where the t_{max} is the time stamp for which the maximum current and voltage product is measured at the ith cycle.

Discharging Features:

Discharging Time

During the discharging process, the time for which the battery terminal voltage reaches its minimum voltage.

Maximum Temperature Time

Time which gives the maximum temperature at the discharging process for each cycle.

Area Under Voltage Curve

Area covered by the voltage measured vs. time plot.

Area Under Current Curve

Area covered by the current vs. time plot.

Discharging Capacity

The remaining capacity at each discharging cycle.

When combining the charge cycle and discharge cycle, there are 13 features for one cycle.

C. Generating Labels and Data Normalization

For the training phase of the RUL prediction model, correct labels are necessary after the features have been extracted from the raw data. To obtain the supervised data (x_i,y_i), the appropriate RUL (y_i) for the ith cycle characteristics (x_i) must be calculated. The ith cycle's RUL was determined as

$$y_i = L + 1 - i \quad (1)$$

where L is the total count of charge and discharge cycles.

To mitigate any adverse effects resulting from varying value ranges, data normalization is an essential component of Neural Network models [19]. We used the minimum–maximum normalization technique to rescale all of the dataset's features inside the interval [0–1]. The following is the min–max normalization formula [19].

$$x_{normalized} = \frac{x - x_{min}}{x_{max} - x_{min}} \quad (2)$$

where x_{max} denotes the greatest value of feature x and x_{min} denotes its minimum value.

By ensuring that all features have the same scale, this normalization strategy can help the neural network model perform better and coverage more quickly.

D. Memory Features

Time Series Analysis can be used to characterize the patterns in the data; therefore, memory-based characteristics spanning numerous cycles—which have not been used much—can be applied here. Utilizing a window that spans many cycles, extracted features are used with memory to capture the properties seen in the preceding n cycles. By increasing the number of preceding cycles (n), testing loss was decreased.

For instance, in order to predict the RUL for the ith cycle, y_i, all of the features from the previous n cycles, $\{x_i, x_{i-1}, x_{i-2}, x_{i-3}, \ldots, x_{i-n}\}$, were used in addition to the features of the current cycle, x_i. Several window sizes were used to test the proposed DNN in order to increase the number of cycles (n).

E. Feature Fusion

Adding memory features to the DNN model increases the number of input features, leading to potential redundancy, higher computational complexity, and inefficiency. To address this, we reduced the dimensionality of the input data using two proven techniques: Principal Component Analysis (PCA), Nonlinear PCA, and an autoencoder.

(1) Principal Component Analysis (PCA)

In this project, to handle the high-dimensional dataset and reduce the risk of errors such as overfitting, we used Principal Component Analysis (PCA) as the first encoding technique. PCA simplifies the dataset by identifying new variables, known as principal components (PCs), which are linear combinations of the original features. These components retain the most significant information from the original data while reducing dimensionality. The process of applying PCA involves the following steps [20]:

Standardization: The data is standardized to ensure all features have a mean of zero and a standard deviation of one, preventing any feature from dominating the analysis.

Covariance matrix calculation: A covariance matrix is computed to measure how different features vary together, identifying relationships between them.

Eigen decomposition: The eigenvalues and eigenvectors of the covariance matrix are calculated to determine the directions (eigenvectors) with the highest variance (eigenvalues).

Selection of principal components: The principal components with the largest eigenvalues are selected, capturing the most variance and ensuring that only the most meaningful information is retained.

Projection: The original dataset is projected onto the space defined by the selected principal components, resulting in a reduced-dimensional representation of the data for further analysis. Figure 4 illustrates the original data compared with the decoded data for the case of n = 3 in PCA.

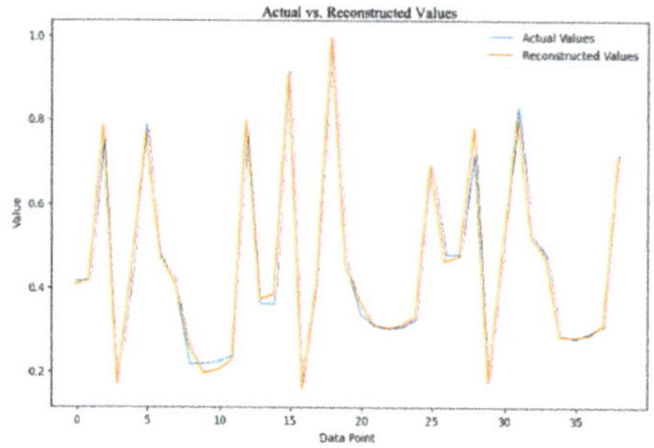

Figure 4. Original Data vs. Decoded Data from PCA.

(2) Nonlinear PCA

In this study, Nonlinear PCA was not used due to the large size of the dataset, making it computationally impractical to handle. Instead, we employed an autoencoder, which provides a scalable and efficient solution for dimensionality reduction by learning nonlinear representations of the data.

(3) Autoencoder

An autoencoder is a type of neural network used for unsupervised learning, primarily for dimensionality reduction and feature extraction [21]. It aims to learn an efficient, compressed representation of input data by encoding it into a lower-dimensional space and then reconstructing it back to the original form. The autoencoder consists of two main parts:

- Encoder: Compresses the input data into a lower-dimensional latent space, capturing the most essential features.
- Decoder: Reconstructs the original data from the compressed representation, ensuring that the important information is retained.

In this project, we only consider the encoder, as the encoded representation is used as input to the DNN model. The decoder is only employed to verify the accuracy of the autoencoder model by evaluating how well it reconstructs the original input. Figure 5 illustrates the original data compared with the decoded data for the case of n = 3 in the autoencoder.

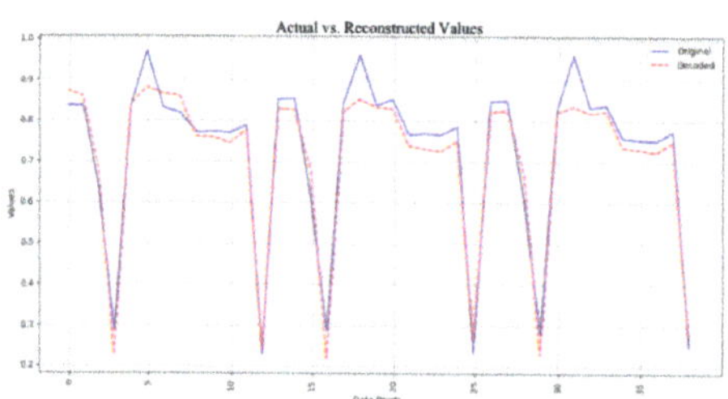

Figure 5. Original data vs. decoded data from autoencoder.

F. Training Neural Network Models with and without encoded Features

Table 1 represents the number of input features for PCA and autoencoder along with their outputs, categorized by different number of previous cycles.

Table 1. Encoded features.

No. of Previous Cycles	No. of Features	No. of Encoded Dimensions
0	13	N/A
1	26	9
2	39	12
3	52	15
4	65	18

The proposed model for remaining useful life prediction is a Deep Neural Network (DNN) that leverages both current and previous cycle features. The output from the encoder serves as input to the DNN, along with the target output, as the DNN operates under a supervised learning framework. In Deep Neural Networks, each input passes through a nonlinear activation function to generate the input for the subsequent layer. The mapping in the ith layer can be expressed as follows:

$$h^{i} = \zeta(Wh^{i} + b) \tag{3}$$

where ζ represents the nonlinear activation function, W denotes the weight matrix, and b corresponds to the bias of the ith layer.

During the training phase, the weights and bias parameters of the layers are optimized interactively to minimize the loss function, which is defined by comparing model output with the target output. After tuning the hyperparameters, the selected DNN model consists of four fully connected layers. Each layer has 10, 7, 4, and 1 neurons, respectively. The ReLU activation function is used for the hidden layers, while the sigmoid function is applied to the output layer. The model's performance during the testing is evaluated using the Root Mean Squared Error (RMSE%) value.

$$\mathrm{RMSE}(\%) = \sqrt{\frac{1}{n} \times \Sigma_{i=1}^{n} \left(\frac{y_{i,\mathrm{prediction}} - y_{i,\mathrm{target}}}{y_{i,\mathrm{target}}} \right)^{2}} \tag{4}$$

2.2. *Nissan Leaf Gen 01 Battery Module*

A. Introduction

The adoption of electric vehicles (EVs) has surged rapidly in recent years. In 2022 alone, 10.5 million new EVs and plug-in hybrid vehicles were introduced to the market. This represents a significant growth in market share, with EVs accounting for 14% of global vehicle sales in 2022, up from 9% in 2021. Projections suggest that by 2030, EVs could capture up to 35% of the market. Most EVs are powered by lithium-ion battery packs, which are composed of multiple battery modules. These batteries typically reach the end of their automotive service life after approximately 10 years. However, even after this, many still retain 60–67% of their original capacity, making them suitable for secondary applications such as energy storage systems (ESSs), particularly for solar power plants [22].

B. Why Use This Model when BMSs Already Exist?

EVs are equipped with a sophisticated battery management system (BMS), which continuously monitors and estimates the remaining useful life (RUL) of the battery during operation. However, once the battery pack is removed from the vehicle and disconnected from the BMS, the system's memory is reset and the ability to predict the RUL is lost. This presents a significant challenge when repurposing retired EV batteries for second-life applications.

Therefore, this study aims to develop a predictive model for estimating the remaining useful life (RUL) of Nissan Leaf Gen 01 battery modules after their removal from the BMS.

The proposed method focuses on utilizing simple tests to predict the battery's remaining life, ensuring the feasibility of second-life applications in energy storage systems.

C. About the Battery Module

The Nissan Leaf Generation 01 battery pack consists of 48 modules connected in series, with each module comprising four lithium-ion cells. The anode material is a combination of $LiMn_2O_4$ and $LiNiO_2$, while the cathode is composed of graphite. The configuration of each battery module is 2P2S, meaning two parallel sets are connected in series, resulting in an overall pack configuration of 2P-96S. The nominal capacity of the battery pack is 66.2 Ah (24 kWh) at a 0.3C rate, where the C-rate defines the rate of charge or discharge relative to the total capacity. For instance, a 1C rate would fully charge or discharge the battery in one hour, while a 2C rate would complete the process in 30 min. Due to high current requirements managed by the battery management system (BMS), the usable capacity is set to 65.6 Ah. Each module has an internal resistance of 1 mΩ, and the series resistance across the pack is 2 mΩ. The operating voltage range for a single cell is 2.8 V to 4.2 V, with a mean cell voltage of 3.8 V, yielding a typical module voltage of 7.6 V and a maximum module voltage of 8.4 V. Each module weighs approximately 3.8 kg, with an energy density of 213 Wh/L and a specific energy of 132 Wh/kg. Table 2 summarizes the battery module parameters.

Table 2. Nissan Leaf Gen 01 battery specifications.

Module Configuration	2P-2S
Module Capacity	500 Wh
Module Voltage	5.6 V–8.4 V (7.4 V Mean)
Min Voltage (Per Cell)	2.8 V–4.2 V (3.7 V Mean)
Weight	3.8 kg
Energy Density	213 Wh/L
Specific Energy	132 Wh/kg.

D. Data Collection

1. Charging Process

Due to the difference in capacity between the Nissan Leaf Gen 01 battery module and the training set, it was necessary to ensure that 1.5 A was driven through each cell. Given the 2P-2S configuration of the module, a total current of 3 A was applied during the charging process.

Charging was carried out using a RIGOL DP 932U DC power supply in constant current mode until the battery voltage reached 8.4 V. Once this voltage reached that value, the current gradually decreased while the voltage kept constant. The charging process was stopped when the current was reduced up to 40 mA.

2. Discharging Process

Discharging was conducted using a constant current method at 4 A, with the assumption that each cell in the module drains 2 A, consistent with the training dataset. This process was carried out using a KIKUSUI PLZ1205W electronic load. Data collection was performed using version 5.1.0 of the SD023-PLZ-5W (Wavy for PLZ-5W) software, provided by KIKUSUI.

Figure 6 illustrates the complete charging and discharging setups used in the laboratory for the data collation process for Nissan Leaf Gen 01 battery modules.

E. Data Normalization

The charging and discharging current and voltage curves over time of the Nissan Leaf module exhibit the same pattern as those of the 18650 battery datasets. The only difference between the training dataset and the Nissan Leaf Gen 01 battery module lies in the capacity when comparing their performance. Therefore, normalization was performed using standard data for each battery type. This process brings both battery values to a scale between 0 and 1, making the model well-suited for predicting the remaining useful life (RUL) of Nissan Leaf battery modules. These methods ensure that predictions remain robust despite the constraints encountered during data collection. It is important to note that this approach does not consider the battery's chemistry or physical structure. Figure 7 illustrates the charge and discharge curves plotted using the gathered data. The standard times can be calculated as follows:

$$18650\text{ battery} = \frac{2\text{ Ah}}{1.5\text{ A}} \times 3600 \quad (5)$$

where 2 Ah is the capacity and 1.5 A is the charging current for the 18650 battery.

$$\text{Nissan Leaf Gen 1 Module} = \frac{24 \times 10^3\text{ Wh}}{48 \times 3\text{ A} \times 8.4\text{ V}} \times 3600 \quad (6)$$

where 24 kW is the capacity, 48 is the number of modules in a pack, 3 A is the charging current, and 8.4 V is the max voltage of a Nissan Leaf battery module.

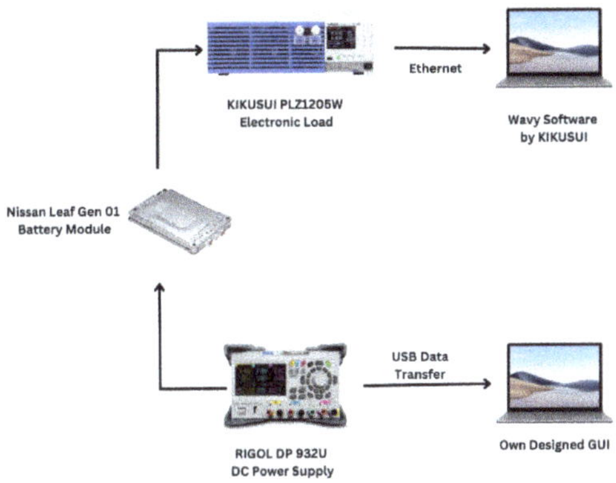

Figure 6. Charging and discharging procedure for Nissan Leaf module.

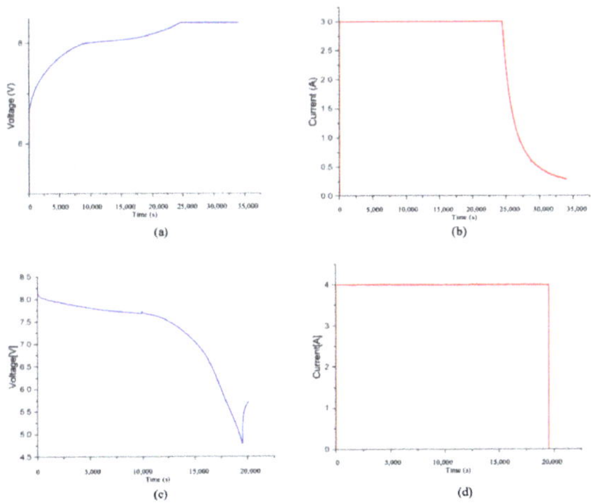

Figure 7. Leaf Gen 01. (**a**) Charge voltage vs. time; (**b**) charge current vs. time; (**c**) discharge voltage vs. time; (**d**) discharge current vs. time.

2.3. Experiment

A. Model Selection

We obtained the lithium-ion battery data from NASA's Prognostic Center of Excellence (PCoE). For our model, we selected four battery cells designated as B0005, B0006, B0007, and B0018. These batteries underwent various operational profiles, including charging, discharging, and impedance testing, all conducted at room temperature. Charging was performed in constant current (CC) mode at 1.5 A until the battery voltage reached 4.2 V, followed by constant voltage (CV) mode until the charge current decreased to 20 mA. Discharging occurred at a constant current (CC) of 2 A until the battery voltages dropped to 2.7 V, 2.5 V, 2.2 V, and 2.5 V for batteries B0005, B0006, B0007, and B0018, respectively.

The experiments were terminated when the batteries met the end-of-life (EOL) criteria, defined as a 30% reduction in rated capacity (from 2 Ah to 1.4 Ah).

We used batteries B0005, B0006, and B0007, which had 167 cycles, to train the model, while battery B0018, with 132 cycles, was utilized for testing. Although the dataset from NASA includes several hundred cycles, the proposed model is capable of functioning effectively with cells that have a higher cycle count, especially since we normalized the target output using min–max normalization.

The DNN model was then trained using the encoded features from batteries B0005, B0006, and B0007, and tested with the encoded features of battery B0018 and CALCE lab data. The predicted results were compared among the DNN, Neural Network with memory features (NNwMF), Support Vector Machine (SVM), and Linear Regression (LR) models using RMSE% values. Under the NNwMF framework, we considered the DNN with PCA encoded memory features, DNN with memory features without encoding, DNN with memory features encoded using an autoencoder, and an LSTM model.

B. Model Retraining

As the above-mentioned model is used to predict the remaining useful life (RUL) of Nissan Leaf batteries, maintaining the same test conditions as those in the training dataset can be challenging. Consequently, measuring certain parameters, such as temperature variation during the charging and discharging processes, becomes difficult. During the data collection phase, we focused solely on charging and discharging currents, voltage, and power over time, while neglecting temperature features. As a result, we had to retrain the most effective model obtained during our initial training phase using the new set of 12 input features, making it suitable for predicting the remaining useful life (RUL) of the Nissan Leaf Gen 01 battery modules.

3. Results and Discussion

A. Results of Encoding Techniques

When implementing memory features, it is essential to compress the input features into lower dimensions without compromising the integrity of the original data, as this could negatively impact the model's accuracy.

i. PCA

PCA is one of the encoding techniques utilized in this study. The accuracy is evaluated by comparing the plot of the original data with the plot generated from the encoded and decoded data. The R-squared method was employed to assess the accuracy of the PCA, with an R-squared value of 100% indicating a perfect match between the graphs. Table 3 presents the accuracy of the PCA for different n values.

Table 3. Accuracy of PCA.

n	Encoded Dimensions	Accuracy (%)
0	N/A	N/A
1	9	98.90
2	12	98.89
3	15	98.87
4	18	98.85

ii. Autoencoder

An autoencoder is a neural network model used as an encoding technique. Accuracy is measured using the RMSE (%) value. Table 4 displays the accuracy of the autoencoder for various values of n.

Table 4. Accuracy of autoencoder.

n	No. of Encoded Dimension	Accuracy (%)
0	N/A	N/A
1	9	89.69
2	12	92.05
3	15	94.77
4	18	94.71

B. Results for Different ML Models

Initially, we developed three machine learning models: Linear Regression, Support Vector Machine (SVM), and a Deep Neural Network (DNN).

These models were trained using data from the B0005, B0006, and B0007 batteries, and predictions were made for the B0018 battery. The RMSE values were calculated to compare the models and identify the one with the highest accuracy.

Table 5 illustrates the accuracies of the three models. The DNN model was chosen due to its lowest validation loss, leading to further optimization of the model. Figure 8 shows the result for the selected DNN model before implementing memory features (MFs).

Table 5. Accuracy of different ML models.

Method	RMSE (%)	Accuracy (%)
DNN	9.14%	90.86%
SVM	10.56%	89.84%
Linear Regression	11.96%	88.04%

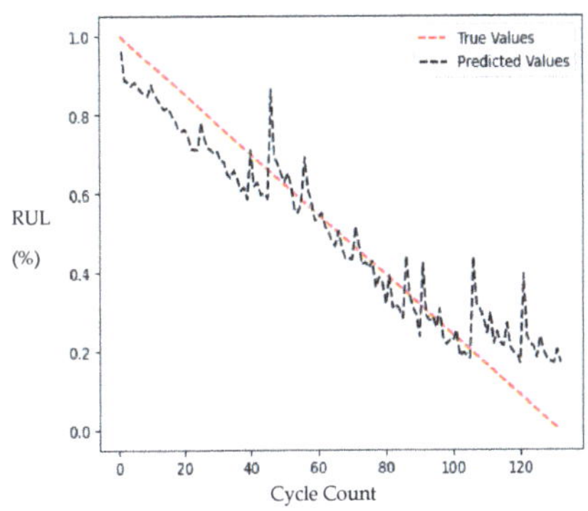

Figure 8. Output of DNN without memory features.

C. Performance Analysis of Neural Network Models with Memory Features

Multiple experiments were conducted with the incorporation of memory features, yielding promising results. The process was repeated for different n values, where n represents the number of previous cycles considered for predicting the RUL. Table 6 presents how the RMSE value varies across the DNN model with an autoencoder, the DNN model with PCA, the DNN model without PCA, and the LSTM model as the number of previous cycles increases.

Table 6. Accuracy of different neural network models.

n	RMSE			
	DNNwMF with Autoencoder	DNNwMF with PCA	DNNwMF Without PCA	LSTM
0	N/A	N/A	9.14%	N/A
1	7.89%	8.77%	9.41%	8.66%
2	6.21%	8.33%	9.63%	8.39%
3	6.22%	7.83%	10.30%	7.89%
4	6.90%	7.72%	10.33%	7.81%

Figure 9 presents the optimal Predicted RUL compared to the True RUL for each NN model, where subfigure (a) shows the performance of the DNN with autoencoder for n = 2 with an RMSE value of 6. 21%, (b) illustrates the DNN with PCA for n = 4 with an RMSE value of 7.72%, and (c) shows the LSTM for n = 4 with an RMSE of 7.81%. Each model demonstrates its best accuracy at the corresponding n values.

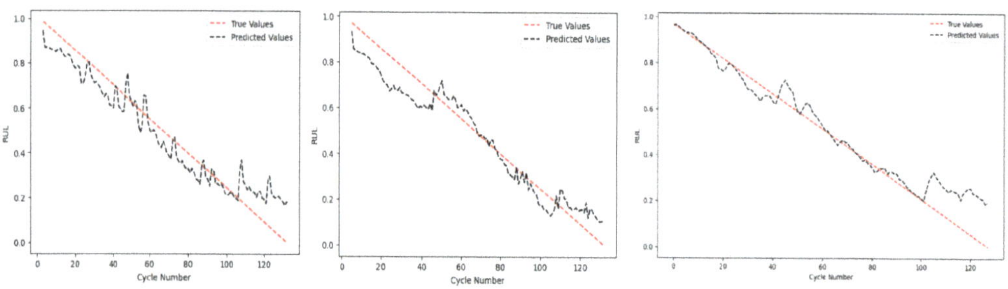

Figure 9. Model outputs. (**a**) DNN with autoencoder for n = 2; (**b**) DNN with PCA for n = 4; (**c**) LSTM for n = 4.

D. Nissan Leaf Battery Predictions compared to BMS reading

Since the DNN with an autoencoder demonstrated the highest accuracy, achieving the lowest RMSE value of 6.61% at n = 2, it was utilized for predicting the RUL of the recently retired Nissan Leaf battery module after retraining the model. The RMSE of the retrained model was 7.89%. The predicted values were compared against the BMS readings of the battery pack, assuming that the battery modules share the same RUL as the packs. Three battery modules (B1, B2, B3) were selected from different state of health (SOH) ranges. Each Nissan Leaf battery underwent complete charging and discharging processes several times: B1 completed five full cycles, while B2 and B3 completed four cycles each. As we incorporated memory features for n = 2, data from three consecutive cycles were required (including two prior cycles). For example, with B1, if the cycles are named C1, C2, C3, C4, and C5:

Set 1 considers the state of C3, using C2 and C1 as memory features.

Set 2 considers the state of C4, using C3 and C2 as memory features.

Set 3 considers the state of C5, using C4 and C3 as memory features.

Similarly, for B2 and B3, two tests were performed for each battery module, following the same logic.

Altogether, for B1, we performed three predictions, and for B2 and B3, we performed two predictions each. The results for each prediction using Deep Neural Network are presented in Table 7.

Table 7. Nissan Leaf battery module prediction.

	B1	B2	B3
Total Cycles	5	4	4
BMS Reading	76.89	56.45	32.00
Prediction for Set 01	79.53	51.52	30.94
Prediction for Set 02	77.72	51.49	29.41
Prediction for Set 03	77.11	-	-

Figure 10 shows the remaining useful life (RUL) displayed by the integrated battery management system (BMS) of Nissan Leaf cars at the time of battery removal. This BMS estimates the RUL by tracking the history of the charging and discharging cycles. Sub figures (a), (b), and (c) show the readings for the B1, B2, and B3 batteries, respectively.

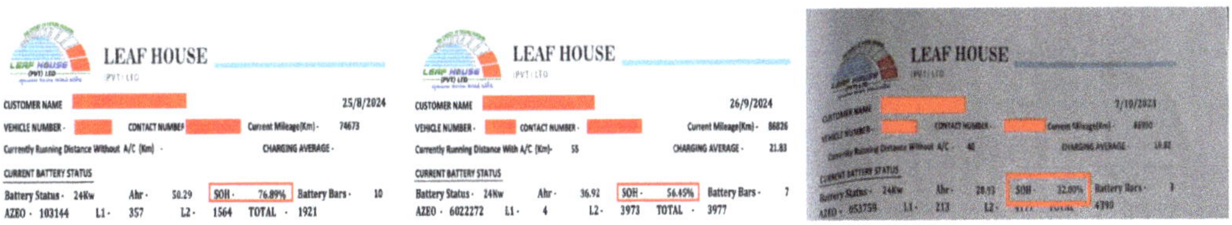

(a) (b) (c)

Figure 10. BMS readings for battery. (**a**) B1; (**b**) B2; (**c**) B3. Red box indicates State of Health at removal.

4. Conclusions

This study presents a novel deep learning approach for predicting the remaining useful life (RUL) of lithium-ion battery (LIB) cells. The methodology involves a feature extraction process that reveals meaningful patterns from time series data, demonstrating the effectiveness of the model in improving RUL prediction accuracy in a normalized manner. Through experimentation, it was found that the Deep Neural Network (DNN) model with memory features (DNNwMF) combined with an autoencoder is optimal for this task, outperforming various machine learning techniques, including RNN (LSTM), SVM, and Linear Regression.

The optimized model achieved a Root Mean Squared Error (RMSE) of 6.61% during testing with the training dataset and demonstrated a prediction accuracy of 92.11% for the retrained model used to predict the RUL of Nissan Leaf battery modules. This predictive capability highlights its suitability for practical applications, including second-life uses for retired batteries. The proposed method's robust performance over traditional models and its practical applicability make it a promising tool for enhancing battery management systems and extending the lifespan of lithium-ion batteries across diverse applications.

However, the current methodology has certain limitations. The time required to complete a full charge–discharge cycle is approximately two days, which poses a constraint for large-scale or real-time implementations. Additionally, the model has only been validated on Nissan Leaf Gen 1 battery modules, limiting its generalizability across different battery models and chemistries.

In real-world scenarios, this model can be integrated into advanced battery management systems (BMSs) to enable predictive maintenance, reduce unexpected battery failures, and support the design of energy-efficient charging and discharging strategies. It can also inform decisions in electric vehicle fleet management, grid storage optimization, and circular economy initiatives by accurately identifying end-of-life batteries suitable for secondary use. Furthermore, the methodological framework of combining memory features with autoencoders opens up avenues for future research in developing generalizable models across different battery chemistries and operational conditions.

Future work will focus on optimizing the model to function effectively with a reduced number of previous cycle data points (e.g., memory features with n = 1 or n = 2), which can significantly lower the data acquisition time and make the model more feasible for real-time applications. Additionally, efforts will be made to generalize the model across various Nissan Leaf battery modules and explore lightweight architectures suitable for edge deployment. Uncertainty quantification and safety-driven RUL models under extreme conditions will also be considered to ensure more reliable and interpretable outcomes.

Author Contributions: Conceptualization, S.M.W., D.M.P.A., S.A.D.S. and V.L.; methodology, S.M.W.; validation, D.M.P.A.; formal analysis, S.A.D.S.; resources, C.W.; data curation, S.M.W.; writing—original draft preparation, S.M.W.; writing—review and editing, S.A.D.S.; visualization, D.M.P.A.; supervision, V.L. and C.W.; funding acquisition, C.W. All authors have read and agreed to the published version of the manuscript.

Funding: This research received no external funding.

Data Availability Statement: The CALCE laboratory data used in this study are publicly available on the official CALCE Lab website at https://calce.umd.edu. The NASA dataset is accessible through the NASA open data portal at https://data.nasa.gov/organization/nasa. The Leaf battery datasets used and/or analyzed during the current study are available from the corresponding author upon reasonable request.

Acknowledgments: We thank NASA labs for providing the data used in this project. We also express our gratitude to Michael Pecht, founder and director of CALCE labs at the University of Maryland, for his valuable advice and for providing lab data. Additionally, we appreciate LEAF HOUSE (PVT) LTD for supplying the Nissan Leaf batteries essential for this work.

Conflicts of Interest: The authors declare no conflicts of interest.

Abbreviations

The following abbreviations are used in this manuscript:

CALCE	Center for Advanced Life Cycle Engineering

References

1. Wickramaarachchi, S.M.; Suraweera, S.A.D.; Akalanka, D.M.P.; Logeeshan, V.; Wanigasekara, C. Accurate Prediction of Remaining Useful Life for Lithium-ion Battery Cells Using Deep Neural Networks. In Proceedings of the 2024 IEEE World AI IoT Congress (AIIoT), Seattle, WA, USA, 29–31 May 2024; pp. 562–568.
2. Ellis, B.L.; Lee, K.-T.; Nazar, L.F. Positive electrode materials for Li-Ion and Li-Batteries. *Chem. Mater.* **2010**, *22*, 691–714. [CrossRef]
3. Vermeer, W.; Mouli, G.R.C.; Bauer, P. A comprehensive review on the characteristics and modeling of Lithium-Ion battery aging. *IEEE Trans. Transp. Electrification* **2022**, *8*, 2205–2232. [CrossRef]
4. Han, X.; Lu, L.; Zheng, Y.; Feng, X.; Li, Z.; Li, J.; Ouyang, M. A review on the key issues of the lithium ion battery degradation among the whole life cycle. *eTransportation* **2019**, *1*, 100005. [CrossRef]
5. Tsiropoulos, I.; Tarvydas, D.; Natalia, L. *Li-ion Batteries for Mobility and Stationary Storage Applications*; EU Publications: Luxembourg, 2018.

6. Wang, Z.; Liu, Y.; Wang, F.; Wang, H.; Su, M. Capacity and remaining useful life prediction for lithium-ion batteries based on sequence decomposition and a deep-learning network. *J. Energy Storage* **2023**, *72*, 108085. [CrossRef]
7. Hasib, S.A.; Islam, S.; Chakrabortty, R.K.; Ryan, M.J.; Saha, D.K.; Ahamed, M.H.; Moyeen, S.I.; Das, S.K.; Ali, F.; Islam, R.; et al. A comprehensive review of available battery datasets, RUL prediction approaches, and advanced battery management. *IEEE Access* **2021**, *9*, 86166–86193. [CrossRef]
8. Pang, X.; Huang, R.; Wen, J.; Shi, Y.; Jia, J.; Zeng, J. A lithium-ion battery RUL prediction method considering the capacity regeneration phenomenon. *Energies* **2019**, *12*, 2247. [CrossRef]
9. Pan, C.; Huang, A.; He, Z.; Chang, L.; Sun, Y.; Zhao, S.; Wang, L. Prediction of remaining useful life for lithium-ion battery based on particle filter with residual resampling. *Energy Sci. Eng.* **2021**, *9*, 1115–1133. [CrossRef]
10. Ren, L.; Li, Z.; Hong, S.; Zhao, S.; Wang, H.; Zhang, L. Remaining useful life prediction for Lithium-Ion Battery: A deep learning approach. *IEEE Access* **2018**, *6*, 50587–50598. [CrossRef]
11. Zhang, Y.; Xiong, R.; He, H.; Pecht, M.G. Long Short-Term Memory Recurrent Neural Network for Remaining Useful Life Prediction of Lithium-Ion Batteries. *IEEE Trans. Veh. Technol.* **2018**, *67*, 5695–5705. [CrossRef]
12. Liu, J.; Saxena, A.; Goebel, K.; Saha, B.; Wang, W. An Adaptive Recurrent Neural Network for Remaining Useful Life Prediction of Lithium-ion Batteries. In Proceedings of the Annual Conference of the PHM Society, Portland, OR, USA, 10–16 October 2010; Volume 2.
13. Wen, J.; Yu, Y.; Chen, C. A Review on Lithium-Ion Batteries Safety Issues: Existing Problems and Possible Solutions. *Mater. Express* **2012**, *2*, 197–212. [CrossRef]
14. Xu, X.; Chen, N. A state-space-based prognostics model for lithium-ion battery degradation. *Reliab. Eng. Syst. Saf.* **2017**, *159*, 47–57. [CrossRef]
15. Zhang, Y.; Xiong, R.; He, H.; Pecht, M.G. Lithium-Ion Battery Remaining Useful Life Prediction With Box–Cox Transformation and Monte Carlo Simulation. *IEEE Trans. Ind. Electron.* **2019**, *66*, 1585–1597. [CrossRef]
16. Nuhic, A.; Terzimehic, T.; Soczka-Guth, T.; Buchholz, M.; Dietmayer, K. Health diagnosis and remaining useful life prognostics of lithium-ion batteries using data-driven methods. *J. Power Sources* **2013**, *239*, 680–688. [CrossRef]
17. Kandadi, T.; Shankarlingam, G. Drawbacks of LSTM Algorithm: A Case Study. 2025. Available online: https://ssrn.com/abstract=5080605 (accessed on 6 June 2025).
18. Yeh, C.-N.; Rose, J.; Thaman, H.; Narasimhan, S.; Huang, W.-Y.; Sun, W.; Huang, W.; Zhang, Z.; Chueh, W.C. Lithium Plating on Graphite Electrodes in Lithium-Ion Batteries. In *ECS Meeting Abstracts*; The Electrochemical Society, Inc.: Pennington, NJ, USA, 2024; Volume MA2024-02, p. 532.
19. Pranolo, A.; Setyaputri, F.U.; Paramarta, A.K.I.; Triono, A.P.P.; Fadhilla, A.F.; Akbari, A.K.G.; Utama, A.B.P.; Wibawa, A.P.; Uriu, W. Enhanced Multivariate Time Series Analysis Using LSTM: A Comparative Study of Min-Max and Z-Score Normalization Techniques. *Ilk. J. Ilm.* **2024**, *16*, 210–220. [CrossRef]
20. Thorstensen, N.; Segonne, F.; Keriven, R. Normalization and preimage problem in gaussian kernel PCA. In Proceedings of the 2008 15th IEEE International Conference on Image Processing, San Diego, CA, USA, 12–15 October 2008; pp. 741–744.
21. Guan, P.; Zhang, T.; Zhou, L. RUL Prediction of Rolling Bearings Based on Multi-Information Fusion and Autoencoder Modeling. *Processes* **2024**, *12*, 1831. [CrossRef]
22. Gao, W.; Cao, Z.; Kurdkandi, N.V.; Fu, Y.; Mi, C. Evaluation of the second-life potential of the first-generation Nissan Leaf battery packs in energy storage systems. *eTransportation* **2024**, *20*, 100313. [CrossRef]

computation

MDPI

Article

Subsequential Continuity in Neutrosophic Metric Space with Applications

Vishal Gupta [1,†], Nitika Garg [1,†] and Rahul Shukla [2,*,†]

[1] Department of Mathematics, MMEC, Maharishi Markandeshwar (Deemed to be University), Mullana, Ambala 133207, Haryana, India; vgupta@mmumullana.org (V.G.); nitika.mmdu@gmail.com (N.G.)
[2] Department of Mathematical Sciences and Computing, Walter Sisulu University, Mthatha 5117, South Africa
* Correspondence: rshukla@wsu.ac.za
† These authors contributed equally to this work.

Abstract: This paper introduces two concepts, subcompatibility and subsequential continuity, which are, respectively, weaker than the existing concepts of occasionally weak compatibility and reciprocal continuity. These concepts are studied within the framework of neutrosophic metric spaces. Using these ideas, a common fixed point theorem is developed for a system involving four maps. Furthermore, the results are applied to solve the Volterra integral equation, demonstrating the practical use of these findings in neutrosophic metric spaces.

Keywords: compatible maps (CM); fuzzy metric space (FMS); intuitionistic fuzzy set (IFS); neutrosophic metric space (NMS); coincidence point (CP)

1. Introduction

Zadeh introduced FSs in 1965 [1], and the concept of FMSs has been extensively explored by numerous researchers through various approaches. Kramosil and Michalek initially introduced FMS in 1975 [2], laying the foundation for further developments. Later, in 1994, George and Veeramani refined this concept by introducing significant modifications and investigating the Hausdorff topology for these spaces [3]. Over the years, researchers have expanded on these ideas, introducing statistical FMS, fuzzy pseudo metric spaces, and other related notions [2,4–6]. Various studies have contributed to the advancement of fuzzy metric concepts, drawing from different perspectives [5,7–11].

Several researchers, including [2,12–19], have contributed to the study of commuting mappings and FPTs for compatible and subcompatible maps in FMSs [20,21]. These theorems serve as a significant extension and generalization of various FPTs originally formulated for contractive-type mappings in metric spaces and similar structures. Furthermore, the work of [22] was instrumental in introducing the concept of type (β) compatibility within FMS. Their research established links between compatible maps and those classified under types (α) and (β), while also formulating a series of FPTs specifically tailored for type (β) compatible maps in FMS.

Grabiec [19], in 1988, expanded the classical FPTs initially proposed by Banach and later refined by Edelstein in 1962 [23], extending their applicability to FMS as outlined by the definitions provided by Kramosil and Michalek.

In 1983, Krassimir Atanassov [24,25] introduced the concept of IFSs as an extension of Lotfi Zadeh's FS theory, broadening the conventional understanding of set structures. Later, in 2004, Park [26] extended FMSs, originally formulated by George and Veeramani in

https://doi.org/10.3390/computation13040087

1994 [3], by proposing IFM-spaces. This development provided a natural progression in the field, linking these spaces to existing results in metric spaces (MS) [24–27].

Further advancements followed in 2006 when Gregori et al. [28] analyzed the convergence of topologies induced by fuzzy metrics and IFM. Expanding on this, Saadati et al. [29] gave the idea of modified IFMSs. After that Saadati, Sedghi, and Shobe [29] refined the IFMS framework of Park's work [26] and the foundational ideas of George and Veeramani [3], leading to the development of modified IFMSs. Numerous researchers have since explored various aspects of IFMS, employing diverse methodologies [30,31]. Several other researchers [32] have explored additional fixed point results within the context of NMSs.

A major advancement in this field came with Smarandache's work in 1999, which introduced the concept of measuring dilemmas while also generalizing existing mathematical structures that represent imprecision. Many researchers have contributed to the development of neutrosophic theory, including those who formulated neutrosophic logic [33] and the Dombi neutrosophic graph [34]. Ongoing research continues to expand the notion of NSs and their wide-ranging applications.

In neutrosophic set theory, each event is characterized by three key components: truthfulness (T), indeterminacy (I), and falsity (F), as originally introduced by Smarandache in 2003. NMSs further extend these ideas by utilizing continuous triangular norms (CTN) and continuous triangular conorms (CTC) to facilitate their study and application. In the present paper, Section 2 presents the idea of NS, and NMS [35] is then defined with the help of CTC and CTN. Additionally, a definition of Cauchy sequences in NMS is provided.

Moving to Section 3, some definitions and examples of weakly commuting, compatible mappings, as well as occasionally weakly compatible, subsequentially continuous, and subcompatible mappings in NMS, are introduced. In Section 4, FPT is established by using subsequentially continuous and subcompatible mappings in NMS. Section 5 focuses on illustrating the practical applications of the results, presenting examples to validate the findings. Section 6 provides the conclusion of the study. Lastly, the abbreviations and references used in the paper are given.

2. Preliminaries

In this section, some preliminaries are given that will be used later on.

Definition 1 ([7]). *A CTN is a binary operator $\uplus : [0,1] \times [0,1] \mapsto [0,1]$ if $\uplus$ satisfies the following criteria:*
For $p, l, f, t \in [0,1]$,

1. *$\uplus$ is continuous,*
2. *if $p \leqslant f$ and $l \leqslant t$, then $p \uplus l \leqslant f \uplus t$,*
3. *$p \uplus 1 = p$, and*
4. *$\uplus$ is associative and commutative.*

Example 1 ([7]). *(i) $\iota \uplus \nu = \iota\nu$ (ii) $\iota \uplus \nu = min(\iota, \nu)$ $\forall$ $\iota, \nu \in [0,1]$.*

Definition 2 ([7]). *A CTC is a binary operator $\odot : [0,1] \times [0,1] \mapsto [0,1]$ if $\odot$ satisfies the following criteria:*
For $p, l, f, t \in [0,1]$,

1. *$\odot$ is continuous,*
2. *If $p \leqslant f$ and $l \leqslant t$, then $p \odot l \leqslant f \odot t$,*
3. *$p \odot 0 = p$,*
4. *$\odot$ is associative and commutative.*

Example 2 ([7]). *(i)* $g \odot h = g + h - gh$ *(ii)* $g \odot h = max(g, h)$ *for all* $g, h \in [0, 1]$

Definition 3 ([35]). *Let* $\mathfrak{A}$ *be an arbitrary set. Then* $\aleph = < l, P(l), Q(l), R(l) >: l \in \mathfrak{A}$ *is an NS such that* $\aleph : \mathfrak{A} \times \mathfrak{A} \times \mathbb{R}^+ \mapsto [0, 1]$. *Let* $\uplus$ *be a CTN and let* $\odot$ *be the CTC. Then* $(\mathfrak{A}, \aleph, \uplus, \odot)$ *is NMS if the following criteria are satisfied.* $\forall\, l, m, v \in \mathfrak{A}$,

1. $0 \leqslant P(l, m, t) \leqslant 1, 0 \leqslant Q(l, m, t) \leqslant 1, 0 \leqslant R(l, m, t) \leqslant 1$, *for all* $t \in \mathbb{R}^+$,
2. $P(l, m, t) + Q(l, m, t) + R(l, m, t) \leqslant 3$, *(for* $t \in \mathbb{R}^+$*)*,
3. $P(l, m, t) = 1$ *(for* $t > 0$*) iff* $l = m$,
4. $P(l, m, t) = P(m, l, t)$ *(for* $t > 0$*)*,
5. $P(l, m, t) \uplus P(m, v, s) \leqslant P(l, v, t + s)(\forall t, s > 0)$,
6. $P(l, m, .)$:$[0, \infty) \mapsto [0, 1]$ *is continuous,*
7. $lim_{t \mapsto \infty} P(l, m, t) = 1(\forall t > 0)$,
8. $Q(l, m, t) = 0$ *(for* $t > 0$*) iff* $l = m$,
9. $Q(l, m, t) = Q(m, l, t)$ *(for* $t > 0$*)*,
10. $Q(l, m, t) \odot Q(m, v, s) \geqslant Q(l, v, t + s)(\forall t, s > 0)$,
11. $Q(l, m, .)$:$[0, \infty) \mapsto [0, 1]$ *is continuous,*
12. $lim_{t \mapsto \infty} Q(l, m, t) = 0(\forall t > 0)$,
13. $R(l, m, t) = 0$ *(for* $t > 0$*) iff* $l = m$,
14. $R(l, m, t) = R(m, l, t)$ *(for* $t > 0$*)*,
15. $R(l, m, t) \odot R(m, v, s) \geqslant B(l, v, t + s)(\forall t, s > 0)$,
16. $R(l, m, .)$:$[0, \infty) \mapsto [0, 1]$ *is continuous,*
17. $lim_{t \mapsto \infty} R(l, m, t) = 0$ *(for all* $t > 0$*), and*
18. *if* $t \leqslant 0$, *then* $P(l, m, t) = 0, Q(l, m, t) = 1$ *and* $R(l, m, t) = 1$.

Thus, $\aleph = (P, Q, R)$ is called neutrosophic metric (NM) on $\mathfrak{A}$.

The functions $P(l, m, t), Q(l, m, t), R(l, m, t)$ denote the nearness degree, neutralness degree, and non-nearness degree between l and m with respect to t, respectively. .

Definition 4 ([35]). *Consider an NMS* $(\mathfrak{A}, \aleph, \uplus, \odot)$. *A sequence* $\{a_n\}$ *cgs* $a \in \mathfrak{A}$ *iff, for* $\varepsilon > 0$ *and* $l \in (0, 1)$, $\exists\, m \in \mathbb{N}$ *such that* $\forall\, n \geq m$

$$
\begin{aligned}
&P(a_n, a, \varepsilon) > 1 - l, \\
&Q(a_n, a, \varepsilon) < l, \\
&Q(a_n, a, \varepsilon) < l
\end{aligned}
$$

or alternatively,

$$
\begin{aligned}
&\lim_{n \to \infty} P(a_n, a_m, \varepsilon) = 1, \\
&\lim_{n \to \infty} Q(a_n, a_m, \varepsilon) = 0, \\
&\lim_{n \to \infty} Q(a_n, a_m, \varepsilon) = 0
\end{aligned}
$$

as $\varepsilon \mapsto \infty$.

Definition 5 ([35]). *Consider an NMS* $(\mathfrak{A}, \aleph, \uplus, \odot)$. *A sequence* $\{a_n\}$ *in* $\mathfrak{A}$ *is termed as a Cauchy sequence, if for a given* $l > 0$ *and* $\varepsilon > 0$, $\exists\, n_0 \in \mathbb{N}$ *such that*

$$
P(a_l, a_r, \varepsilon) > 1 - l, \quad Q(a_l, a_r, \varepsilon) < l, \quad R(a_l, a_r, \varepsilon) < l,
$$

for all $l, r \geq n_0$.

Definition 6 ([35]). *If every Cauchy sequence is convergent, then an NMS $(\mathfrak{A}, \aleph, \uplus, \odot)$ is complete.*

In the next section, key definitions and illustrative examples of subcompatibility and subsequential continuity within the framework of NMS are provided. These definitions and examples serve as the groundwork for the theoretical development and will be utilized in later sections to establish fixed point results and demonstrate their applications in solving practical problems within the framework of NMS.

3. Subcompatibility and Subsequential Continuity in NMS

Definition 7. *Let ζ and υ be two maps within NMS $(\mathfrak{A}, \aleph, \uplus, \odot)$. We define ζ and υ as weakly commuting when the following conditions holds: $\mathsf{P}(\zeta\upsilon b, \upsilon\zeta b, \varrho) \geq \mathsf{P}(\zeta b, \upsilon b, \varrho)$, $\mathsf{Q}(\zeta\upsilon b, \upsilon\zeta b, \varrho) \leq \mathsf{Q}(\zeta b, \upsilon b, \varrho)$, $\mathsf{R}(\zeta\upsilon b, \upsilon\zeta b, \varrho) \leq \mathsf{R}(\zeta b, \upsilon b, \varrho)$, for all $b \in \mathfrak{A}$ and $\varrho > 0$.*

Example 3. *Let $\mathfrak{A} = \mathbb{R}$ and consider the NMS $(\mathfrak{A}, \aleph, \uplus, \odot)$, where $\aleph = (\mathsf{P}, \mathsf{Q}, \mathsf{R})$ represents the neutrosophic metric functions given as $\mathsf{P}(\mathfrak{x}, \mathfrak{y}, \varrho) = \frac{\varrho}{1+|\mathfrak{x}-\mathfrak{y}|}$, $\mathsf{Q}(\mathfrak{x}, \mathfrak{y}, \varrho) = \frac{|\mathfrak{x}-\mathfrak{y}|}{1+|\mathfrak{x}-\mathfrak{y}|}$, and $\mathsf{R}(\mathfrak{x}, \mathfrak{y}, \varrho) = 1 - \mathsf{P}(\mathfrak{x}, \mathfrak{y}, \varrho) - \mathsf{Q}(\mathfrak{x}, \mathfrak{y}, \varrho)$. Define the mappings $\zeta, \upsilon : A \to A$ as $\zeta(b) = b + 1$ and $\upsilon(b) = 2b$*

Now, the following conditions are verified: AS $\zeta\upsilon(b) = \zeta(2b) = 2b + 1$ and $\upsilon\zeta(b) = \upsilon(b + 1) = 2(b + 1) = 2b + 2$. Thus,

$$\mathsf{P}(\zeta\upsilon b, \upsilon\zeta b, \varrho) = \frac{\varrho}{1 + |(2b+1) - (2b+2)|} = \frac{\varrho}{1+1} = \frac{\varrho}{2},$$

and

$$\mathsf{P}(\zeta b, \upsilon b, \varrho) = \frac{\varrho}{1 + |(b+1) - (2b)|} = \frac{\varrho}{1 + |b-1|}.$$

Clearly, $\mathsf{P}(\zeta\upsilon b, \upsilon\zeta b, \varrho) \geq \mathsf{P}(\zeta b, \upsilon b, \varrho)$ holds.

$$\mathsf{Q}(\zeta\upsilon b, \upsilon\zeta b, \varrho) = \frac{|(2b+1) - (2b+2)|}{1 + |(2b+1) - (2b+2)|} = \frac{1}{2},$$

and

$$\mathsf{Q}(\zeta b, \upsilon b, \varrho) = \frac{|(b+1) - (2b)|}{1 + |(b+1) - (2b)|} = \frac{|b-1|}{1 + |b-1|}.$$

Clearly, $\mathsf{Q}(\zeta\upsilon b, \upsilon\zeta b, \varrho) \leq \mathsf{Q}(\zeta b, \upsilon b, \varrho)$ holds.

Since $\mathsf{R}(\mathfrak{x}, \mathfrak{y}, \varrho) = 1 - \mathsf{P}(\mathfrak{x}, \mathfrak{y}, \varrho) - \mathsf{Q}(\mathfrak{x}, \mathfrak{y}, \varrho)$, it can be verified that

$$\mathsf{R}(\zeta\upsilon b, \upsilon\zeta b, \varrho) \leq \mathsf{R}(\zeta b, \upsilon b, \varrho).$$

Thus, ζ and υ satisfy all the conditions.

Definition 8. *Assume an NMS $(\mathfrak{A}, \aleph, \uplus, \odot)$. Assume ζ and υ are maps. These maps are compatible, if, for any $\varrho > 0$, the following axioms are fulfilled:*

$$\lim_{n\to\infty} \mathsf{P}(\zeta\upsilon a_n, \upsilon\zeta a_n, \varrho) = 1, \lim_{n\to\infty} \mathsf{Q}(\zeta\upsilon a_n, \upsilon\zeta a_n, \varrho) = 0$$

and

$$\lim_{n\to\infty} \mathsf{R}(\zeta\upsilon a_n, \upsilon\zeta a_n, \varrho) = 0,$$

whenever a sequence $\{a_n\}$ in $\mathfrak{A}$ such that both $\lim_{n\to\infty} \zeta a_n$ and $\lim_{n\to\infty} v a_n$ converge to the same point $\mathsf{b} \in \mathfrak{A}$.

Example 4. *Assume $\mathfrak{A} = \mathbb{R}$ and the maps $\zeta(\mathfrak{x}) = 2\mathfrak{x}$ and $v(\mathfrak{x}) = \frac{\mathfrak{x}}{2}$ for $\mathfrak{x} \in \mathbb{R}$.*
Consider a sequence $\{a_n\}$ defined by $a_n = \frac{1}{n}$. Then for $\varrho > 0$,

$$\mathsf{P}(\zeta v a_n, v\zeta a_n, \varrho) \to 1, \quad \mathsf{Q}(\zeta v a_n, v\zeta a_n, \varrho) \to 0, \quad \textit{and} \quad \mathsf{R}(\zeta v a_n, v\zeta a_n, \varrho) \to 0, \textit{ as } n \to \infty.$$

Also,

$$\lim_{n\to\infty} \zeta a_n = \lim_{n\to\infty} 2 \cdot \frac{1}{n} = 0, \quad \lim_{n\to\infty} v a_n = \lim_{n\to\infty} \frac{1}{2n} = 0.$$

Both mappings ζa_n and $v a_n$ converge to 0. Thus, these maps are compatible in NMS.

Definition 9. *Two mappings ζ and v of an NMS $(\mathfrak{A}, \aleph, \uplus, \odot)$ are called reciprocal continuous if $\zeta v a_n \to \zeta b$ and $v\zeta a_n \to v b$, whenever $\{a_n\}$ is a sequence such that $\zeta a_n, v a_n \to b$ for some b in $\mathfrak{A}$.*

Example 5. *Let $\mathfrak{A} = \mathbb{R}$ and consider the NMS $(\mathfrak{A}, \aleph, \uplus, \odot)$, where*
$\aleph = (\mathsf{P}, \mathsf{Q}, \mathsf{R})$ represents the neutrosophic metric functions given as
$\mathsf{P}(\mathfrak{x}, \mathfrak{y}, \varrho) = \frac{\varrho}{1+|\mathfrak{x}-\mathfrak{y}|}$, $\mathsf{Q}(\mathfrak{x}, \mathfrak{y}, \varrho) = \frac{|\mathfrak{x}-\mathfrak{y}|}{1+|\mathfrak{x}-\mathfrak{y}|}$, and $\mathsf{R}(\mathfrak{x}, \mathfrak{y}, \varrho) = 1 - \mathsf{P}(\mathfrak{x}, \mathfrak{y}, \varrho) - \mathsf{Q}(\mathfrak{x}, \mathfrak{y}, \varrho)$.
Define the mappings $\zeta, v : \mathfrak{A} \to \mathfrak{A}$ as $\zeta(b) = b + 1$ and $v(b) = 2b$
Now, let $\{a_n\}$ be a sequence in $\mathfrak{A}$ such that

$$a_n = \frac{1}{n}, \quad \textit{so that } a_n \to 0 \textit{ as } n \to \infty.$$

Also,

$$\zeta a_n = a_n + 1 = \frac{1}{n} + 1, \quad v a_n = 2a_n = \frac{2}{n}.$$

As $n \to \infty$, both $\zeta a_n \to 1$ and $v a_n \to 0$.
Now, the condition $\zeta a_n, v a_n \to b$ is verified for some $b \in \mathfrak{A}$: Let $b = 0$. For the given sequence $\{a_n\}$, $\zeta a_n \to b + 1 = 1$, and $v a_n \to 2b = 0$, which satisfies the condition.
Now,

$$\zeta v a_n = \zeta(2a_n) = 2a_n + 1 = \frac{2}{n} + 1, \quad v\zeta a_n = v(a_n + 1) = 2(a_n + 1) = \frac{2}{n} + 2.$$

As $n \to \infty$, $\zeta v a_n \to \zeta b = 1$ and $v\zeta a_n \to v b = 0$.
Since both limits are consistent, ζ and v are reciprocal continuous.

Remark 1. *When both ζ and v are continuous, it is evident that they exhibit reciprocal continuity. However, it is important to note that this reciprocity does not guarantee continuity in return. Moreover, within the context of the typical FPT applied to a compatible pair of mappings that satisfy contractive conditions, the continuity of one of the mappings either ζ or v implies their reciprocal continuity, but the converse is not true.*

Example 6. *Let $\mathfrak{A} = \mathbb{R}$, and define NMS $(\mathfrak{A}, \aleph, \uplus, \odot)$ where $\mathsf{P}(\mathfrak{x}, \mathfrak{y}, \varrho) = \frac{\varrho}{1+|\mathfrak{x}-\mathfrak{y}|}$, $\mathsf{Q}(\mathfrak{x}, \mathfrak{y}, \varrho) = \frac{|\mathfrak{x}-\mathfrak{y}|}{1+|\mathfrak{x}-\mathfrak{y}|}$, and $\mathsf{R}(\mathfrak{x}, \mathfrak{y}, \varrho) = 1 - \mathsf{P}(\mathfrak{x}, \mathfrak{y}, \varrho) - \mathsf{Q}(\mathfrak{x}, \mathfrak{y}, \varrho)$. Define $\zeta, v : \mathfrak{A} \to \mathfrak{A}$ mappings as*
$\zeta(\mathfrak{x}) = \mathfrak{x} + 1$ and $v(\mathfrak{x}) = 2\mathfrak{x}$.
Both ζ and v are continuous.
Since both mappings ζ and v are continuous, they will exhibit reciprocal continuity. That is, for any sequence $\{a_n\}$ such that $\zeta a_n \to b$ and $v a_n \to b$ as $n \to \infty$, we will have

$$\zeta v a_n \to \zeta b \quad \textit{and} \quad v\zeta a_n \to v b.$$

For example, if $a_n = \frac{1}{n}$, *then* $\zeta a_n = \frac{1}{n} + 1 \to 1$ *and* $v a_n = \frac{2}{n} \to 0$.

Thus, we have $\zeta v a_n = \zeta(\frac{2}{n}) = \frac{2}{n} + 1 \to 1$ *and* $v\zeta a_n = v\left(\frac{1}{n} + 1\right) = \frac{2}{n} + 2 \to 2$.

Therefore, the mappings satisfy reciprocal continuity.

However, ζ *and* v *are continuous, and this does not guarantee that they will be reciprocal continuous in every case without additional conditions.*

Thus, the continuity of ζ *and* v *ensures their reciprocal continuity, but reciprocal continuity does not necessarily imply continuity for these mappings.*

Definition 10. *Consider an NMS* $(\mathfrak{A}, \aleph, \uplus, \odot)$. *Let* ζ *and* v *be self-maps on the set* $\mathfrak{A}$. *A point* a *within* $\mathfrak{A}$ *is defined as a CP of* ζ *and* v *if and only if* $\zeta(a) = v(a)$. *In such a case, the value* $w = \zeta(a) = v(a)$ *is known as a coincidence point for both* ζ *and* v.

Definition 11. *Consider an NMS denoted as* $(\mathfrak{A}, \aleph, \uplus, \odot)$. *A pair of self-mappings denoted as* (ζ, v) *is said to be WC if it exhibits commutativity at the point of coincidence. In other words, if* $\exists$ *a point* u *in* $\mathfrak{A}$ *such that* $\zeta(\mathrm{u}) = v(\mathrm{u})$, *then* $\zeta(v(\mathrm{u})) = v(\zeta(\mathrm{u}))$.

Example 7. *Let* $\mathfrak{A} = \mathbb{R}$, *and define an NMS* $(\mathfrak{A}, \aleph, \uplus, \odot)$ *where*
$\mathsf{P}(\mathfrak{x}, \mathfrak{y}, \varrho) = \frac{\varrho}{1+|\mathfrak{x}-\mathfrak{y}|}$, $\mathsf{Q}(\mathfrak{x}, \mathfrak{y}, \varrho) = \frac{|\mathfrak{x}-\mathfrak{y}|}{1+|\mathfrak{x}-\mathfrak{y}|}$, *and* $\mathsf{R}(\mathfrak{x}, \mathfrak{y}, \varrho) = 1 - \mathsf{P}(\mathfrak{x}, \mathfrak{y}, \varrho) - \mathsf{Q}(\mathfrak{x}, \mathfrak{y}, \varrho)$.
Define two mappings $\zeta, v : \mathfrak{A} \to \mathfrak{A}$ *as* $\zeta(\mathfrak{x}) = \mathfrak{x} + 2$ *and* $v(\mathfrak{x}) = \mathfrak{x} + 2$. *To check if* (ζ, v) *are weakly compatible, we need to verify if* $\exists$ *a point* $\mathrm{u} \in \mathfrak{A}$ *such that* $\zeta(\mathrm{u}) = v(\mathrm{u})$, *and if so, whether* $\zeta(v(\mathrm{u})) = v(\zeta(\mathrm{u}))$. *Thus, to find* u *where* $\zeta(\mathrm{u}) = v(\mathrm{u})$

$$\zeta(\mathrm{u}) = \mathrm{u} + 2, \quad v(\mathrm{u}) = \mathrm{u} + 2.$$

Clearly, $\zeta(\mathrm{u}) = v(\mathrm{u})$ *for all* $\mathrm{u} \in \mathfrak{A}$, *because both mappings are identical.*

Now commutativity can be verified at u. *For any* $\mathrm{u} \in \mathfrak{A}$,

$$\zeta(v(\mathrm{u})) = \zeta(\mathrm{u} + 2) = (\mathrm{u} + 2) + 2 = \mathrm{u} + 4,$$

and

$$v(\zeta(\mathrm{u})) = v(\mathrm{u} + 2) = (\mathrm{u} + 2) + 2 = \mathrm{u} + 4.$$

Thus, $\zeta(v(\mathrm{u})) = v(\zeta(\mathrm{u}))$ *holds for all* $\mathrm{u} \in \mathfrak{A}$.

Since $\zeta(\mathrm{u}) = v(\mathrm{u})$ *for all* $\mathrm{u} \in \mathfrak{A}$, *and* $\zeta(v(\mathrm{u})) = v(\zeta(\mathrm{u}))$ *for all* $\mathrm{u} \in \mathfrak{A}$, *the pair* (ζ, v) *is weakly compatible.*

Thus, the mappings $\zeta(\mathfrak{x}) = \mathfrak{x} + 2$ *and* $v(\mathfrak{x}) = \mathfrak{x} + 2$ *are weakly compatible because they satisfy the condition of commutativity at the point of coincidence. Specifically, since* $\zeta(\mathrm{u}) = v(\mathrm{u})$ *for all* u, *they exhibit commutativity at every point, satisfying the definition of weak compatibility in an NMS.*

Remark 2. *Two maps that are compatible also satisfy the condition of being weakly compatible, but the reverse statement is not necessarily true.*

Definition 12. *Two self-maps denoted as* ζ *and* v *within the framework of an NMS represented as* $(\mathfrak{A}, \aleph, \uplus, \odot)$ *are termed occasionally weakly compatible (OWC) if* $\exists$ *a point* $a \in \mathfrak{A}$ *that is a coincidence point for both* ζ *and* v, *and at this point both* ζ *and* v *exhibit commutativity.*

Example 8. *Let* $\mathfrak{A} = \mathbb{R}$, *and define an NMS* $(\mathfrak{A}, \aleph, \uplus, \odot)$, *where*
$\mathsf{P}(\mathfrak{x}, \mathfrak{y}, \varrho) = \frac{\varrho}{1+|\mathfrak{x}-\mathfrak{y}|}$, $\mathsf{Q}(\mathfrak{x}, \mathfrak{y}, \varrho) = \frac{|\mathfrak{x}-\mathfrak{y}|}{1+|\mathfrak{x}-\mathfrak{y}|}$, *and* $\mathsf{R}(\mathfrak{x}, \mathfrak{y}, \varrho) = 1 - \mathsf{P}(\mathfrak{x}, \mathfrak{y}, \varrho) - \mathsf{Q}(\mathfrak{x}, \mathfrak{y}, \varrho)$.

Define two mappings $\zeta, v : \mathfrak{A} \to \mathfrak{A}$ *as* $\zeta(\mathfrak{x}) = \mathfrak{x} + 1$ *and* $v(\mathfrak{x}) = \mathfrak{x} + 1$.

Now,

$$\zeta(a) = a + 1, \quad v(a) = a + 1.$$

Clearly, $\zeta(a) = v(a)$ *for all* $a \in \mathfrak{A}$*, so every* $a \in \mathfrak{A}$ *is a coincidence point.*

Again, for any $a \in \mathfrak{A}$*,*

$$\zeta(v(a)) = \zeta(a+1) = (a+1)+1 = a+2,$$

and

$$v(\zeta(a)) = v(a+1) = (a+1)+1 = a+2.$$

Since $\zeta(v(a)) = v(\zeta(a))$*,* ζ *and* v *exhibit commutativity at every coincidence point.*

Thus, both maps are OWC.

Definition 13. *Consider an NMS* $(\mathfrak{A}, \aleph, \uplus, \odot)$*, self-maps* ζ *and* v *on the set* $\mathfrak{A}$ *are defined to be subcompatible if* $\exists$ *a sequence* $\{a_n\}$ *in* $\mathfrak{A}$ *such that* $\lim_{n\to\infty} \zeta a_n = \lim_{n\to\infty} v a_n = b, b \in \mathfrak{A}$ *and satisfy* $\lim_{n\to\infty} \mathsf{P}(\zeta v a_n, v\zeta a_n, \varrho) = 1, \lim_{n\to\infty} \mathsf{Q}(\zeta v a_n, v\zeta a_n, \varrho) = 0, \lim_{n\to\infty} \mathsf{R}(\zeta v a_n, v\zeta a_n, \varrho) = 0.$

Example 9. *Consider the set* $\mathfrak{A} = [0,1]$*, and define the neutrosophic metric functions* $\mathsf{P}, \mathsf{Q}, \mathsf{R} : \mathfrak{A} \times \mathfrak{A} \times [0,\infty) \to [0,1]$ *as follows:*

$\mathsf{P}(\mathfrak{x}, \mathfrak{y}, \varrho) = 1 - |\mathfrak{x} - \mathfrak{y}|, \mathsf{Q}(\mathfrak{x}, \mathfrak{y}, \varrho) = |\mathfrak{x} - \mathfrak{y}|, \mathsf{R}(\mathfrak{x}, \mathfrak{y}, \varrho) = |\mathfrak{x} - \mathfrak{y}|.$

Let the operations $\uplus$ *and* $\odot$ *be defined as the standard addition and multiplication on* $[0,1]$ *modulo 1, respectively.*

Define the self-maps ζ *and* v *on* A *as* $\zeta(\mathfrak{x}) = \frac{\mathfrak{x}}{2}$ *and* $v(\mathfrak{x}) = \frac{\mathfrak{x}}{3}$*.*

Now, take the sequence $\{a_n\}$ *in* $\mathfrak{A}$ *as* $a_n = \frac{1}{n}$ *for* $n \geq 1$*.*

Now, convergence of ζa_n *and* $v a_n$ *can be verified:* $\zeta(a_n) = \frac{1}{2n}$ *and* $v(a_n) = \frac{1}{3n}$*.*

As $n \to \infty$*,* $\lim_{n\to\infty} \zeta(a_n) = 0$ *and* $\lim_{n\to\infty} v(a_n) = 0$*.*

Thus, $\lim_{n\to\infty} \zeta(a_n) = \lim_{n\to\infty} v(a_n) = b = 0$*, where* $b \in \mathfrak{A}$*.*

Now, subcompatibility conditions can be evaluated:

$\zeta v(a_n) = \zeta\left(\frac{1}{3n}\right) = \frac{1}{6n}$ *and* $v\zeta(a_n) = v\left(\frac{1}{2n}\right) = \frac{1}{6n}$*.*

Thus,

$\lim_{n\to\infty} \mathsf{P}(\zeta v(a_n), v\zeta(a_n), \varrho) = 1 - \left|\frac{1}{6n} - \frac{1}{6n}\right| = 1$, $\lim_{n\to\infty} \mathsf{Q}(\zeta v(a_n), v\zeta(a_n), \varrho) = \left|\frac{1}{6n} - \frac{1}{6n}\right| = 0$*, and* $\lim_{n\to\infty} \mathsf{R}(\zeta v(a_n), v\zeta(a_n), \varrho) = \left|\frac{1}{6n} - \frac{1}{6n}\right| = 0$*.*

Thus, the maps ζ *and* v *satisfy the conditions for subcompatibility in the neutrosophic metric space* $(\mathfrak{A}, \aleph, \uplus, \odot)$ *with the given sequence* $\{a_n\}$*.*

Thus, it is evident that two occasionally weakly compatible maps are also subcompatible, but the reverse statement is not always true. The example provided below illustrates that there can be instances of subcompatible maps that do not qualify as occasionally weakly compatible (OWC).

Example 10. *Consider an MS* $(\mathfrak{A}, d)$*, where* d *is defined as* $d(\varkappa, \varsigma) = |\varkappa - \varsigma|$*,* $\varkappa, \varsigma \in A = [0,\infty)$ *and, for any positive value* $\varrho \in (0,\infty)$*, we have the operators* $\uplus$ *and* $\odot$ *defined as follows: The TN operator is denoted by* $\uplus$ *with its default operation being the minimum, i.e., TN* $\mathfrak{x} \uplus \mathfrak{y} = \min(\mathfrak{x}, \mathfrak{y})$*, and the TC operator is denoted by* $\odot$ *with its default operation being the maximum, i.e., TC* $\mathfrak{x} \odot \mathfrak{y} = \max(\mathfrak{x}, \mathfrak{y})$*. Define*

$\mathsf{P}(\varkappa, \varsigma, \varrho) = \{ \begin{array}{cc} \frac{\varrho}{\varrho + |\varkappa - \varsigma|} & \varrho > 0 \\ 0 & \varrho = 0 \end{array}$, $\mathsf{Q}(\varkappa, \varsigma, \varrho) = \{ \begin{array}{cc} \frac{\varkappa - \varsigma}{\varrho + |\varkappa - \varsigma|} & \varrho > 0 \\ 1 & \varrho = 1 \end{array}$ *and* $\mathsf{R}(\varkappa, \varsigma, \varrho) = \{ \begin{array}{cc} \frac{|\varkappa - \varsigma|}{\varrho} & \varrho > 0 \\ 0 & \varrho = 0 \end{array}$*. Clearly,* $(\mathfrak{A}, \aleph, \uplus, \odot)$ *is a complete NMS.*

Define ζ and υ as follows:

$$\zeta(\varkappa) = \varkappa^2 \text{ and } \upsilon(\varkappa) = \begin{cases} \varkappa+2 & \varkappa \in [0,4] \uplus (9,\infty) \\ \varkappa+12 & \varkappa \in (4,9] \end{cases}.$$

Consider the sequence $\{\varkappa_n\}$ in set $\mathfrak{A}$ defined as $\varkappa_n = 2 + \frac{1}{n}$ for $n = 1,2,3,\ldots$.

As n approaches infinity, the limits are as follows:

- $\lim_{n\to\infty} \zeta\varkappa_n = \lim_{n\to\infty} \upsilon\varkappa_n = 4$, *so 4 is an element of set $\mathfrak{A}$.*
- *Additionally, $\zeta\upsilon\varkappa_n$ approaches 16 and $\upsilon\zeta$ also tends to 16 as n approaches infinity.*

Thus, $\lim_{n\to\infty} \mathsf{P}(\zeta\upsilon\varkappa_n, \upsilon\zeta\varkappa_n, \varrho) = 1, \lim_{n\to\infty} \mathsf{Q}(\zeta\upsilon\varkappa_n, \upsilon\zeta\varkappa_n, \varrho) = 0$ *and* $\lim_{n\to\infty} \mathsf{R}(\zeta\upsilon\varkappa_n, \upsilon\zeta\varkappa_n, \varrho) = 0$.

Thus, the subcompatibility of ζ and υ is proved. However, $\zeta\varkappa = \upsilon\varkappa$ if and only if $\varkappa = 2$ and $\zeta\upsilon(2) \neq \upsilon\zeta(2)$. Therefore, ζ and υ do not satisfy the OWC property.

Our next goal is to introduce the concept of subsequential continuity within the framework of NMS. This concept is more relaxed than the previously established notion of reciprocal continuity, which was firstly given by Pant [36]. A similar notion was also introduced by H. Boudhadjera [20] within the framework of MS.

Definition 14. *Let $(\mathfrak{A}, \aleph, \uplus, \odot)$ be NMS. Self-maps ζ and υ defined on the set $\mathfrak{A}$ are called subsequentially continuous iff $\exists$ a sequence $\{a_n\}$ in $\mathfrak{A}$ such that $\lim_{n\to\infty} \zeta a_n = \lim_{n\to\infty} \upsilon a_n = b, b \in \mathfrak{A}$ and satisfy $\lim_{n\to\infty} \zeta\upsilon a_n = \zeta b, \lim_{n\to\infty} \upsilon\zeta a_n = \upsilon b$.*

It is evident that, if both ζ and υ are continuous or reciprocally continuous, then they are subsequentially continuous. However, the subsequent example demonstrates that $\exists$ pairs of maps that are subsequentially continuous, but do not meet the criteria of being continuous or reciprocally continuous.

Example 11. *Consider an MS $(\mathfrak{A}, d)$, where the metric d is defined as $d(\varkappa, \varsigma) = |\varkappa - \varsigma|$. For any elements $\varkappa$ and ς in $\mathfrak{A} = [0,\infty)$ and for any positive value $\varrho \in (0,\infty)$, we have the operators $\uplus$ and $\odot$ defined as follows:*

TN $\mathsf{x} \uplus \mathsf{y} = \min.(\mathsf{x},\mathsf{y})$ *and TC* $\mathsf{x} \odot \mathsf{y} = \max.(\mathsf{x},\mathsf{y})$. *Define*

$$\mathsf{P}(\varkappa,\varsigma,\varrho) = \begin{cases} \frac{\varrho}{\varrho+|\varkappa-\varsigma|} & \varrho > 0 \\ 0 & \varrho = 0 \end{cases}, \mathsf{Q}(\varkappa,\varsigma,\varrho) = \begin{cases} \frac{\varkappa-\varsigma}{\varrho+|\varkappa-\varsigma|} & \varrho > 0 \\ 1 & \varrho = 1 \end{cases} \text{ and } \mathsf{R}(\varkappa,\varsigma,\varrho) =$$

$$\begin{cases} \frac{|\varkappa-\varsigma|}{\varrho} & \varrho > 0 \\ 0 & \varrho = 0 \end{cases}.$$ *Clearly, $(\mathfrak{A}, \aleph, \uplus, \odot)$ is a complete NMS.*

Define ζ and υ as follows: $$\zeta(\varkappa) = \begin{cases} 1+\varkappa & \varkappa \in [0,1] \\ 2\varkappa-1 & \varkappa \in [1,\infty). \end{cases}$$

and $$\upsilon(\varkappa) = \begin{cases} 1-\varkappa & \varkappa \in [0,1] \\ 3\varkappa-2 & \varkappa \in [1,\infty). \end{cases}$$ *Clearly ζ and υ are discontinuous at $\varkappa = 1$.*

Consider the sequence $\{\varkappa_n\}$ in set $\mathfrak{A}$, defined as $\varkappa_n = \frac{1}{n}$ for $n = 1,2,3,\ldots$.

As n approaches infinity, the limits are as follows:

- $\lim_{n\to\infty} \zeta\varkappa_n = \lim_{n\to\infty} \upsilon\varkappa_n = 1$, *so 1 is an element of set $\mathfrak{A}$.*
- *Additionally, $\zeta\upsilon\varkappa_n$ approaches 2 (which is $\zeta(1)$) and $\upsilon\zeta$ also tends to 1 (which is $\upsilon(1)$) as n approaches infinity.*

Therefore, ζ and υ exhibit subsequential continuity.

Now, consider the sequence $\{\varkappa_n\}$ in set $\mathfrak{A}$ defined as $\varkappa_n = 1 + \frac{1}{n}$ for $n = 1,2,3,\ldots$. In this case, as n approaches infinity for the sequence $\{\varkappa_n\}$ in set $\mathfrak{A}$, defined as $\varkappa_n = 1 + \frac{1}{n}$ for $n = 1,2,3,\ldots$:

$\lim_{n\to\infty} \zeta\varkappa_n = \lim_{n\to\infty} \upsilon\varkappa_n = 1$, *so 1 is an element of set $\mathfrak{A}$. However, $\zeta\upsilon\varkappa_n$ approaches 1 (which is $\zeta(1)$), not 2.*

As a result, when n approaches infinity, ζ and v do not exhibit reciprocal continuity as $\zeta v \varkappa_n$ does not converge to $\zeta(1)$.

Lemma 1. *Consider the sequence $\{u_n\}$ within the NMS $(\mathfrak{A}, \aleph, \uplus, \odot)$. If $\exists$ a constant k in the open interval $(0,1)$ such that*

$$\mathsf{P}(u_n, u_{n+1}, k\varrho) \geq \mathsf{P}(u_{n-1}, u_n, \varrho), \mathsf{Q}(u_n, u_{n+1}, k\varrho) \leq \mathsf{Q}(u_{n-1}, u_n, \varrho)$$

and

$$\mathsf{R}(u_n, u_{n+1}, k\varrho) \leq \mathsf{R}(u_{n-1,u_n,\varrho}),$$

$\forall \varrho > 0$ and $n = 1,2,3....$ Then $\{u_n\}$ is a Cauchy sequence in $\mathfrak{A}$.

Proof. Consider the following conditions: $\mathsf{P}(u_n, u_{n+1}, k\varrho) \geq \mathsf{P}(u_{n-1}, u_n, \varrho)$, $\mathsf{Q}(u_n, u_{n+1}, k\varrho) \leq \mathsf{Q}(u_{n-1}, u_n, \varrho)$, and $\mathsf{R}(u_n, u_{n+1}, k\varrho) \leq \mathsf{R}(u_{n-1}, u_n, \varrho)$.

These imply that
$\{\mathsf{P}(u_n, u_{n+1}, k\varrho)\}$ is a non-decreasing sequence bounded above by 1, and
$\{\mathsf{Q}(u_n, u_{n+1}, k\varrho)\}$ and $\{\mathsf{R}(u_n, u_{n+1}, k\varrho)\}$ are non-increasing sequences bounded below by 0.

By the monotone convergence theorem,

$$\mathsf{P}(u_n, u_{n+1}, k\varrho) \to l_{\mathsf{P}}, \quad \mathsf{Q}(u_n, u_{n+1}, k\varrho) \to l_{\mathsf{Q}}, \quad \mathsf{R}(u_n, u_{n+1}, k\varrho) \to l_{\mathsf{R}},$$

where $l_{\mathsf{P}} \in [0,1]$, $l_{\mathsf{Q}} \in [0,1]$, and $l_{\mathsf{R}} \in [0,1]$.

Additionally, for $m > n$, using the properties of the neutrosophic metric, we have

$$\mathsf{P}(u_m, u_n, \varrho) \geq \mathsf{P}(u_{m-1}, u_m, k^{m-n}\varrho),$$

$$\mathsf{Q}(u_m, u_n, \varrho) \leq \mathsf{Q}(u_{m-1}, u_m, k^{m-n}\varrho),$$

$$\mathsf{R}(u_m, u_n, \varrho) \leq \mathsf{R}(u_{m-1}, u_m, k^{m-n}\varrho).$$

$\Longrightarrow$

$$\mathsf{P}(u_{m-1}, u_m, k^{m-n}\varrho) \to l_{\mathsf{P}}, \quad \mathsf{Q}(u_{m-1}, u_m, k^{m-n}\varrho) \to l_{\mathsf{Q}}, \quad \mathsf{R}(u_{m-1}, u_m, k^{m-n}\varrho) \to l_{\mathsf{R}},$$

as $m, n \to \infty$.

Additionally, for $\epsilon > 0$, N is chosen such that, for all $m, n \geq N$,

$$\mathsf{P}(u_{m-1}, u_m, k^{m-n}\varrho) > 1 - \epsilon, \quad \mathsf{Q}(u_{m-1}, u_m, k^{m-n}\varrho) < \epsilon, \quad \mathsf{R}(u_{m-1}, u_m, k^{m-n}\varrho) < \epsilon.$$

By the triangle inequality,

$$\mathsf{P}(u_m, u_n, \varrho) \to 1, \quad \mathsf{Q}(u_m, u_n, \varrho) \to 0, \quad \mathsf{R}(u_m, u_n, \varrho) \to 0.$$

Thus, $\{u_n\}$ is a Cauchy sequence in $\mathfrak{A}$. □

Lemma 2. *Consider the NMS denoted as $(\mathfrak{A}, \aleph, \uplus, \odot)$. For all elements $\mathfrak{a}$ and $\mathfrak{b}$ belonging to $\mathfrak{A}$ as well as for any positive number ϱ, if $\exists$ a constant k in $(0,1)$, such that*

$$\mathsf{P}(\mathfrak{a}, \mathfrak{b}, k\varrho) \geq \mathsf{P}(\mathfrak{a}, \mathfrak{b}, \varrho), \mathsf{Q}(\mathfrak{a}, \mathfrak{b}, k\varrho) \leq \mathsf{Q}(\mathfrak{a}, \mathfrak{b}, \varrho), \mathsf{R}(\mathfrak{a}, \mathfrak{b}, k\varrho) \leq \mathsf{R}(\mathfrak{a}, \mathfrak{b}, \varrho),$$

then $\mathfrak{a} = \mathfrak{b}$.

Proof. If $\mathsf{P}(\mathfrak{a},\mathfrak{b},k\varrho) \geq \mathsf{P}(\mathfrak{a},\mathfrak{b},\varrho)$, $\mathsf{Q}(\mathfrak{a},\mathfrak{b},k\varrho) \leq \mathsf{Q}(\mathfrak{a},\mathfrak{b},\varrho)$ and $\mathsf{R}(\mathfrak{a},\mathfrak{b},k\varrho) \leq \mathsf{R}(\mathfrak{a},\mathfrak{b},\varrho)$ for all $t > 0$ and some constant $0 < k < 1$, then

$$\mathsf{P}(\mathfrak{a},\mathfrak{b},\mathfrak{s}) \geq \mathsf{P}\left(\mathfrak{a},\mathfrak{b},\frac{\mathfrak{s}}{k}\right) \geq \mathsf{P}\left(\mathfrak{a},\mathfrak{b},\frac{\mathfrak{s}}{k^2}\right) \geq \cdots \geq \mathsf{P}\left(\mathfrak{a},\mathfrak{b},\frac{\mathfrak{s}}{k^n}\right),$$

$$\mathsf{Q}(\mathfrak{a},\mathfrak{b},\mathfrak{s}) \leq \mathsf{Q}\left(\mathfrak{a},\mathfrak{b},\frac{\mathfrak{s}}{k}\right) \leq \mathsf{Q}\left(\mathfrak{a},\mathfrak{b},\frac{\mathfrak{s}}{k^2}\right) \leq \cdots \leq \mathsf{Q}\left(\mathfrak{a},\mathfrak{b},\frac{\mathfrak{s}}{k^n}\right)$$

and

$$\mathsf{R}(\mathfrak{a},\mathfrak{b},\mathfrak{s}) \leq \mathsf{R}\left(\mathfrak{a},\mathfrak{b},\frac{\mathfrak{s}}{k}\right) \leq \mathsf{R}\left(\mathfrak{a},\mathfrak{b},\frac{\mathfrak{s}}{k^2}\right) \leq \cdots \leq \mathsf{R}\left(\mathfrak{a},\mathfrak{b},\frac{\mathfrak{s}}{k^n}\right)$$

for all $\mathfrak{s} > 0$ and $\mathfrak{a},\mathfrak{b} \in \mathfrak{A}$. Letting $n \to \infty$, we have $\mathsf{P}(\mathfrak{a},\mathfrak{b},\mathfrak{s}) = 1$, $\mathsf{Q}(\mathfrak{a},\mathfrak{b},\mathfrak{s}) = 0$, and $\mathsf{R}(\mathfrak{a},\mathfrak{b},\mathfrak{s}) = 0$, so

$$\mathfrak{a} = \mathfrak{b}.$$

□

Now, we move forward to formulate the main theorem by leveraging the concepts of subcompatible and subsequentially continuous maps. These definitions, introduced earlier, form the basis for deriving significant fixed point results in NMS.

4. Result and Discussion

Theorem 1. *Consider four self-maps ζ, ψ, υ and τ of NMS $(\mathfrak{A}, \aleph, \uplus, \odot)$ with continuous TN $\uplus$ and continuous TC $\odot$ defined by $\varrho \uplus \varrho \geq \varrho$ and $(1-\varrho) \odot (1-\varrho) \leq (1-\varrho)$ $\forall \varrho \in [0,1]$. If the pairs (ζ, υ) and (ψ, τ) are both compatible and subsequentially continuous, then the following holds:*

1. *ζ and υ possess a CP.*
2. *ψ and τ possess a CP.*
3. *Let $\forall a, b \in A$, with $k \in (0,1)$ and $\varrho > 0$,*

$$\begin{aligned}
\mathsf{P}(\zeta a, \psi b, k\varrho) \geq{}& \mathsf{P}(\upsilon a, \tau b, \varrho) \uplus \mathsf{P}(\zeta a, \upsilon a, \varrho) \uplus \mathsf{P}(\psi b, \tau b, \varrho) \uplus \mathsf{P}(\psi b, \upsilon a, 2\varrho) \\
&\uplus \mathsf{P}(\zeta a, \tau b, \varrho), \\
\mathsf{Q}(\zeta a, \psi b, k\varrho) \leq{}& \mathsf{Q}(\upsilon a, \tau b, \varrho) \odot \mathsf{Q}(\zeta a, \upsilon a, \varrho) \odot \mathsf{Q}(\psi b, \tau b, \varrho) \odot \mathsf{Q}(\psi b, \upsilon a, 2\varrho) \\
&\odot \mathsf{Q}(\zeta a, \tau b, \varrho), \\
\mathsf{R}(\zeta a, \psi b, k\varrho) \leq{}& \mathsf{R}(\upsilon a, \tau b, \varrho) \odot \mathsf{R}(\zeta a, \upsilon a, \varrho) \odot \mathsf{R}(\psi b, \tau b, \varrho) \odot \mathsf{R}(\psi b, \upsilon a, 2\varrho) \\
&\odot \mathsf{R}(\zeta a, \tau b, \varrho).
\end{aligned}$$

Thus, ζ, ψ, τ and υ have a unique CFP.

Proof. Given that (ζ, υ) and (ψ, τ) are both subcompatible and subsequentially continuous, it follows that there are two sequences denoted as $\{a_n\}$ and $\{b_n\}$ within the set $\mathfrak{A}$ such that $\lim_{n\to\infty} \zeta a_n = \lim_{n\to\infty} \upsilon a_n = c, c \in A$, which satisfies

$$\lim_{n\to\infty} \mathsf{P}(\zeta \upsilon a_n, \upsilon \zeta a_n, \varrho) = \mathsf{P}(\zeta c, \upsilon c, \varrho) = 1,$$

$$\lim_{n\to\infty} \mathsf{Q}(\zeta \upsilon a_n, \upsilon \zeta a_n, \varrho) = \mathsf{Q}(\zeta c, \upsilon c, \varrho) = 0$$

and

$$\lim_{n\to\infty} \mathsf{R}(\zeta \upsilon a_n, \upsilon \zeta a_n, \varrho) = \mathsf{R}(\zeta c, \upsilon c, \varrho) = 0.$$

Additionally, $\lim_{n\to\infty}\psi b_n = \lim_{n\to\infty}\tau b_n = c', c' \in A$, which satisfies

$$\lim_{n\to\infty} \mathsf{P}(\psi\tau b_n, \tau\psi b_n, \varrho) = \mathsf{P}(\psi c', \tau c', \varrho) = 1,$$
$$\lim_{n\to\infty} \mathsf{Q}(\psi\tau b_n, \tau\psi b_n, \varrho) = \mathsf{Q}(\psi c', \tau c', \varrho) = 0$$

and

$$\lim_{n\to\infty} \mathsf{R}(\psi\tau b_n, \tau\psi b_n, \varrho) = \mathsf{R}(\psi c', \tau c', \varrho) = 0.$$

Therefore, $\zeta c = \upsilon c$ and $\psi c' = \tau c'$, i.e., c is a CP of ζ and υ and c' is a CP of ψ and τ.

Now, we will prove that $c = c'$. By condition (3), we have taken $a = a_n$ and $b = b_n$,

$$\begin{aligned}\mathsf{P}(\zeta a_n, \psi b_n, k\varrho) &\geq \mathsf{P}(\upsilon a_n, \tau b_n, \varrho) \uplus \mathsf{P}(\zeta a_n, \upsilon a_n, \varrho) \uplus \mathsf{P}(\psi b_n, \tau b_n, \varrho) \uplus \mathsf{P}(\psi b_n, \upsilon a_n, 2\varrho) \\ &\uplus \mathsf{P}(\zeta a_n, \tau b_n, \varrho), \\ \mathsf{Q}(\zeta a_n, \psi b_n, k\varrho) &\leq \mathsf{Q}(\upsilon a_n, \tau b_n, \varrho) \odot \mathsf{Q}(\zeta a_n, \upsilon a_n, \varrho) \odot \mathsf{Q}(\psi b_n, \tau b_n, \varrho) \odot \mathsf{Q}(\psi b_n, \upsilon a_n, 2\varrho) \\ &\odot \mathsf{Q}(\zeta a_n, \tau b_n, \varrho)\end{aligned}$$

and

$$\begin{aligned}\mathsf{R}(\zeta a_n, \psi b_n, k\varrho) &\leq \mathsf{R}(\upsilon a_n, \tau b_n, \varrho) \odot \mathsf{R}(\zeta a_n, \upsilon a_n, \varrho) \odot \mathsf{R}(\psi b_n, \tau b_n, \varrho) \odot \mathsf{R}(\psi b_n, \upsilon a_n, 2\varrho) \\ &\odot \mathsf{R}(\zeta a_n, \tau b_n, \varrho).\end{aligned}$$

Assuming the limit is $n \to \infty$, we have

$$\mathsf{P}(c, c', k\varrho) \geq \mathsf{P}(c, c', \varrho) \uplus \mathsf{P}(c, c, \varrho) \uplus \mathsf{P}(c', c', \varrho) \uplus \mathsf{P}(c', c, 2\varrho) \uplus \mathsf{P}(c, c', \varrho),$$
$$\mathsf{Q}(c, c', k\varrho) \leq \mathsf{Q}(c, c', \varrho) \odot \mathsf{Q}(c, c, \varrho) \odot \mathsf{Q}(c', c', \varrho) \odot \mathsf{Q}(c', c, 2\varrho) \odot \mathsf{Q}(c, c', \varrho)$$

and

$$\mathsf{R}(c, c', k\varrho) \leq \mathsf{R}(c, c', \varrho) \odot \mathsf{R}(c, c, \varrho) \odot \mathsf{R}(c', c', \varrho) \odot \mathsf{R}(c', c, 2\varrho) \odot \mathsf{R}(c, c', \varrho).$$

$$\Longrightarrow \mathsf{P}(c, c', k\varrho) \geq \mathsf{P}(c, c', \varrho), \mathsf{Q}(c, c', k\varrho) \leq \mathsf{Q}(c, c', \varrho)$$

and

$$\mathsf{R}(c, c', k\varrho) \leq \mathsf{R}(c, c', \varrho).$$

By Lemma 2, we have $c = c'$.

Furthermore, we will prove that $\zeta c = c$. To establish this claim, we utilize inequality (3) by selecting $a = c$ and $b = b_n$. This gives

$$\begin{aligned}\mathsf{P}(\zeta c, \psi b_n, k\varrho) &\geq \mathsf{P}(\upsilon c, \tau b_n, \varrho) \uplus \mathsf{P}(\zeta c, \upsilon c, \varrho) \uplus \mathsf{P}(\psi b_n, \tau b_n, \varrho) \uplus \mathsf{P}(\psi b_n, \upsilon c, 2\varrho) \\ &\uplus \mathsf{P}(\zeta c, \tau b_n, \varrho), \\ \mathsf{Q}(\zeta c, \psi b_n, k\varrho) &\leq \mathsf{Q}(\upsilon c, \tau b_n, \varrho) \odot \mathsf{Q}(\zeta c, \upsilon c, \varrho) \odot \mathsf{Q}(\psi b_n, \tau b_n, \varrho) \odot \mathsf{Q}(\psi b_n, \upsilon c, 2\varrho) \\ &\odot \mathsf{Q}(\zeta c, \tau b_n, \varrho)\end{aligned}$$

and

$$\begin{aligned}\mathsf{R}(\zeta c, \psi b_n, k\varrho) &\leq \mathsf{R}(\upsilon c, \tau b_n, \varrho) \odot \mathsf{R}(\zeta c, \upsilon c, \varrho) \odot \mathsf{R}(\psi b_n, \tau b_n, \varrho) \odot \mathsf{R}(\psi b_n, \upsilon c, 2\varrho) \\ &\odot \mathsf{R}(\zeta c, \tau b_n, \varrho).\end{aligned}$$

Assuming the limit is $n \to \infty$, one can obtain

$$\begin{aligned}\mathsf{P}(\zeta c, c', k\varrho) &\geq \mathsf{P}(\zeta c, c', \varrho) \uplus \mathsf{P}(\zeta c, \zeta c, \varrho) \uplus \mathsf{P}(c', c', \varrho) \uplus \mathsf{P}(c', \zeta c, 2\varrho)\\ &\quad \uplus \mathsf{P}(\zeta c, c', \varrho),\\ \mathsf{Q}(\zeta c, c', k\varrho) &\leq \mathsf{Q}(\zeta c, c', \varrho) \odot \mathsf{Q}(\zeta c, \zeta c, \varrho) \odot \mathsf{Q}(c', c', \varrho) \odot \mathsf{Q}(c', \zeta c, 2\varrho)\\ &\quad \odot \mathsf{Q}(\zeta c, c', \varrho)\end{aligned}$$

and

$$\begin{aligned}\mathsf{R}(\zeta c, c', k\varrho) &\leq \mathsf{R}(\zeta c, c', \varrho) \odot \mathsf{R}(\zeta c, \zeta c, \varrho) \odot \mathsf{R}(c', c', \varrho) \odot \mathsf{R}(c', \zeta c, 2\varrho)\\ &\quad \odot \mathsf{R}(\zeta c, c', \varrho).\end{aligned}$$

$$\implies \mathsf{P}(\zeta c, c', k\varrho) \geq \mathsf{P}(\zeta c, c', \varrho), \mathsf{Q}(\zeta c, c', k\varrho) \leq \mathsf{Q}(\zeta c, c', \varrho),$$

and

$$\mathsf{R}(\zeta c, c', k\varrho) \leq \mathsf{R}(\zeta c, c', \varrho).$$

By Lemma 2, we have $\zeta c = c' = c$.

Again, we claim that $\psi c = c$. By inequality (3) of Theorem 1, assuming $a = c$ and $b = c$, we obtain

$$\begin{aligned}\mathsf{P}(\zeta c, \psi c, k\varrho) &\geq \mathsf{P}(\upsilon c, \tau c, \varrho) \uplus \mathsf{P}(\zeta c, \upsilon c, \varrho) \uplus \mathsf{P}(\psi c, \tau c, \varrho) \uplus \mathsf{P}(\psi c, \upsilon c, 2\varrho)\\ &\quad \uplus \mathsf{P}(\zeta c, \tau c, \varrho),\\ \mathsf{Q}(\zeta c, \psi c, k\varrho) &\leq \mathsf{Q}(\upsilon c, \tau c, \varrho) \odot \mathsf{Q}(\zeta c, \upsilon c, \varrho) \odot \mathsf{Q}(\psi c, \tau c, \varrho) \odot \mathsf{Q}(\psi c, \upsilon c, 2\varrho)\\ &\quad \odot \mathsf{Q}(\zeta c, \tau c, \varrho)\end{aligned}$$

and

$$\begin{aligned}\mathsf{R}(\zeta c, \psi c, k\varrho) &\leq \mathsf{R}(\upsilon c, \tau c, \varrho) \odot \mathsf{R}(\zeta c, \upsilon c, \varrho) \odot \mathsf{R}(\psi c, \tau c, \varrho) \odot \mathsf{R}(\psi c, \upsilon c, 2\varrho)\\ &\quad \odot \mathsf{R}(\zeta c, \tau c, \varrho).\end{aligned}$$

$$\begin{aligned}\implies \mathsf{P}(c, \psi c, k\varrho) &\geq \mathsf{P}(c, \psi c, \varrho) \uplus \mathsf{P}(\zeta c, \zeta c, \varrho) \uplus \mathsf{P}(\psi c, \psi c, \varrho) \uplus \mathsf{P}(\psi c, c, 2\varrho)\\ &\quad \uplus \mathsf{P}(c, \psi c, \varrho),\\ \mathsf{Q}(c, \psi c, k\varrho) &\leq \mathsf{Q}(c, \psi c, \varrho) \odot \mathsf{Q}(\zeta c, \zeta c, \varrho) \odot \mathsf{Q}(\psi c, \psi c, \varrho) \odot \mathsf{Q}(\psi c, c, 2\varrho)\\ &\quad \odot \mathsf{Q}(c, \psi c, \varrho)\end{aligned}$$

and

$$\begin{aligned}\mathsf{R}(c, \psi c, k\varrho) &\leq \mathsf{R}(c, \psi c, \varrho) \odot \mathsf{R}(\zeta c, \zeta c, \varrho) \odot \mathsf{R}(\psi c, \psi c, \varrho) \odot \mathsf{R}(\psi c, c, 2\varrho)\\ &\quad \odot \mathsf{R}(c, \psi c, \varrho).\end{aligned}$$

By Lemma 2, we have $c = \psi c = \tau c$.

Therefore, $c = \zeta c = \psi c = \upsilon c = \tau c$; i.e., c is a common FP of ζ, ψ, υ and τ.

Uniqueness: Now suppose $\exists$ another FP w of ζ, ψ, υ and τ.

Under condition (3) of Theorem 1, if we set $a = c$ and $b = w$, we obtain,

$$\begin{aligned}\mathsf{P}(\zeta c, \psi w, k\varrho) &\geq \mathsf{P}(\upsilon c, \tau w, \varrho) \uplus \mathsf{P}(\zeta c, \upsilon c, \varrho) \uplus \mathsf{P}(\psi w, \tau w, \varrho) \uplus \mathsf{P}(\psi w, \upsilon c, 2\varrho)\\ &\quad \uplus \mathsf{P}(\zeta c, \tau w, \varrho),\\ \mathsf{Q}(\zeta c, \psi w, k\varrho) &\leq \mathsf{Q}(\upsilon c, \tau w, \varrho) \odot \mathsf{Q}(\zeta c, \upsilon c, \varrho) \odot \mathsf{Q}(\psi w, \tau w, \varrho) \odot \mathsf{Q}(\psi w, \upsilon c, 2\varrho)\\ &\quad \odot \mathsf{Q}(\zeta c, \tau w, \varrho)\end{aligned}$$

and

$$R(\zeta c, \psi w, k\varrho) \leq R(vc, \tau w, \varrho) \odot R(\zeta c, vc, \varrho) \odot R(\psi w, \tau w, \varrho) \odot R(\psi w, vc, 2\varrho)$$
$$\odot R(\zeta c, \tau w, \varrho).$$
$$\Longrightarrow P(c, w, k\varrho) \geq P(c, w, \varrho), Q(c, w, k\varrho) \leq Q(c, w, \varrho)$$

and

$$R(c, w, k\varrho) \leq R(c, w, \varrho).$$

Therefore, in accordance with Lemma 2, it can be concluded that $c = w$.

When we substitute $v = \tau$ in the above theorem, the following result emerges. □

Corollary 1. *Let us consider three self-maps ζ, ψ, and v of NMS $(\mathfrak{A}, \aleph, \uplus, \odot)$ with continuous TN $\uplus$ and continuous TC $\odot$ defined by $\varrho \uplus \varrho \geq \varrho$ and $(1-\varrho) \odot (1-\varrho) \leq (1-\varrho)$ $\forall \varrho \in [0,1]$. If the pairs (ζ, v) and (ψ, v) are compatible and subsequentially continuous, then*

1. *ζ and v have a CP, and*
2. *ψ and v have a CP.*
3. *Further, let $\forall a, b \in \mathfrak{A}, k \in (0,1), \varrho > 0$,*

$$P(\zeta a, \psi b, k\varrho) \geq P(va, vb, \varrho) \uplus P(\zeta a, va, \varrho) \uplus P(\psi b, vb, \varrho) \uplus P(\psi b, va, 2\varrho)$$
$$\uplus P(\zeta a, vb, \varrho),$$
$$Q(\zeta a, \psi b, k\varrho) \leq Q(va, vb, \varrho) \odot Q(\zeta a, va, \varrho) \odot Q(\psi b, vb, \varrho) \odot Q(\psi b, va, 2\varrho)$$
$$\odot Q(\zeta a, vb, \varrho)$$

and

$$R(\zeta a, \psi b, k\varrho) \leq R(va, vb, \varrho) \odot R(\zeta a, va, \varrho) \odot R(\psi b, vb, \varrho) \odot R(\psi b, va, 2\varrho)$$
$$\odot R(\zeta a, vb, \varrho).$$

Then, ζ, ψ and v have a unique common FP.

Proof. The proof is the same as in the above theorem. If $v = \tau$, the desired result will be obtained. □

Remark 3. *We can also establish the validity of this theorem by substituting subsequential continuity of the pairs with reciprocal continuity of the pairs.*

Remark 4. *The conclusions of the previously mentioned theorems remain valid when we replace compatibility with subcompatibility and subsequential continuity with reciprocal continuity while maintaining all other hypotheses unchanged.*

5. Application

Let us take an example of volterra I.E and apply FPT to find the solution.

Consider the following I.E, which is a Volterra I.E of the first kind:

$$u(\mathfrak{z}) = \mathfrak{z} + \varrho \int_0^{\mathfrak{z}} e^{-(\mathfrak{z}-\varpi)} u(\varpi) d\varpi,$$

where • $u(\mathfrak{z})$ is the unknown function,

- ϱ is a given constant and
- $0 \leq \mathfrak{z} \leq 1$.

We want to prove that this I.E has a unique solution on the interval $[0,1]$.

Step 1: Define the Operator:

We define an operator $\mathfrak{M}$ as follows:

$$\mathfrak{M}(u)(\mathfrak{z}) = \mathfrak{z} + \varrho \int_0^{\mathfrak{z}} e^{-(\mathfrak{z}-\varpi)} u(\varpi) d\varpi.$$

To prove that $\mathfrak{M}$ is continuous, we will show that, if a sequence of functions $\{u_n\}$ converges to some function u (pointwise or in some other suitable norm), then the sequence of transformed functions $\mathfrak{M}(u_n)$ converges to $\mathfrak{M}(u)$.

Let us consider a sequence of functions $\{u_n\}$ that converges to u pointwise:

$$u_n(\mathfrak{z}) \to u(\mathfrak{z}) \text{ as } n \to \infty.$$

We will show that

$$\mathfrak{M}(u_n)(\mathfrak{z}) \to \mathfrak{M}(u)(\mathfrak{z}) \text{ as } n \to \infty.$$

For this, we can break down $\mathfrak{M}(u_n)(\mathfrak{z})$:

$$\mathfrak{M}(u_n)(\mathfrak{z}) = \mathfrak{z} + \varrho \int_0^{\mathfrak{z}} e^{-(\mathfrak{z}-\varpi)} u_n(\varpi) d\varpi.$$

Now, we will use the concept of dominated convergence. For this we will show that

1. $u_n(\varpi)$ converges pointwise to $u(\varpi)$ as $n \to \infty$ for each ϖ in the interval $[0,\mathfrak{z}]$.
2. $\exists$ a dominating function $g(\mathfrak{z})$ such that $|u_n(\varpi)| \leq g(\mathfrak{z})$ $\forall$ n and ϖ in $[0,\mathfrak{z}]$ and $g(\mathfrak{z})$ is integrable on $[0,\mathfrak{z}]$.
3. The dominated convergence theorem (DCT) is used to justify interchanging the limit and the integral sign in $\mathfrak{M}(u_n)(\mathfrak{z})$.

By the DCT, we can conclude that

$$\mathfrak{M}(u_n)(\mathfrak{z}) \to \mathfrak{M}(u)(\mathfrak{z}) \text{ as } n \to \infty.$$

This establishes the subsequential continuity of the operator $\mathfrak{M}$ when sequence of functions $\{u_n\}$ converges pointwise to u.

Step 2: Show $\mathfrak{M}$ is a Contraction Mapping:

To apply the FPT, we have to show that $\mathfrak{M}$ is a contraction mapping on a suitable MS. For this purpose, we can use the L^∞ norm, which measures the supremum of the absolute values of the function over the interval $[0,1]$.

Now, to prove that $\mathfrak{M}$ is a contraction mapping, we will prove that $\exists$ a constant $0 \leq k < 1$ such that

$$|\mathfrak{M}(u) - \mathfrak{M}(v)|_\infty \leq k|u - v|_\infty,$$

where $|u|_\infty = \sup_{0 \leq \mathfrak{z} \leq 1} |u(\mathfrak{z})|$ is the L^∞ norm.

By analyzing $|\mathfrak{M}(u)(\mathfrak{z}) - \mathfrak{M}(v)(\mathfrak{z})|$, we can derive an expression involving the difference $|u(\mathfrak{z}) - v(\mathfrak{z})|$. By using the Mean Value Theorem for integrals, we can find a k such that the contraction condition holds.

Step 3: Apply the Fixed-Point Theorem:

Once we have established that $\mathfrak{M}$ is a contraction mapping, we can apply the FPT. This theorem guarantees that $\exists$ a unique function u in the MS of continuous functions on $[0,1]$ such that $\mathfrak{M}(u) = u$. This function u is the unique solution to the original integral equation.

This method shows that the I.E has a unique solution on the interval $[0,1]$ by applying the FPT and using the concept of a contraction mapping with subcompatibility or subsequential continuity.

Implementation by taking a mathematical example

Step 1: Defining the Operator:

Consider the sequence of functions $\{u_n(\mathfrak{z})\} = \frac{\mathfrak{z}^n}{n}$ for $n \geq 1$ on the interval $[0,1]$. We aim to show that $u_n(\mathfrak{z})$ converges pointwise to $u(\mathfrak{z}) = 0$ on $[0,1]$.

(i) Pointwise Convergence:

For any fixed $\mathfrak{z}$ in $[0,1]$, as n approaches infinity, $\frac{\mathfrak{z}^n}{n}$ converges to 0. Since the numerator $\mathfrak{z}^n$ grows slower than the denominator, n goes to infinity. Therefore, $u_n(\mathfrak{z})$ converges pointwise to $u(\mathfrak{z}) = 0$.

(ii) Existence of Dominating Function:

We will find a dominating function $g(\mathfrak{z})$ such that $|u_n(\mathfrak{z})| \leq g(\mathfrak{z})$ for all n and $\mathfrak{z}$ in $[0,1]$.

Since $u_n(\mathfrak{z}) = \frac{\mathfrak{z}^n}{n}$ and $0 \leq \mathfrak{z} \leq 1$, we have $|u_n(\mathfrak{z})| \leq \frac{1}{n}$ for all n.

Now, choose $g(\mathfrak{z}) = 1$. Then $|u_n(\mathfrak{z})| \leq \frac{1}{n} \leq 1$ for all n and $\mathfrak{z}$ in $[0,1]$. Hence, $g(\mathfrak{z}) = 1$ is a dominating function.

(iii) Dominated Convergence Theorem (DCT):

With $g(\mathfrak{z}) = 1$, which is integrable over $[0,1]$, we can apply the DCT to justify the interchange of the limit and the integral sign.

Thus,

$$\mathfrak{M}(u_n)(\mathfrak{z}) = \mathfrak{z} + \varrho \int_0^{\mathfrak{z}} e^{-(\mathfrak{z}-\varpi)} u_n(\varpi) d\varpi = \mathfrak{z} + \varrho \int_0^{\mathfrak{z}} e^{-(\mathfrak{z}-\varpi)} \frac{\varpi^n}{n} d\varpi.$$

Since $e^{-(\mathfrak{z}-\varpi)}$ is bounded on $[0,1]$, we can replace $u_n(\varpi)$ with $u(\varpi) = 0$ by the DCT. Therefore, $\mathfrak{M}(u_n)(\mathfrak{z})$ converges to $\mathfrak{M}(u)(\mathfrak{z})$ as $n \mapsto \infty$.

This establishes the subsequential continuity of the operator $\mathfrak{M}$ when functions u_n converges pointwise to u.

Step 2: Show $\mathfrak{M}$ is a Contraction Mapping:

To prove that $\mathfrak{M}$ is a contraction mapping, we need to find a constant $0 \leq k < 1$ such that for any two functions $u(\mathfrak{z})$ and $v(\mathfrak{z})$ in the function space, the operator $\mathfrak{M}$ satisfies the contraction condition:

$$|\mathfrak{M}(u) - \mathfrak{M}(v)|_\infty \leq k|u - v|_\infty,$$

where $|f|_\infty = \sup_{\mathfrak{z}\in[0,1]} |f(\mathfrak{z})|$ represents the supremum norm over the interval $[0,1]$.

Let $\mathfrak{M}(u)$ and $\mathfrak{M}(v)$ be

$$\mathfrak{M}(u)(\mathfrak{z}) = \mathfrak{z} + \varrho \int_0^{\mathfrak{z}} e^{-(\mathfrak{z}-\varpi)} u(\varpi) d\varpi.$$

$$\mathfrak{M}(v)(\mathfrak{z}) = \mathfrak{z} + \varrho \int_0^{\mathfrak{z}} e^{-(\mathfrak{z}-\varpi)} v(\varpi) d\varpi.$$

Thus, the difference $\mathfrak{M}(u)(\mathfrak{z}) - \mathfrak{M}(v)(\mathfrak{z})$ is

$$\mathfrak{M}(u)(\mathfrak{z}) - \mathfrak{M}(v)(\mathfrak{z}) = \varrho \int_0^{\mathfrak{z}} e^{-(\mathfrak{z}-\varpi)} (u(\varpi) - v(\varpi))\, d\varpi.$$

Now, $|\mathfrak{M}(u) - \mathfrak{M}(v)|_\infty$ is

$$\begin{aligned} |\mathfrak{M}(u) - \mathfrak{M}(v)|_\infty &= \sup_{\mathfrak{z}\in[0,1]} |\mathfrak{M}(u)(\mathfrak{z}) - \mathfrak{M}(v)(\mathfrak{z})| \\ &= \sup_{\mathfrak{z}\in[0,1]} \left| \varrho \int_0^{\mathfrak{z}} e^{-(\mathfrak{z}-\varpi)} (u(\varpi) - v(\varpi)) d\varpi \right|. \end{aligned}$$

Substituting the expression for $\mathfrak{M}(u)(\mathfrak{z}) - \mathfrak{M}(v)(\mathfrak{z})$,

$$|\mathfrak{M}(u) - \mathfrak{M}(v)|_\infty = \sup_{\mathfrak{z}\in[0,1]} \left| \varrho \int_0^{\mathfrak{z}} e^{-(\mathfrak{z}-\varpi)} (u(\varpi) - v(\varpi))\, d\varpi \right|.$$

The absolute value of the integral can be bounded by the integral of the absolute value:

$$|\mathfrak{M}(u) - \mathfrak{M}(v)|_\infty \leq \sup_{\mathfrak{z}\in[0,1]} \varrho \int_0^{\mathfrak{z}} e^{-(\mathfrak{z}-\varpi)} |u(\varpi) - v(\varpi)|\, d\varpi.$$

Since $e^{-(\mathfrak{z}-\varpi)} \leq 1$ for all $\mathfrak{z}, \varpi \in [0,1]$, we have

$$|\mathfrak{M}(u) - \mathfrak{M}(v)|_\infty \leq \sup_{\mathfrak{z}\in[0,1]} \varrho \int_0^{\mathfrak{z}} |u(\varpi) - v(\varpi)|\, d\varpi.$$

By the definition of the supremum norm,

$$|u(\varpi) - v(\varpi)| \leq |u - v|_\infty, \quad \forall \varpi \in [0,1].$$

Thus,

$$|\mathfrak{M}(u) - \mathfrak{M}(v)|_\infty \leq \sup_{\mathfrak{z}\in[0,1]} \varrho \int_0^{\mathfrak{z}} |u - v|_\infty\, d\varpi.$$

Since $|u - v|_\infty$ is independent of ϖ, it can be factored out:

$$|\mathfrak{M}(u) - \mathfrak{M}(v)|_\infty \leq \varrho |u - v|_\infty \sup_{\mathfrak{z}\in[0,1]} \int_0^{\mathfrak{z}} 1\, d\varpi.$$

Simplifying the integral $\int_0^{\mathfrak{z}} 1\, d\varpi = \mathfrak{z}$, it follows that

$$|\mathfrak{M}(u) - \mathfrak{M}(v)|_\infty \leq \varrho |u - v|_\infty \sup_{\mathfrak{z}\in[0,1]} \mathfrak{z}.$$

Since $\mathfrak{z} \leq 1$ for $\mathfrak{z} \in [0,1]$, we get

$$|\mathfrak{M}(u) - \mathfrak{M}(v)|_\infty \leq \varrho |u - v|_\infty.$$

If $\varrho < 1$, we can set $k = \varrho$, where $0 \leq k < 1$. Thus, $\mathfrak{M}$ satisfies the contraction condition:

$$|\mathfrak{M}(u) - \mathfrak{M}(v)|_\infty \leq k |u - v|_\infty.$$

Step 3: Apply the Fixed-Point Theorem:

The Fixed-Point Theorem states:

If Y is a complete metric space and $\mathfrak{M} : Y \to Y$ is a contraction mapping with contraction constant $k < 1$, then $\mathfrak{M}$ has a unique FP u^* in Y such that $\mathfrak{M}(u^*) = u^*$.

Here, Y is the space of continuous functions equipped with the supremum norm $|f|_\infty$ over the interval $[0,1]$, and $\mathfrak{M} : Y \to Y$ is the operator defined as

$$\mathfrak{M}(u)(\mathfrak{z}) = \mathfrak{z} + \varrho \int_0^{\mathfrak{z}} e^{-(\mathfrak{z}-\varpi)} u(\varpi) d\varpi.$$

We have already shown that $\mathfrak{M}$ is a contraction mapping with contraction constant $k = \varrho$, which satisfies $0 \leq \varrho < 1$.

Now, as $\mathfrak{M}$ is a contraction mapping on a complete MS, $\exists$ a unique FP u^* such that $\mathfrak{M}(u^*) = u^*$. In other words, $\exists$ a unique function $u(\mathfrak{z})$ satisfying the I.E:

$$u(\mathfrak{z}) = \mathfrak{z} + \varrho \int_0^{\mathfrak{z}} e^{-(\mathfrak{z}-\varpi)} u(\varpi) d\varpi.$$

To find the solution, let $u_0(\mathfrak{z}) = 0$ by the Picard iteration method. Find $u_1(\mathfrak{z})$:

$$u_{n+1}(\mathfrak{z}) = \mathfrak{z} + \varrho \int_0^{\mathfrak{z}} e^{-(\mathfrak{z}-\varpi)} u_n(\varpi) d\varpi$$

Since $u_0(\mathfrak{z}) = 0$, the integral term becomes zero, and we have

$$u_1(\mathfrak{z}) = \mathfrak{z} + \varrho \int_0^{\mathfrak{z}} e^{-(\mathfrak{z}-\varpi)} \cdot 0 \, d\varpi$$

$$u_1(\mathfrak{z}) = \mathfrak{z}$$

Therefore, $u_1(\mathfrak{z}) = \mathfrak{z}$ is the first approximation in the Picard iteration method when the initial guess is $u_0(\mathfrak{z}) = 0$.

To find $u_2(\mathfrak{z})$, the second approximation in the Picard iteration method, we use $u_1(\mathfrak{z}) = \mathfrak{z}$ obtained from the previous iteration as the input function in the iteration formula:

$$u_{n+1}(\mathfrak{z}) = \mathfrak{z} + \varrho \int_0^{\mathfrak{z}} e^{-(\mathfrak{z}-\varpi)} u_n(\varpi) d\varpi$$

$$u_2(\mathfrak{z}) = \mathfrak{z} + \varrho \int_0^{\mathfrak{z}} e^{-(\mathfrak{z}-\varpi)} \cdot \varpi \, d\varpi$$

We will compute this integral to find $u_2(\mathfrak{z})$:

$$u_2(\mathfrak{z}) = \mathfrak{z} + \varrho \left[-\frac{1}{e^{\mathfrak{z}-\varpi}} \cdot \varpi \Big|_0^{\mathfrak{z}} + \int_0^{\mathfrak{z}} \frac{1}{e^{\mathfrak{z}-\varpi}} \cdot 1 \, d\varpi \right]$$

$$u_2(\mathfrak{z}) = \mathfrak{z} + \varrho \left[-\frac{1}{e^{\mathfrak{z}-\mathfrak{z}}} \cdot \mathfrak{z} + \int_0^{\mathfrak{z}} \frac{1}{e^{\mathfrak{z}-\varpi}} \, d\varpi \right]$$

$$u_2(\mathfrak{z}) = \mathfrak{z} + \varrho \left[-\frac{\mathfrak{z}}{1} + \left(-\frac{1}{e^{\mathfrak{z}-\varpi}} \Big|_0^{\mathfrak{z}} \right) \right]$$

$$u_2(\mathfrak{z}) = \mathfrak{z} + \varrho \left[-\mathfrak{z} + 1 - \frac{1}{e^{\mathfrak{z}}} \right]$$

$$u_2(\mathfrak{z}) = (1 - \varrho)\mathfrak{z} + \varrho - \varrho \frac{1}{e^{\mathfrak{z}}}$$

Therefore, $u_2(\mathfrak{z}) = (1 - \varrho)\mathfrak{z} + \varrho - \varrho \frac{1}{e^{\mathfrak{z}}}$. This is the second approximation in the Picard iteration method.

By using the boundary conditions, we can calculate the $u(\mathfrak{z})$, which is the unique solution to the I.E on $[0, 1]$.

Therefore, by applying the FPT, we have established the existence and uniqueness of the solution to the I.E. This completes the proof that the given Volterra I.E has a unique solution on the interval $[0, 1]$.

Now we are giving an example in decision theory.

Example 12. *Application in Decision Theory:*

In decision-making problems involving uncertainty, neutrosophic metric spaces (NMSs) provide a robust framework to evaluate alternatives by considering degrees of membership (T), non-membership (F), and indeterminacy (I). This framework is particularly useful in situations where the available information is incomplete, inconsistent, or vague, such as selecting suppliers for a sustainable supply chain.

For example, a company needs to choose the best supplier from four candidates (S_1, S_2, S_3, S_4) *based on three criteria:*

1. *cost efficiency* (f),
2. *delivery time* (g), *and*
3. *environmental sustainability* (h).

Each supplier's performance on these criteria is evaluated in the neutrosophic metric space, where

T represents the degree of membership (e.g., how well a supplier meets the criterion),
F represents the degree of non-membership (e.g., how poorly a supplier performs), and
I represents the degree of indeterminacy (e.g., uncertainty or ambiguity in the evaluation).

The overall performance of a supplier is mapped using k, which combines the three criteria into a single score.

Now, the mappings f *(cost efficiency) and g (delivery time) are subcompatible if their evaluations align sufficiently, meaning there is no strong contradiction between their outputs. For example, if a supplier scores high on cost efficiency* (f) *but moderately on delivery time* (g), *their neutrosophic evaluations should overlap in a way that allows meaningful aggregation into k (overall performance). Subcompatibility ensures that combining* f, g, *and h into k results in a coherent overall evaluation. Again, if a sequence of evaluations for a supplier (e.g., periodic assessments over time) converges to a certain neutrosophic value under mappings* f *and g, then k should reflect this consistency; i.e., gradual changes in criterion evaluations should lead to gradual changes in the overall performance k, avoiding abrupt or discontinuous shifts.*

Numerical Example

Consider supplier S_1 *evaluated as follows:*

- $f(S_1) = (0.8, 0.1, 0.1)$ *for cost efficiency,*
- $g(S_1) = (0.7, 0.2, 0.1)$ *for delivery time, and*
- $h(S_1) = (0.6, 0.2, 0.2)$ *for environmental sustainability.*

The overall performance $k(S_1)$ *is calculated as*

$$k(S_1) = \max\{f(S_1), g(S_1), h(S_1)\}.$$

Using the component-wise maximum,

$$k(S_1) = (\max(0.8, 0.7, 0.6), \max(0.1, 0.2, 0.2), \max(0.1, 0.1, 0.2)),$$

$$k(S_1) = (0.8, 0.2, 0.2).$$

Here,

- $T = 0.8$: *the supplier* S_1 *has a high overall membership degree;*
- $F = 0.2$: *there is a moderate degree of non-membership;*
- $I = 0.2$: *some indeterminacy exists in the evaluation.*

Now, subcompatibility and sequential continuity are used:

1. ***Subcompatibility:*** $f(S_1)$ *and* $g(S_1)$ *are subcompatible if their neutrosophic evaluations do not strongly contradict each other. For example,* $f(S_1) = (0.8, 0.1, 0.1)$ *and* $g(S_1) = (0.7, 0.2, 0.1)$ *align well because their T, F, and I values are close and compatible.*

2. ***Sequential Continuity:*** *If the evaluations of $f(S_1)$, $g(S_1)$, and $h(S_1)$ change gradually over time (e.g., $f(S_1) \to (0.85, 0.05, 0.1)$), then $k(S_1)$ should also change gradually, ensuring that the overall performance mapping remains consistent.*

Thus, in NMSs, the decision-making process accounts for uncertainty and inconsistency in supplier evaluations. Subcompatibility ensures the coherent aggregation of criteria into overall performance, while sequential continuity maintains consistency in evaluations over time, making NMS an effective tool for solving complex, uncertain problems such as supplier selection.

6. Conclusions

Within this study, some innovative concepts, such as specific subcompatibility and subsequential continuity, are presented. They offer a less restrictive framework compared to OWC and reciprocal continuity within the context of NMS. Leveraging these concepts, a common fixed point theorem applicable to four mappings is formulated. Our findings are further extended within the NMS framework. To showcase the practical relevance of this study, illustrative examples were provided to validate the new results and demonstrate their applicability in integral equations.

Author Contributions: N.G.: writing—review, conceptualization, formal analysis, writing—original draft and editing, data curation, validation, software, visualization, and investigation. V.G.: conceptualization, supervision, writing—original draft and editing, methodology, project administration, and investigation. R.S.: writing—original draft and editing and validation. All the authors contributed equally to the preparation of this paper. All authors have read and agreed to the published version of the manuscript.

Funding: This work was supported by Directorate of Research and Innovation, Walter Sisulu University, South Africa.

Informed Consent Statement: All authors provide consent for the publication of identifiable details, including those within the text ("Material"), in this journal. This article does not involve any studies with human participants or animals conducted by any of the authors, so informed consent is not required.

Data Availability Statement: My manuscript has no associated data. The code used in this study is accessible from the corresponding author upon request.

Acknowledgments: The authors express their gratitude to all the reviewers for their valuable feedback, which greatly contributed to enhancing the completeness and significance of our paper.

Conflicts of Interest: The authors declare no conflicts of interest.

Abbreviations

MS	Metric space
CM	Compatible Maps
FP	Fixed Point
FPT	Fixed point theorem
FMS	Fuzzy metric space
IFS	Intuitionistic fuzzy set
NS	Neutrosophic set
NMS	Neutrosophic metric space
CTN	Continous triangular norm
CTC	Continous triangular conorm
IFM	Intuitionistic fuzzy metric
IFMS	Intuitionistic fuzzy metric space

CP	Coincidence point
OWC	Occasionally weakly compatible
I.E	Integral Equation
DCT	Dominatyed Convergence Theorem

References

1. Zadeh, L.A. Fuzy sets. *Inf. Control* **1965**, *8*, 338–353.
2. Kramosil, I.; Michalek, J. Fuzzy metric and statistical spaces. *Kibernetica* **1975**, *11*, 326–334.
3. George, A.; Veeramani, P. On some results in fuzzy metric spaces. *Fuzzy Sets Syst.* **1994**, *64*, 395–399.
4. Deng, Z.-K. Fuzzy pseudo-metric spaces. *J. Math. Anal. Appl.* **1982**, *86*, 74–95.
5. Kaleva, O.; Seikkala, S. On fuzzy metric spaces. *Fuzzy Sets Syst.* **1984**, *12*, 225–229.
6. Bandyopadhyay, T.; Samanta, S.K.; Das, P. Fuzzy metric spaces redefined and a fixed point theorem. *Bull. Cal. Math. Soc.* **1989**, *81*, 247–252.
7. Menger, K.M. Statistical metrics. *Proc. Natl. Acad. Sci. USA* **1942**, *28*, 535–537.
8. Gupta, V.; Gondhi, A.; Shukla, R. Fixed Point Results in Modified Intuitionistic Fuzzy Soft Metric Spaces with Application. *Mathematics* **2024**, *12*, 1154. [CrossRef]
9. Shukla, S.; Dubey, N.; Shukla, R.; Meznik, I. Coincidence point of Edelstein type mappings in fuzzy metric spaces and application to the stability of dynamic markets. *Axioms* **2023**, *12*, 854. [CrossRef]
10. Mani, N.; Pingale, M.; Shukla, R.; Pathak, R. Fixed point theorems in fuzzy b-metric spaces using two different t-norms. *Adv. Fixed Point Theory* **2023**, *13*, 29.
11. Shukla, S.; Rai, S.; Shukla, R. Some Fixed Point Theorems for α-Admissible Mappings in Complex-Valued Fuzzy Metric Spaces. *Symmetry* **2023**, *15*, 1797. [CrossRef]
12. Jungck, G. Commuting maps and fixed points. *Am. Math.* **1976**, *83*, 261–263.
13. Jungck, G. Compatible mappings and common fixed points. *Int. J. Math. Math. Sci.* **1986**, *9*, 771–779.
14. Jungck, G.; Murthy, P.P.; Cho, Y.J. Compatible mapping of type (a) and common fixed points. *Math. Jpn.* **1993**, *38*, 381–390.
15. Jungck, G.; Rhoades, B.E. Some fixed point theorems for compatible maps. *Int. J. Math. Math. Sci.* **1993**, *3*, 417–428.
16. Pathak, H.K.; Cho, Y.J.; Kang, J.M.; Madharia, B. Compatible mappings of type (c) and common fixed point theorems of gregus type. *Demonstr. Math.* **1998**, *31*, 499–518.
17. Sharma, S.; Deshp, E.B. Common fixed points of compatible maps of type (β) on fuzzy metric spaces. *Demonstr. Math.* **2002**, *35*, 165–174.
18. Mishra, S.N.; Sharma, N.; Singh, S.L. Common fixed points of maps on fuzzy metric spaces. *Int. J. Math. Math. Sci.* **1994**, *17*, 253–258.
19. Grabiec, M. Fixed points in fuzzy metric spaces. *Fuzzy Sets Syst.* **1988**, *27*, 385–389. [CrossRef]
20. Bouhadjera, H.; Godet-Thobie, C. Common fixed theorems for pairs of sub compatible maps. *arXiv* **2009**, arXiv:0906.3159v1.
21. Manro, S.; Bouhadjera, H.; Singh, S. A common fixed point theorem in intuitionistic fuzzy metric space by using subcompatible maps. *Int. J. Contemp. Math. Sci.* **2010**, *5*, 2699–2707.
22. Cho, Y.J.; Pathak, H.K.; Kang, S.M.; Jung, J.S. Common fixed points of compatible maps of type (β) on fuzzy metric spaces. *Fuzzy Sets Syst.* **1998**, *93*, 99–111.
23. Edelstein, M. On fixed and periodic points under contractive mappings. *J. London Math. Soc.* **1962**, *37*, 74–79.
24. Naidu, S.V.R.; Rao, K.P.P.; Srinivasarao, N. On convergent sequences and fixed point theorems in D-metric spaces. *Int. J. Math. Sci.* **2005**, *12*, 1969–1988.
25. Atanassov, K.; Stoeva, S. Intuitionistic fuzzy sets. In Proceedings of the Polish Symposium on Interval and Fuzzy Mathematics, Poznan, Poland, 23–26 August 1983.
26. Park, J.H. Intuitionistic fuzzy metric spaces. *Chaos Solitons Fractals* **2004**, *22*, 1039–1046.
27. Johnsy, J.; Jeyaraman, M.; Shukla, R.; Venkatesan, R. Exploring profit opportunities in intuitionistic fuzzy metric spaces via Edelstein type mappings. *Int. J. Anal. Appl.* **2024**, *22*, 143.
28. Gregori, V.; Romaguera, S.; Veeramani, P. A Note on Intuitionistic Fuzzy Metric Spaces. *Chaos Solitons Fractals* **2006**, *28*, 902–905.
29. Saadati, R.; Sedghi, S.; Shobe, N. Modified intuitionistic fuzzy metric spaces and some fixed point theorems. *Chaos Solitons Fractals* **2008**, *38*, 36–47.
30. Miah, S.S. An in-depth exploration of intuitionistic fuzzy T_0 in the context of bitopology. *Notes Intuitionistic Fuzzy Sets* **2024**, *30*, 66–76. [CrossRef]
31. Miah, S.S.; Miah, J.; Amin, R.; Sultana, N. Intuitionistic fuzzy normal bi-topological space-approach of intuitionistic fuzzy open sets. *Notes Intuitionistic Fuzzy Sets* **2024**, *30*, 230–241. [CrossRef]
32. Miah, S.S.; Lily, F.T.; Amin, R.; Karim, R.; Akbar, M.A. Separation axioms on fuzzy neutrosophic bitopological spaces using fuzzy neutrosophic open sets. *J. Umm -Qura Univ. Appl. Sci.* **2024**. [CrossRef]

33. Smarandache, F. Neutrosophic set-a generalization of the intuitionistic fuzzy set. *Int. J. Pure Appl. Math.* **2005**, *24*, 287.
34. Lakhwani, T.S.; Mohanta, K.; Dey, A.; Mondal, S.P.; Pal, A. Some operations on Dombi neutrosophic graph. *J. Ambient. Intell. Humaniz. Comput. Intell. Humaniz. Comput.* **2021**, *13*, 425–443.
35. Kirisci, M.; Simsek, N. Neutrosophic metric spaces. *Math. Sci.* **2020**, *14*, 241–248.
36. Pant, R.P.; Jha, K. A remark on common fixed points of four mappings in a fuzzy metric space. *J. Fuzzy Syst.* **2004**, *12*, 433–438.

computation

MDPI

Article

FPGA Implementation of Synergetic Controller-Based MPPT Algorithm for a Standalone PV System

Abdul-Basset A. Al-Hussein [1], Fadhil Rahma Tahir [1] and Viet-Thanh Pham [2,*]

1 Department of Electrical Engineering, University of Basrah, Basrah 61001, Iraq; abdulbasset.jasim@uobasrah.edu.iq (A.-B.A.A.-H.); fadhil.rahma@uobasrah.edu.iq (F.R.T.)
2 Faculty of Electronics Technology, Industrial University of Ho Chi Minh City, Ho Chi Minh City 70000, Vietnam
* Correspondence: phamvietthanh@iuh.edu.vn

Abstract

Photovoltaic (PV) energy is gaining traction due to its direct conversion of sunlight to electricity without harming the environment. It is simple to install, adaptable in size, and has low operational costs. The power output of PV modules varies with solar radiation and cell temperature. To optimize system efficiency, it is crucial to track the PV array's maximum power point. This paper presents a novel fixed-point FPGA design of a nonlinear maximum power point tracking (MPPT) controller based on synergetic control theory for driving autonomously standalone photovoltaic systems. The proposed solution addresses the chattering issue associated with the sliding mode controller by introducing a new strategy that generates a continuous control law rather than a switching term. Because it requires a lower sample rate when switching to the invariant manifold, its controlled switching frequency makes it better suited for digital applications. The suggested algorithm is first emulated to evaluate its performance, robustness, and efficacy under a standard benchmarked MPPT efficiency (η_{MPPT}) calculation regime. FPGA has been used for its capability to handle high-speed control tasks more efficiently than traditional micro-controller-based systems. The high-speed response is critical for applications where rapid adaptation to changing conditions, such as fluctuating solar irradiance and temperature levels, is necessary. To validate the effectiveness of the implemented synergetic controller, the system responses under variant meteorological conditions have been analyzed. The results reveal that the synergetic control algorithm provides smooth and precise MPPT.

Keywords: PV system; synergetic control theory; FPGA; MPPT; fixed-point representation; Xilinx system generator; DC-DC boost converter

1. Introduction

To secure a long-term and sustainable energy supply, it is crucial to prioritize the widespread adoption and effective utilization of renewable energy sources. Resources like solar, wind, hydropower, and biomass not only provide an inexhaustible energy supply but also minimize environmental harm compared to fossil fuels. Transitioning to these sustainable alternatives at a much larger scale can mitigate climate change, reduce carbon emissions, and ensure energy security for future generations. For many years, environmental contamination has been a major concern on a worldwide scale. The demand for sustainable energy is still an ongoing challenge. To address this issue, massive resources are needed to provide a variety of sustainable energy sources. Solar photovoltaics (PV) is predicted to be the most popular renewable energy source because of its availability, simplicity of installation, and near-zero maintenance requirements. Furthermore, because solar energy is so accessible, it seems to be the most popular green energy source. Nevertheless, the cost of solar electricity remains greater than that of fossil fuels due to the low conversion efficiency of PV solar systems. PV systems have low efficiency, where the photovoltaic generator (PVG) converts light into electricity with about a 12 to 20% efficiency [1,2]. Losses occur during the transmission of energy from the solar panel to the load unit. These losses can be attributed to a variety of factors, including fluctuating load values, nonlinear power-voltage characteristics of the photovoltaic generator (PVG), and mismatches between the load and the PVG. The goal is to keep the photovoltaic system running as efficiently as possible by detecting the maximum power point always and reducing oscillation significantly to avoid the issues that are often associated with regular MPPT algorithms. Therefore, improving the maximum power point tracking (MPPT) strategy is one practical method to boosting the energy conversation efficiency [3].

In recent times, a substantial number of MPPT algorithms, characterized by varying levels of efficacy and complexity, have been devised and presented in the scientific community. These algorithms have been designed to optimize performance, and their development reflects the ongoing advancements and diverse approaches in the field. The first algorithms were based on measuring voltage and current, which were thought to be straightforward but unreliable; their disadvantage was that power loss resulted from PV module shorting and opening circuiting in order to measure voltage and current, respectively, for reference as a crucial step [4]. Among other conventional MPPT approaches and more complicated instances are as the perturb and observe (P&O), incremental conductance (IC), and the hill climbing (HC), which continuously track and determine the MPP direction by detecting the variation in the PV module power due to the PV module voltage small change or perturbation employed by the control strategy. These control methods are widely used since they are simple and easy to implement, but they have also same limitations: they are vulnerable to facing variant atmospheric conditions and fail under fast-varying climatic conditions, which causes system instability [5,6]. Conversely, certain MPPT approaches perform well in both static and dynamic states, while they require certain information and the understanding of some subjects, like fuzzy logic and neural networks [7], particle swarm optimization [8], etc.

AI-based MPPT techniques outperform conventional methods such as perturb and observe (P&O) and incremental conductance (INC) by dynamically adapting to rapid changes in irradiance and temperature without causing oscillations around the MPP [9]. Traditional MPPT algorithms often suffer from trade-offs between tracking speed and steady-state stability, leading to energy losses in fluctuating conditions. In contrast, AI-driven MPPT methods can predict optimal operating points by analyzing historical and real-time data, allowing them to make intelligent decisions that enhance energy conversion efficiency. However, AI-based MPPT techniques, such as artificial neural networks (ANNs) and fuzzy logic controllers (FLCs), require extensive real-time computations to accurately track the maximum power point (MPP) under varying environmental conditions [9].

Of all the methods mentioned above, the sliding-mode control (SMC)-based MPPT algorithm is one of the most significant due to its advantages, which include stability, resistance to fluctuation in parameters, quick dynamic reaction, and ease of implementation [10]. Sliding-mode control theory is mostly used to drive the electrical power converter systems which constitute variable structure design [11]. Furthermore, some of those techniques have been utilized by PV systems, primarily to control the amount of current fed into the grid. Ref. [12] has addressed a sliding-mode current-based MPPT strategy that is based on a combination of a standard P&O MPPT technique and an SMC. In this work, SMC is used by Bianconi et al. to synchronous boost in order to control the input capacitor current to the current reference that is acquired by P&O [12].

It is well known that the SMC nonlinear approach has high performance attributes including resilience, fast dynamic response, and simplicity of implementation . However, the chattering problem, which results in undesired oscillations, is its primary disadvantage [13].

All of these challenges, particularly the oscillation behavior, resilience, and speed of the MPPT in tracking the ideal power, which was sparked by the aforementioned study, have directed efforts to enhance the PV system's performance. One of the most attractive and reliable control strategies, called synergetic control theory (SCT), is recommended to accomplish this aim. Synergetic control theory is one of the recently evolved technologies used to solve the previously mentioned problems. It is a nonlinear control-based strategy that was first initiated by Kolesnikov [14]. Synergetic control reduces chattering more effectively than sliding-mode control. Chattering is a common issue in sliding-mode control, causing high-frequency oscillations that can lead to wear and tear on the system. Synergetic control, on the other hand, provides smoother control signals, which helps to minimize chattering and needs less filtering. However, it is well-suited for digital implementation due to its analytical nature. This makes it more practical for modern control systems, which often rely on digital controllers. In contrast, sliding-mode control can be more challenging to implement digitally. In addition, synergetic control provides constant switching frequency operation, which is beneficial for maintaining system stability and reducing wear on the switching components. Sliding mode control, by contrast, can have varying switching frequencies, which can lead to instability and increased wear. Moreover, synergetic control offers a more direct method for generating control laws, making it more efficient in the digital design process. This flexibility is valuable in high-performance applications where speed controllers need to provide not only accuracy but also flexibility and efficiency [15].

In addition to being effective for controlling nonlinear systems, the suggested synergetic control approach is regarded as a very effective robust control technique [16]. It eliminates the chattering phenomenon but has the invariance concept of the sliding-mode control. Recently, it has been proficiently employed in various applications such as the m-parallel connected DC-DC buck converters [17], in a maximum power point tracking for a standalone solar power system [2], and in the design of power system stabilizers [18]. In [19,20], the authors used the synergetic control for chaos suppression in different power systems. The authors of [21] used this theory to control the endocrine glucose–insulin regulatory system. On the other hand, the hardware implementation of synergetic control was proposed using the dSPACE RTI 1104 processor, which is a 64-bit floating-point processor as given in [22]. The design was used to validate the MPPT controller for autonomous PV system maximum power extracting.

Field Programmable Gate Arrays (FPGAs) offer a powerful and efficient hardware solution for implementing complex Maximum Power Point Tracking (MPPT) techniques in photovoltaic (PV) systems. Unlike traditional micro-controllers and digital signal processors (DSPs), FPGAs provide high-speed parallel processing, low-latency computations, and reconfigurable architectures, making them ideal for handling the complex computations associated with MPPT applications [23]. By leveraging FPGA hardware acceleration, the control models can execute with enhanced precision and minimal computational delays, ensuring improved efficiency in energy harvesting compared to conventional MPPT methods [24].

The integration of MPPT techniques into FPGA platforms also offers scalability and adaptability for modern PV applications. As energy systems become more complex with the inclusion of microgrids and distributed energy resources, FPGA-based controllers can accommodate multiple input variables, optimizing power extraction across different PV module configurations. Additionally, FPGAs enable hardware-accelerated deep learning models for advanced MPPT strategies, allowing for real-time adjustments based on weather forecasts and grid demand. Unlike fixed hardware controllers, FPGA architectures can be reprogrammed to support evolving MPPT strategies, ensuring long-term adaptability without requiring costly hardware replacements [25]. Inspired from the above work, and noting that none of the previous works on synergistic control theory were implemented using fixed-point representation on FPGA, this paper proposes the following aspects:

- PV system and DC-DC boost converter modeling.
- Propose a novel FPGA-based controller that employs the synergetic control strategy to track the MPP for a standalone photovoltaic power system under different meteorological states. The suggested MPPT controller's primary objective is to concurrently guarantee system stability at maximum power, strong robustness, and quick dynamic response.
- The MPPT Synergetic algorithm is designed, investigated, and mathematically explained in the paper. The elaborated synergetic MPPT algorithm has been implemented both in simulations and using the Xilinx System Generator as a hardware-in-the-loop platform.
- Fixed-point representations are provided to optimize the FPGA resource utilization and to achieve timing constraints such as positive worst negative slack (WNS).
- The complicated VHDL code developed from a Xilinx's blockset design was then utilized to set up the intended FPGA board. When generating an FPGA programming file, all downstream FPGA development processes, such as synthesis and place and route, are carried out, respectively.

This paper outlines the study in five sections. Following this introduction, Section 2 introduces the overall PV system components, mathematical modeling of the PV generator, and DC-DC boost converter. In Section 3, different aspects and derivation of the synergetic control theory are described. In Section 4, the implementation procedure and the simulation results are given in addition to the FPGA hardware requirements. The main conclusions and discussion inspired from this work are provided in Section 5.

2. Photovoltaic System Description

2.1. Overall System Description

The overall schematic diagram of the proposed photovoltaic (PV) system is given in Figure 1. At its core, this system consists of a PV array, a direct current DC-DC boost converter, MPPT algorithm, and a resistive type load. The key innovation of this setup lies in its ability to optimize the power extracted by the PV system. It is well known that the solar panels operate most efficiently when they operate at their Maximum Power Point (MPP), which varies depending on factors such as sunlight intensity and temperature. MPPT technology continuously monitors and adjusts the electrical load connected to the panels to ensure they operate as close as possible to their MPP, thereby maximizing the energy harvested from the sunlight. Overall, a PV system with MPPT enhances the overall performance and energy yield of solar installations, making it a preferred choice for residential, commercial, and industrial applications seeking to harness solar power effectively and efficiently. The FPGA platform implements the MPPT algorithm to maximize the efficiency of solar energy conversion as well as to generate signal control for the DC-DC boost converter.

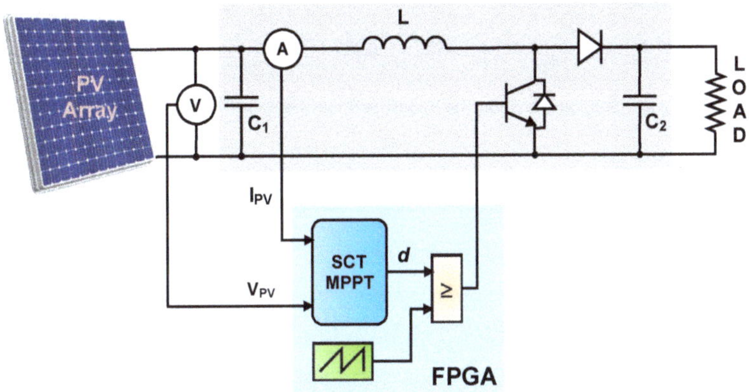

Figure 1. Photovoltaic system block diagram.

2.2. PV Cell Modeling

In essence, a photovoltaic solar unit is a p-n junction that directly transforms solar radiation into electrical energy. Photons from the cell are absorbed by semiconductor atoms when it is exposed to sunlight, which releases electrons from the negative layer. Through an external circuit, these electrons make their way to the positive layer, where they create an electric current [26].

The most popular representation of the photovoltiac generator unit is the single-diode model, which is usually employed because of its well-accurateness and ease of analysis. As seen in Figure 2, this model comprises a current source that is regulated by the amount of light hitting the PV unit surface, a diode that represents the solar cell's PN junction, and the losses caused by the resistance of the PV connection or material, which can be represented by series and parallel resistors.

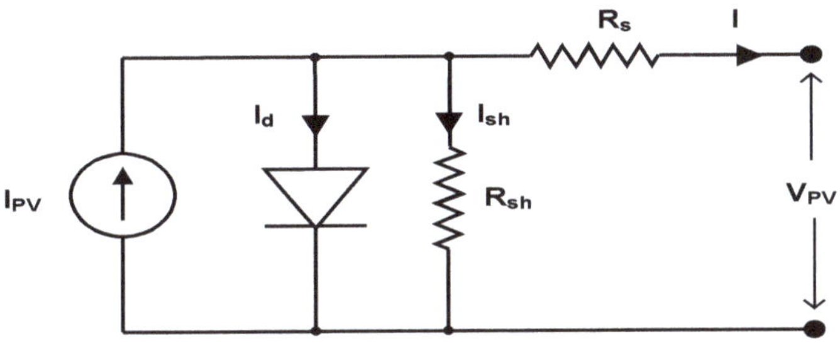

Figure 2. The electrical PV solar cell model.

The general mathematical representation of the PV cell is provided using the following Equation [26]:

$$I = I_{ph} - I_d - I_{sh} \tag{1}$$

where I_{ph} denotes the photo current, I_d defines the diode current, and I_{sh} a shunt current.

The solar photo current mathematical model can be given as follows:

$$I_{ph} = G_k\left[I_{sc} + k_I\left(T_{op} - T_{\mathrm{ref}}\right)\right] \tag{2}$$

The current of the shunt resistor branch I_{sh} is evaluated by the following model:

$$I_{sh} = \frac{V_{pv} + I_{pv}R_s}{R_{sh}} \tag{3}$$

The I_d that stands for the current passing through the model diode shown in Figure 2 is given by the following mathematical equation:

$$I_d = I_s\left[\exp\left(q\frac{V_{pv} + R_S I_{pv}}{V_t}\right) - 1\right] \tag{4}$$

The reverse saturation current I_s often referred to as leakage current in practical diode circuits and flows through the diode when it is reverse-biased, meaning the voltage applied is in the opposite direction to the diode's forward bias. It increases exponentially with temperature, as shown in the following formula:

$$I_s = I_{rs}\left(\frac{T_{op}}{T_{ref}}\right)^3 e^{\left[\frac{qEg}{nk}\left(\frac{1}{T_{op}} - \frac{1}{T_{ref}}\right)\right]} \tag{5}$$

Eventually, the output current may be written as follows:

$$I = I_{ph} - I_s\left[\exp\left(\frac{qV_{pv} + R_S I_{pv}}{V_t}\right) - 1\right] - \frac{V_{pv} + I_{pv}R_S}{R_{Sh}} \tag{6}$$

The specifications of the PV array used in this work are detailed in Table 1.

Table 1. Electrical characteristics of the SunPower SPR-305E-WHT-D cell.

Parameters	Symbols	Values	Units
Maximum power	P_{max}	305.226	W
Open-circuit voltage	V_{oc}	64.2	V
Short-circuit current	I_{sc}	5.96	A
Optimum operating voltage	V_{mpp}	54.7	V
Optimum operating current	I_{mpp}	5.58	A
Temperature coefficient of I_{sc}	K_i	0.061745	%/°C
Temperature coefficient of V_{oc}	K_v	−0.2727	%/°C

The I-V and P-V characteristics of the photovoltaic cell under constant temperature and varying solar radiation levels are displayed in Figure 3. Moreover, the PV array's I-V and P-V characteristics at fixed irradiance and varying temperature levels are displayed in Figure 4.

It is evident that the maximum power point of the PV cell exhibits nonlinear properties. The maximum power point is sensitive to temperature and light intensity. As a result, when the temperature level drops or the irradiance rises, the PV panel power increases. Therefore, an appropriate control algorithm is required to guarantee that the photovoltaic solar system works at its maximum output power point. And this is the aim of this study.

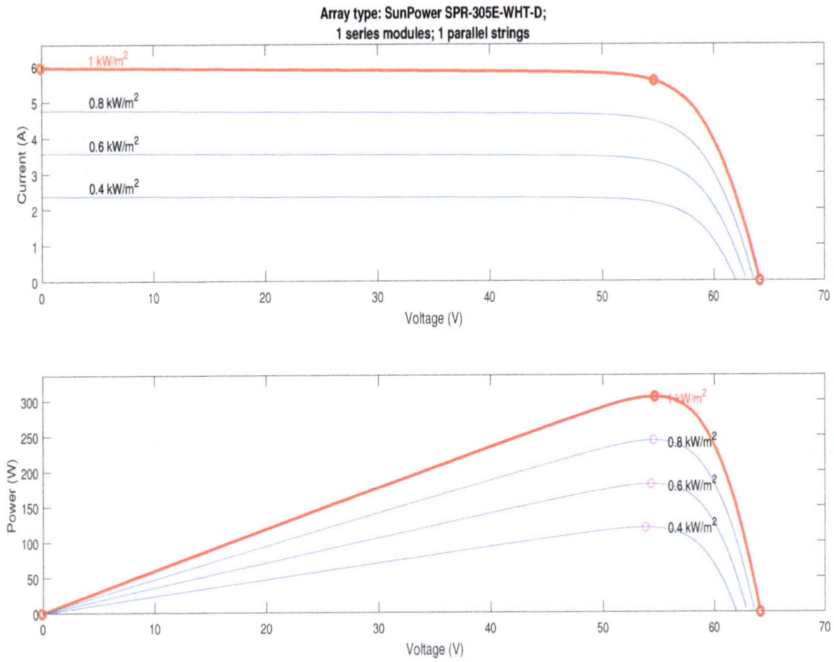

Figure 3. I-V and P-Vd electrical characteristics of SunPower SPR-305E-WHT-D module, at different irradiance.

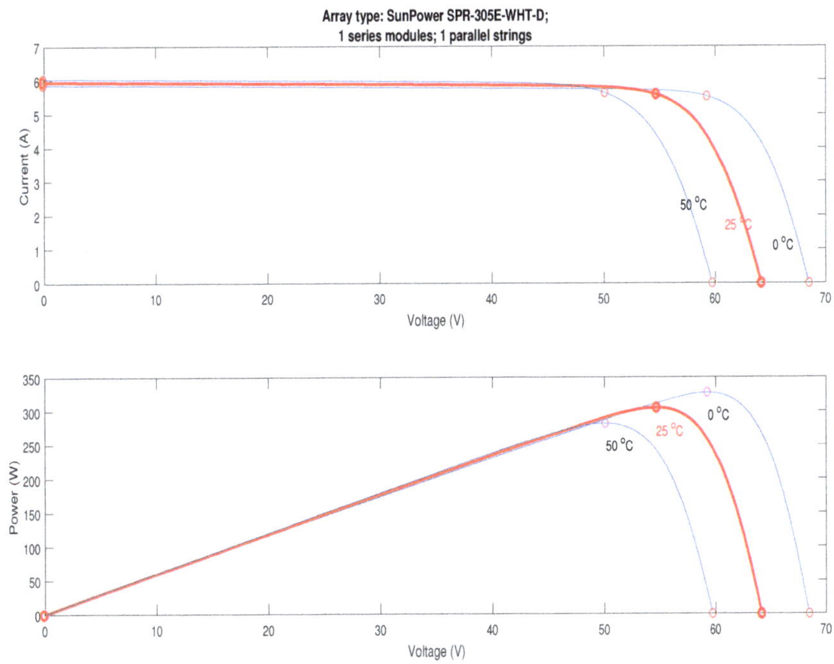

Figure 4. I-V and P-V electrical characteristics of SunPower SPR-305E-WHT-D module, at different temperatures.

2.3. DC-DC Boost Converter

A DC-DC boost converter is an electrical device that steps up (increases) a DC voltage from a lower level to a higher level. It achieves this by using a combination of inductors, capacitors, diodes, and switches (typically transistors) arranged in a specific circuit configuration, as shown in Figure 5. Current passes through the inductor when the switch is closed, and during this state the energy is stored in the inductor magnetic field. When the switch opens, the inductor's magnetic field decreases, generating a voltage higher than the input voltage, which forward-biases the diode and allows the energy to flow to the output capacitor. The capacitor smooths the voltage, providing a stable higher output voltage. This process repeats rapidly, continuously boosting the voltage. Modeling a DC-DC boost converter involves analyzing its behavior in different operating conditions to understand how it converts voltage efficiently. The key aspects of modeling include circuit equations, duty cycle, and switching modes. The complete mathematical expression of the DC-DC boost converter could, therefore, be represented by (7) [2,5]:

$$\begin{cases} \dfrac{dI_L}{dt} = \dfrac{1}{L}V_{PV} - \dfrac{1}{L}(1-d)V_{dc} \\ \dfrac{dV_o}{dt} = \dfrac{1}{C_2}(1-d)I_L - \dfrac{1}{RC_2}V_{dc} \end{cases} \tag{7}$$

where the parameter d refers to the duty cycle. Assume $x_1 = I_L$ and $x_2 = V_{dc}$ are state variables. Then, (7) can be written as follows:

$$\begin{cases} \dot{x}_1 = \dfrac{1}{L}V_{PV} - \dfrac{1}{L}(1-d)x_2 \\ \dot{x}_2 = \dfrac{1}{C_2}(1-d)x_1 - \dfrac{1}{RC_2}x_2 \end{cases} \tag{8}$$

where (8) is the state space's representation of the considered boost converter. The above mathematical model (8) can be represented as the following system mathematically:

$$\dot{x} = \frac{dx}{dt} = f(x,t) + g(x,t)d \tag{9}$$

where $x = [x_1\ x_2]^T$, $f(x,t) = \left[\frac{1}{L}(V_{PV} - V_{dc})\ \frac{1}{C_2}\left(I_L - \frac{V_{dc}}{R}\right)\right]^T$, $g(x,t) = \left[\frac{V_{dc}}{L}\ -\frac{I_L}{C_2}\right]^T$.

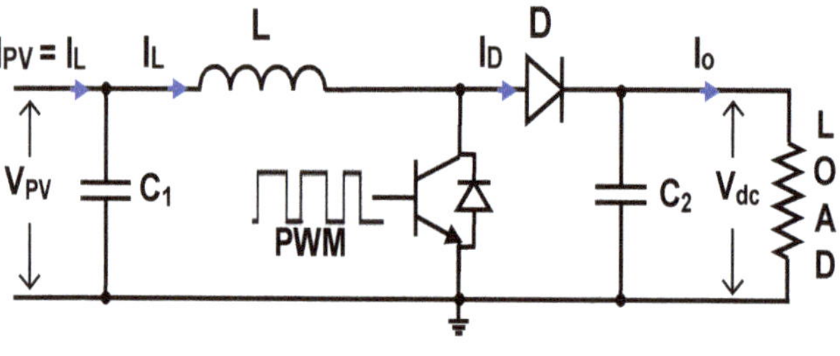

Figure 5. DC-DC boost converter schematic.

The DC-DC boost converter has been designed using the parameters listed in Table 2.

Table 2. DC-DC boost converter parameters.

Parameters	Symbol	Values	Units
Inductance	L	5	mH
Input capacitance	C_1	220	µF
Output capacitance	C_2	330	µF
Switching frequency	F	20	KHz
Load	R	18	Ω

3. Synergetic Control Theory (SCT)

A significantly innovative approach in contemporary nonlinear control theory is the Synergetic Control Theory (SCT). It is founded on concepts from contemporary mathematics and synergetics, which study how systems build functional structures. This approach is designed to handle complex systems and ensure stability and control in various applications, including robotics, power systems, and chemical reactors. Consider the following nonlinear system:

$$\dot{x} = f(x,t) + g(x,t)d \tag{10}$$

where $x \in R^n$ is the vector of the nonlinear system states, $f(x,t) \in R^n$ expresses the system dynamics represented with a smooth nonlinear function, $g(x,t) \neq 0$ is the gain of the control function, and finally the required control input is denoted by d, which should be $\in R$.

The synergetic control algorithm, which guarantees that the dynamics of the derived system progress from any initial state to the invariant manifold and then toward the system (10) origin, is the basis for determining the control vector, d, in practice. The specific macro variables ψ, often known as aggregated variables, determine the control that is built. The dynamic evolving of these macro variables ψ, which can be expressed as a function of the dynamical system's state variables, needs to be appropriately selected by the designer and should meet the following evolution constraint [21,27,28]:

$$T\dot{\psi} + \theta(\psi) = 0 \tag{11}$$

where T is a specific designer chosen parameter that determines the rate of convergence speed to the invariant manifold $\psi(x,t) = 0$ specified by the macro-variable ψ. And $\theta(\psi)$ is defined a smooth differentiable function of ψ that has to be selected, such that [21,27]:

(1) invertible and differentiable;
(2) $\theta(0) = 0$;
(3) $\theta(\psi)\psi > 0, \forall\psi \neq 0$.

It is clear that if the function $\theta(\psi)$ is selected in the form of (12), then the chosen $\theta(\psi)$ guarantees the mentioned constraints.

$$\theta(\psi) = \psi(x,t) \tag{12}$$

As demonstrated in the literature [2,22], the process mentioned previously may be used with DC-DC boost converters. The matter at hand is figuring out the control law (duty cycle d) that the MPPT controller should produce instantaneously, to precisely track the targeted maximum power point. Assume that the invariant manifold defined as follows (13):

$$\psi = \frac{\partial P_{PV}}{\partial I_L} = 0. \tag{13}$$

Hence,

$$\frac{\partial(V_{PV} I_L)}{\partial I_L} = I_L \frac{\partial V_{PV}}{\partial I_L} + V_{PV} = 0 \tag{14}$$

By chain rule, one can write the following:

$$\frac{d\psi}{dt} = \left(\frac{d\psi}{dI_L}\right)\left(\frac{dI_L}{dt}\right) \tag{15}$$

Replacing (12) and (15) in (11) gives the following:

$$T\left(\frac{d\psi}{dI_L}\right)\left(\frac{dI_L}{dt}\right)+\psi=0 \tag{16}$$

Since

$$\frac{d\psi}{dI_L}=2\frac{\partial V_{PV}}{\partial I_L}+I_L\frac{\partial^2 V_{PV}}{\partial^2 I_L} \tag{17}$$

Combining together the boost converter state space Equations (8) and (17) in Equation (16) gives the following:

$$\begin{aligned}&\left[2\frac{\partial V_{PV}}{\partial I_L}+I_L\frac{\partial^2 V_{PV}}{\partial^2 I_L}\right]\left[\frac{1}{L}V_{PV}-\frac{1}{L}(1-d)V_{dc}\right]\\&=-\frac{1}{T}\left[V_{PV}+I_L\frac{\partial V_{PV}}{\partial I_L}\right]\end{aligned} \tag{18}$$

Thus, the control law:

$$d=1-\frac{V_{PV}}{V_{dc}}-\frac{V_{PV}+I_L\frac{\partial V_{PV}}{\partial I_L}}{T\frac{V_{dc}}{L}\left[2\frac{\partial V_{PV}}{\partial I_L}+I_L\frac{\partial^2 V_{PV}}{\partial^2 I_L}\right]} \tag{19}$$

The chattering problem can be minimized or eliminated since the control rule produced by the synergetic control theory is continuous rather than a switching term, as shown by (19).

The asymptotic stability of the PV solar system with the synergetic-based MPPT algorithm is achieved by employing a Lyapunov function candidate, which serves as a mathematical tool to analyze the stability properties of a dynamical system. By constructing a suitable Lyapunov function, it is possible to demonstrate that the system's trajectories converge to an equilibrium point over time. This approach involves showing that the Lyapunov function is positive definite and its derivative along the system's trajectories is negative definite, thereby ensuring that the system's state asymptotically approaches the desired equilibrium.

Theorem 1. *Consider the nonlinear DC-DC boost converter with a PV module standalone power system* (8)*; the system will converge to the invariant manifolds* $\psi=0$ *under the action of the control laws* (19). *And the PV system will track the MPP accurately.*

Proof. Define a Lyapunov candidate function as follows:

$$W=\frac{1}{2}\psi_1^2 \tag{20}$$

then, the time derivative of W is as follows:

$$\dot{W}=(\psi\dot{\psi}) \tag{21}$$

substituting (11) and (12) into (21) yields the following:

$$\dot{W}=\psi\left(\frac{d\psi}{dt}\right)=\psi\left[\left(-\frac{1}{T}\right)\psi\right] \tag{22}$$

consequently, we have:

$$\dot{W}=\left(-\frac{1}{T}\right)\psi^2\leq 0 \tag{23}$$

Therefore, $\dot{W}\leq 0$.

Consequently, the standalone PV system is asymptotically stable. And this concludes the proof. □

Figure 6 shows the flowchart of this algorithm and provides a systematic representation of its step-by-step operation, illustrating the key steps, beginning by voltage and current measurement, power computation, synergetic control law application, and duty cycle adjustment for the DC-DC converter. By following this structured approach, the synergetic MPPT ensures optimal energy harvesting under varying environmental conditions, making it a reliable solution for PV applications.

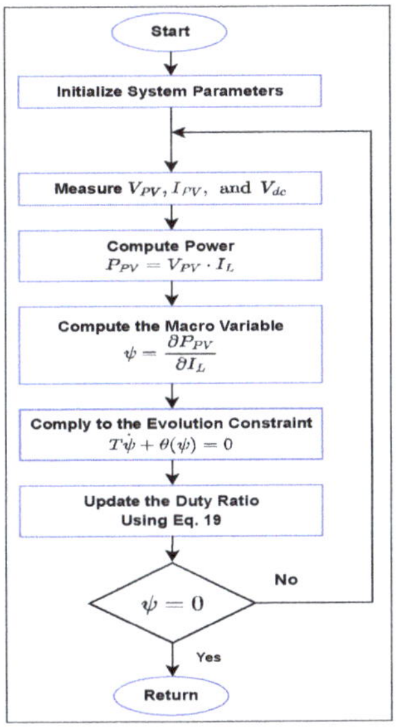

Figure 6. Flowchart diagram of the proposed synergetic control-based MPPT algorithm.

4. Implementation Aspects

This part presents the outcomes of the simulation experiments, which were designed to evaluate the performance of the proposed MPPT synergetic controller system under different scenarios. Experiments were designed to test various scenarios and parameters to understand their impact on the system's performance. The results are categorized and discussed in detail to highlight key findings and trends. The aims through these simulations were to provide a comprehensive evaluation of the proposed MPPT synergetic controller, as shown in Figure 1, under different conditions, thereby offering insights into its robustness, efficiency, and potential areas for improvement.

4.1. FPGA 32-Bits Fixed-Point Implementation

Fixed-point representation is often used on FPGAs due to its efficiency and performance benefits. Fixed-point arithmetic typically requires fewer hardware resources and consumes less power compared to floating-point arithmetic. This efficiency is crucial for FPGAs, which have limited resources. Additionally, fixed-point arithmetic can be faster and has more predictable timing behavior, making it suitable for real-time applications.

Another advantage of fixed-point representation is its simplicity. Fixed-point arithmetic is easier to implement and understand, reducing the likelihood of design errors. FPGA design tools also provide good support for fixed-point arithmetic, facilitating efficient synthesis and optimization. Moreover, many FPGA applications, such as digital signal processing, communications, and control systems, can tolerate or prefer fixed-point arithmetic due to the nature of the algorithms and the required precision. Fixed-point representation allows designers to choose the exact number of bits for the integer and fractional parts, providing custom precision tailored to the application's needs.

A prevalent signed fixed-point encoding notation is $Qm.n$, which provides m integer bits, n fractional bits, and 1 sign bit. Its accuracy is 2^{-n}, and its corresponding limit is between -2^m and $2^m - 2^{-n}$. In this work, a Q16.16 fixed-point data format is used to represent V_{PV}, I_{PV}, and V_{dc} signals of the PV system.

To determine the appropriate fixed-point representation for a signal, we started by analyzing the signal's characteristics. We identified the dynamic range by finding the minimum and maximum values of the signals inside that the MPPT synergetic controller can take, and assessed the precision requirements. This initial analysis helped us understand the needs of our signal processing task.

Choosing the total number of bits, or word length, for the fixed-point representation, requires balancing precision, dynamic range, and resource usage. We allocated bits between the integer and fractional parts. For the integer part, we had to ensure enough bits to cover the entire dynamic range of the signal, where the number of integer bits n should satisfy $2^n \geq \max(\text{absolute value of signal})$. The remaining bits were used for the fractional part, increasing precision but reducing the dynamic range.

4.2. Simulation Results

The PV system and the MPPT algorithm were modeled and simulated using the Xilinx System Generator's blockset for seamless integration, as shown in Figure 7. The sampling time was selected as $Ts = 1 \times 10^{-6}$ s. In synergetic control theory, the parameter T plays a crucial role in shaping the system's transient response and stability, particularly in MPPT applications for photovoltaic (PV) systems. It determines the speed at which the system converges to the MPP, where a smaller T results in a faster response but may introduce instability or oscillations, while a larger T ensures smoother tracking at the cost of slower convergence. Typically, $0.01\text{ s} \leq T \leq 0.1$ s is selected to balance speed and stability. Improper selection of T can lead to excessive duty cycle variations, affecting power tracking efficiency. To determine an optimal T, simulation-based tuning is recommended, where different values can be tested to evaluate convergence speed, power oscillations, and steady-state error. By fine-tuning T, the synergetic MPPT controller can achieve a balance between rapid tracking and robust stability, ensuring efficient power extraction under dynamic environmental conditions. The convergence time for the synergistic controller is chosen as $T = 0.05$ s in this study. The duty cycle control law given by (19) is realized, as shown in Figure 8. Using delay blocks in the designed model is a crucial technique for equalizing time delays across different paths in FPGA designs. Delay blocks introduce a specified number of clock cycles delay into a signal path, thereby balancing timing across various paths. Equalizing the time delay for all paths in an FPGA design using a Xilinx System Generator is crucial for maintaining data integrity, ensuring proper synchronization, and achieving reliable operation. Unequal time delays can cause data corruption as different parts of the data may arrive at different times, leading to incorrect data interpretation. The algorithms were rigorously simulated to ensure accuracy and effectiveness in managing the PV system's output.

Two factors are taken into consideration while evaluating the simulation results for the suggested MPPT strategy: temperature fluctuation and adaptability to irradiance, under standard climate conditions (SCC) of temperature 25 °C and irradiance = 1000 W/m^2.

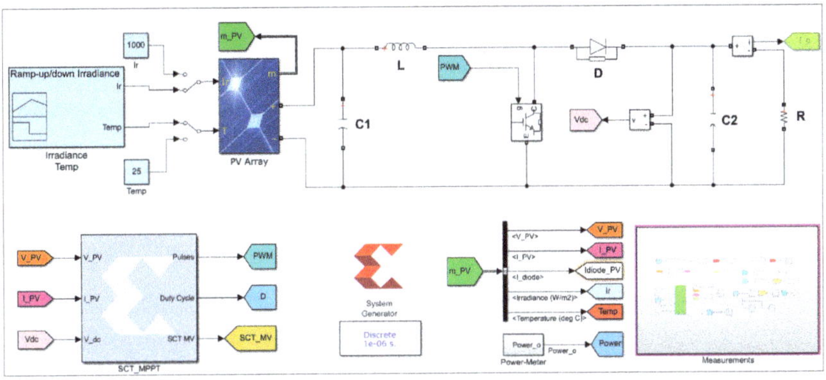

Figure 7. The overall PV system design and the synergetic control-based MPPT algorithm.

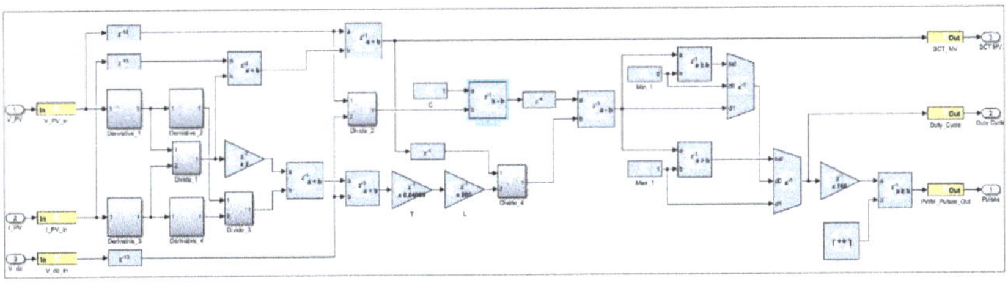

Figure 8. The inside detail of the SCT_MPPT subsystem in Figure 7.

Figure 9a shows the output power under the standard climate condition SCC. The results confirm a good performance and high effectiveness for the suggested controller, in both steady and transient states. Obviously, it is noted in a transient state that the proposed synergetic algorithm ascertains fast convergence to the MPP and the operating point moves on the synergetic manifold in the correct direction. At the same time, the manipulated variable or the duty cycle of the proposed technique converges to the optimal value in limited time as, shown in Figure 9b, and the aggregated synergetic variable is maintained very close to zero, as shown in Figure 9c. This will guarantee the ability to reach the optimum point ($dP_{pv}/dI_{pv} = 0$). A zero macro-variable indicates stable system operation, and the system is operating at its desired equilibrium point, which is aligned with a maximum power output from the PV array. Moreover, in a steady state, once the output power of the PV system is maintained at the maximum, a significant reduction in the oscillation around the MPP appeared and, as a result, the power extracted using the synergetic approach was much larger. In addition, the PV system voltages and currents are given in Figure 9d.

To examine the energy harvesting performance of the proposed MPPT controller under irradiance and temperature variations, in the beginning, the temperature remained constant at 25 °C during the first 2 s, as shown part in Figure 10b, while the irradiance levels dropped abruptly, mimicking real-world conditions. This type of change can be used to simulate sudden changes in weather conditions, such as a cloud passing over the solar panel or the sudden onset of a shadow. The irradiance level jumps instantaneously from one value to another. To test the irradiance effect, the irradiance levels reduced from 1000 W/m^2 to 500 W/m^2 at $t = 0.38$ s. A smooth ramp increase in irradiance was applied at $t = 1$ s to recover the original 1000 W/m^2. This change represents a gradual rise in the intensity of sunlight over a period of time. This type of change can be used to simulate the natural increase in sunlight during sunrise or the gradual clearing of clouds. The irradiance level increases linearly from one value to another over a specified duration. After that, an abrupt change in the temperature was applied by increasing it from 25 °C to 50 °C at

$t = 2$ s, while keeping the irradiance at 1000 W/m^2 and the load remained the same during the simulation time. The irradiance and temperature profiles are shown in Figure 10a and Figure 10b, respectively. The tracking results of these changes are shown in Figure 10.

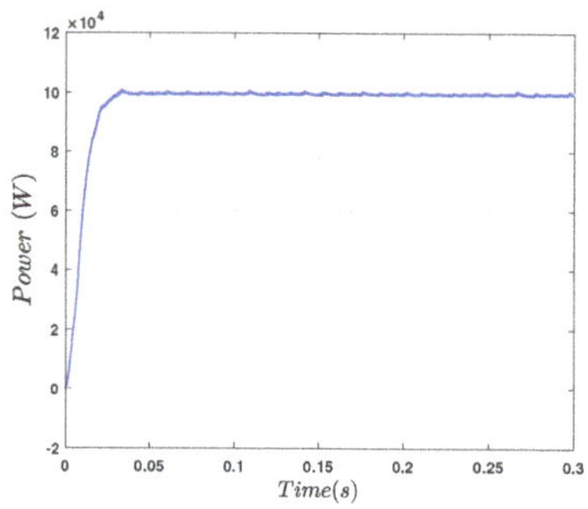

(**a**) Output power.

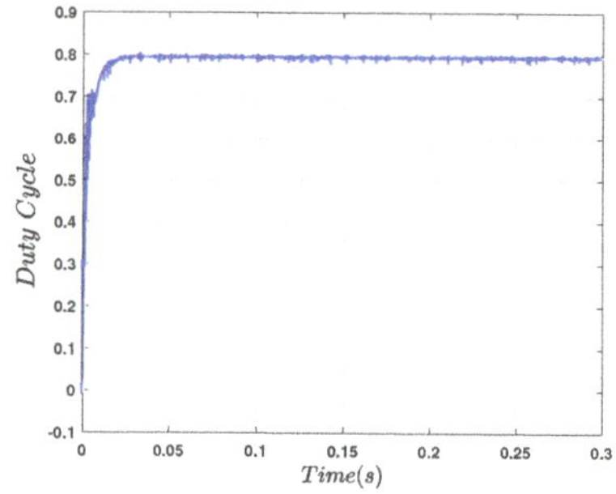

(**b**) Duty cycle.

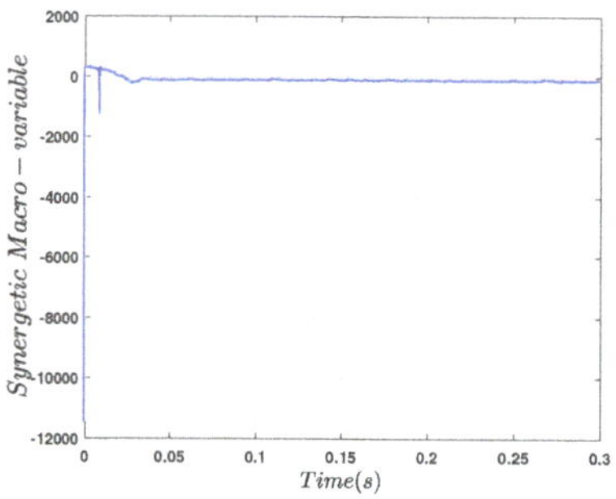

(**c**) Aggregated synergetic macro-variable.

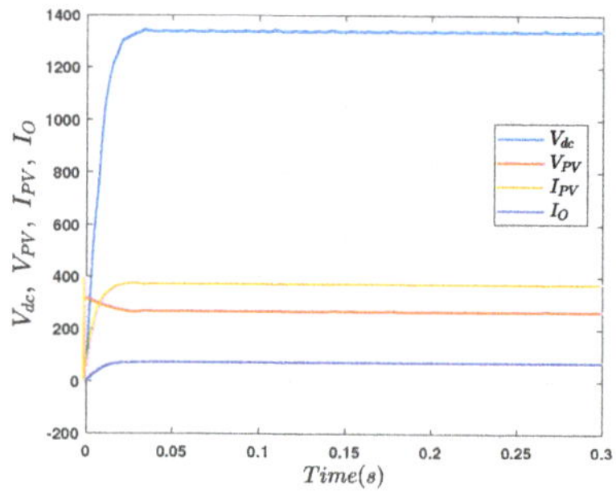

(**d**) PV system voltages and currents.

Figure 9. Standard meteorological conditions test results, where irradiance = 1000 W/m^2 and temperature = 25 °C.

The power extracted from the PV generator is shown in Figure 10c; when the irradiance level sharply changes at time $t = 0.38$ s, the MPPT synergetic controller can quickly track the maximum power point at both 1000 W/m^2 and 500 W/m^2 irradiance levels, respectively. The same is applicable when applying a ramp variation in the irradiance power at time $t = 1$ s. From these result, it is clear to conclude that the developed MPPT synergetic algorithm is robust to abrupt changes in illumination.

The synergetic macro-variable always lies on the attractor vicinity ($\psi = 0$), as illustrated in Figure 10d. This denotes the robustness of using the new approach. The duty cycle of the drive signal generated using the proposed FPGA MPPT controller is shown in Figure 10e. The drive PMW signal applied to the boost DC-DC converter successfully achieved the control objective of maintaining the movement toward the MPP, despite the disturbances applied to the irradiance levels and temperature value. Figure 10f illustrates the output voltage (V_{dc}), the PV generator voltage (V_{PV}), the PV generator current (I_{PV}), and the load current (I_O).

All the simulation results above confirm that the control approach based on synergetic theory is able to ensure output at the optimum point in transient and steady-state conditions and can provide strong robustness against disturbances in the external conditions without inversely affecting the output power. Moreover, all the results show that the responses are chatter-free, with smooth signals.

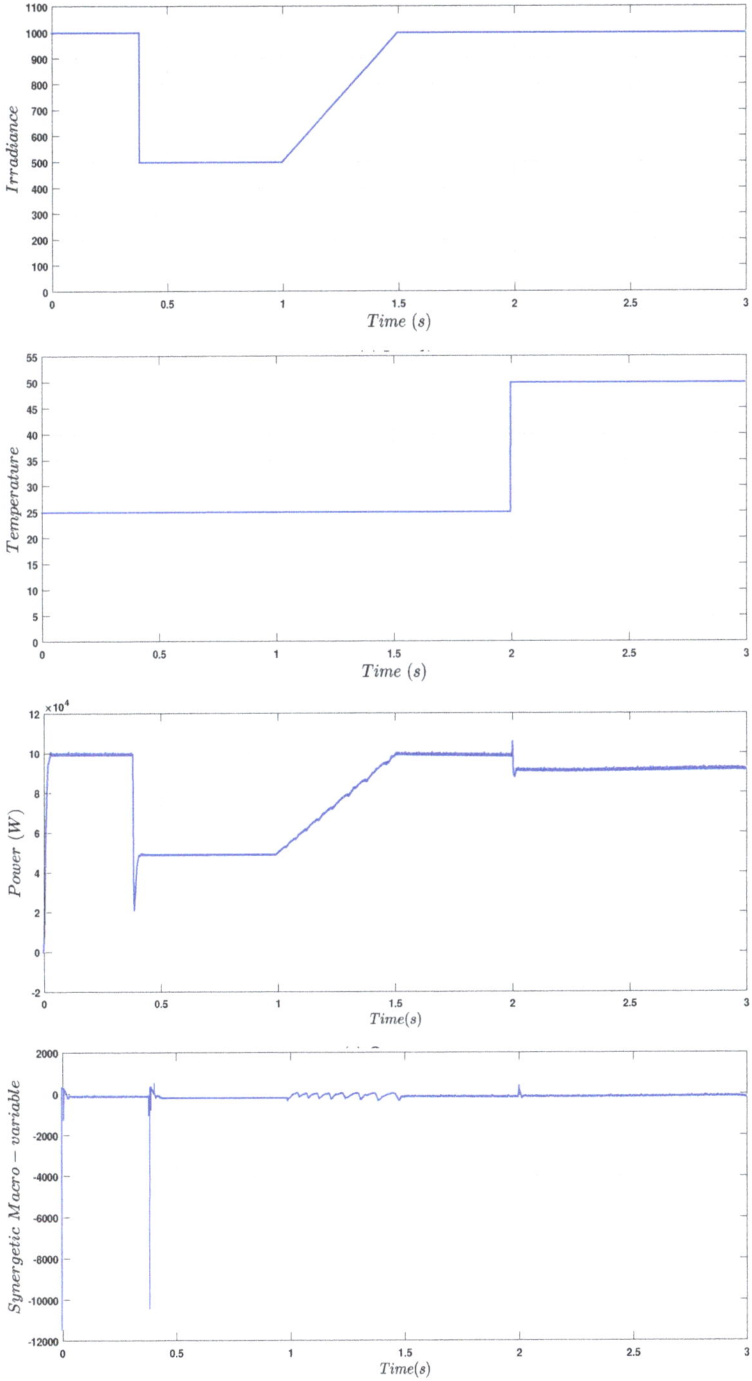

Figure 10. *Cont.*

(**d**) The synergetic macro-variable time waveform.

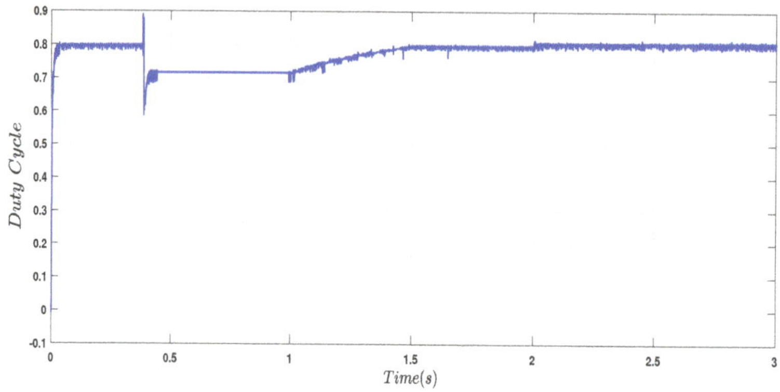

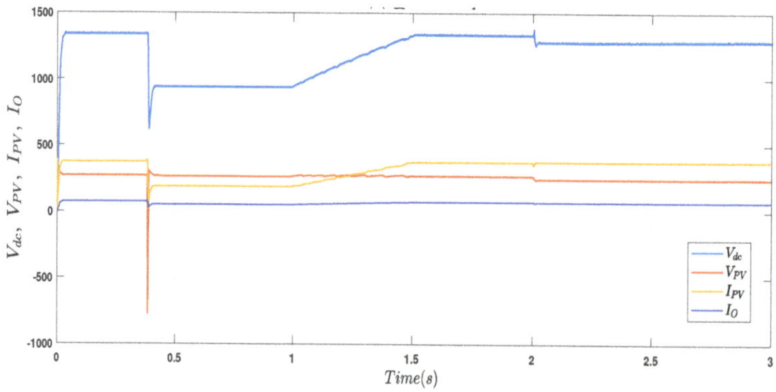

(f) The standalone PV system voltages and current measurements.

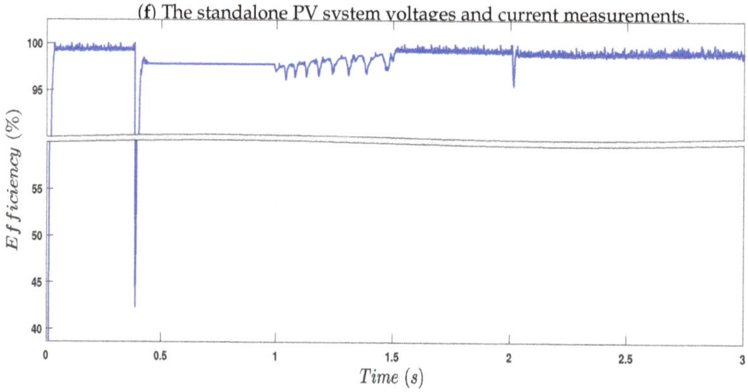

(g) PV system's efficiency.

Figure 10. Results of the PV system under irradiance and temperature variations.

The integration of photovoltaic (PV) systems with boost converters demonstrates remarkable efficiency, even in the face of various disturbances such as fluctuating irradiance and temperature changes, as shown in Figure 10g. At the core of this enhanced performance lies the synergy between the PV panels and the boost converter, which serves to regulate and optimize the voltage and current output to maximize the extracted power from the PV system. This optimization is primarily driven by the suggested synergetic MPPT algorithms, which ensure that the PV panels operate at their peak power point regardless of external conditions by continuously adjusting the duty cycle to enable the system to maximize energy capture from the sunlight.

The average efficiency of extracting power from a photovoltaic (PV) system is remarkably high, reaching an impressive $\eta_{MPPT} = 98.11\%$, ensuring that the majority of the captured sunlight is effectively utilized. This efficiency not only enhances the overall performance of the PV system but also contributes to its sustainability and cost-effectiveness. With such a high efficiency rate, PV systems can provide reliable and clean energy, reducing dependence on conventional fossil fuels and mitigating environmental impact. To evaluate the effectiveness of our proposed MPPT method, a comparative analysis was conducted against various state-of-the-art techniques reported in the literature as given in Table 3. The comparison considers key performance metrics, including MPPT tracking time, steady-state oscillation, and overall efficiency. Our work demonstrates superior performance in terms of MPPT (Maximum Power Point Tracking) time and steady-state oscillations, compared to other approaches. The MPPT time in our work is the shortest (0.03 s), outperforming methods like FLC-based MPPT (0.30 s) and PSO and hybrid intelligent methods (>1 s). Additionally, our approach achieves the lowest steady-state oscillation (0.1%), which is significantly lower than the oscillations seen in other techniques such as PSO (1.6%) and FLC-based MPPT (1.0%). The use of a Boost converter in our method ensures efficient power conversion. Furthermore, our MPPT efficiency is 98.11%, which is higher than most other reported methods. While the FLC-based MPPT achieves 98% efficiency, our approach still surpasses it. Other techniques, such as Hybrid Intelligent Controller and Feedforward ANN, exhibit lower efficiencies, exceeding only 91% and 90%, respectively. These results highlight the effectiveness of our MPPT strategy in achieving faster convergence, reduced power fluctuations, and higher overall efficiency, making it a promising alternative to existing solutions.

Table 3. Comparative studies of synergetic MPPT with other MPPT recent implementations.

Reference	Algorithm	DC-DC Converter	MPPT Time (s)	Steady-State Oscillation (%)	MPPT Efficiency (%)
[29]	FLC-based MPPT	Boost	0.3	±1.0	98.00
[30]	Feed forward ANN	Boost	0.03	±0.7	>90.00
[18]	PSO	Buck	>1	±1.6	97.00
[31]	Hybrid intelligent controller	Cuk	>1	±0.4	>91.00
Proposed Work	Synergetic MPPT	Boost	0.03	±0.1	98.11

4.3. Hardware Co-Simulation of the Suggested MPPT Algorithm

The hardware co-simulation framework allows for the integration of detailed simulation models with hardware implementations, facilitating a more comprehensive evaluation of control strategies. This approach enables the exploration of complex control algorithms and their real-world performance without the need for extensive hardware prototyping. The hardware co-simulation was then performed to test the control algorithms on an FPGA in real-time, ensuring the simulated performance matched the hardware implementation. The Xilinx System Generator facilitated the automatic generation of HDL code from the Simulink models, which was synthesized and implemented on an FPGA for high-speed, real-time control. The control logic was optimized for efficiency and responsiveness, integrating it meticulously with the PV system to achieve optimal performance. Extensive testing and validation were conducted to ensure the control law's stability, efficiency and reliability under various operating conditions, resulting in a robust and high-performing PV system.

The proposed algorithm was designed using the FPGA ZedBoard Zynq xc7z020-1clg484 Evaluation and Development Kit. The full system with hardware co-simulation model for the FPGA design is shown in Figures 11 and 12. The JTAG (Joint Test Action

Group) interface, typically used for debugging and programming FPGA devices, is connected to the PC via USB, as shown in Figure 13. In this setup, JTAG acts as a bridge between the FPGA board and the MATLAB/Simulink environment. When the system operates, the FPGA continuously reads V_{dc}, V_{PV}, and I_{PV} signals. These measurements are transmitted in real-time through the JTAG port. Then, serial samples were returned to the PC using Simulink/Matlab R2020b. The viewer recorded the output drive PWM signal. This allowed for real-time testing and verification of the design in a simulated environment that closely mirrors actual hardware behavior. Overall, this setup leverages the JTAG port for bidirectional communication between the FPGA hardware and MATLAB/Simulink, enabling thorough testing and validation of the FPGA-based control systems in real-time applications.

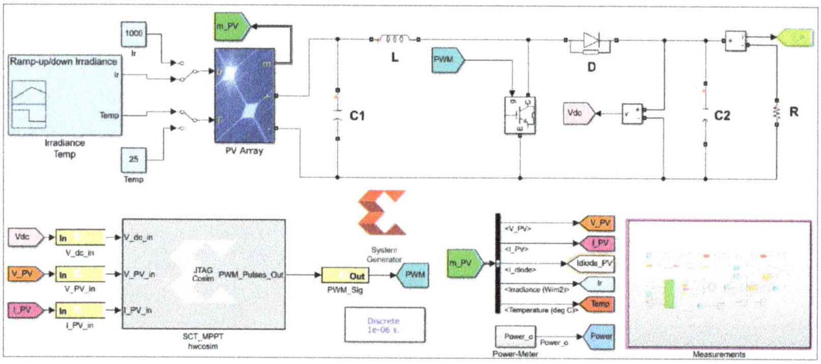

Figure 11. The hardware co-simulation overall design.

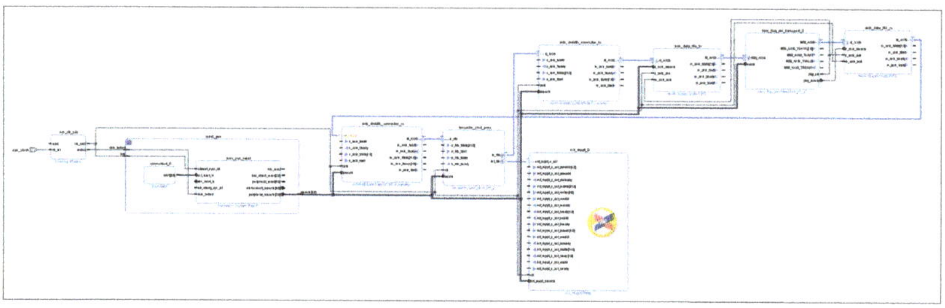

Figure 12. The inside details of the SCT_MPPT subsystem in Figure 11, implemented on the FPGA ZedBoard kit.

Figure 13 illustrates the hardware co-simulation involving the FPGA Xilinx ZedBoard, an essential process in validating and optimizing FPGA designs. This co-simulation integrates both hardware and software components, demonstrating their interaction and performance in a real-world scenario. This approach not only confirms the design's functionality but also ensures compatibility and efficiency across various operational situations, underscoring its vital role in FPGA development workflows. In addition to the hardware co-simulation, Figure 13 shows the modeling of photovoltaic (PV) systems and the implementation of the Maximum Power Point Tracking (MPPT) algorithm in Simulink. The PV model in Simulink captures the electrical characteristics and behavior of solar panels under diverse environmental conditions, providing insights into their efficiency and output. The MPPT algorithm, which dynamically adjusts the operating point to maximize power extraction, is integrated within this simulation. This combination enables the detailed analysis and optimization of solar energy systems, ensuring that the PV system operates at peak efficiency despite variations in sunlight and temperature.

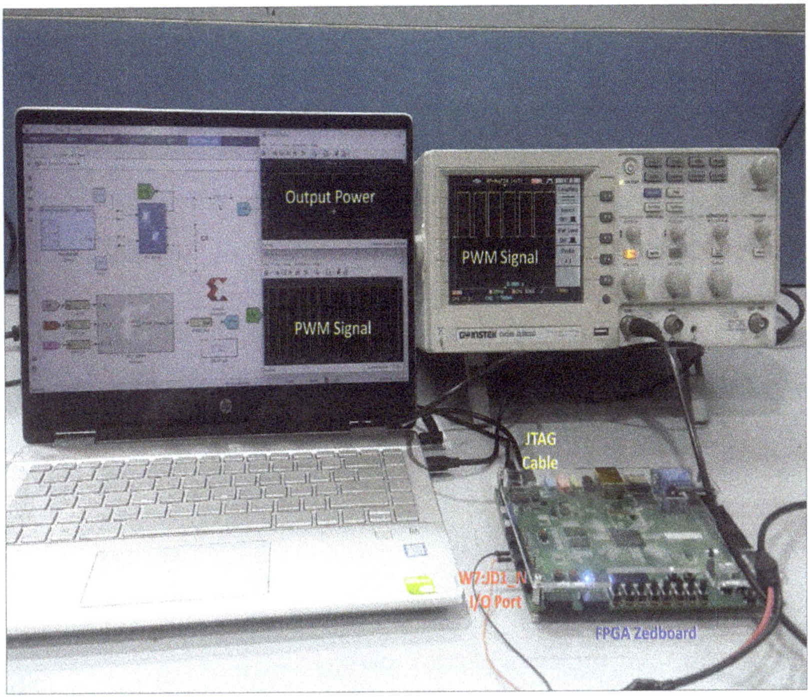

Figure 13. The experimental real-time hardware-in-the-loop implementation of the proposed synergetic MPPT algorithm.

Figure 13 further depicts the generation of the output PWM signal used to drive the boost converter, represented both in Simulink and on the oscilloscope screen. The PWM (Pulse Width Modulation) signal is crucial for regulating the operation of the boost converter, ensuring that the output power meets the specified requirements. This simulation showcases the precise timing and duty cycle adjustments necessary for maintaining stable power levels from variable input sources. Additionally, Figure 13 shows the JTAG cable connecting the PC to the Xilinx ZedBoard, facilitating seamless communication for programming, debugging, and testing FPGA designs. This robust connection allows developers to transfer data and configuration files directly to the ZedBoard, enabling real-time modifications and diagnostics, thus streamlining the development process and enhancing the overall design and testing efficiency.

A summary of the system resource utilization, power consumption, and timing constraints of the proposed MPPT controller are all shown in Figure 14. Overall, the comprehensive insights offered by the Timing, Power, and Utilization Report in Vivado are invaluable for achieving an optimal balance between performance, power efficiency, and resource usage. The FPGA design demonstrates remarkable efficiency across multiple dimensions, ensuring optimal resource utilization and high performance. The design achieves a balanced use of logic elements, utilizing only 65% of the available capacity. This indicates a well-structured and optimized logic implementation, minimizing redundancy and maximizing the functionality within the given resources. The sequential logic, represented by the flip-flops, is utilized at a moderate 41%, showcasing effective clock management and a careful consideration of timing constraints. These metrics highlight our design's ability to maintain a high level of complexity without overburdening the FPGA's logic capacity, ensuring reliable and efficient operation. Additionally, our design excels in memory and computational efficiency. With block RAM usage at 65%, we have effectively leveraged the FPGA's memory resources to support data-intensive operations while maintaining a balance that prevents resource exhaustion. The use of DSP slices stands at 23%, indicating a proficient allocation of these resources for mathematical and signal processing tasks. This balanced usage demonstrates our design's capability to handle complex computations and data manipulations efficiently. Furthermore, the I/O pin utilization at 49% provides ample room for scalability and future expansion, reflecting thoughtful planning and resource management. Overall, these metrics collectively underscore the efficiency and robustness of our FPGA design, positioning it well for both current performance needs and future growth. The resource utilization metrics suggest that the FPGA implementation is not only effective but also efficient in terms of hardware usage.

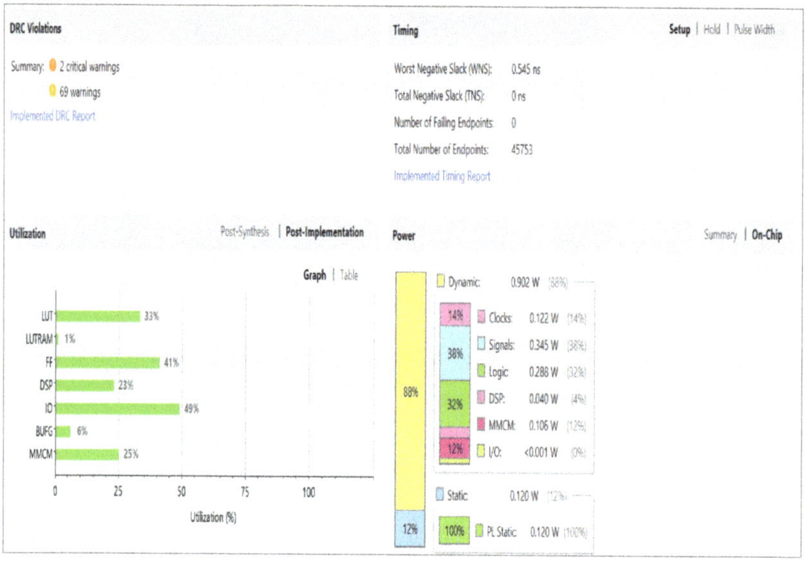

Figure 14. FPGA timing, utilization, and power reports.

The RTL (Register-Transfer Level) elaborated schematic generated by Vivado v2020.2 software is shown in Figure 15 and provides a visual representation of the synergetic MPPT controller digital design at a high level of abstraction.

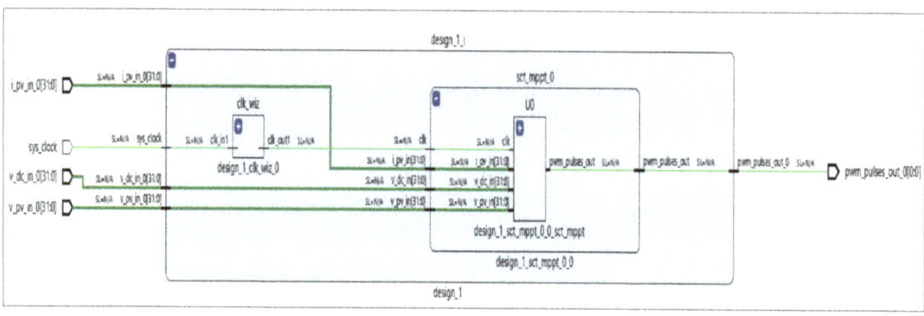

Figure 15. FPGA RTL elaborated schematic.

5. Conclusions

On a final note, this work presents a novel FPGA-based implementation of a synergetic control algorithm for maximum power point tracking (MPPT) in photovoltaic (PV) systems. The Zedboard Zynq xc7z020-1clg484 development board was used to implement the design for the real-time evaluation of the developed system. The proposed MPPT model, which integrates the photovoltaic module, boost converter, SCT algorithm, and PWM drive signal, has been designed and tested under varying environmental conditions. The performance evaluation highlights the effectiveness of the FPGA-based synergetic MPPT controller in tracking the MPP accurately and robustly. A comparative analysis of key performance metrics—including MPPT tracking time, steady-state oscillation, and overall efficiency—demonstrates the superior performance of the proposed approach. The FPGA-based synergetic algorithm significantly reduces MPPT tracking time, minimizes oscillations around the MPP, and improves the overall energy harvesting efficiency compared to conventional MPPT techniques. The ability of FPGA to execute high-speed parallel computations enhances the controller's responsiveness, making it highly suitable for dynamic environmental conditions. The use of FPGA in MPPT control offers several advantages, including real-time processing capabilities, low-latency execution, and high computational efficiency. These benefits make FPGA a promising platform for advanced renewable energy applications. Looking ahead, AI-driven techniques like machine learning and deep learning techniques can be leveraged to further optimize the synergetic MPPT algorithm. AI-driven predictive models can enhance real-time decision making, improving tracking accuracy and adapting the controller to complex environmental variations. Moreover, extending this work beyond standalone PV systems, future developments will focus on integrating the proposed FPGA-based MPPT controller within smart grids and hybrid renewable energy systems. Additionally, large-scale experimental validation will be conducted to assess the controller's feasibility in real-world smart grid applications.

Author Contributions: Conceptualization, A.-B.A.A.-H.; Investigation, F.R.T.; Methodology, A.-B.A.A.-H.; Resources, V.-T.P.; Supervision, F.R.T.; Validation, F.R.T.; Visualization, V.-T.P.; Writing—original draft, A.-B.A.A.-H.; Writing—review and editing, V.-T.P. All authors have read and agreed to the published version of the manuscript.

Funding: This research received no external funding.

Data Availability Statement: The authors declare that the data supporting the findings of this study are all available within the article.

Conflicts of Interest: The authors have declared no conflict of interest.

Nomenclature

PV	Photovoltaic
MPP	Maximum power point
$MPPT$	Maximum power point tracking
η_{MPPT}	MPPT efficiency
PVG	Photovoltaic generator
$P\&O$	Perturb and Observe
IC	Incremental conductance
HC	Hill climbing
SMC	Sliding-mode control
SCT	Synergetic control theory
$FPGA$	Field-programmable gate array
WNS	Worst negative slack (ns)

I_{ph}	Diode photo current (A)
I_d	Diode current (A)
I_{sh}	Diode shunt current (A)
I_s	Reverse saturation current (A)
P_{ma}	Maximum power (W)
V_{oc}	Open-circuit voltage (V)
V_{mp}	Optimum operating voltage (V)
I_{mp}	Optimum operating current (A)
K_i	Temperature coefficient of Isc %/°C
K_v	Temperature coefficient of Voc %/°C
d	Duty cycle
L	Inductance (H)
C_1	Input capacitance (F)
C_2	Output capacitance (F)
F	Switching frequency (Hz)
R	Load resistance (Ω)
ψ	Macro-variables
T	Designer chosen parameter that determines the rate of convergence
SCC	Standard climate conditions
V_{dc}	Output voltage (V)
V_{PV}	PV voltage (V)
I_{PV}	PV current (A)
TNS	Total Negative Slack (ns)

References

1. Farh, H.M.; Eltamaly, A.M. Maximum power extraction from the photovoltaic system under partial shading conditions. In *Modern Maximum Power Point Tracking Techniques for Photovoltaic Energy Systems*; Springer: Cham, Switzerland, 2020; pp. 107–129.
2. Taissala, A.; Goron, D.; Nisso, N.; Kidmo, D.K.; Ekam, P.S.N.; Mbakop, F.K.; Djongyang, N. An Optimized Synergetic Nonlinear Controller (OSNC) based maximum power point tracking for a standalone photovoltaic system using a boost converter. *Energy Rep.* **2022**, *8*, 107–122. [CrossRef]
3. Ahmed, J.; Salam, Z. A modified P&O maximum power point tracking method with reduced steady-state oscillation and improved tracking efficiency. *IEEE Trans. Sustain. Energy* **2016**, *7*, 1506–1515.
4. Zegaoui, A.; Aillerie, M.; Petit, P.; Sawicki, J.; Charles, J.; Belarbi, A. Dynamic behaviour of PV generator trackers under irradiation and temperature changes. *Sol. Energy* **2011**, *85*, 2953–2964. [CrossRef]
5. Radjai, T.; Gaubert, J.P.; Rahmani, L.; Mekhilef, S. Experimental verification of P&O MPPT algorithm with direct control based on Fuzzy logic control using CUK converter. *Int. Trans. Electr. Energy Syst.* **2015**, *25*, 3492–3508.
6. Ouberri, Y.; Yatimi, H.; Aroudam, E. Design of a robust sliding mode controller for MPPT based on automation PLC for PV applications. *Int. Trans. Electr. Energy Syst.* **2020**, *30*, e12296. [CrossRef]
7. Salah, C.B.; Ouali, M. Comparison of fuzzy logic and neural network in maximum power point tracker for PV systems. *Electr. Power Syst. Res.* **2011**, *81*, 43–50. [CrossRef]
8. Ishaque, K.; Salam, Z.; Amjad, M.; Mekhilef, S. An improved particle swarm optimization (PSO)–based MPPT for PV with reduced steady-state oscillation. *IEEE Trans. Power Electron.* **2012**, *27*, 3627–3638. [CrossRef]
9. Yap, K.Y.; Sarimuthu, C.R.; Lim, J.M.Y. Artificial intelligence based MPPT techniques for solar power system: A review. *J. Mod. Power Syst. Clean Energy* **2020**, *8*, 1043–1059.
10. Belkaid, A.; Gaubert, J.P.; Gherbi, A. Design and implementation of a high-performance technique for tracking PV peak power. *IET Renew. Power Gener.* **2017**, *11*, 92–99. [CrossRef]
11. Bianconi, E.; Calvente, J.; Giral, R.; Petrone, G.; Ramos-Paja, C.A.; Spagnuolo, G.; Vitelli, M. A fast current-based MPPT technique based on sliding mode control. In Proceedings of the 2011 IEEE International Symposium on Industrial Electronics, Gdansk, Poland, 27–30 June 2011; pp. 59–64.
12. Bianconi, E.; Calvente, J.; Giral, R.; Mamarelis, E.; Petrone, G.; Ramos-Paja, C.A.; Spagnuolo, G.; Vitelli, M. Perturb and observe MPPT algorithm with a current controller based on the sliding mode. *Int. J. Electr. Power Energy Syst.* **2013**, *44*, 346–356. [CrossRef]
13. Abdelaziz, A.Y.; Almoataz, Y. *Modern Maximum Power Point Tracking Techniques for Photovoltaic Energy Systems*; Springer: Cham, Switzerland, 2020.

14. Kolesnikov, A.; Veselov, G.; Kolesnikov, A. *Modern Applied Control Theory: Synergetic Approach in Control Theory*; TRTU: Taganrog, Moscow, 2000; pp. 4477–4479.
15. Erenturk, K.; Draou, A.; AlKassem, A. Design and comparison of different types of synergetic controllers for islanded DC microgrids. *Sustainability* **2022**, *14*, 8792. [CrossRef]
16. Jiang, Z. Design of a nonlinear power system stabilizer using synergetic control theory. *Electr. Power Syst. Res.* **2009**, *79*, 855–862. [CrossRef]
17. Kondratiev, I.; Santi, E.; Dougal, R.; Veselov, G. Synergetic control for m-parallel connected DC-DC buck converters. In Proceedings of the 2004 IEEE 35th Annual Power Electronics Specialists Conference (IEEE Cat. No. 04CH37551), Aachen, Germany, 20–25 June 2004; Volume 1, pp. 182–188.
18. Li, H.; Yang, D.; Su, W.; Lü, J.; Yu, X. An overall distribution particle swarm optimization MPPT algorithm for photovoltaic system under partial shading. *IEEE Trans. Ind. Electron.* **2018**, *66*, 265–275. [CrossRef]
19. Al-Hussein, A.B.A.; Tahir, F.R.; Ouannas, A.; Sun, T.C.; Jahanshahi, H.; Aly, A.A. Chaos suppressing in a three-buses power system using an adaptive synergetic control method. *Electronics* **2021**, *10*, 1532. [CrossRef]
20. Al-Hussein, A.B.A.; Tahir, F.R.; Boubaker, O. Chaos elimination in power system using synergetic control theory. In Proceedings of the 2021 18th International Multi-Conference on Systems, Signals & Devices (SSD), Monastir, Tunisia, 22–25 March 2021; pp. 340–345.
21. Al-Hussein, A.B.A.; Tahir, F.R.; Pham, V.T. Fixed-time synergetic control for chaos suppression in endocrine glucose–insulin regulatory system. *Control Eng. Pract.* **2021**, *108*, 104723. [CrossRef]
22. Ayat, R.; Bouafia, A.; Gaubert, J.P. Experimental validation of synergetic approach based MPPT controller for an autonomous PV system. *IET Renew. Power Gener.* **2021**, *15*, 1515–1527. [CrossRef]
23. Ilyas, A.; Khan, M.R.; Ayyub, M. FPGA based real-time implementation of fuzzy logic controller for maximum power point tracking of solar photovoltaic system. *Optik* **2020**, *213*, 164668. [CrossRef]
24. Koutroulis, E.; Kalaitzakis, K.; Tzitzilonis, V. Development of an FPGA-based system for real-time simulation of photovoltaic modules. *Microelectron. J.* **2009**, *40*, 1094–1102. [CrossRef]
25. Prathap, J.A.; Anandhi, T. A novel parallel duty cycle control algorithm for photovoltaic voltage regulator system using FPGA. *Microprocess. Microsyst.* **2019**, *65*, 107–120. [CrossRef]
26. Mars, N.; Grouz, F.; Essounbouli, N.; Sbita, L. Synergetic MPPT controller for photovoltaic system. *J. Electr. Electron. Syst.* **2017**, *6*, 232. [CrossRef]
27. Kondratiev, I.; Santi, E.; Dougal, R. Robust nonlinear synergetic control for m-parallel-connected DC-DC boost converters. In Proceedings of the 2008 IEEE Power Electronics Specialists Conference, Rhodes, Greece, 15–19 June 2008; pp. 2222–2228.
28. Kolesnikov, A.A. Introduction of synergetic control. In Proceedings of the 2014 American Control Conference, Portland, OR, USA, 4–6 June 2014; pp. 3013–3016.
29. Youssef, A.; El Telbany, M.; Zekry, A. Reconfigurable generic FPGA implementation of fuzzy logic controller for MPPT of PV systems. *Renew. Sustain. Energy Rev.* **2018**, *82*, 1313–1319. [CrossRef]
30. Jyothy, L.P.; Sindhu, M. An artificial neural network based MPPT algorithm for solar PV system. In Proceedings of the 2018 4th International Conference on Electrical Energy Systems (ICEES), Chennai, India, 7–9 February 2018; pp. 375–380.
31. Vimalarani, C.; Kamaraj, N. Improved method of maximum power point tracking of photovoltaic (PV) array using hybrid intelligent controller. *Optik* **2018**, *168*, 403–415.

computation

MDPI

Article

Model Predictive Control of Spatially Distributed Systems with Spatio-Temporal Logic Specifications

Ikkei Komizu, Koichi Kobayashi * and Yuh Yamashita

Graduate School of Information Science and Technoloty, Hokkaido University, Sapporo 060-0814, Japan
* Correspondence: k-kobaya@ssi.ist.hokudai.ac.jp; Tel.: +81-11-706-6452

Abstract: In this paper, for spatially distributed systems, we propose a new method of model predictive control with spatio-temporal logic specifications. We formulate the finite-time control problem with specifications described by SSTL$_f$ (signal spatio-temporal logic over finite traces) formulas. In the problem formulation, the feasibility is guaranteed by representing control specifications as a penalty in the cost function. Time-varying weights in the cost function are introduced to satisfy control specifications as well as possible. The finite-time control problem can be written as a mixed integer programming (MIP) problem. According to the policy of model predictive control (MPC), the control input can be generated by solving the finite-time control problem at each discrete time. The effectiveness of the proposed method is presented through a numerical example.

Keywords: feasibility; model predictive control; spatially distributed systems; spatio-temporal logic specifications

1. Introduction

A spatially distributed system is a system whose state dynamically changes over time and space [1,2]. This system represents the temporal changes in the states of other related locations using measurement values collected at a specific location. Spatially distributed systems appear in various issues such as smart buildings, advanced road traffic systems, and vibration control [3–6]. Therefore, it is important to contemplate the control problem of spatiotemporal patterns in spatially distributed systems.

In recent years, temporal logic has been employed in control issues related to IoT and cyber-physical systems. Temporal logic is a logic system where the truth value of a proposition changes over time [7]. In temporal logic, temporal operators are added to conventional logical operators, allowing the description of propositions in relation to time. In order to handle continuous signals, signal temporal logic (STL) has been proposed in [8]. In STL, specifications of properties of dense time and real-valued signals can be described. Control methods using STL have been widely studied (see, e.g., [9–16]). Moreover, signal spatio-temporal logic (SSTL) has been proposed for spatially distributed systems [17]. In SSTL, spatial operators are introduced to temporal logic. In [18], SSTL has been applied to the monitoring and planning of robotic tasks. Furthermore, SSTL$_f$ has been proposed in the case of finite traces [6].

In [6], the finite-time optimal control problem with SSTL$_f$ formulas for spatially distributed systems is formulated and is reduced to a mixed-integer programming (MIP) problem. When the dynamics in a spatially distributed system are linear, this problem is reduced to a mixed integer linear programming (MILP) problem. However, in [6], only the finite-time optimal control problem has been considered, and model predictive control (MPC) has not been focused on. MPC is a control method that generates the control input by solving the finite-time optimal control problem at each time and has various applications (see, e.g., [19–23]). MPC for spatially distributed systems has been studied in, e.g., [24]. To the best of our knowledge, MPC with spatio-temporal logical specifications for spatially distributed systems has not been studied.

In this paper, we propose a new method of MPC for spatially distributed systems. A control specification is described by an SSTL$_f$ formula. We suppose that an SSTL$_f$ formula is given for a sufficiently long time interval. An SSTL$_f$ formula and spatial constraints in the finite-time optimal control problem are derived from a given SSTL$_f$ formula. In the finite-time optimal control problem studied in this paper, an SSTL$_f$ formula and spatial constraints are considered as a penalty in the cost function. Hence, the feasibility of the finite-time optimal control problem can be guaranteed. In other words, the control input can be necessarily generated. In a similar way to the method in [6], the finite-time optimal control problem can be reduced to an MIP problem. The proposed method provides us with an efficient control method for complex systems.

This paper is organized as follows. In Section 2, a spatially distributed system is introduced. In Section 3, SSTL$_f$ is summarized. In Section 4, the finite-time optimal control problem is formulated. In Section 5, the reduction of the finite-time optimal control problem to an MIP problem is explained. In Section 6, a procedure of MPC is proposed. In Section 7, a numerical example is explained to show the effectiveness of the proposed method. In Section 8, we conclude this paper.

Notation: Let $\mathcal{R}$ denote the set of real numbers. For the finite set A, let $|A|$ denote the number of elements in A.

2. Spatially Distributed Systems

Consider a multi-dimensional Euclidean space partitioned into a grid, represented as an undirected graph $\mathcal{G} = (\mathcal{L}, \mathcal{E})$, where $\mathcal{L}$ is the set of nodes and $\mathcal{E} \subseteq \mathcal{L} \times \mathcal{L}$ is the set of edges. The state of the node l at time t is denoted by $\mathrm{x}(t,l) \in \mathcal{R}^n$. Let $\mathcal{L}' \subseteq \mathcal{L}$ denote the set of nodes without control inputs. Let $\mathcal{B}(l) := \{i_1^l, \ldots, i_{|\mathcal{B}(l)|}^l\} \subseteq \mathcal{L}$ denote neighborhoods of the node l. A discrete-time spatially distributed system on graph $\mathcal{G}$ is given by

$$\mathrm{x}(t+1,l) = \begin{cases} g_l(\mathrm{x}(t,l), \mathrm{x}(t,i_1^l), \ldots, \mathrm{x}(t,i_{|\mathcal{B}(l)|}^l), \mathrm{u}(t,l)) & \text{if } l \in \mathcal{L} \setminus \mathcal{L}' \\ g_l(\mathrm{x}(t,l), \mathrm{x}(t,i_1^l), \ldots, \mathrm{x}(t,i_{|\mathcal{B}(l)|}^l)) & \text{if } l \in \mathcal{L}', \end{cases} \tag{1}$$

where $\mathrm{u}(t,l) \in \mathcal{U} \subseteq \mathcal{R}^m$ is the control input ($\mathcal{U}$ is a set representing input constraints), and g_l is a real-valued continuous function. We suppose that the centralized controller calculates the control inputs by collecting the states.

3. SSTL$_f$

We explain the syntax of SSTL$_f$ (see [6] for further details).

The syntax of SSTL$_f$ is defined over a set of m atomic predicates

$$M = \{\mu_j(x_1, \ldots, x_n) \mid j \in \{1, \ldots, m\},\ \mu_j(x_1, \ldots, x_n) \equiv (f_j(x_1, \ldots, x_n)) \geq 0)\}.$$

An SSTL$_f$ formula is recursively defined by the following syntax:

$$\varphi ::= \mathrm{True} \mid \neg\varphi \mid \varphi_1 \wedge \varphi_2 \mid \mathcal{F}_{[t_1,t_2]}\varphi \mid \mathcal{G}_{[t_1,t_2]}\varphi \mid \Diamond^l_{[d_1,d_2]}\varphi \mid \boxdot^l_{[d_1,d_2]}\varphi,$$

where φ, φ_1, and φ_2 are the SSTL$_f$ fomula, t_1, t_2 are times such that $t_1 \leq t_2$, and $d_1, d_2 \in \mathcal{R}_{\geq 0}$ with $d_1 \leq d_2$. Temporal operators $\mathcal{F}_{[t_1,t_2]}$ and $\mathcal{G}_{[t_1,t_2]}$ are called *eventually* and *globally* operators, respectively. Within the time interval $[t_1, t_2]$, $\mathcal{F}_{[t_1,t_2]}\varphi$ denotes that φ is satisfied at least once, while $\mathcal{G}_{[t_1,t_2]}\varphi$ denotes that φ is satisfied at all times. Spatial operators $\Diamond^l_{[d_1,d_2]}$ and $\boxdot^l_{[d_1,d_2]}$ are called *somewhere* and *everywhere* operators, respectively. Define $L^l_{[d_1,d_2]} := \{l' \in \mathcal{L} \mid d_1 \leq d(l,l') \leq d_2\}$, where $d(l,l')$ denotes the distance between l and l'. The spatial operator $\Diamond^l_{[d_1,d_2]}\varphi$ denotes that at least one node within $L^l_{[d_1,d_2]}$ satisfies φ, while $\boxdot^l_{[d_1,d_2]}\varphi$ denotes that all nodes within $L^l_{[d_1,d_2]}$ satisfy φ.

For a given finite spatio-temporal trace x, the satisfaction of an SSTL$_f$ φ formula at the time t and the location l, which is denoted by $(x,t,l) \models \varphi$, is defined recursively as follows:

$$
\begin{aligned}
(x,t,l) \models \mu_j &\Leftrightarrow (f_j(x_1,\ldots,x_n) \geq 0) \\
(x,t,l) \models \neg\varphi &\Leftrightarrow (x,t,l) \not\models \varphi \\
(x,t,l) \models \varphi_1 \wedge \varphi_2 &\Leftrightarrow (x,t,l) \models \varphi_1 \wedge (x,t,l) \models \varphi_2 \\
(x,t,l) \models \varphi_1 \mathcal{U}_{[t_1,t_2]} \varphi_2 &\Leftrightarrow \exists t' \in \{t_1,\ldots,t_2\}.\,(x,t',l) \models \varphi_2 \\
&\qquad \wedge (\forall t'' \in \{t_1,\ldots,t'-1\}.\,(x,t'',l) \models \varphi_1) \\
(x,t,l) \models \mathcal{G}_{[t_1,t_2]}\varphi &\Leftrightarrow \forall t' \in \{t_1,\ldots,t_2\}.\,(x,t',l) \models \varphi \\
(x,t,l) \models \mathcal{F}_{[t_1,t_2]}\varphi &\Leftrightarrow \exists t' \in \{t_1,\ldots,t_2\}.\,(x,t',l) \models \varphi \\
(x,t,l) \models \Diamond^{l}_{[d_1,d_2]}\varphi &\Leftrightarrow \exists l' \in L.\,(d_1 \leq d(l,\,l') \leq d_2) \wedge (x,t,l') \models \varphi \\
(x,t,l) \models \boxdot^{l}_{[d_1,d_2]}\varphi &\Leftrightarrow (x,t,l) \models \neg(\Diamond^{l}_{[d_1,d_2]}\neg\varphi).
\end{aligned}
$$

By utilizing SSTL$_f$ formulas, control specifications for the system (1) can be described.

4. Problem Formulation

The time interval for control is defined as $\{0,1,\ldots,H\}$. For this interval, we assume that the SSTL$_f$ formula φ is given as a control specification. In MPC, we solve the finite-time optimal control problem in the time interval $\{t,t+1,\ldots,t+N\}$, where t is the current time, and N is the prediction horizon. To generate the control input, this problem is solved until $t = H-1$.

Assume that from the SSTL$_f$ formula φ, the SSTL$_f$ formula $\varphi_F(t,l)$ that should be satisfied in the time interval $\{t,t+1,\ldots,t+N\}$ can be derived. Assume also that from the SSTL$_f$ formula φ, the spatial constraint $\varphi_T(k,l)$ at time $k = t,t+1,t+N$ such that φ is easily satisfied in the time interval $\{t+N+1,t+N+2,\ldots,t+H\}$ can be derived. Let $z_{\varphi_F}(t,l)$ and $z_{\varphi_T}(k,l)$ denote binary variables, where $z_{\varphi_F}(t,l)$ ($z_{\varphi_T}(k,l)$) is 1 if $\varphi_F(t,l)$ ($\varphi_T(k,l)$) is true, otherwise 0 (see also Section 5.1).

Under these preparations, consider the following finite-time optimal control problem.

Problem 1. *For the system* (1)*, suppose that the current time t, the current state $x(t,l)$, the previous control input $u(t-1,l)$ ($u(-1,l)=0$), the SSTL$_f$ formula $\varphi_F(t,l)$, the spatial constraint $\varphi_T(k,l)$, and the prediction horizon N are given. Then, find a control input sequence $u(t,l), u(t+1,l),\ldots,u(t+N-1,l) \in \mathcal{U}$ minimizing the following cost function:*

$$
\begin{aligned}
J = &\sum_{k=t}^{t+N-1} \alpha_k \sum_{l\in L/L'} |u(k,l) - u(k-1,l)| \\
&+ \sum_{k=t}^{t+N} \left\{ \sum_{l\in L} \beta_{k,l}(1 - z_{\varphi_F}(t,l)) + \sum_{l\in L} \gamma_{k,l}(1 - z_{\varphi_T}(k,l)) \right\},
\end{aligned}
\tag{2}
$$

where α_k, $\beta_{k,l}$, and $\gamma_{k,l}$ are time-varying weighting coefficients.

The communication cost between the controller and the actuators can be reduced by introducing the term weighted by α_k in the cost function (2).

We suppose that there is no constraint at time $t+N$ when Problem 1 is solved at some time t. Depending on a given SSTL$_f$ formula, when Problem 1 is solved at the next time $t+1$, a constraint at time $t+N+1$ may be newly imposed. In such a case, Problem 1 at time $t+1$ may become infeasible. To overcome this technical issue, constraints related to the SSTL$_f$ formula φ are represented by using terms weighted by $\beta_{k,l}$ and $\gamma_{k,l}$. Hence, the feasibility of Problem 1 is always guaranteed. There is a possibility that the SSTL$_f$ formula φ is not satisfied. The SSTL$_f$ formula φ is satisfied as well as possible by adjusting $\beta_{k,l}$ and $\gamma_{k,l}$.

5. Reduction of Problem 1 to an MIP Problem

In this section, we consider reducing Problem 1 to an MILP problem.

First, we consider modeling the graph structure in the system (1) and introducing binary variables. Next, we consider transforming an SSTL$_f$ formula into a set of linear inequalities. See [6] for further details. The procedure of transforming a logic formula into linear inequalities has been widely studied. See, e.g., [25,26] for further details.

5.1. Introduction of Binary Variables

Consider the system (1). For each $l_i \in L$, introduce $|L|$ binary vectors $v_{l_i} \in \{0,1\}^{|L|}$. Here, $v_{l_i,i} = 1$, meaning the i-th element of v_{l_i} is 1, and for $i \neq j$, $v_{l_i,j} = 0$. The matrix $D \in \mathbb{R}^{|L|\times|L|}$ is a matrix representing distances, where the (i,j)-th element $D_{i,j}$ is given by

$$D_{i,j} = \begin{cases} d(l_i,\ l_j) & \text{if } \Sigma(l_i,\ l_j) \neq 0, \\ M^d & \text{otherwise,} \end{cases}$$

where M^d is a sufficiently large positive number such that $M^d \geq \max\{d(l_i,l_j) \mid l_i,l_j \in L, \Sigma(l_i,l_j) \neq 0\}$. To convert SSTL$_f$ expressions into linear inequalities, introduce the following binary variables $z_\varphi(t,l)$ for each $t \in \mathbb{T}$ and $l \in L$, where φ represents an SSTL$_f$ expression. For a given spatiotemporal trace x,

$$z_\varphi(t,l) = \begin{cases} 1 & \text{if } (x,t,l) \models \varphi, \\ 0 & \text{otherwise.} \end{cases}$$

5.2. Atomic Predicates, Boolean Operators

Next, we consider converting atomic predicates and Boolean operators into linear inequalities.

Consider an atomic predicate $\varphi = \mu_j(x_1,\ldots,x_n)$. The satisfaction of φ is represented as

$$\begin{aligned} f_j(x(t,\ l)) &\leq M^{\mu_j} z_\varphi(t,l) - \epsilon, \\ -f_j(x(t,\ l)) &\leq M^{\mu_j}(1 - z_\varphi(t,l)) - \epsilon, \end{aligned}$$

where M^{μ_j} is a sufficiently large positive number compared to the maximum value of f_j for $j \in \{1,\ldots,m\}$, and ϵ is a sufficiently small number.

Next, we consider converting Boolean operators into linear inequalities. Let $\varphi = \neg\psi$ denote the logical operator representing negation. Then, we can obtain

$$z_\varphi(t,l) = 1 - z_\psi(t,l).$$

Let $\varphi = \bigwedge_{k=1}^{K} \psi_k$ denote the logical operator representing conjunction Then, we can obtain

$$\begin{aligned} z_\varphi(t,l) &\leq z_{\psi_k}(t,l),\ \forall k \in [1,\ K], \\ z_\varphi(t,l) &\geq 1 - K + \sum_{k=1}^{K} z_{\psi_k}(t,l). \end{aligned}$$

Let $\varphi = \bigvee_{k=1}^{K} \psi_k$ denote the logical operator representing logical disjunction. Then, we can obtain

$$\begin{aligned} z_\varphi(t,l) &\geq z_{\psi_k}(t,l),\ \forall k \in [1,\ K], \\ z_\varphi(t,l) &\leq \sum_{k=1}^{K} z_{\psi_k}(t,l). \end{aligned}$$

Thus, any Boolean operators can be converted into linear inequalities as described above.

5.3. Temporal Operators

Next, we consider transforming temporal operators into linear inequalities for finite traces over $\{0,1,\ldots,H\}$. We remark that there are instances where temporal operators change within the time interval for control $\{0,1,\ldots,H\}$ and the actual computation interval for prediction $\{t,t+1,\ldots,t+N\}$.

Consider the global operator $\varphi = \mathcal{G}_{[t_1,t_2]}\psi$ with $t_1 \geq t_2$. Then, over the time interval $\{0,1,\ldots,H\}$, φ represents the logical conjunction of ψ. In this case, we can obtain

$$z_\varphi(t,l) = \begin{cases} \bigwedge_{k=t+t_1}^{t+t_2} \psi(k,l) & \text{if } t \in \{0,\ldots,H-t_2\}, \\ 0 & \text{otherwise.} \end{cases}$$

For the global operator, the linear inequalities remain unchanged within the prediction interval as well.

Consider the eventual operator $\varphi = \mathcal{F}_{[t_1,t_2]}\psi$ with $t_1 \leq t_2$. Then, over the time interval $\{0,1,\ldots,H\}$, φ represents the logical disjunction of ψ. In this case,

$$z_\varphi(t,l) = \begin{cases} \bigvee_{k=t+t_1}^{t+t_2} \psi(k,l) & \text{if } t \in \{0,\ldots,H-t_1\}, \\ 0 & \text{otherwise.} \end{cases}$$

Also, when $t+N < t_2$ in the predicted interval$\{t,t+1,\ldots,t+N\}$, or when $t_1 < t < t_2 \leq t+N$ and $\bigvee_{k=t_1}^{t} \psi(k,l) = 1$, there are no constraints imposed by the temporal operator. Specifically, if $t_1 \leq t$ and $t+N < t_2$ with $\bigvee_{k=t_1}^{t} \psi(k,l) = 1$, there are no constraint conditions even beyond $t+N$ into the future. Also, we can obtain

$$z_\varphi(t,l) = \begin{cases} \bigvee_{k=t}^{t+t_2} \psi(k,l) & \text{if } (\bigvee_{k=t_1}^{t} \psi(k,l) = 0) \wedge (t_1 < t < t_2 \leq t+N), \\ \bigvee_{k=t+t_1}^{t+t_2} \psi(k,l) & \text{if } (t \leq t_1) \wedge (t_2 \leq t+N), \\ 0 & \text{otherwise.} \end{cases}$$

5.4. Spatial Operators

Third, we consider converting spatial operators into linear inequalities. The 'somewhere' operator $\varphi = \Diamond_{[d_1,d_2]}^{l}\psi$ can be represented by

$$z_\varphi(t,l) = \bigvee_{l' \,:\, d_1 \leq v_l^\top D v_l' \leq d_2} z_\psi(t,l').$$

The 'everywhere' operator $\varphi = \Box_{[d_1,d_2]}^{l}\psi$ can be represented by

$$z_\varphi(t,l) = \bigwedge_{l' \,:\, d_1 \leq v_l^\top D v_l' \leq d_2} z_\psi(t,l').$$

5.5. MIP Problem

Let $LE(\varphi_F(t))$ denote the linear inequalities obtained by transforming the SSTL$_f$ formula $\varphi_F(t)$ using the above method. Problem 1 can be equivalently reduced to the following MIP problem.

Problem 2. *Suppose that the current time t, the current state $x(t,l)$, and the previous input $u(t-1,l)$ are given. Then, find a control input sequence $u(t,l), u(t+1,l), \ldots, u(t+N-1,l) \in \mathcal{U}$ minimizing the cost function* (2) *subject to conditions of $LE(\varphi_F(t))$ and $z_{\varphi_F(t)} = 1$.*

If the function g_l in the system (1) is linear with respect to the state and the control input, then Problem 2 is an MILP problem.

6. Model Predictive Control

In this section, we propose a procedure of MPC using Problem 1. MPC is a control method where the control input is generated by solving the finite-time optimal control problem. We can obtain a time sequence of the control input by solving the finite-time optimal control problem. In the conventional MPC, the first one in the obtained input sequence is applied to the plant.

When a control specification is given by an SSTL_f formula, a control specification is changed at each time, because the time interval considered in the finite-time optimal control problem is shifted. Hence, a procedure of MPC under an SSTL_f formula is different from that of the conventional MPC. Based on this fact, we propose a procedure of MPC using Problem 1.

Procedure for model predictive control:

Step 1: Set $t = 0$, $\mathrm{x}(0, l) = \mathrm{x}_{0,l}$, and an SSTL_f formula.

Step 2: Derive an SSTL_f formula and spatial constraints at time t from a given SSTL_f formula.

Step 3: Solve Problem 2.

Step 4: Apply the control input $\mathrm{u}(t, l)$ obtained by solving Problem 1.

Step 5: Measure $\mathrm{x}(t + 1, l)$.

Step 6: Update $t := t + 1$. If $t = H$, then the procedure is terminated, otherwise go to Step 2.

Since Problem 2 is always feasible, we can guarantee that the control input until $t = H - 1$ is calculated.

7. Numerical Example

Consider a room in a 2-dimensional Euclidean space with seven heaters and two windows, where the temperature distribution is controlled according to specifications described by an SSTL_f formula. The room is partitioned into a 10×10 grid, and is modeled by an undirected graph. Figure 1 illustrates the room setup for this simulation. By the discretization of the heat conduction equation, the dynamics of the room temperature are derived as follows:

$$T(t+1,l) = (1 - V \cdot A_l)T(t,l) + Vu(t,l) + \frac{W}{|\mathcal{B}(l)|} \sum_{l' \in \mathcal{B}(l)} (T(t,l') - T(t,l)), \; l \in \mathcal{L}_h,$$

$$T(t+1,l) = (1 - V \cdot A_l)T(t,l) + \frac{W}{|\mathcal{B}(l)|} \sum_{l' \in \mathcal{B}(l)} (T(t,l') - T(t,l)), \; l \in \mathcal{L} \setminus \mathcal{L}_h,$$

where $T(t,l)$ denotes the temperature of the location l at time t, $\mathcal{L}$ is the set of partitioned areas ($|\mathcal{L}| = 100$), and A_l, V, and W are constant. See [6] for further details. In this simulation, we set $V = 1$, $W = 0.4$, and

$$A_l = \begin{cases} 0.05 & \text{if } l \in \mathcal{L}_w, \\ 0 & \text{otherwise.} \end{cases}$$

We also set $H = 99$, $N = 15$, and $T(0,l) = 15$.

The atomic propositions μ_i are defined as $\mu_1 \equiv (x - 18 \geq 0)$ and $\mu_2 \equiv (x - 22 > 0)$. We give two control specifications. The first specification is that the temperature in the locations where people are present and their surroundings must be between 18 °C and 22 °C. The second specification is that in the specified location $l_{2,7} \in \mathcal{L}$ and its surroundings, there must be at least one location where the temperature is between 18 °C and 22 °C at least once during the time interval $15 \leq t \leq 99$. These specifications are represented by the following SSTL$_f$ formulas ($\bar{l} \in \overline{\mathcal{L}} = \{l_{4,3}, l_{5,4}, l_{6,5}\}$):

$$\begin{aligned}
&(T, \bar{l}) \models \varphi_{\bar{l}} = \mathcal{G}_{[30,59]} \boxdot^{l_{6,5}}_{[0,1]} \phi \wedge \mathcal{G}_{[40,69]} \boxdot^{l_{5,4}}_{[0,1]} \phi \wedge \mathcal{G}_{[50,79]} \boxdot^{l_{4,3}}_{[0,1]} \phi, \\
&(T, l_{2,7}) \models \varphi_{l_{2,7}} = \mathcal{F}_{[15,99]} \diamondsuit^{l_{2,7}}_{[0,1]} \phi, \\
&\phi = \mu_1 \wedge \neg \mu_2.
\end{aligned}$$

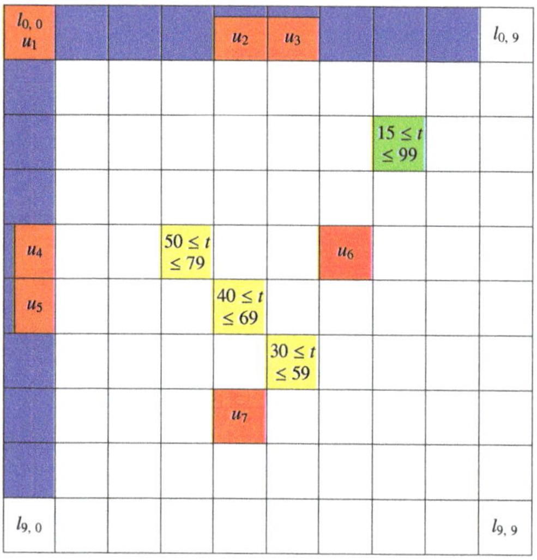

Figure 1. Grid model of the room. Red locations $\mathcal{L}_h = \{l_{0,0}, l_{0,4}, l_{0,5}, l_{4,0}, l_{5,0}, l_{4,6}, l_{6,4}\}$ have a heater with a control input. Blue locations $\mathcal{L}_w = \{l_{0,1}, \ldots, l_{0,8}, l_{1,0}, \ldots, l_{8,0}\}$ face a window. In yellow locations $\overline{\mathcal{L}} = \{l_{4,3}, l_{5,4}, l_{6,5}\}$, we suppose that there are some persons in the time interval shown. A constraint is imposed for also the green location $l_{2,7}$.

The number of spatial constraints is four. The following four spatial constraints are imposed for Problem 1:

$$\boxdot^{l_{6,5}}_{[0,1]} \phi, \quad \boxdot^{l_{5,4}}_{[0,1]} \phi, \quad \boxdot^{l_{4,3}}_{[0,1]} \phi, \quad \diamondsuit^{l_{2,7}}_{[0,1]} \phi.$$

We consider $\varphi = \boxdot^{l_{6,5}}_{[0,1]} \phi$ as an example of transforming a spatial constraint into linear inequalities. This constraint can be rewritten as

$$z_{\varphi}(t, l_{6,5}) = z_{\phi}(t, l_{5,5}) \wedge z_{\phi}(t, l_{6,4}) \wedge z_{\phi}(t, l_{6,5}) \wedge z_{\phi}(t, l_{6,6}) \wedge z_{\phi}(t, l_{7,5}),$$

which is equivalent to the following linear inequalities:

$$\begin{aligned}
&z_{\varphi}(t, l_{6,5}) \leq z_{\phi}(t, l_{5,5}), \\
&z_{\varphi}(t, l_{6,5}) \leq z_{\phi}(t, l_{6,4}), \\
&z_{\varphi}(t, l_{6,5}) \leq z_{\phi}(t, l_{6,5}), \\
&z_{\varphi}(t, l_{6,5}) \leq z_{\phi}(t, l_{6,6}), \\
&z_{\varphi}(t, l_{6,5}) \leq z_{\phi}(t, l_{7,5}), \\
&z_{\varphi}(t, l_{6,5}) \geq 1 - 5 + z_{\phi}(t, l_{5,5}) + z_{\phi}(t, l_{6,4}) + z_{\phi}(t, l_{6,5}) + z_{\phi}(t, l_{6,6}) + z_{\phi}(t, l_{7,5}).
\end{aligned}$$

We remark that these spatial constraints are not necessarily satisfied at each time because these constraints are considered as the penalty in the cost function. For $\gamma_{t,l}$ in the cost function (2), consider two cases: i) $\gamma_{t,l} = 0$ and ii) $\gamma_{t,l} = -0.02(t - t_{1,l})^2 + 10$, where $t_{1,l_{6,5}} = 30$, $t_{1,l_{5,4}} = 40$, $t_{1,l_{4,3}} = 50$, and $t_{1,l_{2,7}} = 15$. Other coefficients α_k and $\beta_{t,l} = 10$ are set as $\alpha_k = 1$ and $\beta_{t,l} = 10$, respectively. These are set through a trial and error process. One of the future efforts is to design these function/parameters in a systematic way.

In addition, when Problem 1 is solved at the initial time, no SSTL_f formula is imposed. For example, at time 10, the following SSTL_f formula is considered as a control specification (note that the prediction horizon N is given by $N = 15$):

$$(T, \bar{l}) \models \varphi_{\bar{l}} = \mathcal{G}_{[10,25]} \boxdot^{l_{6,5}}_{[0,1]} \phi,$$
$$\phi = \mu_1 \wedge \neg\mu_2.$$

If $\Diamond^{l_{2,7}}_{[0,1]} \phi$ is not satisfied until time 83, then after time 84, we impose the constraint that this spatial constraint is satisfied at least one time.

We present the computation result. Figures 2 and 3 show control inputs in two cases. From these figures, we see that the control inputs are changed to satisfy constraints depending on $\gamma_{t,l}$.

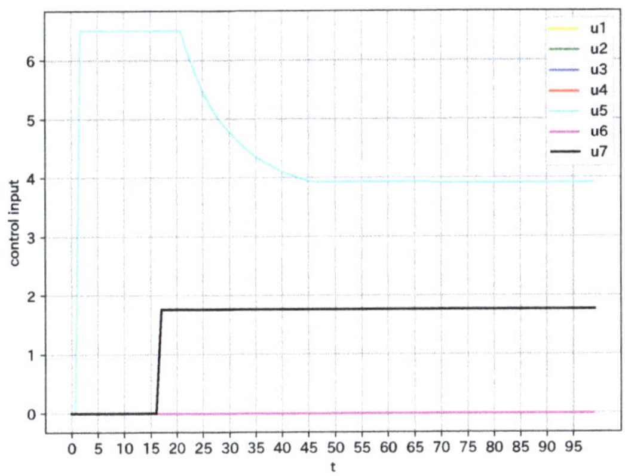

Figure 2. Control inputs in the case of $\gamma_{t,l} = 0$, where control inputs except for u_5 and u_7 are always zero.

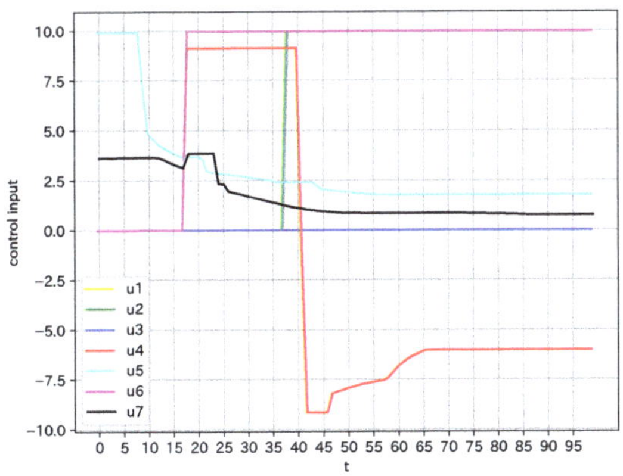

Figure 3. Control inputs in the case of $\gamma_{t,l} = -0.02(t - t_{1,l})^2 + 10$, where u_1 and u_3 are always zero.

Next, we check whether the constraints are satisfied or not. Figures 4 and 5 show whether constraints are satisfied or not in two cases. From Figure 4, we see that constraints are not satisfied at locations $l_{4,3}$ and $l_{5,4}$ in the case of $\gamma_{t,l} = 0$. From Figure 4, we see that this technical issue is overcome by introducing a time-varying weight. Furthermore, spaces and time intervals satisfying certain conditions are explicitly characterized. Based on this characterization, we validate the proposed approach. In Case (i), the percentage that certain conditions for space/time are satisfied is 97.8%. In Case (ii), this percentage is 33.0%. Thus, it becomes easier to satisfy the SSTL$_f$ formula by introducing a time-varying weighting coefficient.

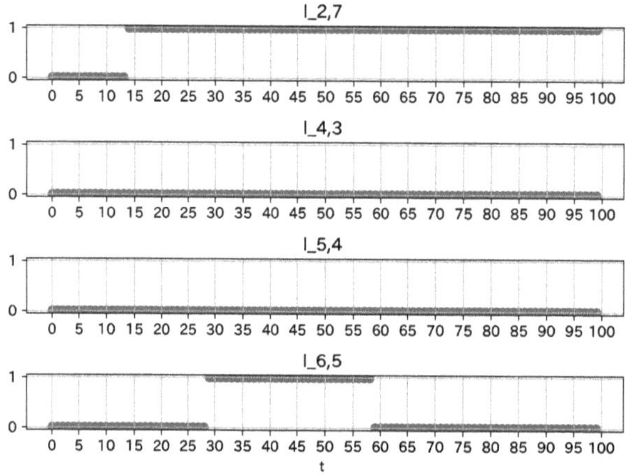

Figure 4. Results whether constraints are satisfied or not in the case of $\gamma_{t,l} = 0$ (1: the constraint is satisfed, 0: the constraint is not satisfed).

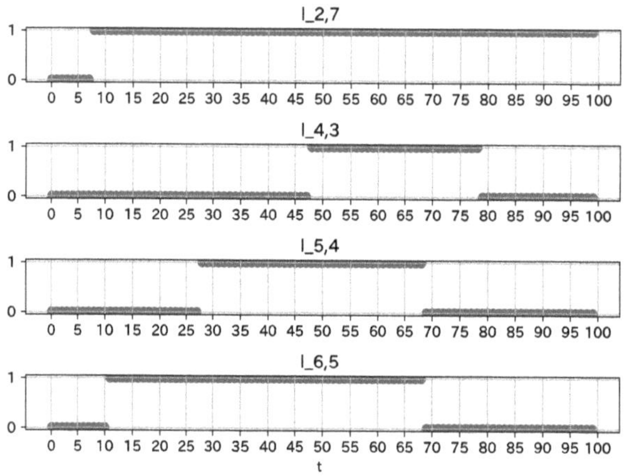

Figure 5. Results whether constraints are satisfied or not in the case of $\gamma_{t,l} = -0.02(t - t_{1,l})^2 + 10$ (1: the constraint is satisfed, 0: the constraint is not satisfed).

Finally, we comment the computation time for solving the problem at each time. The mean computation time and the worst computation time were 8.7 s and 29.4 s, respectively. Here, we used the computer with CPU: Intel Core i5-12600K 3.69 GHz and Memory: 16 GB, and used the CBC (COIN-OR Brand-and-Cut) 2.10.3 [27] https://github.com/coin-or/Cbc

(accessed on 1 September 2024) as an MILP solver. Reducing the computation time is one of the future efforts.

8. Conclusions

In this paper, we proposed a new method of MPC for spatially distributed systems. A control specification is given by an $SSTL_f$ formula. To satisfy it, several conditions and time-varying weighting coefficients were introduced for the finite-time optimal control problem. The proposed method was demonstrated by a numerical example.

One of the future efforts is to develop a general procedure to derive constraint conditions and time-varying weighting coefficients in the finite-time optimal control problem. In addition, it is also important to apply the proposed method to practical and real systems. In order to implement practical and real systems, it is significant to develop a method to reduce the computation time for solving an MIP problem in spatially distributed systems.

Author Contributions: Conceptualization, I.K., K.K. and Y.Y.; methodology, I.K. and K.K.; software, I.K.; writing, I.K. and K.K. All authors have read and agreed to the published version of the manuscript.

Funding: This work was partly supported by JSPS KAKENHI Grant Numbers JP21H04558, JP22K04163, JP23H01430.

Data Availability Statement: Data is contained within the article.

Conflicts of Interest: The authors declare no conflicts of interest.

References

1. Jovanović, M.R. Modeling, Analysis, and Control of Spatially Distributed Systems. Ph.D. Thesis, University of California, Santa Barbara, CA, USA, 2004.
2. Lee, R.; Kiremidjian, A.S. Uncertainty and correlation for loss assessment of spatially distributed systems. *Earthq. Spectra* **2007**, *23*, 753–770. [CrossRef]
3. Potami, R.; Demetriou, M.A.; Grigoriadis, K.M. Actuator switching for vibration control of spatially distributed systems. In Proceedings of the 2007 American Control Conference, New York, NY, USA, 9–13 July 2007; pp. 4981–4986.
4. Malings, C.; Pozzi, M. Value of information for spatially distributed systems: Application to sensor placement. *Reliab. Eng. Syst. Saf.* **2016**, *154*, 219–233. [CrossRef]
5. Li, T.; Liu, J.; Kang, J.; Sun, H.; Yin, W.; Chen, X.; Wang, H. STSL: A novel spatio-temporal specification language for cyber-physical systems. In Proceedings of the 2020 IEEE 20th International Conference on Software Quality, Reliability and Security (QRS), Macau, China, 11–14 December 2020; pp. 309–319.
6. Kinugawa, T.; Ushio, T. Finite-Horizon Optimal Spatio-Temporal Pattern Control under Spatio-Temporal Logic Specifications. *IEICE Trans. Inf. Syst.* **2022**, *105*, 1658–1664. [CrossRef]
7. Gabbay, D.M.; Reynolds, M.A.; Finger, M. *Temporal Logic: Mathematical Foundations and Computational Aspects*; Oxford University Press: Oxford, UK, 2000.
8. Maler, O.; Nickovic, D. Monitoring temporal properties of continuous signals. In Proceedings of the International Symposium on Formal Techniques in Real-Time and Fault-Tolerant Systems, Grenoble, France, 22–24 September 2004; pp. 152–166.
9. Cairoli, F.; Fenu, G.; Pellegrino, F.A.; Salvato, E. Model predictive control of glucose concentration based on signal temporal logic specifications. In Proceedings of the 2019 6th International Conference on Control, Decision and Information Technologies (CoDIT), Paris, France, 23–26 April 2019; pp. 714–719.
10. Péni, T.; Csutak, B.; Szederkényi, G.; Röst, G. Nonlinear model predictive control with logic constraints for COVID-19 management. *Nonlinear Dyn.* **2020**, *102*, 1965–1986. [CrossRef] [PubMed]
11. Sun, D.; Chen, J.; Mitra, S.; Fan, C. Multi-agent motion planning from signal temporal logic specifications. *IEEE Robot. Autom. Lett.* **2022**, *7*, 3451–3458. [CrossRef]
12. Hashimoto, W.; Hashimoto, K.; Takai, S. Stl2vec: Signal temporal logic embeddings for control synthesis with recurrent neural networks. *IEEE Robot. Autom. Lett.* **2022**, *7*, 5246–5253. [CrossRef]
13. Meng, Y.; Fan, C. Signal temporal logic neural predictive control. *IEEE Robot. Autom. Lett.* **2023**, *8*, 7719–7726. [CrossRef]
14. Yu, X.; Dong, W.; Li, S.; Yin, X. Model predictive monitoring of dynamical systems for signal temporal logic specifications. *Automatica* **2024**, *160*, 111445. [CrossRef]
15. Gu, Z.; Guo, R.; Yates, W.; Chen, Y.; Zhao, Y.; Zhao, Y. Walking-by-logic: Signal temporal logic-guided model predictive control for bipedal locomotion resilient to external perturbations. In Proceedings of the 2024 IEEE International Conference on Robotics and Automation (ICRA), Yokohama, Japan, 13–17 May 2024; pp. 1121–1127.

16. Vlahakis, E.E.; Lindemann, L.; Dimarogonas, D.V. Distributed sequential receding horizon control of multi-agent systems under recurring signal temporal logic. In Proceedings of the 2024 European Control Conference (ECC), Stockholm, Sweden, 15–25 June 2024; pp. 305–310.
17. Nenzi, L.; Bortolussi, L.; Ciancia, V.; Loreti, M.; Massink, M. Qualitative and quantitative monitoring of spatio-temporal properties with SSTL. *Log. Methods Comput. Sci.* **2018**, *14*, 21–37.
18. Pek, C.; Schuppe, G.F.; Esposito, F.; Tumova, J.; Kragic, D. SpaTiaL: monitoring and planning of robotic tasks using spatio-temporal logic specifications. *Auton. Robot.* **2023**, *47*, 1439–1462. [CrossRef]
19. Bersani, C.; Ouammi, A.; Sacile, R.; Zero, E. Model predictive control of smart greenhouses as the path towards near zero energy consumption. *Energies* **2020**, *13*, 3647. [CrossRef]
20. Elsisi, M.; Tran, M.Q.; Hasanien, H.M.; Turky, R.A.; Albalawi, F.; Ghoneim, S.S. Robust model predictive control paradigm for automatic voltage regulators against uncertainty based on optimization algorithms. *Mathematics* **2021**, *9*, 2885. [CrossRef]
21. Garcia-Torres, F.; Zafra-Cabeza, A.; Silva, C.; Grieu, S.; Darure, T.; Estanqueiro, A. Model predictive control for microgrid functionalities: Review and future challenges. *Energies* **2021**, *14*, 1296. [CrossRef]
22. Schwenzer, M.; Ay, M.; Bergs, T.; Abel, D. Review on model predictive control: An engineering perspective. *Int. J. Adv. Manuf. Technol.* **2021**, *117*, 1327–1349. [CrossRef]
23. Castelletti, A.; Ficchì, A.; Cominola, A.; Segovia, P.; Giuliani, M.; Wu, W.; Lucia, S.; Ocampo-Martinez, C.; De Schutter, B.; Maestre, J.M. Model predictive control of water resources systems: A review and research agenda. *Annu. Rev. Control.* **2023**, *55*, 442–465. [CrossRef]
24. Wang, M.; Li, N.; Li, S.; Zhang, W. Model Predictive Control Design for Spatially-Distributed System based on Input-Output Data Sets. *IFAC Proc. Vol.* **2011**, *44*, 3641–3646. [CrossRef]
25. Biere, A.; Heljanko, K.; Junttila, T.; Latvala, T.; Schuppan, V. Linear encodings of bounded LTL model checking. *Log. Methods Comput. Sci.* **2006**, *2*, 1–64. [CrossRef]
26. Williams, H.P. *Model Building in Mathematical Programming*; John Wiley & Sons: Hoboken, NJ, USA, 2013.
27. Forrest, J.; Lougee-Heimer, R. CBC user guide. In *Emerging Theory, Methods, and Applications*; INFORMS: Catonsville, MD, USA, 2005; pp. 257–277.

computation

MDPI

Article

The Effect of Proportional, Proportional-Integral, and Proportional-Integral-Derivative Controllers on Improving the Performance of Torsional Vibrations on a Dynamical System

Khalid Alluhydan [1], Ashraf Taha EL-Sayed [2,*] and Fatma Taha El-Bahrawy [2]

1 Department of Mechanical Engineering, College of Engineering, King Saud University, P.O Box 800, Riyadh 11421, Saudi Arabia; kalluhydan@ksu.edu.sa

2 Department of Basic Science, Modern Academy for Engineering and Technology, Elmokattam 11439, Egypt; fatma.taha@eng.modern-academy.edu.eg

* Correspondence: atelsayed@eng.modern-academy.edu.eg

Abstract: The primary goal of this research is to lessen the high vibration that the model causes by using an appropriate vibration control. Thus, we begin by implementing various controller types to investigate their impact on the system's reaction and evaluate each control's outcomes. The controller types are presented as proportional (P), proportional-integral (PI), and proportional-integral-derivative (PID) controllers. We employed PID control to regulate the torsional vibration behavior on a dynamical system. The PID controller aims to increase system stability after seeing the impact of P and PI control. This kind of control ensures that there are no unstable components in the system. By using the multiple time scale perturbation (MTSP) technique, a first-order approximate solution has been obtained. Using the frequency response function approach, the stability and steady-state response of the system at the primary resonance scenario ($\Omega_1 \cong \omega_1, \Omega_2 \cong \omega_2$) are considered as the worst resonance and addressed. Additionally examined are the nonlinear dynamical system's chaotic response and the numerical solution for various parameter values. The MATLAB programs are utilized to attain simulation outcomes.

Keywords: MSPT; P; PI; PID controllers; nonlinear differential equations; active control; stability; torsional vibration

1. Introduction

Torsional vibration occurs in some form in all rotating machinery. Even when the vibration is nearing destructive amplitude, there are situations in which it cannot be identified without specialized monitoring equipment. After the shaft bending stiffness and diametral moment of inertia have been replaced by the twisting stiffness and polar moment of inertia, respectively, many elements of torsional vibration are equivalent to shaft vibration. When something mediates the connection between the vibration and the ground, or when gear teeth or coupling jaws are empty, torsional vibration can be detected by the noise level and vibration (perceptible to touch). Torsional vibration can interact with the ground through gear sets used to change the speed of power transmission systems; in reciprocating machines, the path to the ground is provided by sliding crank mechanisms found in engines and compressors. Typically, torsional vibration manifests as a complicated vibration signal with numerous frequency components. Some systems experience brief torsional vibrations due to shock from sudden starts and the unloading of gear teeth; synchronous electric motor systems may also experience torsional resonance at startup.

Conventional PID controllers have been widely adopted in numerous industrial applications due to their simple design, affordable price, simplicity of maintenance, and there being ready-made modules [1–3]. Ref. [4] offers the implementation of nonlinear state-dependent (SDP-PID+) control employing the SDP transfer function model, a type of nonlinear description of dynamical structures. Fine-tuning traditional PID control is problematic owing to the specific properties of numerous procedures, including binary sample time delays, longer durations, higher-order TF models, and nonlinearities [5–7]. Sayed et al. [8] developed a nonlinear resilient SDP PID control approach for a discrete transfer function with nonlinear properties. This research emphasized robust response processes, for which the robust PID and SDP-PID techniques were specifically designed. Dano and Julli'ere [9] studied how MFC actuators controlled oscillations in a composite structure. Kumar and Ray [10] examined vibrations in sandwich shells with between one and three piezoelectric composites and layering damping techniques. The PD controller is designed to decrease oscillations of a hung Jeffcott rotor through two pairs of poles [11]. A PD controller can effectively relax a beam system's steady-state amplitude vibrations [12]. Eissa et al. [13,14] suggested a PD controller and a time-delayed PD controller to reduce the vibrations of magnetic systems with cubic and quadratic nonlinear coefficients underneath parametric principal forces. Bauomy and El-Sayed employed a PD controller to control the behavior of the MFC laminated shell structure. The purpose of employing the PD controller is to improve system stability by increasing control, as it can forecast future errors in the framework response [15]. More than 90% of industries still utilize PID controllers due to their simplicity, functionality, and ease of usage [16]. PID controller gains are acquired by matching the frequency response of the closed-loop control system [17]. Recently, a systematic approach was used to select PID parameters for nonlinear uncertain structures [18]. PID controllers offer advantages over passive approaches for controlling semi-active suspension systems [19–21]. Ref. [22] investigates the control of a quarter-car semi-active suspension system utilizing a PID controller. The typical PID controller is constructed using the Ziegler–Nichols approach and is used to regulate the suspension system. The torsional vibrations of a one-degree-of-freedom nonlinear dynamical structure are regulated with active control [23]. Wenzhi and Zhiyong [24] suggested an active control to decrease torsional vibration in a big turbogenerator with a rotor shaft. Whole-state feedback control using a linear quadratic regulator (LQR) effectively reduces torsional vibration energy and response in the turbogenerator shaft system. El-Sayed and Bauomy [25] they succeeded in reducing the torsional vibration of a nonlinear dynamical system using passive and active control methods. The research study [26] proposes an adaptive PI event-triggered control approach for MIMO nonlinear systems with unpredictable input delay. An adaptive proportional/proportional-integral (P/PI) control strategy is proposed for a solar-driven volumetric methane/steam reforming reactor (SVMSR) with passive thermal management. The strategy aims to stabilize product components and reduce fluctuations in the hydrogen production rate under fluctuating radiation conditions [27]. Previous research, such as studies [28–30], has demonstrated the successful application of the multiple-scale perturbation technique to derive approximate solutions for various vibrating systems. These studies often utilize MATLAB programs to analyze and solve vibration problems.

A cantilever beam model was explored and derived to load an intermediate lumped mass under harmonic excitation. The vibration suppression can be succeeded by using IRC+ NSC controller. To determine the unstable and stable zones for each frequency response curve, numerical stability research was carried out [31].This research investigates the use of a nonlinear spring pendulum for the vibration control of ship roll motion. Three second-order nonlinear differential equations—one for the rotation angle, one for the relative elongation of the absorber spring, and one for the elongation of the absorber spring—make up the mathematical model that depicts the ship roll motion with the absorber. The authors use a series solution in which they account for terms up to the fourth order in trigonometric functions of the rotational angle. According to the authors, the nonlinear spring-pendulum system's two modes may be made to respond to multi-parametric excitation forces in a way that reduces their maximum values by 8.8% and 0.02% [32]. The PPF control of the nonlinear GMA framework has been described in [33]. The basic resonance and framework amplitude stability can be successfully constrained by tuning the PPF limitations. A few experiments have been carried out to verify the accuracy of the findings. The investigation illustrated the growth of the framework and contrasted its usefulness to earlier research. The 3D plot improves and illustrates the work's correctness. Ref. [34] suggests using NIPPF controllers to manage the nonlinear vibration of a spinning shaft's primary resonance vibration. Among these is a comparison between the controllers for the FRCs under study, NIPPF, and ANIPPF. A two-degree-of-freedom system, counting quadratic and cubic nonlinearities among the parametric and external forces, demonstrate the calculated system. Multiple scales are joined in a connected manner to analyze the stability of the measured structure and obtain approximations of solutions. From the mathematical solution, every resonance is retrieved. The Runge–Kutta fourth-order process is used to gauge the system's performance. Within the numerical results, the examined structure's scheduled frequency response curves are examined for influences including significant coefficients [35]. A low-speed and high-torque permanent magnet synchronous motor powers the semi-direct drive-cutting gearbox system of a shearer, which uses nonlinear integral positive position feedback (NIPPF) and adaptive nonlinear integral positive position feedback (ANIPPF) controllers. Using the averaging technique to solve the nonlinear differential equations and modeling the system with controllers yields an analytic solution in the case of primary and 1:1 internal resonance. The MATLAB program was used to compare the numerical and analytical solutions for time history and FRCs in order to verify their comparability [36].

In this work, we utilized PID control to suppress the torsional vibration after studying the model on a website [37]. A two-degree-of-freedom system under multiple excitations results from this. To provide an estimated solution up to the first-order approximations, MSPT is employed throughout. Using frequency response functions, the stability of the system is examined in the vicinity of the principal resonance case. A few suggestions on the system's various parameters are given. Numerical examples are provided to show how active controllers affect the behavior of the system. A comparison is shown between PID control and additional controllers.

2. Mathematical Modeling

2.1. System Dynamics without Control

This section is presented to illustrate the investigation of the torsional vibration dynamical system. The dynamical model in this work consists of two coupled parts, as shown in Figure 1. θ_1 and θ_2 represent the angular positions (generalized coordinates) within the system. In this nonlinear dynamical system, the following hold:

- I_1 and I_2 represent the polar mass moments of inertia.
- k_1 is the linear spring stiffness of the first part.
- k_2 represents the spring stiffness of the second part, which comprises the following:
    - k_{21}: a linear component.
    - k_{22}: nonlinear quadratic and cubic components.
- $F_1^{\bullet}$ and $F_2^{\bullet}$ denote the generalized excitation forces.

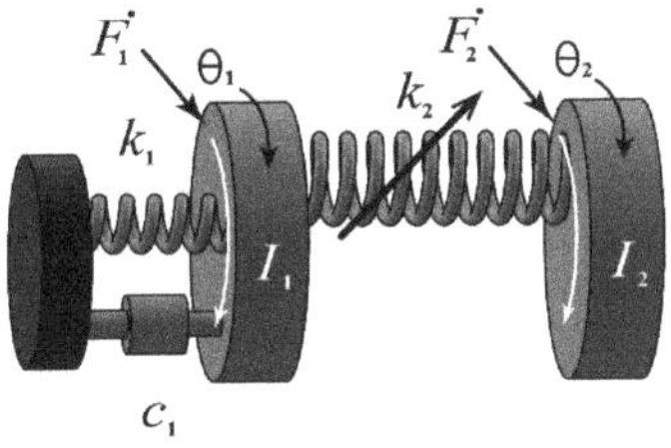

Figure 1. Model of schematic diagram of main system.

Therefore, the equations of the motions of the free body system found in Figure 1 can be constructed in the same manner as those in [25,37]:

$$I_1\ddot{\theta}_1 + k_1\theta_1 + c_1\dot{\theta}_1 + k_{21}(\theta_1 - \theta_2) + k_{22}(\theta_1 - \theta_2)^2 + k_{23}(\theta_1 - \theta_2)^3 = F_1^\bullet, \quad (1)$$

$$I_2\ddot{\theta}_2 + k_{21}(\theta_2 - \theta_1) - k_{22}(\theta_1 - \theta_2)^2 - k_{23}(\theta_1 - \theta_2)^3 = F_2^\bullet, \quad (2)$$

$$\ddot{\theta}_1 + \frac{k_1}{I_1}\theta_1 + \frac{c_1}{I_1}\dot{\theta}_1 + \frac{k_{21}}{I_1}(\theta_1 - \theta_2) + \frac{k_{22}}{I_1}(\theta_1 - \theta_2)^2 + \frac{k_{23}}{I_1}(\theta_1 - \theta_2)^3 = \frac{F_1^\bullet}{I_1}, \quad (3)$$

$$\ddot{\theta}_1 + \left(\frac{k_1 + k_{21}}{I_1}\right)\theta_1 + \frac{c_1}{I_1}\dot{\theta}_1 - \frac{k_{21}}{I_1}\theta_2 + \frac{k_{22}}{I_1}(\theta_1 - \theta_2)^2 + \frac{k_{23}}{I_1}(\theta_1 - \theta_2)^3 = \frac{F_1^\bullet}{I_1}, \quad (4)$$

$$\ddot{\theta}_2 + \frac{k_{21}}{I_2}(\theta_2 - \theta_1) - \frac{k_{22}}{I_2}(\theta_1 - \theta_2)^2 - \frac{k_{23}}{I_2}(\theta_1 - \theta_2)^3 = \frac{F_2^\bullet}{I_2}, \quad (5)$$

$$\frac{\ddot{\theta}_1}{\theta_0} + \left(\frac{k_1 + k_{21}}{I_1}\right)\frac{\theta_1}{\theta_0} + \frac{c_1}{I_1}\frac{\dot{\theta}_1}{\theta_0} - \frac{k_{21}}{I_1}\frac{\theta_2}{\theta_0} + \frac{k_{22}\theta_0}{I_1}\frac{(\theta_1 - \theta_2)^2}{\theta_0^2} + \frac{k_{23}\theta_0^2}{I_1}\frac{(\theta_1 - \theta_2)^3}{\theta_0^3} = \frac{F_1^\bullet}{I_1}, \quad (6)$$

$$\frac{\ddot{\theta}_2}{\theta_0} + \frac{k_{21}}{I_2}\frac{(\theta_2 - \theta_1)}{\theta_0} - \frac{k_{22}\theta_0}{I_2}\frac{(\theta_1 - \theta_2)^2}{\theta_0^2} - \frac{k_{23}\theta_0^2}{I_2}\frac{(\theta_1 - \theta_2)^3}{\theta_0^3} = \frac{F_2^\bullet}{I_2}. \quad (7)$$

We will now introduce the dimensionless forms of the parameters used in this analysis.

$$\varphi_j = \frac{\theta_j}{\theta_0}(j = 1, 2), \omega_1^2 = \frac{k_1 + k_{21}}{I_1}, \zeta = \frac{c_1}{I_1}, \beta = \frac{k_{21}}{I_1}, \alpha_1 = \frac{k_{22}\theta_0}{I_1}, \alpha_2 = \frac{k_{23}\theta_0^2}{I_1}\omega_2^2 = \frac{k_{21}}{I_2}, \alpha_3 = \frac{k_{22}\theta_0}{I_2},$$
$$\alpha_4 = \frac{k_{23}\theta_0^2}{I_2}, \ f_j\sin(\Omega_j t) = \frac{F_j^\bullet}{I_j}.$$

Based on the above parameters, we can obtain the following equations of motion in their dimensionless forms:

$$\ddot{\varphi}_1 + \omega_1^2\varphi_1 + \zeta\dot{\varphi}_1 - \beta\varphi_2 + \alpha_1(\varphi_1 - \varphi_2)^2 + \alpha_2(\varphi_1 - \varphi_2)^3 = f_1\sin(\Omega_1 t), \quad (8)$$

$$\ddot{\varphi}_2 + \omega_2^2(\varphi_2 - \varphi_1) - \alpha_3(\varphi_1 - \varphi_2)^2 - \alpha_4(\varphi_1 - \varphi_2)^3 = f_2\sin(\Omega_2 t). \quad (9)$$

2.2. System Dynamics with PID Control

The goal of the present section is to propose PID controllers to reduce harmful torsional vibration on the dynamical system in this work at one of the worst resonance cases, as depicted in Figure 2. Furthermore, the control in our work is represented as two net control forces F_{C1} and F_{C2} that are generated to suppress the torsional oscillations in two directions.

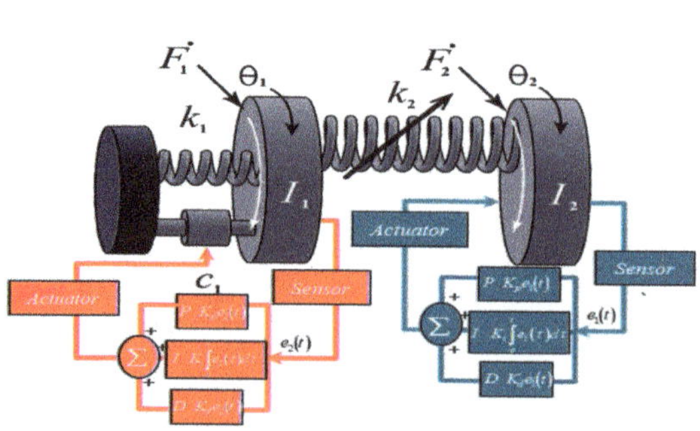

Figure 2. Model of schematic diagram of main system with PID controllers.

Here, K_p, K_i, and K_d denote the proportional feedback control gain, integral feedback control gain, and derivative feedback control gain, respectively. Also, $e_1(t)$ and $e_2(t)$ denote the error value with zero steady-state step error.

The equations of motion utilizing the PID controllers coupled to the nonlinear dynamical system as depicted in Figure 2 can be expressed as follows:

$$\ddot{\varphi}_1 + \omega_1^2\varphi_1 + \varepsilon\zeta\dot{\varphi}_1 - \varepsilon\beta\varphi_2 + \varepsilon\alpha_1(\varphi_1 - \varphi_2)^2 + \varepsilon\alpha_2(\varphi_1 - \varphi_2)^3 = \varepsilon f_1 \sin(\Omega_1 t) + \varepsilon F_{C1}, \quad (10)$$

$$\ddot{\varphi}_2 + \omega_2^2(\varphi_2 - \varphi_1) - \varepsilon\alpha_3(\varphi_1 - \varphi_2)^2 - \varepsilon\alpha_4(\varphi_1 - \varphi_2)^3 = \varepsilon f_2 \sin(\Omega_2 t) + \varepsilon F_{C2}, \quad (11)$$

$$F_{C1} = -K_p\varphi_1 - K_i\int_0^t \varphi_1(\tau)d\tau - K_d\dot{\varphi}_1, \quad (12a)$$

$$F_{C2} = -K_p\varphi_2 - K_i\int_0^t \varphi_2(\tau)d\tau - K_d\dot{\varphi}_2, \quad (12b)$$

$$\begin{array}{l}\ddot{\varphi}_1 + \omega_1^2\varphi_1 + \varepsilon\zeta\dot{\varphi}_1 - \varepsilon\beta\varphi_2 + \varepsilon\alpha_1(\varphi_1 - \varphi_2)^2 + \varepsilon\alpha_2(\varphi_1 - \varphi_2)^3 = \varepsilon f_1 \sin(\Omega_1 t) \\ -\varepsilon K_p\varphi_1 - \varepsilon K_i\int_0^t \varphi_1(\tau)d\tau - \varepsilon K_d\dot{\varphi}_1\end{array}, \quad (13)$$

$$\begin{array}{l}\ddot{\varphi}_2 + \omega_2^2(\varphi_2 - \varphi_1) - \varepsilon\alpha_3(\varphi_1 - \varphi_2)^2 - \varepsilon\alpha_4(\varphi_1 - \varphi_2)^3 = \varepsilon f_2 \sin(\Omega_2 t) \\ -\varepsilon K_p\varphi_2 - \varepsilon K_i\int_0^t \varphi_2(\tau)d\tau - \varepsilon K_d\dot{\varphi}_2\end{array}. \quad (14)$$

3. Analytical Investigations

3.1. Perturbation Analysis

The multiple-scales perturbation technique (MSPT) is applied within this section to obtain an approximation solution of the nonlinear dynamical system with the proposal control (i.e., PID control) given by Equations (13) and (14). Correspondingly, we were able to find a first-order approximate solution to Equations (13) and (14), proposed as follows [28,29]:

$$\varphi_n = \varphi_{n0} + \varepsilon\varphi_{n1} + O\left(\varepsilon^2\right), \ (n = 1, 2) \quad (15)$$

where the minor perturbation parameter ε is located in the range of $0 < \varepsilon \ll 1$. Let us define two time scales, T_0 and T_1, where $T_0 = t$ represents a fast scale while $T_1 = \varepsilon t$ is the slow one. The derivatives of time are converted into the following:

$$\frac{d}{dt} = \frac{dT_0}{dt}\frac{\partial}{\partial T_0} + \frac{dT_1}{dt}\frac{\partial}{\partial T_1} + \ldots = D_0 + \varepsilon D_1 + \ldots, \quad (16)$$

$$\frac{d^2}{dt^2} = \frac{d}{dt}\left(\frac{dT_0}{dt}\frac{\partial}{\partial T_0} + \frac{dT_1}{dt}\frac{\partial}{\partial T_1} + \ldots\right) = D_0^2 + 2\varepsilon D_0 D_1 + \ldots. \quad (17)$$

where $D_j = \frac{\partial}{\partial T_j}$ $(j = 0, 1)$.

The following set of ordinary differential equations was constructed by substituting Equations (15) and (16) into Equations (13) and (14) and equating the coefficients of the same power of ε in both sides:

$O(\varepsilon^0)$:

$$\left(D_0^2 + \omega_1^2\right)\varphi_{10} = 0, \quad (18a)$$

$$\left(D_0^2 + \omega_2^2\right)\varphi_{20} = \omega_2^2\varphi_{10}. \quad (18b)$$

$O(\varepsilon^1)$:

$$(D_0^2+\omega_1^2)\varphi_{11} = -2D_0D_1\varphi_{10} - \zeta D_0\varphi_{10} + \beta\varphi_{20} - \alpha_1(\varphi_{10}-\varphi_{20})^2 - \alpha_2(\varphi_{10}-\varphi_{20})^3 + f_1\sin(\Omega_1 t) - K_p\varphi_{10} - K_i\int_0^t \varphi_{10}(\tau)d\tau - K_dD_0\varphi_{10}, \tag{19a}$$

$$(D_0^2+\omega_2^2)\varphi_{21} = \omega_2^2\varphi_{11} - 2D_0D_1\varphi_{20} + \alpha_3(\varphi_{10}-\varphi_{20})^2 + \alpha_4(\varphi_{10}-\varphi_{20})^3 + f_2\sin(\Omega_2 t) - K_p\varphi_{20} - K_i\int_0^t \varphi_{20}(\tau)d\tau - K_dD_0\varphi_{20}. \tag{19b}$$

The zeroth order approximation is represented by the general solution of Equations (18a) and (18b), which can be expressed as follows:

$$\varphi_{10} = A_1(T_1)\exp(i\omega_1T_0) + cc., \tag{20a}$$

$$\varphi_{20} = A_2(T_1)\exp(i\omega_2T_0) + \Gamma A_1(T_1)\exp(i\omega_1T_0) + cc. \tag{20b}$$

where cc denotes the complex conjugate of the preceding components, A_m is the complex function in T_1, and $\Gamma = \left(\frac{\omega_2^2}{\omega_2^2-\omega_1^2}\right)$.

Substituting Equation (20) into Equation (19a), we have

$$\begin{aligned}
(D_0^2+\omega_1^2)\varphi_{11} = {} & \left[\begin{array}{l} -2i\omega_1D_1A_1 - i\omega_1\zeta A_1 + \Gamma\beta A_1 - \alpha_2\left(\begin{array}{c} 6(1-\Gamma)A_1A_2\overline{A}_2 \\ +3(1-\Gamma)^3A_1^2\overline{A}_1 \end{array}\right) \\ -\left(K_p - i\frac{K_i}{\omega_1} + K_di\omega_1\right)A_1 \end{array}\right]\exp(i\omega_1T_0) \\
& + \left[-\alpha_1(1-\Gamma)^2A_1^2\right]\exp(2i\omega_1T_0) + \left[-\alpha_2(1-\Gamma)^3A_1^3\right]\exp(3i\omega_1T_0) + [\beta A_2 \\
& + \alpha_2\left(3A_2^2\overline{A}_2 + 6(1-\Gamma)^2A_1\overline{A}_1A_2\right)]\exp(i\omega_2T_0) + \left[-\alpha_1A_1^2\right]\exp(2i\omega_2T_0) \\
& + \left[\alpha_2A_2^3\right]\exp(3i\omega_2T_0) + [2\alpha_1(1-\Gamma)A_1A_2]\exp(i(\omega_1+\omega_2)T_0) \\
& + \left[2\alpha_1(1-\Gamma)A_1\overline{A}_2\right]\exp(i(\omega_1-\omega_2)T_0) + \left[3\alpha_2(1-\Gamma)^2A_1^2A_2\right]\exp(i(2\omega_1+\omega_2)T_0) \\
& + \left[3\alpha_2(1-\Gamma)^2A_1^2\overline{A}_2\right]\exp(i(2\omega_1-\omega_2)T_0) + \left[-3\alpha_2(1-\Gamma)A_1A_2^2\right]\exp(i(\omega_1+2\omega_2)T_0) \\
& + \left[-3\alpha_2(1-\Gamma)A_1\overline{A}_2^2\right]\exp(i(\omega_1-2\omega_2)T_0) + \left[-\alpha_1\left((1-\Gamma)^2A_1\overline{A}_1 + A_2\overline{A}_2\right) - iK_i\frac{A_1}{\omega_1}\right] \\
& + \left[\frac{-if_1}{2}\right]\exp(i\Omega_1T_0) + cc.,
\end{aligned} \tag{21}$$

To obtain the solvability condition of Equation (21), the closeness term of the excitation frequencies (Ω_1) and natural frequency (ω_1) is described via employing the dimensionless detuning parameterσ_1, as in the following:

$$\Omega_1 = \omega_1 + \varepsilon\sigma_1. \tag{22}$$

By substituting Equation (22) into Equation (21) and canceling the term that leads to secular ones, we obtain the particular solution of the first approximation (φ_{11}) as the following:

$$\begin{aligned}
\varphi_{11} = {} & M_1\exp(2i\omega_1T_0) + M_2\exp(3i\omega_1T_0) + M_3\exp(i\omega_2T_0) + M_4\exp(2i\omega_2T_0) \\
& + M_5\exp(3i\omega_2T_0) + M_6\exp(i(\omega_1+\omega_2)T_0) + M_7\exp(i(\omega_1-\omega_2)T_0) \\
& + M_8\exp(i(2\omega_1+\omega_2)T_0) + M_9\exp(i(2\omega_1-\omega_2)T_0) + M_{10}\exp(i(\omega_1+2\omega_2)T_0) \\
& + M_{11}\exp(i(\omega_1-2\omega_2)T_0) + M_{12} + cc.
\end{aligned}, \tag{23}$$

Here, M_i $(i = 1, 2, \ldots, 12)$ is presented in Appendix A.

Substituting Equations (20) and (23) into Equation (19b), we have

$$\begin{array}{l}(D_0^2+\omega_2^2)\varphi_{21}=\left[-2i\omega_1 D_1\Gamma A_1+\alpha_4\left(3(1-\Gamma)^3A_1^2\overline{A}_1+6(1-\Gamma)A_1A_2\overline{A}_2\right)\right.\\ \left.-\left(K_p-i\frac{K_i}{\omega_1}+i\omega_1 K_d\right)\Gamma A_1\right]\exp(i\omega_1 T_0)+\left[\omega_2^2M_1+\alpha_3(1-\Gamma)^2A_1^2\right]\exp(2i\omega_1 T_0)\\ +\left[\omega_2^2M_2+\alpha_4(1-\Gamma)^3A_1^3\right]\exp(3i\omega_1 T_0)+\left[\omega_2^2M_3-2i\omega_2 D_1A_2\right.\\ \left.-\left(K_p-i\frac{K_i}{\omega_2}+i\omega_2 K_d\right)A_2-\alpha_4\left(3A_2^2\overline{A}_2+6(1-\Gamma)^2A_1\overline{A}_1A_2\right)\right]\exp(i\omega_2 T_0)\\ +\left[\omega_2^2M_4+\alpha_3A_2^2\right]\exp(2i\omega_2 T_0)+\left[\omega_2^2M_5-\alpha_4A_2^3\right]\exp(3i\omega_2 T_0)\\ +\left[\omega_2^2M_6-2\alpha_3(1-\Gamma)A_1A_2\right]\exp(i(\omega_1+\omega_2)T_0)+\left[\omega_2^2M_7-2\alpha_3(1-\Gamma)A_1\overline{A}_2\right]\\ \times\exp(i(\omega_1-\omega_2)T_0)+\left[\omega_2^2M_8-3\alpha_4(1-\Gamma)^2A_1^2A_2\right]\exp(i(2\omega_1+\omega_2)T_0)\\ +\left[\omega_2^2M_9-3\alpha_4(1-\Gamma)^2A_1^2\overline{A}_2\right]\exp(i(2\omega_1-\omega_2)T_0)+\left[\omega_2^2M_{10}+3\alpha_4(1-\Gamma)A_1A_2^2\right]\\ \times\exp(i(\omega_1+2\omega_2)T_0)+\left[\omega_2^2M_{11}+3\alpha_4(1-\Gamma)A_1\overline{A}_2^2\right]\exp(i(\omega_1-2\omega_2)T_0)\\ +\left[\omega_2^2M_{12}+\alpha_3\left((1-\Gamma)^2A_1\overline{A}_1+A_2\overline{A}_2\right)-K_i\left(i\frac{A_2}{\omega_2}+i\frac{\Gamma A_1}{\omega_1}\right)\right]+\left[\frac{-if_2}{2}\right]\exp(i\Omega_2T_0)+cc.\end{array} \quad (24)$$

To obtain the second solvability condition of Equation (24), the closeness term of excitation frequencies (Ω_2) and natural frequency (ω_2) is described via employing the dimensionless detuning parameter σ_2 as the following:

$$\Omega_2=\omega_2+\varepsilon\sigma_2. \quad (25)$$

By substituting Equation (25) into Equation (24) and canceling the term which leads to the secular ones, we obtain the particular solution of the first approximation (φ_{21}) as the following:

$$\begin{array}{l}\varphi_{21}=N_1\exp(i\omega_1T_0)+N_2\exp(2i\omega_1T_0)+N_3\exp(3i\omega_1T_0)+N_4\exp(2i\omega_2T_0)\\ +N_5\exp(3i\omega_2T_0)+N_6\exp(i(\omega_1+\omega_2)T_0)+N_7\exp(i(\omega_1-\omega_2)T_0)\\ +N_8\exp(i(2\omega_1+\omega_2)T_0)+N_9\exp(i(2\omega_1-\omega_2)T_0)+N_{10}\exp(i(\omega_1+2\omega_2)T_0)\\ +N_{11}\exp(i(\omega_1-2\omega_2)T_0)+N_{12}+cc.\end{array} \quad (26)$$

Here, N_i $(i=1,2,\ldots,12)$ is presented in Appendix A.

After inserting Equations (22) and (25) into Equations (21) and (24) and deleting the secular term, the conditions of solvability can be gained as follows:

$$2i\omega_1D_1A_1=\left[\begin{array}{l}\left(-i\omega_1\zeta+\Gamma\beta-K_p+i\frac{K_i}{\omega_1}-K_di\omega_1\right)A_1+(-6\alpha_2(1-\Gamma))A_1A_2\overline{A}_2\\ +\left(-3\alpha_2(1-\Gamma)^3\right)A_1^2\overline{A}_1\\ +\left[\frac{-if_1}{2}\right]\exp(i\sigma_1T_1)\end{array}\right], \quad (27a)$$

$$2i\omega_2D_1A_2=\left[\begin{array}{l}\left(-\Gamma\beta-K_p+i\frac{K_i}{\omega_2}-i\omega_2K_d\right)A_2+(-3\Gamma\alpha_2-3\alpha_4)A_2^2\overline{A}_2\\ +(-6\Gamma\alpha_2-6\alpha_4)(1-\Gamma)^2A_1\overline{A}_1A_2\\ +\left[\frac{-if_2}{2}\right]\exp(i\sigma_2T_1)\end{array}\right]. \quad (27b)$$

To obtain the amplitude-phase equations of the controlled system, we analyze the solution of Equation (27), exchanging $A_n(T_1)$ by the polar form as

$$A_n=\frac{1}{2}a_n(T_1)e^{i\gamma_n(T_1)},\ (n=1,2). \quad (28)$$

We obtain the governing equations of the amplitudes a_n and the phases γ_n by substituting from Equation (28) into Equation (27) and then separating the real and imaginary components.

$$\dot{a}_1=\left(-\frac{\zeta}{2}+\frac{K_i}{2\omega_1^2}-\frac{K_d}{2}\right)a_1+\left[\frac{-f_1}{2\omega_1}\right]\cos(\psi_1), \quad (29a)$$

$$a_1\dot{\gamma}_1 = \left[\left(-\frac{\Gamma\beta}{2\omega_1} + \frac{K_p}{2\omega_1}\right)a_1 + \left(\frac{3\alpha_2(1-\Gamma)}{4\omega_1}\right)a_1 a_2^2 + \left(\frac{3\alpha_2(1-\Gamma)^3}{8\omega_1}\right)a_1^3\right] + \left[\frac{-f_1}{2\omega_1}\right]\sin(\psi_1), \quad (29b)$$

$$\dot{a}_2 = \left(\frac{K_i}{2\omega_2^2} - \frac{K_d}{2}\right)a_2 + \left[\frac{-f_2}{2\omega_2}\right]\cos(\psi_2), \quad (30a)$$

$$\begin{aligned} a_2\dot{\gamma}_2 &= \left[\left(\frac{\Gamma\beta}{2\omega_2} + \frac{K_p}{2\omega_2}\right)a_2 + \left(\frac{3\Gamma\alpha_2+3\alpha_4}{8\omega_2}\right)a_2^3 + \left(\frac{3\Gamma\alpha_2+3\alpha_4}{4\omega_2}\right)(1-\Gamma)^2 a_1^2 a_2\right] \\ &+ \left[\frac{-f_2}{2\omega_2}\right]\sin(\psi_2) \end{aligned} \quad (30b)$$

where

$$\psi_1 = \sigma_1 T_1 - \gamma_1, \psi_2 = \sigma_2 T_1 - \gamma_2. \quad (31)$$

The fixed points in Equations (29)–(30) correspond to the steady-state solutions of the system, which in turn correspond to $\dot{a}_n = 0$ and $\dot{\psi}_n = 0$.

From Equation (31), we indicate that $\dot{\gamma}_1 = \sigma_1$ and $\dot{\gamma}_2 = \sigma_2$.

As a result, $\dot{a}_n = 0$ and $\dot{\psi}_n = 0$; the practical case's frequency response equations (FRE) ($a_1 \neq 0$, $a_2 \neq 0$) are provided as

$$0 = \left(-\frac{\zeta}{2} + \frac{K_i}{2\omega_1^2} - \frac{K_d}{2}\right)a_1 + \left[\frac{-f_1}{2\omega_1}\right]\cos(\psi_1), \quad (32a)$$

$$a_1\sigma_1 = \left[\left(-\frac{\Gamma\beta}{2\omega_1} + \frac{K_p}{2\omega_1}\right)a_1 + \left(\frac{3\alpha_2(1-\Gamma)}{4\omega_1}\right)a_1 a_2^2 + \left(\frac{3\alpha_2(1-\Gamma)^3}{8\omega_1}\right)a_1^3\right] + \left[\frac{-f_1}{2\omega_1}\right]\sin(\psi_1), \quad (32b)$$

$$0 = \left(\frac{K_i}{2\omega_2^2} - \frac{K_d}{2}\right)a_2 + \left[\frac{-f_2}{2\omega_2}\right]\cos(\psi_2), \quad (33a)$$

$$\begin{aligned} a_2\sigma_2 &= \left[\left(\frac{\Gamma\beta}{2\omega_2} + \frac{K_p}{2\omega_2}\right)a_2 + \left(\frac{3\Gamma\alpha_2+3\alpha_4}{8\omega_2}\right)a_2^3 + \left(\frac{3\Gamma\alpha_2+3\alpha_4}{4\omega_2}\right)(1-\Gamma)^2 a_1^2 a_2\right] \\ &+ \left[\frac{-f_2}{2\omega_2}\right]\sin(\psi_2) \end{aligned}. \quad (33b)$$

3.2. *Stability Analysis via Linearizing the above System*

In order to examine the stability of the given fixed points nonlinear solution, let

$$\left.\begin{aligned} a_m &= a_{m0} + a_{m1}, \\ \psi_m &= \psi_{m0} + \psi_{m1} \end{aligned}\right\} \quad (34)$$

where a_{m1} and ψ_{m1} are perturbations that are thought to be tiny in comparison to a_{m0} and ψ_{m0}. Here, a_{m0} and ψ_{m0} are the solutions of Equations (29) and (30). Equation (34) is substituted into Equations (29) and (30) with Equation (31), retaining only the linear terms in a_{m1} and ψ_{m1}. Therefore, the linearized system of Equations (29) and (30) has the forms

$$\dot{a}_{11} = \left[-\frac{\zeta}{2} + \frac{K_i}{2\omega_1^2} - \frac{K_d}{2}\right]a_{11} + \left[\frac{f_1}{2\omega_1}\sin(\psi_{10})\right]\psi_{11}, \quad (35a)$$

$$\begin{aligned} \dot{\psi}_{11} &= \left[\left(\frac{\sigma_1}{a_{10}} + \frac{\Gamma\beta}{2a_{10}\omega_1} - \frac{K_p}{2a_{10}\omega_1}\right) + \left(-\frac{3\alpha_2(1-\Gamma)}{4a_{10}\omega_1}\right)a_{20}^2 + \left(-\frac{9\alpha_2(1-\Gamma)^3}{8\omega_1}\right)a_{10}\right]a_{11} \\ &+ \left[\frac{f_1}{2a_{10}\omega_1}\cos(\psi_{10})\right]\psi_{11} + \left[\left(-\frac{3\alpha_2(1-\Gamma)}{2\omega_1}\right)a_{20}\right]a_{21} \end{aligned}, \quad (35b)$$

$$\dot{a}_{21} = \left[\left(\frac{K_i}{2\omega_2^2} - \frac{K_d}{2}\right)\right]a_{21} + \left[\frac{f_2}{2\omega_2}\sin(\psi_{20})\right]\psi_{21}, \quad (36a)$$

$$\begin{array}{rl}\dot{\psi}_{21} & =\left[-\left(\frac{3\Gamma\alpha_2+3\alpha_4}{2\omega_2}\right)(1-\Gamma)^2 a_{10}\right]a_{11}+\left[\left(\frac{\sigma_2}{a_{20}}-\frac{\Gamma\beta}{2a_{20}\omega_2}-\frac{K_p}{2a_{20}\omega_2}\right)\right. \\ & \left.-\left(\frac{9\Gamma\alpha_2+9\alpha_4}{8\omega_2}\right)a_{20}-\left(\frac{3\Gamma\alpha_2+3\alpha_4}{4a_{20}\omega_2}\right)(1-\Gamma)^2 a_{10}^2\right]a_{21}+\left[\frac{f_2}{2\omega_2 a_{20}}\cos(\psi_{20})\right]\psi_{21}\end{array}. \quad (36b)$$

The above Equations (35) and (36) can be described as the following matrix:

$$\begin{bmatrix}\dot{a}_{11} & \dot{\psi}_{11} & \dot{a}_{21} & \dot{\psi}_{21}\end{bmatrix}^T=[J]\begin{bmatrix}a_{11} & \psi_{11} & a_{21} & \psi_{21}\end{bmatrix}^T. \quad (37)$$

Here $[J]$is represented by the appropriate portions of Equations (35) and (36).
The eigenvalues of $[J]$ ascertained using the subsequent equation are as follows:

$$\lambda^4+\Gamma_1\,\lambda^3+\Gamma_2\,\lambda^2+\Gamma_3\lambda+\Gamma_4=0. \quad (38)$$

The coefficients of Equation (38) are denoted as $\Gamma_m\ (m=1,2,\ldots,4)$. The solutions of the system with PID control are stable if the roots' real parts of λ have negative values; if not, they are unstable. It is a necessary and sufficient requirement for a steady-state solution to use the Routh–Hurwitz criterion, which states that all of the roots of Equation (38) must have negative real parts if and only if all of the principal minors and the following determinant D are positive.

$$D=\begin{vmatrix}\Gamma_1 & 1 & 0 & 0\\ \Gamma_3 & \Gamma_2 & \Gamma_1 & 1\\ 0 & \Gamma_4 & \Gamma_3 & \Gamma_2\\ 0 & 0 & 0 & \Gamma_4\end{vmatrix}. \quad (39)$$

4. Results and Discussion

4.1. Time History Performance without Control

To analyze the behavior of the dynamical system the fourth-order Runge–Kutta algorithm (ode45 in MATLAB) [30] is applied to find the numerical solution of the given uncontrolled system of Equations (8) and (9).

The time history performance of the system without any controller at the primary resonance ($\Omega_1\cong\omega_1,\Omega_2\cong\omega_2$) is shown in Figure 3 at the chosen values ($\omega_1=3;\zeta=0.2;\omega_2=2;\beta=0.5\omega_2^2;\alpha_1=0.2;\alpha_2=0.3;f_1=10;\alpha_3=2\alpha_1;\alpha_4=2\alpha_2;f_2=5;\Omega_1=\omega_1;\Omega_2=\omega_2$).

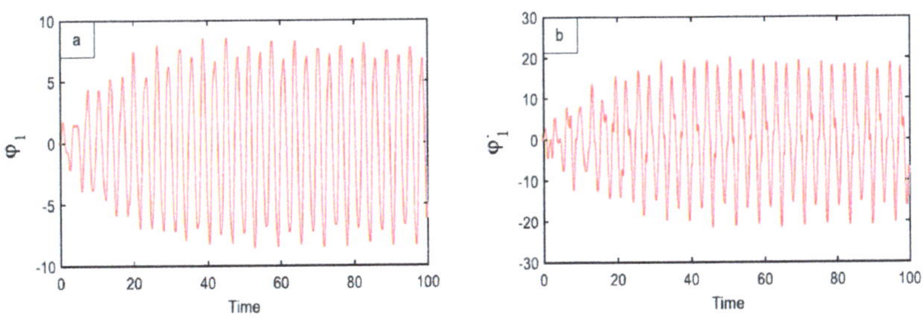

Figure 3. **The** time diagram without any controller (**a**) the first part of the system, φ_1 (**b**) the response of its velocity, $\dot{\varphi}_1$.

Figure 3a,b show the steady-state time response against the amplitude φ_1 for the uncontrolled first system and the velocity $\dot{\varphi}_1$, respectively. Similarly, Figure 4a,b show the uncontrolled second main system and its amplitude φ_2 and velocity $\dot{\varphi}_2$ with the time response.

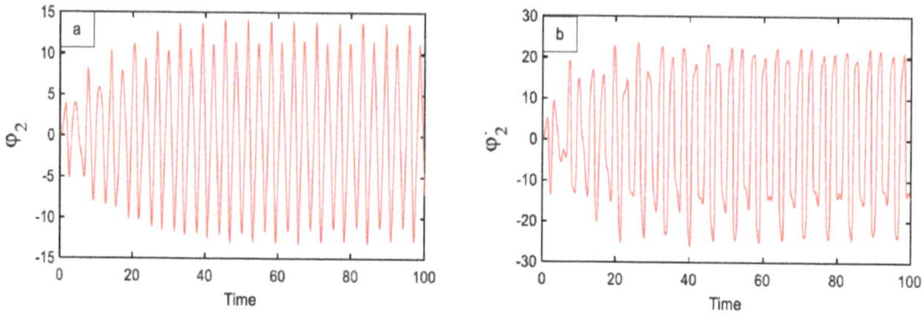

Figure 4. The time diagram without any controller (**a**) the second part of the system, φ_2 (**b**) response of its velocity, $\dot{\varphi}_2$.

4.2. Time History Performance with Different Control

The closed-loop performances of the P, PI, and PID controllers for the two systems φ_1 and φ_2, along with their corresponding velocities $\dot{\varphi}_1$ and $\dot{\varphi}_2$, are displayed in Figure 5. The closed-loop responses of the traditional P and PI controllers are unstable and exhibit peak overshoot. Better closed-loop performance, such as in responses with less peak overshoot and settling time, was supplied by the redesigned PID controller structure, which conveys closed-loop responses with less peak and overshoot and a more stable curve than the others. The study was for the first main system and its velocity, as in Figure 5a,b, and the second main system shown in Figure 5c,d. Figure 5 shows evidence of both steady behavior and the absence of chaos in the produced wavelengths and amplitudes in every section. We utilized the gain values that are depicted in Table 1 to obtain these closed loops using the three control approaches.

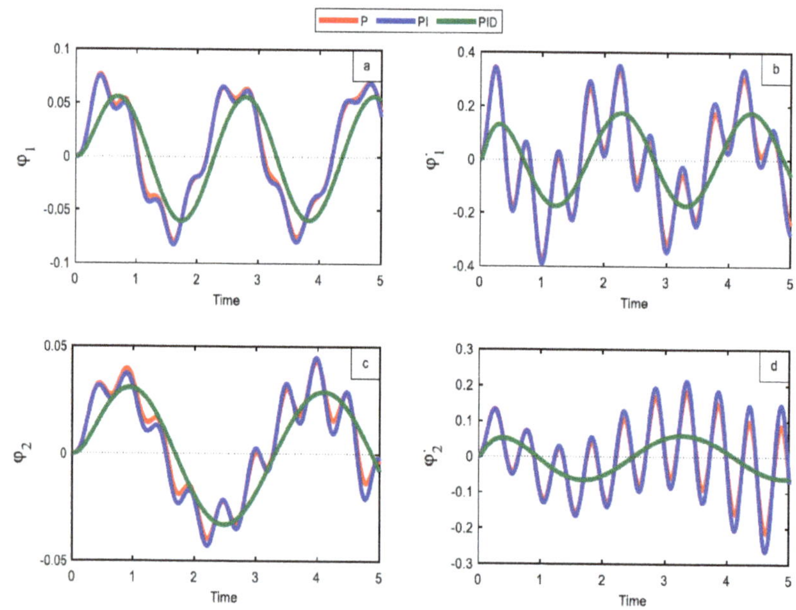

Figure 5. Responses in closed loop using P, PI, and PID controller. (**a**) the first part of the system φ_1 (**b**) the response of its velocity $\dot{\varphi}_1$ (**c**) the second part of the system φ_2 (**d**) the response of its velocity$\dot{\varphi}_2$.

Table 1. Parameters of a PID controller.

Controller		Gain		
		K_p	K_i	K_d
P	**(Red)**	150	-	-
PI	**(Blue)**	150	20	-
PID	**(Green)**	150	20	20

In Figure 6a,b, there is a depiction of the first main system's amplitude decreasing from 7.788 to 0.0569 after the utilization of a time PID controller. This indicates that the controller's effectiveness (E_a = amplitude without control/amplitude with) was equivalent to 136.87 for the first main system φ_1, with a proportional reduction of 99.27%. Likewise, the amplitude φ_2 of the second system, which is equal to 13.59, as shown in Figure 7, decreased to 0.02886, where E_a = 470.89, reflecting a proportional reduction of 99.79%.

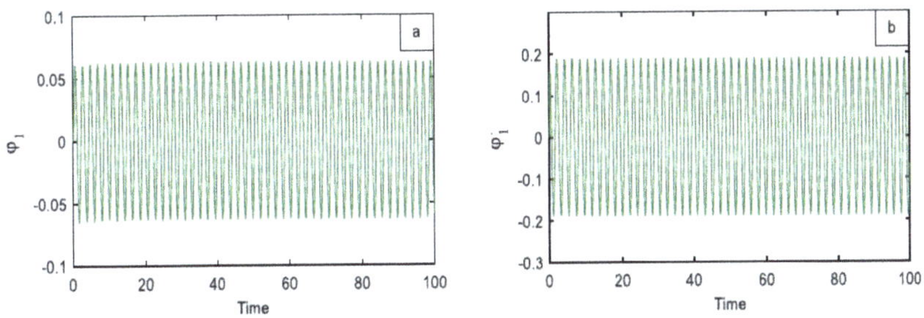

Figure 6. The time diagram in the primary resonance situation with the PID controller (**a**) the first part of the system φ_1 (**b**) the response of its velocity $\dot{\varphi}_1$.

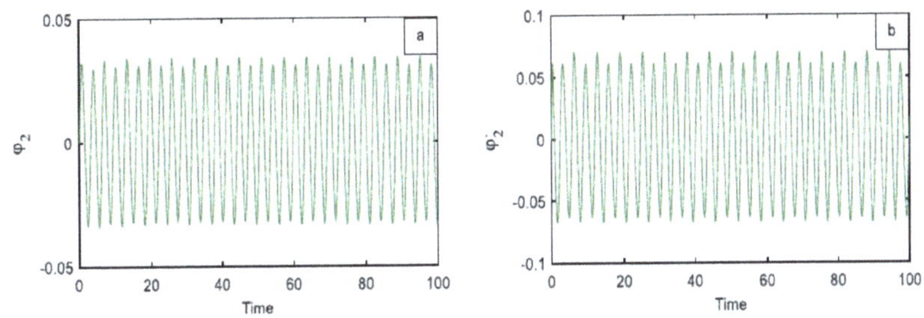

Figure 7. The time diagram in the primary resonance situation with the PID controller (**a**) the second part of the system φ_2 (**b**) the response of its velocity$\dot{\varphi}_2$.

Figure 8 illustrates the phase plane of both main systems before and after adding the PID controller. Figure 8a shows that the first main system φ_1, with a multi-limit cycle in the case of not adding control, and as improved with a limited cycle after adding PID. With the second main system φ_2, as shown in Figure 8b before adding the control, the phase plane is the multi-limit cycle, which decreased after adding PID.

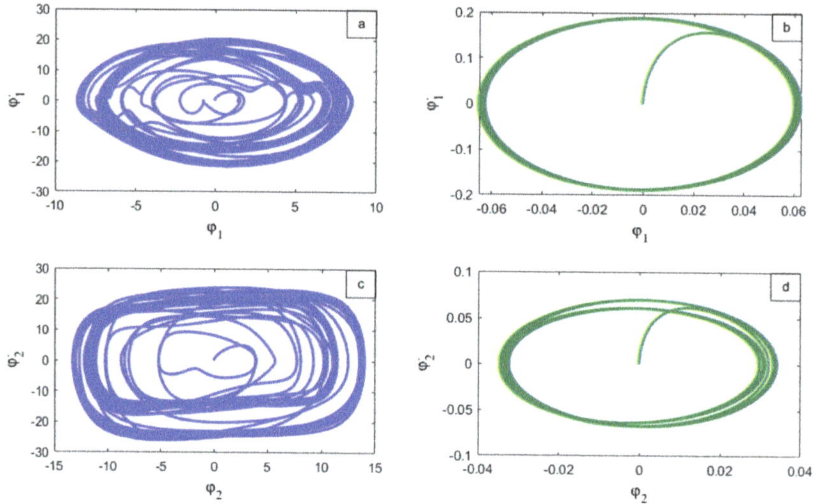

Figure 8. The phase plane of the system's (**a**) φ_1 with angular velocities $\dot{\varphi}_1$ in the primary resonance situation without control (**b**) φ_1 with angular velocities $\dot{\varphi}_1$ in the primary resonance situation with the PID controller (**c**) φ_2 with angular velocities $\dot{\varphi}_2$ in the primary resonance situation without control (**d**) φ_2 with angular velocities $\dot{\varphi}_2$ in the primary resonance situation with the PID controller.

4.3. *Frequency Response Curves (FRC)*

The frequency response curves of Equations (32) and (33) of the first main system a_1, against the detuning parameter σ_1, are illustrated in Figure 9a without the influence of any controller, where the solid black line represents the stable solution while the red line indicates the unstable solution of the same equation. The amplitude of the first main system is fully reduced after the P controller is added; however, as Figure 9b shows, this declining portion of the curve is unstable. The response curve in Figure 9c shows what happens when a PI controller is added. It is discovered that this fully reduces the amplitude of the primary system a_1, yet the curve is absolutely unstable. After adding a PID controller, the first main system's behavior is shown in Figure 9d, where it is discovered that the curve has a monotonically decreasing amplitude and is completely stable. The response curves of the second main system a_2, against the detuning parameter σ_2, are illustrated in Figure 10a without the influence of any controller. The amplitude of the second main system is fully reduced after the P controller is added; however, as Figure 10b shows, this declining portion of the curve is unstable. The response curve in Figure 10c shows what happens when a PI controller is added. It is discovered that this controller reduces the amplitude of the second system a_2, yet the curve behaves in an unstable way. After adding a PID controller, the second main system's behavior is shown in Figure 10d, where it is discovered that the curve has a monotonically decreasing amplitude and is completely stable. Figure 11 clearly illustrates the difference in the curves' responses before and after the PID controller was included for the two primary systems, a_1 and a_2. Figure 11a,b demonstrated how the system is only stable and does not contain any unstable parts, as well as how the addition of a PID controller causes the amplitude to drop with a_1 and disappear with a_2. The amplitude rose for increasing values of the external force f_1 for the first main system a_1, as Figure 12a illustrates, with the first component of the system, a_1. The amplitude of the first main system is shifted to the right and displays a monotonically declining curve as the values of natural frequency ω_1 increase, as seen in Figure 12b.The amplitude decreases monotonically when the damping coefficient ζ values increase, as shown in Figure 12c. As the values of the nonlinear parameter β increased, the amplitude of the first half of the system bent to the left, as illustrated in Figure 12d.

Lastly, Figure 12e illustrates how the nonlinear parameter α_2 behaves for both positive and negative parameter values. For very tiny negative values of α_2, the curve bends left, but for high positive values of α_2, the curve bends right. The second main system's amplitude increased for large values of the external force f_2, as shown in Figure 13a, with the second portion of the system, a_2. As seen in Figure 13b, the second main system's amplitude is moved to the right and exhibits a monotonic declining curve for increased values of the natural frequency ω_2. As seen in Figure 13c, the amplitude remains constant and shifts to the right for extraordinarily high positive values of the nonlinear parameter α_4 and to the left for extraordinarily low negative values of α_4. The response of the gains with the amplitude is examined in Figure 14. Figure 14a establishes the values of K_i and K_d. Upon further examination of the influence of K_p, we discovered that when K_p values increase, the amplitude of both primary systems decreases while remaining steady. With different values of K_i, we observed that the amplitude of both main systems increased indistinguishably for the fixed values of K_p and K_d. However, when $K_i = 80$, both main systems behaved in an unstable manner, as shown in Figure 14b. Lastly, although the other two gains are fixed, Figure 14c shows the improvement of K_d. Painting made it evident that the amplitude is unstable at the initial K_d values and that, in both systems, the amplitude decreases as K_d increases.

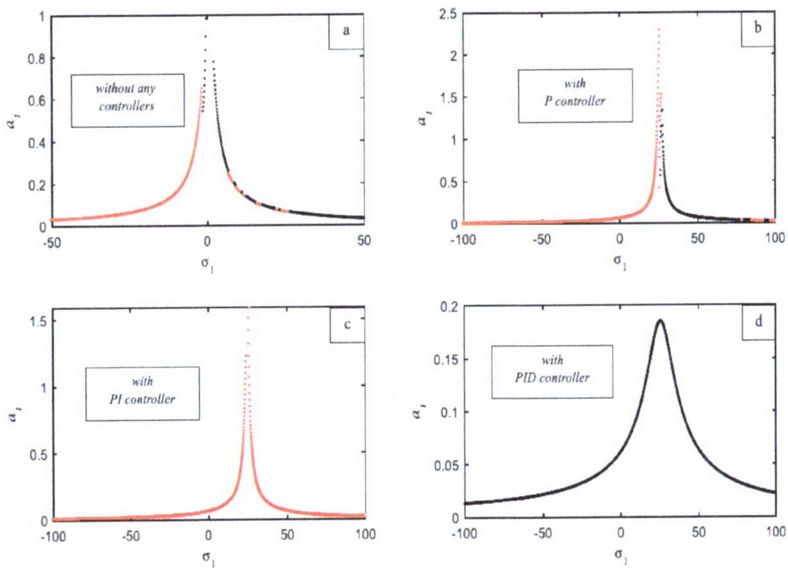

Figure 9. The frequency response curves on the plane σ_1 and the first part of the system (a_1) (**a**) without a controller, (**b**) with a P controller, (**c**) with a PI controller, and (**d**) with a PID controller. (**red color**) unstable region (**black color**) stable region

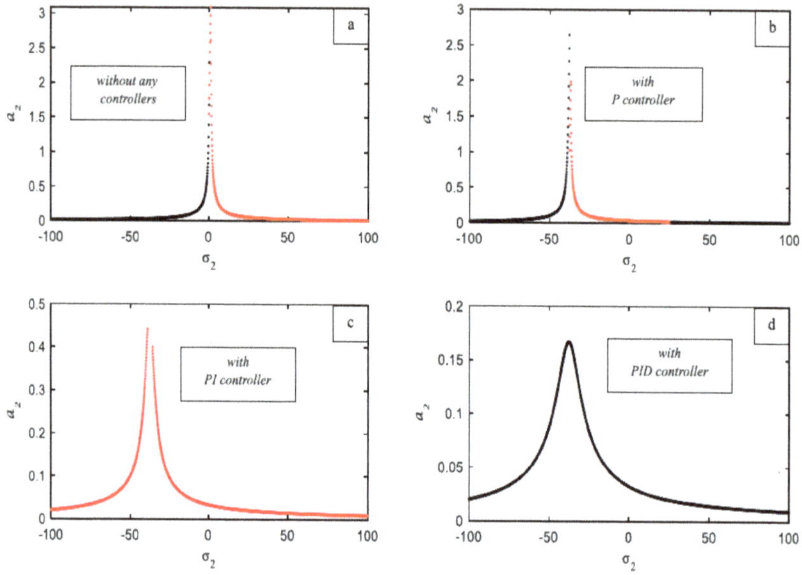

Figure 10. The frequency response curves on plane σ_2 and the first part of the system (a_2) (**a**) without a controller, (**b**) with a P controller, (**c**) with a PI controller, and (**d**) with PID controller. (**red color**) unstable region (**black color**) stable region.

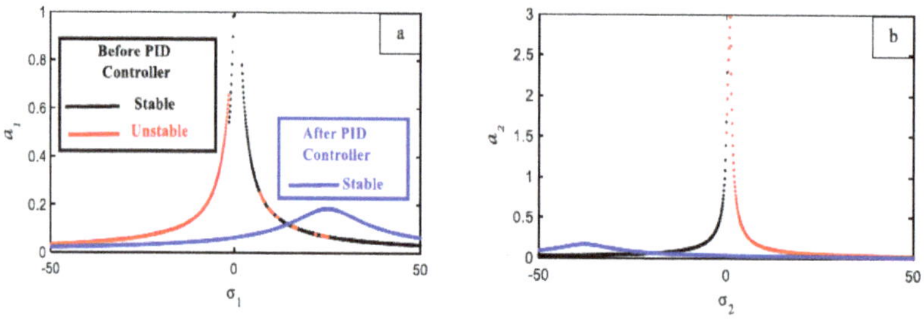

Figure 11. Frequency response before and after PID: (**a**) first main system a_1 and (**b**) first main system a_2.

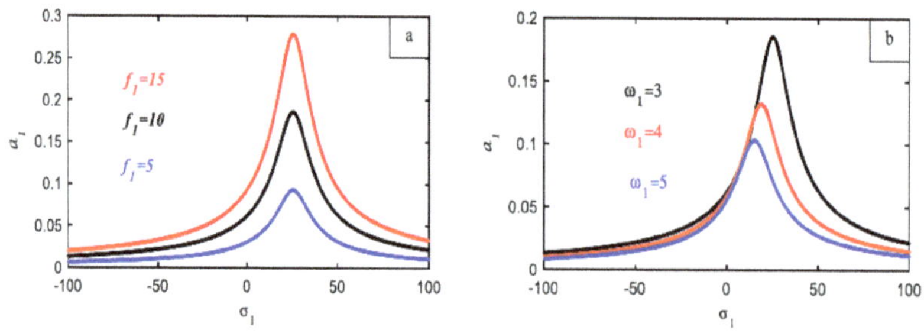

Figure 12. *Cont.*

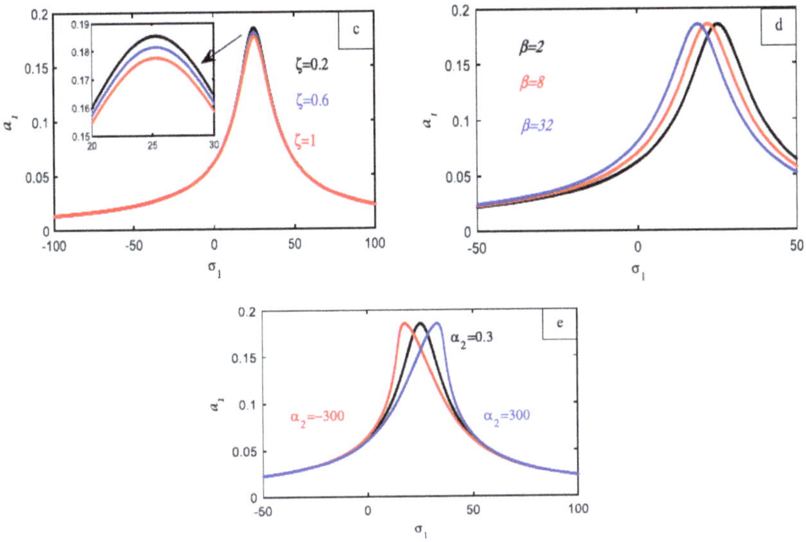

Figure 12. (**a**) The FRC of the external force action f_1. (**b**) Natural frequency ω_1. (**c**) Damping coefficient ζ. (**d**) Linear parameter β. (**e**) Nonlinear parameter α_2. All of these regard the first part of the system a_1.

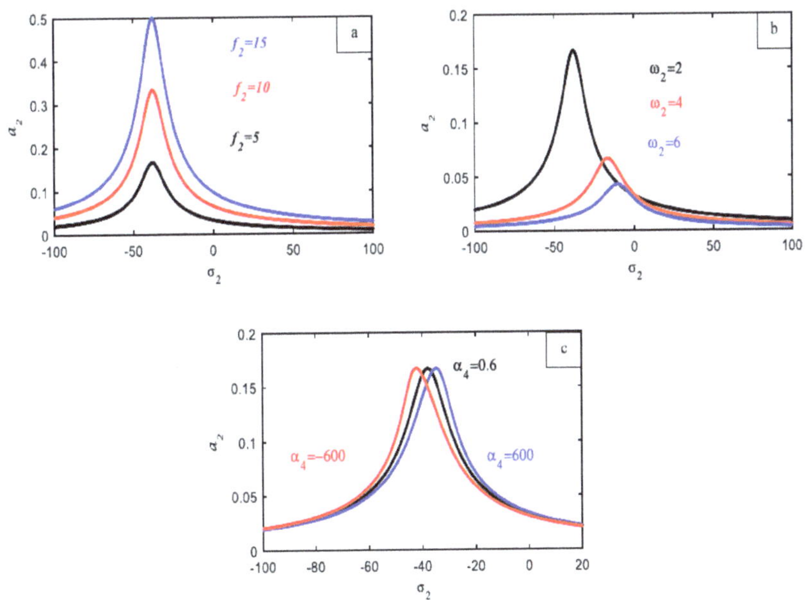

Figure 13. (**a**) The FRC of the external force action f_2. (**b**) Natural frequency ω_2. (**c**) Nonlinear parameter α_4. All of these regard the second part of system a_2.

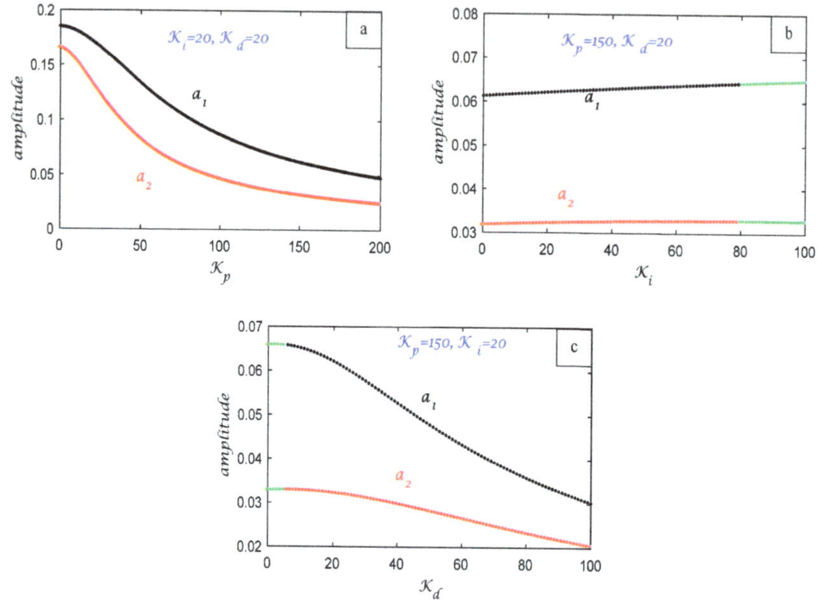

Figure 14. Response curve for the system amplitudes with (**a**)K_p (**b**) K_i (**c**) K_d.

5. Comparison

5.1. Comparison of the Perturbation's Temporal Response Solutions with Numerical Techniques

Analytical solutions to Equations (29) and (30) are graphically represented by (---) lines, which correspond with the numerical solutions of Equations (13) and (14), as displayed in Figure 15a for the first main system, and in Figure 15b for the second main system.

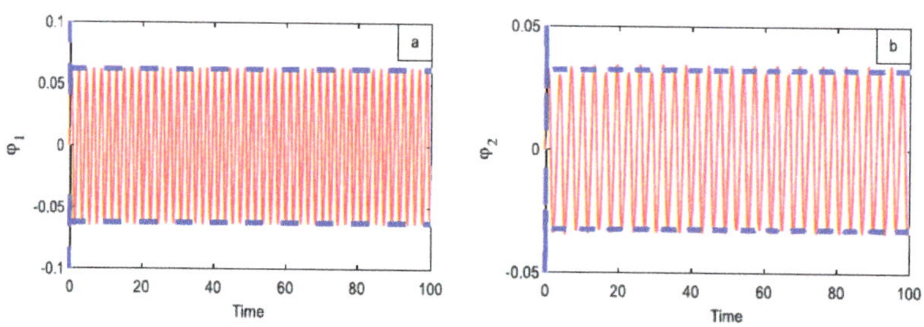

Figure 15. Comparison of numerical simulation and perturbation analysis for both framework modes in PID controllers. (**a**) the first part of the system φ_1 (**b**) the second part of the system φ_2

5.2. Comparison between RK-4 and FRC

Figure 16 shows an acceptable agreement with the numerical solutions of Equations (4) and (5), using (RK-4) highlighted by yellow circles and the frequency response curves (FRC) for the two main systems a_1 in Figure 16a and a_2 in Figure 16b, which are presented with the solid line.

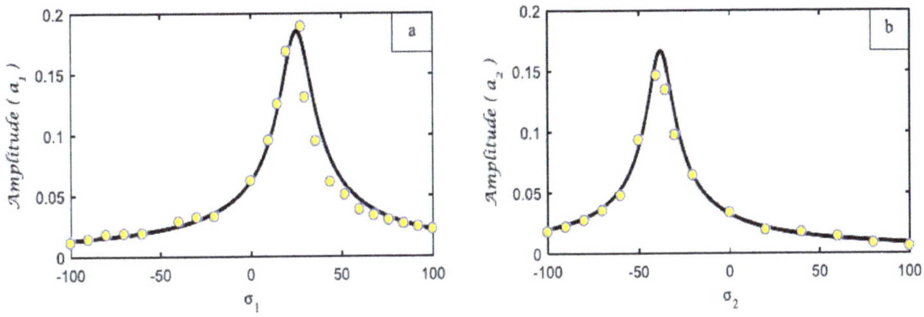

Figure 16. Contrast between the FRC solution and RK- 4 solution for both systems (**a**) the first part of the system a_1 (**b**) the second part of the system a_2.

5.3. Comparison with Published Work

For previous work, the following can be stated:

(1) Torsional vibration was examined in a review of the literature [25] for active and passive control, which is a useful tool for managing the torsional vibration of a nonlinear dynamical system that is exposed to several parametric excitations.
(2) They used the frequency response equations; the stability of the system is examined in the vicinity of the simultaneous sub-harmonic and internal resonances.
(3) The behavior of the system with and without two controllers is numerically integrated and examined.

For this work, after adding control, we compared the time histories of our work and a prior study and discovered that the amplitudes and wavelengths showed that the solutions generated exhibited stable behavior and were devoid of chaos.

6. Conclusions

The torsional vibration control of a nonlinear dynamical system has been tackled within this article. Proportional-integral-derivative (PID) controllers have been proposed to control the harmful torsional vibration of the system, as shown in Figure 2 for one of the worst resonance cases. The multiple-scale perturbation approach is applied to obtain the approximation solution for the coupled controlled system. The time history is drawn to study the steady-state vibration amplitudes and the effectiveness of the applied control algorithms in suppressing vibration. In addition, the stability and effects of different system and control parameters are illustrated in frequency response curves according to the Routh–Hurwitz criterion. Based on the above discussion, the following conclusions can be drawn:

(1) It is noted that the PID controller is operated to reduce the dangerous vibrations in a short time.
(2) This work provided a comparison between P, PI, and PID controllers in the context of FRCs.
(3) Numerous coefficients' effects are examined and shown numerically.
(4) Despite the excitation frequency, the PID controller is the most effective control method for minimizing the vibrations in the framework.
(5) The closed-loop response of relative displacement is obtained with the PID controller, which comprises the peak-overshoot.
(6) The modified structure of the PID controller, such as with the P and PI controllers, is used for the control of the relative displacement of the suspension system. From the results, the PID controller provided better closed-loop performance in terms of peak overshoot and settling time, which are minimized.

Author Contributions: K.A.: resources; methodology; formal analysis; validation; visualization; writing—original draft; writing—review and editing (equal); funding acquisition. A.T.E.-S.: conceptualization; investigation; methodology; data curation; validation; writing—original draft; writing—review and editing. F.T.E.-B.: formal analysis; validation; investigation; methodology; data curation; conceptualization; writing—original draft; writing—review and editing. All authors have read and agreed to the published version of the manuscript.

Funding: This research was funded by the Researchers Supporting Project, grant number (RSPD2024R 588), King Saud University, Riyadh, Saudi Arabia.

Data Availability Statement: All data generated or analyzed during this study are included in this published article.

Acknowledgments: The authors extend their appreciation to the Researchers Supporting Project, grant number (RSPD2024R588), King Saud University, Riyadh, Saudi Arabia.

Conflicts of Interest: The authors have not revealed any conflicting interests.

Nomenclature

I_1, I_2	Polar mass moment of the nonlinear dynamical system
k_1, k_2	Linear spring stiffness of the nonlinear dynamical system
k_{21}, k_{22}, k_{23}	Quadratic and cubic stiffness parts
$F_1^\bullet, F_2^\bullet$	Excitation forces
c_1	Linear damping coefficients of the nonlinear dynamical system
ω_1, ω_2	Natural frequencies
ζ	Damping coefficient
β	Linear parameter
$\alpha_i (i = 1, 2, 3, 4)$	Nonlinear parameter
F_{C1}, F_{C2}	Forced control
K_p	Proportional gain
K_d	Derivative gain
K_i	Integral gain
θ_0	Reference angle

Appendix A

$$M_1 = \left[\frac{\alpha_1(1-\Gamma)^2 A_1^2}{3\omega_1^2}\right], M_2 = \left[\frac{\alpha_2(1-\Gamma)^3 A_1^3}{8\omega_1^2}\right], M_3 = \left[\frac{\beta A_2+\alpha_2\left(3A_2^2\overline{A}_2+6(1-\Gamma)^2 A_1\overline{A}_1 A_2\right)}{\omega_1^2-\omega_2^2}\right]$$

$$M_4 = \left[\frac{-\alpha_1 A_1^2}{\omega_1^2-4\omega_2^2}\right], M_5 = \left[\frac{\alpha_2 A_2^3}{\omega_1^2-9\omega_2^2}\right], M_6 = \left[\frac{2\alpha_1(1-\Gamma)A_1 A_2}{\omega_1^2-(\omega_1+\omega_2)^2}\right], M_7 = \left[\frac{2\alpha_1(1-\Gamma)A_1\overline{A}_2}{\omega_1^2-(\omega_1-\omega_2)^2}\right]$$

$$M_8 = \left[\frac{3\alpha_2(1-\Gamma)^2 A_1^2 A_2}{\omega_1^2-(2\omega_1+\omega_2)^2}\right], M_9 = \left[\frac{3\alpha_2(1-\Gamma)^2 A_1^2\overline{A}_2}{\omega_1^2-(2\omega_1-\omega_2)^2}\right], M_{10} = \left[\frac{-3\alpha_2(1-\Gamma)A_1 A_2^2}{\omega_1^2-(\omega_1+2\omega_2)^2}\right]$$

$$M_{11} = \left[\frac{-3\alpha_2(1-\Gamma)A_1\overline{A}_2^2}{\omega_1^2-(\omega_1-2\omega_2)^2}\right], M_{12} = \left[\frac{-\alpha_1\left((1-\Gamma)^2 A_1\overline{A}_1 + A_2\overline{A}_2\right) - iK_i\frac{A_1}{\omega_1}}{\omega_1^2}\right]$$

$$N_1 = \frac{1}{\omega_2^2-\omega_1^2}\left[-2i\omega_1 D_1\Gamma A_1 + \alpha_4\left(3(1-\Gamma)^3 A_1^2\overline{A}_1 + 6(1-\Gamma)A_1 A_2\overline{A}_2\right) - \left(K_p - \frac{K_i}{\omega_1} + \omega_1 K_d\right)\Gamma A_1\right]$$

$$N_2 = \left[\frac{\omega_2^2 M_1 + \alpha_3(1-\Gamma)^2 A_1^2}{\omega_2^2-4\omega_1^2}\right], N_3 = \left[\frac{\omega_2^2 M_2 + \alpha_4(1-\Gamma)^3 A_1^3}{\omega_2^2-9\omega_1^2}\right]$$

$$N_4 = \left[\frac{-\omega_2^2 M_4 - \alpha_3 A_2^2}{3\omega_2^2}\right], N_5 = \left[\frac{-\omega_2^2 M_5 + \alpha_4 A_2^3}{8\omega_2^2}\right], N_6 = \left[\frac{\omega_2^2 M_6 - 2\alpha_3(1-\Gamma)A_1 A_2}{\omega_2^2 - (\omega_1 + \omega_2)^2}\right]$$

$$N_7 = \left[\frac{\omega_2^2 M_7 - 2\alpha_3(1-\Gamma)A_1 \overline{A}_2}{\omega_2^2 - (\omega_1 - \omega_2)^2}\right], N_8 = \left[\frac{\omega_2^2 M_8 - 3\alpha_4(1-\Gamma)^2 A_1^2 A_2}{\omega_2^2 - (2\omega_1 + \omega_2)^2}\right]$$

$$N_9 = \left[\frac{\omega_2^2 M_9 - 3\alpha_4(1-\Gamma)^2 A_1^2 \overline{A}_2}{\omega_2^2 - (2\omega_1 - \omega_2)^2}\right], N_{10} = \left[\frac{\omega_2^2 M_{10} + 3\alpha_4(1-\Gamma)A_1 A_2^2}{\omega_2^2 - (\omega_1 + 2\omega_2)^2}\right]$$

$$N_{11} = \left[\frac{\omega_2^2 M_{11} + 3\alpha_4(1-\Gamma)A_1 \overline{A}_2^2}{\omega_2^2 - (\omega_1 - 2\omega_2)^2}\right], N_{12} = \left[\frac{\omega_2^2 M_{12} + \alpha_3\left((1-\Gamma)^2 A_1 \overline{A}_1 + A_2 \overline{A}_2\right) - K_i\left(\frac{A_2}{\omega_2} + \frac{\Gamma A_1}{\omega_1}\right)}{\omega_2^2}\right]$$

References

1. Sowmya, V.S.; Dharsini, S.P.; Dharshini, R.P.; Aravind, P. Application of various PID controller tuning techniques for a temperature system. *Int. J. Comput. Appl.* **2014**, *103*, 32–34.
2. Pradeepkannan, D.; Sathiyamoorthy, S. Implementation of Gain Scheduled PID Controller for a Nonlinear Coupled Spherical Tank Process. *Int. J. Mech. Mechatron. Eng.* **2014**, *14*, 93–98.
3. Sabri, L.A.; Hussein, A.A. Implementation of fuzzy and PID controller to water level system using LabView. *Int. J. Comput. Appl.* **2015**, *116*, 6–10.
4. Bashiri, A.H. Empirical study of robust/developed PID control for nonlinear time-delayed dynamical system in discrete time domain. *Heliyon* **2024**, *10*, e29749. [CrossRef] [PubMed]
5. Hamed, A.; Shaban, E.M.; Darwish, R.R.; Abdel Ghany, A.M. Design and implementation of discrete PID control applied to Bitumen tank based on new approach of pole placement technique. *Int. J. Dynam. Control* **2017**, *5*, 604–613. [CrossRef]
6. Shaban, E.M.; Hamed, A.; Darwish, R.R.; Abdel Ghany, A.M. New tuning approach of discrete PI/PID controller applied to bitumen system based on non-minimal state space formulation. In Proceedings of the 25th International Conference on Computer Theory and Applications (ICCTA), Alexandria, Egypt, 24–26 October 2015; pp. 52–57.
7. Hamed, A.R.; Shaban, E.M.; Abdelhaleem, A.M. Industrial implementation of state dependent parameter PID+ control for nonlinear time delayed bitumen tank system. *Iran J. Sci. Technol. Trans. Electr. Eng.* **2022**, *46*, 743–751. [CrossRef]
8. Sayed, H.; Shaban, E.M.; Abdelhamid, A. State-Dependent Parameter PID+ Control Applied to A Nonlinear Manipulator Arm. In *Recent Advances in Engineering Mathematics and Physics*; Farouk, M., Hassanein, M., Eds.; Springer: Cham, Switzerland, 2020.
9. Dano, M.L.; Julli'ere, B. Active control of thermally induced distortion in composite structures using macro fiber composite actuators. *Smart Mater. Struct.* **2007**, *16*, 2315–2322. [CrossRef]
10. Kumar, R.S.; Ray, M.C. Active control of geometrically nonlinear vibrations of doubly curved smart sandwich shells using 1–3 piezoelectric composites. *Compos. Struct.* **2013**, *105*, 173–187. [CrossRef]
11. Saeed, N.; Kamel, M. Nonlinear PD-controller to suppress the nonlinear oscillations of horizontally supported Jeffcott-rotor system. *Int. Non-Linear Mech.* **2016**, *87*, 109–124. [CrossRef]
12. Fey, R.H.B.; Wouters RM, T.; Nijmeijer, H. Proportional and derivative control for steady-state vibration mitigation in a piecewise linear beam system. *Nonlinear Dyn.* **2010**, *60*, 535–649. [CrossRef]
13. Eissa, M.; Kandil, A.; El-Ganaini, W.A.; Kamel, M. Analysis of a nonlinear magnetic levitation system vibrations controlled by a time-delayed proportional derivative controller. *Nonlinear Dyn.* **2015**, *79*, 1217–1233. [CrossRef]
14. Eissa, M.; Kandil, A.; Kamel, M.; El-Ganaini, W.A. On controlling the response of primary and parametric resonances of a nonlinear magnetic levitation system. *Meccanica* **2015**, *50*, 233–251. [CrossRef]
15. Bauomy, H.S.; EL-Sayed, A.T. Act of nonlinear proportional derivative controller for MFC laminated shell. *Phys. Scr.* **2020**, *95*, 095210. [CrossRef]
16. Hote, Y.V.; Jain, S. PID controller design for load frequency control: Past, Present and future challenges. *IFAC-Pap. Online* **2018**, *51*, 604–609. [CrossRef]
17. Darwish, N.M. PID controller design in the frequency domain for time-delay systems using direct method. *Trans. Inst. Meas. Control* **2018**, *40*, 940–950. [CrossRef]
18. Zhao, C.; Guo, L. PID controller design for second order nonlinear uncertain systems. *Sci. China Inf. Sci.* **2017**, *60*, 022201. [CrossRef]
19. Hanafi, D. PID controller design for semi-active car suspension based on model from intelligent system identification. In Proceedings of the IEEE Computer Society, Second International Conference on Computer Engineering and Applications, Bali, Indonesia, 19–21 March 2010; pp. 60–63.

20. Constantin, M.; Popescu, O.S.; Mastorakis, N.E. Testing and simulation of motor vehicle suspension. *Int. J. Syst. Appl. Eng. Dev.* **2009**, *3*, 74–83.
21. Kumar, M.S. Development of Active System for Automobiles using PID Controller. In Proceedings of the World Congress on Engineering, London, UK, 2–4 July 2008; Volume II.
22. Govinda, K.E.; Raghul, S.; Kishore, K.R.; Mathan, K.M.; Prasanth, C. Enhancing the Closed Loop Performance of Semi-active Suspension System with I-PD Controller. *Mater. Sci. Eng.* **2019**, *561*, 012085. [CrossRef]
23. Amer, Y.A.; EL-Sayed, A.T.; El-Bahrawy, F.T. Torsional vibration reduction for rolling mill's main drive system via negative velocity feedback under parametric excitation. *J. Mech. Sci. Technol.* **2015**, *29*, 1581–1589. [CrossRef]
24. Wenzhi, G.; Zhiyong, H. Active control and simulation test study on torsional vibration of large turbo-generator rotor shaft. *Mech. Mach. Theory* **2010**, *45*, 1326–1336. [CrossRef]
25. El-Sayed, A.T.; Bauomy, H.S. Passive and active controllers for suppressing the torsional vibration of multiple degree-of-freedom system. *J. Vib. Control* **2015**, *21*, 2616–2632. [CrossRef]
26. Jianhui, W.; Yushen, W.; Philip Chen, C.L.; Zhi, L.; Wenqiang, W. Adaptive PI event-triggered control for MIMO nonlinear systems with input delay. *Inf. Sci.* **2024**, *677*, 120817.
27. Yang, W.W.; Yang, Y.J.; Tang, X.Y.; Zhang, K.R.; Li, J.C.; Xu, C. An adaptive P/PI control strategy for a solar volumetric methane/steam reforming reactor with passive thermal management. *Chem. Eng. Sci.* **2023**, *281*, 119005. [CrossRef]
28. Kevorkian, J.; Cole, J.D. Multiple Scale and Singular Perturbation Methods. In *Applied Mathematical Sciences*; Springer: Berlin/Heidelberg, Germany, 1996.
29. Nayfeh, A. *Perturbation Methods*; Wiley: New York, NY, USA, 1973.
30. Dukkipati, R.V. *Solving Vibration Analysis Problems Using Matlab*; New Age International Pvt Ltd Publishers: New Delhi, India, 2007.
31. Bauomy, H.S.; El -Sayed, A.T. Mixed controller (IRC+ NSC) involved in the harmonic vibration response cantilever beam model. *Meas. Control* **2020**, *53*, 1954–1967. [CrossRef]
32. Kamel, M.; Eissa, M.; El-sayed, A.T. Vibration reduction of a nonlinear spring pendulum under multi-parametric excitation via a longitudinal absorber. *Phys. Scr.* **2009**, *80*, 025005. [CrossRef]
33. Bauomy, H.S.; El -Sayed, A.T.; Salem, A.M.; El-Bahrawy, F.T. The improved giant magnetostrictive actuator oscillations via positive position feedback damper. *AIMS Math.* **2023**, *8*, 16864–16886. [CrossRef]
34. Bauomy, H.S.; El -Sayed, A.T.; El-Bahrawy, F.T.; Salem, A.M. Safety of a continuous spinning Shaft's structure from nonlinear vibration with NIPPF. *Alex. Eng. J.* **2023**, *67*, 193–207. [CrossRef]
35. Bauomy, H.S.; El -Sayed, A.T. Vibration performance of a vertical conveyor system under two simultaneous resonances. *Arch. Appl. Mech.* **2018**, *88*, 1349–1368. [CrossRef]
36. El-Sayed, A.T.; Bauomy, H.S. NIPPF versus ANIPPF controller outcomes on semi- direct drive cutting transmission system in a shearer. *Chaos Solitons Fractals* **2022**, *156*, 111778. [CrossRef]
37. Forming Equations of Motion for Multiple Degree-of-Freedom Systems. Available online: www.efunda.com/formulae/vibrations/mdof_eom.cfm (accessed on 1 January 2013).

MDPI AG
Grosspeteranlage 5
4052 Basel
Switzerland
Tel.: +41 61 683 77 34

Computation Editorial Office
E-mail: computation@mdpi.com
www.mdpi.com/journal/computation

www.ingramcontent.com/pod-product-compliance
Lightning Source LLC
Chambersburg PA
CBHW061558210926
51850CB00009B/2145
* 9 7 8 3 7 2 5 8 7 9 5 1 9 *